The new criminology:
for a social theory of deviance

International Library of Sociology

Founded by Karl Mannheim

Editor: John Rex, University of Warwick

Arbor Scientific

Arbor Vitae

A catalogue of the books available in the **International Library of Sociology** and other series of Social Science books published by Routledge will be found at the end of this volume

The new criminology:
for a social theory of deviance

Ian Taylor
Criminology Unit, Faculty of Law, University of Sheffield

Paul Walton
Department of Sociology, University of Bradford

Jock Young
Department of Sociology, Middlesex Polytechnic

Routledge & Kegan Paul
London and Boston

*First published in 1973
by Routledge & Kegan Paul Ltd
Broadway House, 68–74 Carter Lane,
London EC4V 5EL and
9 Park Street,
Boston, Mass. 02108, U.S.A.
Printed in Great Britain by
Western Printing Services Ltd
Bristol*

ISBN 0 7100 7472 7 (c)
ISBN 0 7100 7552 9 (p)

32755

To live outside the law you must be honest
I know you always say that you agree
Alright, so where are you tonight . . .?

Bob Dylan: 'Absolutely Sweet Marie'

Contents

Foreword

If any single book can succeed in making 'criminology' intellectually serious, as distinct from professionally respectable, then this study, remarkable for its combination of the analytical with the historical, will do it. It is perhaps the first truly comprehensive critique that we have ever had of the totality, of past and contemporary, of European and American, studies of 'crime' and 'deviance'. It is as meticulous in its treatment of the obscure, unknown theorist as it is of the most fashionable, probing both with a catholic seriousness. It is a critique, again remarkable, for the sure manner in which it combines the craftsmen's grasp of fine-grained detail with a philosophical horizon and reflexivity. As a result, the technical detail never operates within the merely conventional limits of what is worth speaking about, while the philosophical depth does not feed only on itself but also becomes a dwelling place for someone else's world.

The reorienting power of this work, and it *is* a work of *power* whose achievement does not depend upon merely marginal distinctions, derives from its ability to demonstrate that all studies of crime and deviance, however deeply entrenched in their own technical traditions, are inevitably also grounded in larger, more general social theories which are always present (and consequential) even as unspoken silences. What this important study does, then, is this: it redirects the total structure of technical discourse concerning 'crime' and 'deviance'; it does this precisely by breaking this silence, by speaking what is normally unspoken by technicians, by launching a *deliberate discourse* concerning the general, social theory usually only tacit in specialized work in crime and deviance; by exhibiting explicitly the linkages between technical detail and the most basic philosophical positions.

Very rarely, if ever, have crime and deviance studies been subjected to a critique and excavation which is at once comprehensively thorough-going, patiently probing, and systematic. This study, then, begins the work of transforming the self-crippled discourse of technicians, with their essentially unexamined 'way of life', from the standpoint of a larger intellectual rationality, by liberating technical 'topics' into a newly enlivening, larger, more reflective critique.

Here, then, the proper study of criminology is made throughly clear: it is the *critical understanding* of both the larger society and of the broadest social theory; it is not simply the study of some marginal, exotic or esoteric group, be they criminals or criminologists. This study, of what at first seems to be a limited field, is, in point of fact, the occasion for the exhibition of the broadest sociological and philosophical concerns. Clearly what this work is saying and exhibiting is that what matters is not crime and deviance studies but the larger critical theory on which these must rest. And given the state of such technical studies, there are few things more important to say.

It was precisely because there was a hiatus between these levels that many members of my own generation, surfacing after World War II, paid scant attention to studies of crime and deviance. The few exceptions were precisely those that promised to liberate us from technical parochialism, perhaps most especially, the work launched by Robert K. Merton and C. Wright Mills. The critique of Robert Merton's work in the present volume is a powerful and provocative one. If the limits of Merton's work derive in part from its essentially 'liberal' bathos, two other things also need to be said. One is that these limits do not derive only from Merton's *liberal* side but also from his 'rebel' side (to use the author's language); that is, Merton's limits derive as much from the nature of the *rebel horse* he rode, as from the liberal snaffle and curb with which he held it in check. More on this, in a moment. A second qualification that must also be emphasized in passing a serious judgement on Merton's work in this area is that it should be seen *historically*, in terms of what it meant when it first appeared and made the rounds. In this context, it needs emphasis that Merton's work on *anomie* as well as Mills's work on 'social pathology' was a *liberative* work, for those who lived with it as part of a *living* culture as distinct from how it may now appear as part of the mere *record* of that once-lived culture.

There are several reasons for this. One is that both Merton and Mills kept open an avenue of access to Marxist theory. Indeed both of them had a kind of tacit *Marxism*. Mills's Marxism was always much more tacit than his own radical position made it seem, while Merton was always much more *Marxist* than his silences on that question may make it seem. Unlike Parsons, Merton always knew his Marx and knew thoroughly the nuances of controversy in living Marxist culture. Merton developed his generalized analysis of the various forms of deviant behaviour by locating them within a systematic formalization of Durkheim's theory of *anomie*, from which he gained analytic distance by tacitly grounding himself in a Marxian ontology of social *contradiction*. It is perhaps this Hegelian dimension of Marxism that has had the most enduring effect on Merton's *analytic rules*, and which disposed him to view *anomie* as the unanticipated outcome of social institutions that thwarted men in their effort to acquire the very goods and values that these same institutions had encouraged them to pursue. In its openness to the internal contradictions of capitalist *culture* few Lukacians have been more incisive.

Mills, for his part, especially in his critique of 'The Professional Ideology of Social Pathologists', strove to overcome the isolation of 'social problems' analysis in the then current division of academic labour, and to situate it in an historical view of the institutionalized totality of a commercialized industrialism. In this respect, then, both Merton's and Mills's work was liberative because it was a critique of the *encapsulation* of the technical parochialism of crime and deviance studies, seeing them as expressive of larger social theories, and in need of a self-conscious critique from other theoretical perspectives. It is in this way that much of their liberative impact was realized; it is also for this very reason that *limits* were built into the liberation to whose groundwork they contributed so much.

Put it this way: their ability to understand previous, encapsulated studies of deviance and crime as defective instances did not simply expose the *distorted* character of such studies, its crippling defects, but, it also defined them as *instances*, or one might say, as mere *examples* of a larger rationality, and hence as devoid of high value in their own right. To see the conventional isolation of crime and deviance studies as defective because of its theoretical isolation *was* liberative; to see these studies as exemplary instances was to define them in a way, which, if it did not cripple them, might still *stunt* their growth. Given the priority assigned to high-level general theory, it could become difficult to take deviants and deviance seriously, in their own right.

There is then a certain generalized tension between the theoretical centre and the specialized peripheries. Cut off from the theoretical centre, the technical specializations inevitably became the dwelling place of routinized technicians who prattle about their 'autonomy' even as they become the paid auxiliaries of the 'Welfare' State. Yet totally assimilated into the theoretical centre and reduced to a merely exemplary significance—exemplary, that is, of a higher theoretical rationality—specializations easily lose the kind of *intrinsic* worth that might ensure their continued development. In short, instead of simply seeing the relation between theoretical centre and peripheral specializations as one of a mutual 'dependence' of theory and practice or application, as a kind of wedding in which bride and groom live happily ever after, it is also necessary to see this relation between centre and periphery dialectically as having its own *contradictions*— even if these are not antagonistic contradictions.

A few more comments about the potential dangers that a higher level theory may hold for a peripheral specialization may be in order, especially since I share the authors' concern for general theory. A tendency not to view the deviant as important in his own right derives not only from an effort to assert the claims of general theory in an age of specialization but, also, from certain specific substantive suppositions of the general theory used. Specifically, Marxism had viewed deviants and criminals as peripheral relative to its own central concern with power and contention-for-power. Viewing criminals and deviants as a *Lumpenproletariat* that would play no decisive role in the class struggle, and indeed, as susceptible to use by reactionary forces, Marxists were not usually motivated to develop a systematic theory of crime and deviance. In short, being neither proletarian nor bourgeois, and standing off to the periphery of the central *political* struggle, criminals and deviants were at best the butlers and maids, the spear carriers, colourful actors perhaps but nameless, and worst of all, lacking in a historical 'mission'. They could be, indeed, *had* to be, ignored by those devoted to the study of more 'important' issues—power, political struggle, and class conflict. One of the many excellences of this volume is that its authors see this general problem quite clearly and also see it as a problem of *Marxism* in particular, despite the fact that their own work is in part grounded in a reflective reading of Marxism. They have very keenly understood that a mere 'application' of Marxism to crime and deviance studies would be an exemplification of the very uncritical posture which is, at bottom, the position to which they are most relentlessly opposed.

Let me briefly develop a different implication of the foregoing. The great empirical richness of the 'Chicago School's' studies of deviance, particularly of its 'second' generation, trained by E. C. Hughes and Herbert Blumer and now led by men such as Howard Becker, the richness of their researches derives in some part from the fact that they never had to liberate themselves from viewing deviants as a kind of political low-life. The Chicagoans' readiness to attend to the social world of the deviant was grounded in his view of the deviant as no less important, real, or historically valuable than members of any other social world. The Chicagoans could accept the authenticity of the deviant world; they could 'let it be' rather than *depreciate* it by comparing it invidiously with social groups who were said to have a historical mission, and they could *appreciate* it as a form of life no less real or worthy than that of the working class.

Here too, there is a need for a historical perspective. I have often thought that it was only after the radical thrust of the 'thirties had ground to a halt, and after the working class had been assimilated into the 'Welfare' State following World War II, that concern with the deviant achieved a kind of moral significance and a degree of liberative impact. For a while, the deviants had become the untamed underside of bourgeois society—indeed there is a long (and romantic tendency to keep them as such. They became a kind of 'moral equivalent' of the 'corrupted' and pacified proletariat; living a rich and spontaneous existence in the midst of bourgeois greyness and routine; devoid of the domesticated hypocrisy of the respectable who were often seen as using them: e.g. the prostitute helps the 'pure' girl to remain pure, etc.

Rooted in a corrupt and burgeoning Chicago, a corruption that in time came to be taken for granted while the 'reformer' was soon recognized as a kind of hustler, on the make in his own way, it became clear, at least to second-generation Chicagoans, that respectable society was implicated in protecting and condoning crime and deviance. Having no 'illusions' about the present and no real 'hope' for its fundamental change, the Chicagoans did not believe in the moral superiority of the 'respectables' and could view the 'deviants' not as a periphery but as just one more boundaried social world. The pimp, so to speak, was just another kind of salesman. So if the younger Chicago School did not react with moral indignation against the corruption of respectable society, if theirs was a species of accommodation to the *status quo*, they could also immerse themselves without qualm, indeed with dedication, in the night world of the deviant. For the younger Chicagoans, the study of deviant worlds was a way of life, a way in which they might 'drop out' of respectable society with its transparent hypocrisy. For them, the deviant world was an authentic dwelling place, even if not 'home'. They could thus assimilate an understanding of deviant worlds, seeing them from the perspective of the deviant's own experience. If I have elsewhere stressed this school's *accommodation* to the *status quo* perhaps the above properly accents the positive value and social rationality of the second generation of Chicago School studies of deviance.

There is, then, a certain contradication between a Marxist perspective on deviance which looks at it from the outside and as lacking in *historical* value, and the Meadian view of the Chicagoans whose view is internal, and timeless, and without any impulse to *moralize*. If the Marxist refuses to accommodate to the world of established power and respectability, he also has a limited insight into and stunted compassion for the lowly. Only the 'bottom rail' that history intends to make top rail is given attention; but he will not write the sociology of all those many outcasts who have no historical future. Correspondingly, however, the Marxist has few illusions about the 'freedom' or spontaneity of the deviant, no impulse to romanticize his life; and he recongizes that the deviant's existence, however authentic, does not really transcend the limits of the larger society. The Meadian or Chicago view is grounded in a tacit accommodation to this larger society although it has no 'illusions' about it. Yet it is for just this reason that it could accept and assimilate the alien world of the deviant. What becomes increasingly necessary is a theoretical position that accepts the reality of deviance, that has a capacity to explore its *Lebenswelt*, without becoming the technician of the 'Welfare' State and its zoo-keepers of deviance. The work before us strives toward a theoretical perspective that can do that, and more; that can rescue the liberative dimension in both Marxism and Meadianism; it utilizes a critique of crime and deviance to work toward a larger theoretical reconstruction without patronizing the concrete and smaller worlds, without using them simply as 'examples' or 'points of departure'.

ALVIN W. GOULDNER
Sociologisch Instituut,
Universiteit van Amsterdam

Acknowledgments

This book is fundamentally the product of discussions and developments in and around the National Deviancy Conference, a growing body of sociologists and individuals involved in social action in the United Kingdom. We would like to acknowledge conversations we have held, individually and collectively, with Steve Allwyn, Stan Cohen, Jeff Coulter, David Downes, Stuart Hall, Laurie Taylor, and Bridget Pym. We should also like to thank Martha Sonnenberg, of California, for help with several problems in the American literature. We would never have made the deadline with our publishers if it had not been for the unstinting work of Isobel Jackson of the Criminology Unit in the Faculty of Law at Sheffield University, who compiled the references with speed and efficiency; the secretarial staff at Sheffield (Mrs Barbara Holland and Mrs Valerie Royston); the library staff in the Social Science Library at the University of Bradford, and inestimable support from Elizabeth Elston, Judith Heather, Mary Leek and Henrietta Resler. For various reasons, none of this would have ever emerged if it had not been for the State of Acapulco, the Broomhill Tavern (Sheffield), the Karachi Restaurant (Bradford), and the Akiko Restaurant (London). We thank them all. Peter Hopkins of Routledge has been a source of support and of encouragement (in more ways than one) during the two and a half years of writing.

1 Classical criminology and the positivist revolution

The classical school of criminology

The classical school of criminology grew out of the philosophy of the Enlightenment. The central tenet of classicism was that the rights of man had to be protected against the corruption and excesses of existing institutions: and these vagaries were nowhere more evident than in the legal systems of eighteenth-century Europe. Punishment was arbitrary and barbarous, 'due processes' of law being absent or ignored and crime itself being ill-defined and extensive. It was in this context that the Italian Cesare Beccaria first formulated the principles of classical criminology, basing them firmly on the social contract theories of Hobbes,[1] Montesquieu and Rousseau.

Thus, his famous *Essay on Crimes and Punishments* (1804, pp. 5–6) starts with a concise statement of the social contract position on the nature of laws:

> Laws are the conditions, under which men, naturally independent, united themselves in society. Weary of living in a continual state of war, and of enjoying a liberty which became of little value, from the uncertainty of its duration, they sacrificed one part of it, to enjoy the rest in peace and security. The sum of all these portions of the liberty of each individual constituted the sovereignty of a nation; and was deposited in the hands of the sovereign, as the lawful administrator. But it was not sufficient only to establish this deposit; it was also necessary to defend it from the usurpation of each individual, who would always endeavour not only to take away from the mass his own portion, but to encroach on that of others. Some motives, therefore, that strike the senses, were necessary to prevent the despotism of each individual from plunging

society into its former chaos. Such motives are the punishments established against the transgressors of the laws. I say, that motives of this kind are necessary; because experience shows that the multitude adopt no established principle of conduct; and because society is prevented from approaching to that dissolution (to which, as well as all other parts of the physical and moral world, it naturally tends), only by motives that are the immediate objects of sense, and which being continually presented to the mind, are sufficient to counterbalance the effect of the passions of the individual, which oppose the general good. Neither the power of eloquence nor the sublimest truths, are sufficient to restrain, for any length of time, those passions which are excited by the lively impressions of present objects.

Thus men come together and freely create a civil society, it being the function of legal punishment to ensure the continued existence of society. Further, Beccaria believes it is a part of the common interest of all that crimes should not be committed. Punishment, however, though intended to reduce crime, must always be proportional to the degree to which a crime violates the (consensually agreed) sanctity of property, personal well-being and the welfare of the state. Punishment in the excess of this consensus or for alternative ends is illegitimate and contrary to the social contract.

Classical theory can be summed up briefly as follows:

1. all men being by nature self-seeking are liable to commit crime.

2. there is a consensus in society as to the desirability of protecting private property and personal welfare.

3. in order to prevent a 'war of all against all', men freely enter into a contract with the state to preserve the peace within the terms of this consensus.

4. punishment must be utilized to deter the individual from violating the interests of others. It is the prerogative of the state, granted to it by the individuals making up the social contract, to act against these violations.

5. punishments must be proportional to the interests violated by the crime. It must not be in excess of this neither must it be used for reformation; for this would encroach on the rights of the individual and transgress the social contract.

6. there should be as little law as possible, and its implementation should be closely delineated by due process.

7. the individual is responsible for his actions and is equal, no matter what his rank, in the eyes of the law. Mitigating circumstances or excuses are therefore inadmissible.

We can see, therefore, that classical theory is above all a theory of

2

social control (with its theories on human motivation, etc., implicit rather than explicit): it delimits first, the manner in which the state should react to the criminal, second, those deviations which permit individuals to be labelled as criminals, and third, the social basis of criminal law. Like social contract theories in general, the classical theory of crime and social control commanded support amongst the rising bourgeoisie and their legal representatives.

Social contract theory can be seen historically as an ideological framework for the protection of the rising bourgeoisie, in particular against feudal interference. For social contract theory—above all else—insisted on the rewarding of useful activity and the punishment of damaging activity. Positive and negative characteristics were assigned to different kinds of behaviour in terms of their utility in a newly propertied society. Alvin Gouldner has put this well (1971, pp. 62–3):

> The middle-class standard of utility developed in the course
> of its polemic against the feudal norms and aristocratic claims
> of the 'old regimes', in which the rights of men were held to be
> derived from and limited by their estate, class, birth, or lineage:
> in short, by what they 'were' rather than by what they *did*.
> In contrast, the new middle class held in highest esteem those
> talents, skills, and energies of individuals that contributed to
> their own individual accomplishments and achievements. The
> middle-class standard of utility implied that rewards should
> be proportioned to men's work and contribution. The useful-
> ness of men, it was now held, should control the station to
> which they might rise or the work and authority they might
> have, rather than that their station should govern and admit
> them to employment and privileges.

Classical social contract theory—or utilitarianism—can be seen to operate with three important assumptions, all of which are arguable. First, it posits a consensus amongst rational men on the morality and permanence of the present distribution of property. Second, it characterizes all law-breaking behaviour occurring in a society where a social contract has allegedly been struck as essen- tially pathological or irrational, the behaviour of men unable—by virtue of personal inadequacies—to enter into contracts. Third, the clear inference is that the theorists of the social contract themselves had a special access to the criteria by which to judge the rationality or otherwise of an act: and these criteria were the criteria of utility as developed by the theorists themselves. Utilitarianism, therefore, was not a theory of unqualified or unrestricted individual equality. Although men were seen to be equal in the sense of having an equal power to reason, they could not be seen (in a propertied society) to be

3

equal in all other respects. This ambiguity (or contradiction) has been noted by Leon Radzinowicz (1966, p. 5):

> the doctrine of equality, though given great weight, was more cautiously defined . . . it was not prepared to go to the length of attacking inequalities in property or rank. Though men had been equal in a state of nature they could not be so in society: authority and subordination must remain, although they must cease to be abused. Nevertheless the fact that equality could not be expected in wealth and power made it the more vital to recognise it where it did exist—in the very fact of humanity itself.

The contradiction between the defence of equality and the emphasis on property is never fully resolved in utilitarian theory. No real attention is given to the fact that lack of property might make men more likely to commit crime; and no consideration is devoted to the possibility that the rewards held out by the system as rewards might be more easily available to those already in propertied (or otherwise privileged) positions. The democratic stress in early utilitarianism—with its emphasis on equality amongst those who contributed usefully to society—was never more than ideology. It bore little relation to middle-class practice (Gouldner, 1971, p. 71).

> The middle class never believed that its property—derived incomes—its rights to rents, profits, interests—were justified in terms of the utility of property. The middle class insisted that property and men of property were useful to society and deserving of honour and other rewards because of this; but men of property also held that property was sacred in itself, and, in doing so, made a tacit claim that its rewards should not depend only upon its usefulness. The property interests of the middle class have thus always exerted a strain against its own utilitarian values . . .

Formally, however, all men—because of their rationality—were to be equal in the eyes of the law, and this rationality would, it was argued, enable them to realize the beneficial nature of the consensus implicit in the social contract. Men's rationality, however, was in practice always pitted against the passions of an unthinking self-interest. A second contradiction presented itself and continued to present itself in utilitarian thinking. For Beccaria, it was precisely this contradiction in human practice which made necessary the fact of punishment. Punishment, so to speak, was the second line of defence—deterring the individual from offences when his reason failed and his passions tempted him into criminality. Yet, since man has a free choice between the courses of action, he is always to be judged to be responsible and not to be excused by pleas of mitigation or of irresponsibility. Detailed discussion of the nature of criminal motivation is, however, avoided in most classical writings: the focus is rather on the evolution of a legal system, which is seen as embodying a moral calculus circumscribing and detailing appropriate social reaction against the criminal deviant. In avoiding discussion of criminal motivation—in particular any discussion of the relationship between inequality and criminal action—social contract theorists left the moral and rational supremacy of the bourgeoisie unquestioned; and, in concentrating on questions of legal order and disposition, it focused the attention on problems in the administration of control (Vold, 1958, p. 23):

> It seems fair, therefore, to characterize the classical school as 'administrative and legal criminology'. Its great advantage was that it set up a scheme of procedure easy to administer. It made the judge only an instrument to apply the law, and the law undertook to prescribe an exact penalty for every crime and every degree thereof. Puzzling questions about the reasons for or 'causes' of behavior, the uncertainties of motive and intent, the unequal consequences of an arbitrary rule, these were all deliberately ignored for the sake of administrative uniformity. This was the classical conception of justice—an exact scale of punishments for equal acts without reference to the nature of the individual involved and with no attention to the question of special circumstances under which the act came about.

In practice, of course, the fact was that criminal action was very much more concentrated and unequally structured than classical theories would imply. Irrationality, defined in classical terms, was concentrated amongst the 'dangerous classes', a fact that classical theory, unable to highlight the differential distribution of property, could not explain. Beccaria (1804, pp. 80–1), attempting to elaborate a punishment suitable for robbery, confronted the problem in the following terms:

> He who endeavours to enrich himself with the property of another, should be deprived of part of his own. But this crime, alas! is commonly the effect of misery and despair; the crime of that unhappy part of mankind, to whom the right of exclusive property (a terrible and perhaps unnecessary right) has left but a bare existence. Besides, as pecuniary punishments may increase the number of robbers, by increasing the number of poor, and may deprive an innocent family of subsistence, the most proper punishment will be that kind of slavery, which alone

5

can be called just; that is, which makes society, for a time, absolute master of the person, and labour of the criminal, in order to oblige him to repair, by this dependence, the unjust despotism he usurped over the property of another, and his violation of the social compact.

Classicism is exhausted. For if there is a clear reason for theft—the 'right of exclusive property'—then crime cannot be seen as irrational. Moreover, the justice of the social contract itself is thrown into doubt: and deviance from contractual 'obligations' must concomitantly be understood more sympathetically. Finally, once it is seen that an 'unjust despotism' may be hidden by the ideology of social contract utilitarianism, the classical symmetry of crime and punishment, an essential part of the theory itself, is shown to be ineffective and self-contradictory. For if the poor steal from the rich because they are poor, then it follows that punishment involving the deprivation of the criminal's property can only exacerbate the problem. *A system of classical justice of this order could only operate in a society where property was distributed equally.*[2]

Beccaria did not explore these contradictions any further. Instead, he concentrated on providing a corpus of principles for the legislator which makes its appeal to legal convenience rather than theoretical rigour. But the question of criminal motivation (the irrational deviance of those who would defy the social contract) is taken up by the main body of social contract theorists. MacPherson (1962, p. 98) puts well the question the social contract theorists have to answer:

> What of a man without substantial property or hope of acquiring it? Is the lifelong wage-earner, living at bare subsistence level, capable of acknowledging obligation to a sovereign whose main function is to make and enforce the rules which the wage-earner may feel are what have put him and keep him in this precarious position?

Hobbes would answer that this man can acknowledge an obligation if he is taught that the *status quo* is inevitable (cf. MacPherson, 1962, p. 98); the more cautious Locke would argue that, although the labouring classes have an interest in civil society, they could never be full members of it—because of their lack of property (MacPherson, 1962, p. 248). The 'solution' in social contract theory to the problem of inequality—in the final analysis—is an evasion, and is best seen in Locke. He makes a distinction between those members of the poor who have chosen depravity and those who, because of their unfortunate circumstances, were unable to live a 'rational' life (cf. MacPherson, 1962, p. 226). Thus, crime is *either* an irrational choice (a product of the passions) *or* it may be the result of factors militating against the free exercise of rational choice. In neither respect can it be fully rational action in the sense that conforming action is invariably seen to be.

These two alternative views of criminal motivation have dominated criminology (surviving the attack of positivism) ever since. Both views withdraw authenticity and rationality from the criminal act itself, and, also, not unimportantly, establish scholars versed in the study of society and law as 'independent' arbiters of the rationality of action.

Neo-classical revisionism

The classical school of criminology—spelling out as it did the conditions of the social contract and control—had an extraordinary influence on legislation throughout the world. Farner, a nineteenth-century commentator on Beccaria, for example, asserts (1880, p. 46):

> Whatever improvement our penal laws have undergone in the last hundred years is due primarily to Beccaria, and, to an extent that has not always been recognised. Lord Mansfield is said never to have mentioned his name without a sign of respect. Romilly referred to him in the very first speech he delivered in the House of Commons on the subject of law reform. And there is no English writer of that day who, in treating of the criminal law, does not refer to Beccaria.

The actual implementation of classical premises, however, was to be fraught with difficulties. The contradictions in classicism reared their head in the attempt to evolve universal penal measures and in day-to-day practice. It was impossible in practice to ignore the determinants of human action and to proceed as if punishment and incarceration could be easily measured on some kind of universal calculus: apart from throwing the working of the law itself into doubt (e.g. in punishing property crime by deprivation of property) classicism appeared to contradict widely-held commonsensical notions of human nature and motivation. Modifications of classicist principles, therefore, occurred—encouraged by lawyers, on the one hand, and penologists on the other. The resulting neo-classicist scheme—hemmed in and qualified with positivist exceptions, now forms the basis for the majority of legal systems both in the West and in the Soviet bloc.

The central problem involved in implementing 'pure' classicist principles was the classicist concentration on the criminal act—individual differences between criminal actors being ignored, or given only an *ad hoc* consideration. In practice, the particular situation in which the actor was placed, his past history of criminality,

7

and his 'degree' of 'responsibility': all cried out for the attention of the jurist. The neo-classicists, such as Rossi, Garaud and Joly, introduced revisions to account for these problems of practice. In particular, the neo-classicists, first, allowed for mitigating circumstance. Particular attention was to be given in the courtroom to the situation (e.g. the physical and social environment) in which the individual offender had been placed. Second, some allowance was to be given for an offender's past record: the longer an offender's previous record, the more he could be seen to be determined by external circumstance. Finally, some consideration for factors of incompetence, pathology, insanity and impulsive behaviour (the latter negating premeditation) was urged on the jurist. All these considerations were held to be important in modifying the ability of the individual to exercise his free will.

In the neo-classical scheme, man is still held to be accountable for his actions but certain minor reservations are made. The past history and the present situation of the actor are held to affect his likelihood to reform. In other words, the actor is no longer the isolated, atomistic, rational man of pure classicism. A view of the social world emerges which looks something like the following:

1. At the centre are adult, sane individuals—seen to be fully responsible for their actions. They are identical to the ideal type actors of 'pure' classical theory—except that some cognizance is taken of their particular circumstances. These allowances are relevant only to mitigation—they do not form the basis of excusing the actor his responsibility. All men, therefore, as before, are seen to be capable of crime—no particular motivational patterns (e.g. psychological types) or structural circumstances (e.g. crimes of poverty) are recognized.

2. Children and (often) the aged are seen to be less capable of making accountable decisions.

3. A small group of individuals—the insane and the grossly feeble-minded—are seen to be incapable of adult freedom of action. The actions of men in this section of society are explained entirely in terms of predisposing factors. Here actions are determined: there is no question of the actors being responsible for what they do (and, therefore, for what happens to them).

The neo-classicist revisions created an entrée for the non-legal expert—particularly the psychiatrists, and later, the social workers—into the courts. An arena is now recognized where judge, lawyer and jury appraise behaviour in terms of moral choice—various experts on deviancy are called in, as the courts see fit, to propound their determinist explanations of behaviour, as the basis for mitigation (e.g. suspension of sentence) or 'reform' (e.g. changing the offender's predisposing environment by institutionalization).

The revisions in classical thought also encompassed the range of penal measures available to the court. As Radzinowicz (1966, p. 123) has indicated:

the rigidity of the classical school on the Continent of Europe made it almost impossible to develop constructive and imaginative penal measures. Had our system of dealing with crime been confined within the pattern laid down in *Dei delitti e delle pene* virtually all the reforms of which we are most proud would have been excluded because they would have conflicted with the principle that punishment must be closely defined in advance and strictly proportionate to the offence. There would have been no discharge, no adjustment of fines to the means of offenders, no suspended sentences, no probation, no parole, no special measures for young offenders or the mentally abnormal.

Awareness of the effects of incarceration on the criminal, in terms of stigmatization and the consequences of close association between criminals, coupled with the various individual differences observed between criminals (independent of their crimes), brought home to penologists and the judiciary the necessity to revise classicist principles. That is, instead of seeing the sentenced criminal as an atomistic individual who could, and would, connect his crime rationally to his 'just' punishment and draw the appropriate moral conclusions, the neo-classicists came to be aware that:

1. the sentence would have different effects, depending on the individual characteristics of the offender.

2. that to imprison the offender was to place him in an environment which would in itself affect his future propensity to crime.

A central consequence of this revision was that punishment came increasingly to be phrased in terms of punishment appropriate to rehabilitation.[3] There was, however, no radical departure from the free-will model of man involved in the earlier classical premises. *The criminal had to be punished in an environment conducive to his making the correct moral decisions. Choice was (and still is) seen to be a characteristic of the individual actor—but there is now a recognition that certain structures are more conducive to free choice than others.*

The neo-classicists took the solitary rational man of classicist criminology and gave him a past and a future. With an eye to the influence of factors which might determine the commission of a criminal act and the actions of a man subsequent to conviction, they held fast to the notion of human volition. They merely sketched in the structures which might blur or marginally affect the exercise of voluntarism. It is this model—with minor corrections—which remains the major model of human behaviour held to by agencies of social control in all advanced industrial societies (whether in the West or the East) (cf. Hollander, 1969), and it is against the background of this dominant ideology that alternative views of motivation and action will have to struggle. It was against this model, too, that the positive school of criminology attempted to exert its influence.

The positivist revolution

Enrico Ferri, one of the three central figures of the 'positive school', envisaged positivism not merely as a reform movement—a straightforward graft on to the classicist model itself—but as a Copernican transformation of man's conception of crime and human nature (1901, pp. 9, 23 and 36).

> The historical mission of the (Classical) School consisted in a reduction of punishment. . . . We now follow up the practical and scientific mission of the classical school with a still more noble and fruitful mission by adding to the problem of the diminution of penalties the problem of the diminution of crimes.

Positivism saw its role as the systematic elimination of the free will 'metaphysics' of the classical school—and its replacement by a science of society, taking on for itself the task of the eradication of crime. In the words of one of its contemporary adherents (Eysenck, 1970, p. 204), positivism

> holds out to society an altogether different approach to criminality, an approach geared only to practical ends, such as the elimination of anti-social conduct, and not cluttered with irrelevant, philosophical, retributory, and ethicoreligious beliefs.

Since the end of the nineteenth century, courtroom and penal practice has been dominated by a neo-classical model, whilst most psychological and sociological studies of criminal and deviant action have been carried out within a more or less positivist framework. Periodically, the two models clash, and, indeed, the debates about responsibility in penal philosophy bear testimony to the attempts of classicists (Hart, 1962) to resist the positivist incursions (Wootton. 1959; Eysenck, 1970).

It is important to distinguish positivism as used in criminology from the positivism involved in social and psychological theory at large, if only because criminological positivism has been more obviously and clearly framed with a view to immediate practice.[4]

Our intention here, then, is to single out the common elements that are present in the numerous versions of positive criminology. We realize that some individual theories will transcend the limitations of this model in detail: but it is our contention that their general orientation must invariably fall within the parameters of such a model.

Positivism's major attribute—from which its major characteristics may all be deduced—is its insistence on the unity of the scientific method. That is, the premises and instruments which are alleged to be successful in the study of the physical world are seen to be of equal validity and promise in the study of society and man. Insisting on this premise, positivists have proceeded to propound the methods for the quantification of behaviour, have acclaimed the objectivity of the scientist, and have asserted the determinate, law-governed nature of human action. We will deal with each of these three premises in turn, subsequently discussing the six distinct problems we see them to have raised for positivists and the solutions they have offered.

The quantification of behaviour

The physical sciences had sought to discover 'law-like generalities' via measurement and quantification of phenomena. Positivist criminology proceeded along similar lines, seeking to develop accurate and calculable units of crime and deviance as a preliminary to generalization. The problem they faced was that of distinguishing crime and deviancy from normal behaviour on a quantifiable basis, and the immediate and obvious resort was to the criminal statistics, furnishing as they did some details of both the quantity and the types of crimes committed. The contradictions were immediate and obvious:

1. The statistics were categorized in legal terms, terms which might be inadequate for scientific analysis.

2. The statistics were based on 'crimes known to the police' which were (and are) in many instances only a tiny proportion of the total number of criminal acts committed. The total amount of criminality, as represented in the statistics, therefore, could vary considerably according to the degree of police vigilance, the deployment of police resources, the willingness of the public to report particular offences and so on,[5] without there being any real change in the amount of law-breaking.

3. The statistics define crime only in terms of the infraction of laws—but these laws may reflect only the caprice of law-makers or the interests of powerful groups. They may not represent any moral consensus, of a universal or persistent variety, in the population at large.

In the search for a moral yardstick on which to base a positive science, these problems met with two general solutions: a liberal and a radical positivism.

11

Liberal positivism

Liberal positivists admit the inadequacy of the criminal statistics whilst suggesting that certain revisions can be made in order that the statistics can be used in analysis. The assumption is that there is a consensus in a community and that the law represents a formal crystallization of that consensus. Crime by this definition is necessarily extreme deviance. This is basically the position taken by Leslie Wilkins (1964, p. 9) in his search for a statistical model of conformity and deviancy:

> A society in which a large proportion of the population regularly practise a given form of behaviour will tend to permit the behaviour and not define it as 'deviant'. Indeed, on one interpretation of the term 'deviant' it is impossible to conceive of any action being classified as deviant if the majority of the population within a culture regularly behave that way. Owing to inertia within social systems, the official definition of deviance may fall out of line with the definitions of individuals. A ruling minority or powerful group may, for a time, be able to persuade the majority to permit the definitions to remain unamended because they reflect some idealized behaviour patterns to which the majority tend to subscribe. But in democratic countries there is little scope for large differences between the definitions of the majority of the people and the encoded definitions.

At the back of this position, of course, is the implicitly classical notion that sees the legal system as a reflection of freely-chosen contracts between rational men and liberal society. Deviation from these kinds of laws, therefore, provides the criminologist with invaluable information about the fundamental tendency of men to conform or deviate (to social arrangements of the most developed variety): they tell us about the distribution of pathological individuals in a more or less perfect society. Paul Tappan is the clearest exponent of this view of the statistics and their utility (1962, pp. 28–34):

> The behavior prohibited has been considered significantly in derogation of group welfare by deliberative and representative assembly, formally constituted for the purpose of establishing such norms; nowhere else in the field of social control is there directed a comparable rational effort to elaborate standards conforming to the predominant needs, desires, and interests of the community . . .
>
> Adjudicated offenders represent the closest possible approxi-

mation to those who have in fact violated the law, carefully selected by the sieving of the due process of the law; no other province of social control attempts to ascertain the breach of norms with such rigor and precision.

Whilst it is admitted that the figures may be under-representative for minor crimes, it is thought that the more serious offences among minor criminals and the vast majority of major crimes will be reported. The central task is the reformulation of the categories utilized in the official statistics to provide data more in keeping with the interests and objectives of the scientist.[6] This perspective is prevalent primarily amongst government agencies concerned with crime and, for example, government sponsored research. It assumes its most sophisticated form in a study carried out by Sellin and Wolfgang in the 1960s (1969, p. 1):

The purpose of the research was to examine the feasibility of constructing an index of delinquency that would, in contrast with traditional and entrenched methods in use, provide a more sensitive and meaningful measurement of the significance and the ebb and flow of the infractions of law attributable to juveniles, taking into account both the number of these violations and their character and degree of seriousness.

Official statistics of juvenile delinquency, currently published and generally assumed to provide a proper index to that phenomenon, seemed to us to be crude and quite inadequate for that purpose. They were either based on cases brought to court and, thus, ignored the high percentage of delinquencies —often as much as one half or two thirds—disposed of by the police by simple warnings or a referral to some social agency other than the court; or they were based on the number of juveniles charged by the police with specific crimes, the labels of which were supplied by the penal code and juvenile court statutes. We were convinced that police data on delinquency would furnish the best foundation for an index or indexes, but we were also convinced that the principles adopted by police agencies in compiling and publishing delinquency statistics were in need of reformulation.

The authors began by working through the police records in order to expand on the limited data and categorization of the raw statistics. They chose those types of delinquency which would be most likely to be brought to police attention with sufficient regularity that the proportion of such offences made visible would remain reasonably constant over time. The legal code then, was assumed to be a reflection of a consensus in society. Adjustments in categorization and assumptions of constant proportions of visible to non-visible offences made up the preliminary reformulation. But they baulked at assuming that the legal classification reflected accurately the agreed social harm of an offence. Instead, they argued, it was necessary to establish a posited community agreement as to the respective gravity of various offences. Out of this a *real* index of delinquency could be created, its variation representing the *true* extent of deviation amongst juveniles. The offences were therefore rated by a community jury so as to arrive at appropriate weightings for each and thereby a satisfactory index (Sellin and Wolfgang, 1969, p. 6):

> 141 brief descriptions of events so constructed as to take into account characteristic features, such as its circumstance, the injury (if any) inflicted on a victim, intimidation and violence, value of property lost or damaged, etc. These events, as described, were rated on category and magnitude scales by about 750 university students, police line officers, juvenile aid officers, and juvenile court judges. . . . The results of these attitude tests enabled us to give weights to various elements of an event and produce a form for scoring it.

The attempts by the liberal positivists, therefore, to arrive at a moral yardstick on which to build a positive science ultimately concerned with the diminution of unwanted behaviours, rests on the assumptions that there is a more or less prevalent consensus on the nature of morality; that this morality can be described (and ultimately quantified) by any particular mixed group of respondents from the population at large (i.e. that a group of students, police and jurymen are representative of a more general consensus); and that the law in some way can be reformed (and with it the statistics) to ensure that it represents the morality that has been so described. Throughout, the emphasis in liberal positivism is on the existence or the possibility of a social and moral consensus.

Radical positivism

Radical positivism has two wings: a mild version which takes the legal code as representative of a consensus and proceeds to create its own statistics in terms of this measure, but independently of the police and the judiciary (who may not themselves be representative) and a stronger version which derives its statistics from a posited consensus which is held to differ significantly from that enshrined in legal definitions.

Travis Hirschi, like the majority of modern criminologists, adopts the milder version when he writes (1969, p. 47): 'In this study, delinquency is defined by acts, the detection of which is thought to result in the punishment of the person committing them by agents of the wider society.'

The responsibility for evaluating whether an act is to appear as crime or not is shifted either to the wider society in general, or, in the case of self-report studies (cf., for example, Gold, 1970) to the offender himself. The law provides a rough moral yardstick, the statistics representing the willingness of individuals to admit to an act retrospectively, or the extent to which police officers are willing and able to arrest offenders whom they encounter in the course of their work. In this perspective, the stress is on the seriousness with which lawbreaking is viewed, whether by the agency of social control (the policeman) or by the respondent in a self-report study. It is assumed that there is no great disagreement on the morality of law itself.

The predicament which arises in this perspective is that crime, thus defined or quantified, is found to be well-nigh ubiquitous. It is found to occur in all sections of society—amongst the rich and the poor, the young and the old—amongst men and women—and always in greater amounts and in different proportions than was previously assumed (cf. Gold, 1970). Criminological theory, however, has largely worked on the assumption that crime is an overwhelmingly youthful, masculine, working-class activity. Radical positivists—confronting the altogether different picture of criminality arrived at by their own techniques—conclude, not that there is a greater spread and variety of rationality in the society at large (some of which is rational law-breaking) than was previously allowed, but that the effectiveness of social control throughout the society is not all that it has been assumed to be. The police, the social workers and the judiciary are, by implication, accused of exercising non-scientific criteria in the decisions they have made about the disposition of rule-breaking individuals. Reforms are therefore necessary to ensure that social control operates effectively and 'scientifically' in accordance with the objective interests of the consensus. Radical positivism, therefore, is concerned with the operationalization and the enforcement, via the techniques of positive science, of the moral consensus embodied in the body of criminal law.[7]

Certain positivists, however, have come to quarrel with the use of legal criteria of deviancy entirely. Paul Tappan (1962, p. 28) has summarized this position as follows:

> To a large extent it reveals the feeling among social scientists that not all anti-social conduct is proscribed by law (which is probably true), that not all conduct violative of the criminal code is truly anti-social, or is not so to a significant extent (which is also undoubtedly true). Among some students the opposition to the traditional definition of crime as law violation

15

rises from their desire to discover and study wrongs which are absolute and eternal rather than mere violations of a statutory and case law system which varies in time and place; this is essentially the old metaphysical search for the law of nature. They consider the dynamic and relativistic nature of law to be a barrier to the growth of a scientific system of hypotheses possessing universal validity.

In this perspective, the need is for a set of concepts of 'natural crime' independent of the legal system. The radical positivist has three major points of departure from which to evolve a moral calculus autonomous of the law. He can claim, first, that there exist some fundamental human sentiments—violation of which indicates 'real' crime, a concept of crime untainted by the vagaries of the judiciary, the existence of different interest groups in society, and other historically and culturally specific influences on the content of crime and the make-up of the criminal statistics.[8] Or, he can claim, second, that it is possible to specify a consensus which is quite distinct from the edicts of the legal system. Or, finally, he can make his appeal to certain 'real' system-needs, against which certain acts are really, as distinct from hypothetically, dysfunctional.

The early Italian positivist Raffaele Garofalo (1852–1934) was the first to evolve a sophisticated definition of natural crime (1914, pp. 33–44):

> From what has been said . . . we may conclude that the element of immorality requisite before a harmful act can be regarded as criminal by public opinion, is the injury to so much of the moral sense as is represented by one or the other of the elementary altruistic sentiments of *pity* and *probity*. Moreover, the injury must wound these sentiments not in their superior and finer degrees, but in the *average* measure in which they are possessed by a community—a measure which is indispensable for the adaption of the individual to society. Given such a violation of either of these sentiments, and we have what may properly be called *natural crime*.

The basic moral sensibilities appear in a more or less advanced form in all societies and are seen by Garofalo to be essential to the coexistence of individuals in society (Allen, 1960, p. 257). Natural crime is a product, therefore, of the average moral sense in the community in question.[9]

Garofalo is exceptional in that he uses all the three criteria outlined above, in order to establish his autonomous notion of natural crime. At the root of his definition, however, lies the invocation of the moral sensibilities: 'pity' (revulsion against the voluntary

16

infliction of suffering on others) and 'probity' (respect for the property rights of others). These sentiments are seen as performing essential functions in maintaining the existing moral consensus, and thus to find a place in the values protected by law. The parallel with classicist conceptions of law is apparent. Here, too, a consensus is posited: a consensus founded on fear of the Hobbesian war of all against all and a law which enshrines the necessary (functional) arrangements to prevent such an eventuality. Here too, *a priori* assumptions are made about human nature: the morally right choice is also a choice that is functional for the society itself. A tautologous picture of human nature and social order is erected, a picture which has the happy feature of leaving the specifics of social order (the existence of inequality in the ownership of wealth and property) unquestioned.

Classicism and positivism have in common what they ignore, rather than what they include. In the classical picture of man and society, the social order is *willed*: the rational man makes a choice to uphold the given distribution of property. In Garofalo, on the other hand, the moral sentiments, performing the functions they do for a propertied society, are underlying constants. Human nature is not only a constant (as it is in classical accounts); it is also *determined*. It was the determined nature of moral sentiment, in Garofalo, that foreshortened the range of human choice. Gabriel Tarde, a positivist himself, was later (1912, p. 72) to remark of Garofalo's unusual endeavour that 'The most striking thing to be here observed is the sight of an evolutionist making this desperate effort to attach himself at some fixed point in this unfathomable flood of phenomena and cast anchor exactly in what is the most fluid and evasive thing in the world, that is to say, feeling.'

This search for an 'anchor'—which earlier we called the 'moral yardstick'—for an active (reformative) criminology in positivist principles was most clearly threatened by the 'unfathomable flood' of criminal definitions over time and across cultures. The positivists who postulated fundamental tendencies in human nature attempted —rather like the ethnomethodological writers of our own time[10]—to argue that one could discover a variable but identifiable consensus of meanings and morals, which would in turn serve as the elusive yardstick for positive action. Thus, Thorstein Sellin (1962a, p. 8, our emphasis) argues:

For every person, then, there is from the point of view a given group of which he is a member, a normal (right) and an abnormal (wrong) way of reacting, the norm depending upon the social values of the group which formulated it. *Conduct norms are, therefore, found wherever social groups are found, i.e. universally. They are not the creation of any ONE normative group: they are not confined within political boundaries; they are not necessarily embodied in law.*

These facts lead to the inescapable conclusion that the study of conduct norms would afford a sounder basis for the development of scientific categories than a study of crimes as defined in the criminal law. Such study would involve the isolation and classification of norms into *universal categories* transcending political and other boundaries, a necessity imposed by the logic of science. The study of how conduct norms develop, how they are related to each other and to other cultural elements, the study of changes and differentials in norm violations and the relationship of such violations to other cultural phenomena, are certainly questions which the sociologist by training and interest might regard as falling within his field.

In this fashion the social scientist can focus on the empirical variation of norms in a given social group and still be able to generalize about deviancy as a whole. Thus, statistics come to be related to conduct norms, rather than to legal criteria. The problem here, however, is that any such investigation of conduct norms would almost certainly confront important dissensions within the social groups under investigation. There would be a plurality of definitions (and therefore of statistics) available to the commentator and he would have to make his choice, unaided by *a priori* notions of deviancy.

The final appeal to non-legal criteria is to the needs of the society—the system—itself. By definition, this has been the resort largely of sociologists working within the positivist tradition, and is most notable in the work of the so-called structural-functionalist school of American sociology. The fundamental premises here is that values, norms and morality are unproblematic—they are given by the system. The deviant is not a person with an alternative or authentic morality or rationality—he is an undersocialized individual, who, for a variety of reasons, has not suffiiently internalized the appropriate (i.e. the system) morality. As John Horton has noted (1964, p. 294), in this perspective: 'The problem of the perspective of the observer ... is avoided by interpreting values not as political and utopian ideals, but as neutral objects of the social system being observed. The question of whose values, and why, goes unanswered.'

Shifting the responsibility for evaluation to the system itself, the radical positivist may believe that he can proceed neutrally to specify the real basis and distribution of conformity and deviance. He can dissociate himself from the vagaries of judicial processing, from the consequences of police organizational practice, and in the final analysis from the picture of criminality as portrayed by the official statistics; and yet he can still proceed to construct a science of 'real' crime and correction (in terms of system-needs or 'imperatives'). Actually, of course, as Melvin Tumin has shown, this particular path to positive neutrality is strewn with many a problem. Even if one were to accept, with the functionalists, that it is possible to specify the needs of the system in value-neutral fashion, there would still be a problem in deciding on how to weight, and on how to characterize (as functional or dysfunctional) particular social behaviours within that system. Referring to criminal behaviours in general (however defined), to sexual deviance, to social inequality, or to any activity conventionally seen as a 'social problem', Tumin raises the central queries the radical positivists are unable to answer (1965, p. 381):

> On balance, what can one say about the total impact . . . of such practices? On the net balance, are they supportive or destructive of that system, and which system? And how could one test the truth of any such claim? . . . In the end we come out where we started, namely, with a preference—supported by data, of course, but data that have been weighted and added according to our preferences. And there are no rules to determine which is the better or more correct method of toting up the diverse effects.[11]

The positivist's attempt to stand aside from the social arrangements of his time, in particular the inconsistencies of law and social control, burying beneath them for the natural sensibilities of men, the true consensus, or the real needs of the 'system' itself, has so failed to reveal the basis on which the science of positivism might proceed, in the interests of all, and in defiance of none.

Scientific neutrality

The search for a vantage point from which the social world can be measured and assessed without prejudice or bias is closely bound up with the demand for objectivity in positivist thought. Here, once again, two strands in positivism can be detected: a liberal and a radical version. The liberal version solves the problems of objectivity by denying that questions of value are the concern of the scientist. The politicians (who are democratically elected, and, therefore, represent the consensus) decide on the central problems that face a society and the major aims of political and social legislation. The scientist is exclusively concerned with the means whereby certain ends (given politically—by political man) may be achieved. In this version the positive scientist, the willing handmaiden of the *status quo*, is very much a caricature of the noble scientist of society envisaged by the founder of the positive tradition itself.

The radical positivist would find much more favour with Comte. He argues that the scientist exists apart from, and independently of, sectarian interests and value preferences. Although he may have his personal values as citizen, his major task as a scientist is to discover the true consensus. This true consensus is of course to be found in the needs of the system: the advance of society is the advance of men towards harmony within a civilized and balanced society. Standing in the way of this harmony and consensus, however, are the capricious and unscientific (value-laden) activities of the agencies of social control (in particular, in criminological polemics, the judiciary) on the one hand, and the disruptive and asocial activities of the criminal on the other. The radical positivist locates his objectivity in the interests of the people as a whole—against the criminal and judicial minorities. Thus, Enrico Ferri places himself in direct opposition to the classical school (1929, Preface): 'Historically, the principal reason for the rise of the positivistic view of criminal justice was the necessity ... to put a stop to the exaggerated individualism in favour of the criminal in order to obtain a greater respect for the rights of people who constitute a great majority.'

In so far as the positivist (whether liberal or radical in inclination) is interested in the causes of deviance and crime, he is interested in the environmental and psychological reasons for an individual's failure to internalize the norms of a system the majority are alleged to accept.[12] The meaning of behaviour is never problematic: it is to be interpreted in terms of the posited consensus. Every act can therefore be assigned an objective and ultimately a measurable significance (e.g. along a continuum of introversion and extraversion).[13] There is no problem of translation—since, if there were, it would make science impossible.

The positivist in general, therefore, has a world view of a society consisting, in the main, of normal people, who represent the consensus. He places himself with democratic finesse squarely in the middle of this consensus. Deviants he perceives as a small minority existing at the margins of society; and powerful non-scientists he sees also as a minor problem temporarily obstructing the advance of positive science. Vested interests of power and wealth do not represent the collectivity: this is a position he reserves for himself.

Social reaction against the deviant is only a problem in so far as the police and judiciary are inefficient or prejudiced in their task of representing the collectivity at large. Social reaction plays no important part in the explanation of deviance, since, by definition, deviants are under-socialized or pathological individuals unable to take their place in the central arenas of a healthy society. Deviance is by definition that which is reacted against—by, and on behalf of, the majority of (right-minded) men. The major focus of criminology must, therefore, be on the criminal actor (his psychology, his necessarily peculiar environment, etc.) rather than on the criminal law. The liberal positivist, indeed, could never take any other position: for to question the jurisdiction and the consequences of law would be to vacate the role of scientist for that of political man. The radical positivist, on the other hand, could criticize the law tangentially for its failure to represent the consensus or for its failure to implement its punishment in an equitable fashion. But he will still see the social reaction against deviancy and criminality as being essentially non-problematic. For David Matza, this shift (away from the classicist's concern with the nature of contract and the protection of the individual from the state) is central to an understanding of criminological positivism (1964, p. 3).

> The most celebrated and thus the most explicit assumption of positive criminology is the primacy of the criminal actor rather than the criminal law as the major point of departure in the construction of etiological theories. The explanation of crime, according to the positive school, may be found in the motivational and behavioral systems of criminals. Among these systems, the law and its administration is deemed secondary or irrelevant. This quest for explanation in the character and background of offenders has characterized all modern criminology, irrespective of the particular causal factors espoused.

In the final analysis, therefore, the 'quest for objectivity' in positivism reduces itself to a plea for the measurement of individual pathologies and pathogenic circumstances: an objectivity involving the counting of deviant heads. What is ignored is the problem of what is really (objectively) going on in those heads (and the way what is going on there is a reflection of the oppressions of state and the law, the facts of social inequality, and the structures of outside society in general).

The determinism of behaviour

For deviancy to be dealt with scientifically, it must be seen as being subject to discoverable causal laws. The positivists rejected outright the classicists' notion of a rational man capable of exercising free will. Ferri (1886b, p. 244) clearly outlined his differences with the classicist school:

> We speak two different languages. For us, the experimental

(i.e. inductive) method is the key to all knowledge; to them everything derives from logical deductions and traditional opinion. For them, facts should give place to syllogisms; for us the fact governs and no reasoning can occur without starting with facts, for them science needs only paper, pen and ink and the rest comes from a brain stuffed with more or less abundant reading of books made with the same ingredients. For us science requires spending a long time in examining the facts one by one, evaluating them, reducing them to a common denominator, extracting the central idea from them. For them a syllogism or an anecdote suffices to demolish a myriad of facts gathered through years of observation and analysis; for us the reverse is true.

Where the classicist—as armchair scholar—adjudged the criminality of particular acts in terms of his view of the moral calculus implicit in the social contract, assuming that the criminal thus adjudged was necessarily *either* wicked *or* ignorant; the positivist asserted that the criminal automatically revealed himself by his actions and that the criminal was propelled by forces of which he was himself unaware. There was no responsibility to judge, or, therefore, to investigate questions of motivation. Unlike the classicists who endowed the actor with considerable knowledge of his action, the positivists were concerned, as Durkheim put it, that social life should be explained, not by the notions of those who participate in it, but by more profound causes which are unperceived by consciousness.

The classicist and the positivist were both concerned, however, with their own position as expert, over and above the actor himself. The classicist judged the morality of an act (which itself was seen to be freely made) whilst the positivist explained the causes of the action to the actor himself, arguing that he was unconcerned with questions of morality. Ultimately, the positivist school, following the logic of its own position, called for the abolition of the jury system and its replacement by a team of experts well-versed in the science of human behaviour. Experts were necessary to investigate the causes propelling the individual into crime, diagnosing him and prescribing an appropriate therapeutic regime. An assault was also made on the sentencing policy implicit in classicism: the notion of the fixed sentence proportional to the consequences of the (criminal) action. In its place, the positivists argued, there should be a system of indeterminate sentences which would ensure that, once an individual's 'criminality' had been expertly assessed, there was time enough for a cure to be effected. Above all, the positivists advocated the abolition of specifically penal measures: it made no sense to inflict punishment on the criminal if he had no choice in the question of his own reformation.

It is, of course, at this point that thoroughgoing positivism clashes with the ideology of classical law, and the institutions it has spawned. The acceptance of positivism would considerably undermine the judiciary. The implementation of law would be a matter for the scientific expert and would be removed from the realm of politics (the interpretation by laymen and non-scientists of the consensus). This clash would be muted only by the ideological assumptions held in common: the primacy of the actor rather than the criminal law (or the structure of state behind it) as the focus for criminology.

Out of the 'scientific investigation' of crime, certain positive laws were to be developed: the most famous of which was Ferri's 'law of criminal saturation' (1895, pp. 75 et seq.), namely, the 'law' that:

> just as in a given volume of water, at a given temperature, we
> find the solution of a fixed quantity of any chemical substance,
> not an atom more or less, so in a given social environment,
> in certain defined physical conditions of the individual, we
> find the commission of a fixed number of crimes.

The positivist attempts the scientific explanation of crime by social action as having the qualities (no more and no less) of things —or objects in the natural world. With this in mind he denudes action of meaning, or moral choice and of creativity. For human behaviour to be studied scientifically it must be akin to the non-human world, it must be deterministically dominated by law-like regulations, it must be reified—have the quality of 'things'. This, then, is at the centre of the positivist hopes for a science of a crime and it is in this respect that its theoretical approach stands or falls.

Thus, from the initial three *premises* of the scientific method— measurement (quantification), objectivity (neutrality), and causality (determinism)—are derived a number of *postulates*: a consensus view of the world, a focus on the criminal actor rather than the criminal act, a reification of the social world, a doctrine of non-responsibility for actions, the inapplicability of punishment, and a faith in the superior cognitive ability of the scientific expert.

These *postulates* present positivism with a series of problems, some of which it was well capable of solving; others which emerge as crucial stumbling blocks in the development of positivist theory and practice.

Problem of therapeutic nihilism

If the criminal is denied freedom and is seen inevitably to engage in criminal behaviour, then it can be argued that therapy is by definition

23

impossible. A modern positivist, Hans Eysenck (1970, p. 186), takes exception to this viewpoint for:

It certainly would not follow . . . that the complete denial of freedom of will leaves us in a state of therapeutic nihilism; quite the contrary. Because we know that conduct is determined, we are enabled to study scientifically the mechanisms by which it is determined, and thus develop appropriate ways of changing it.

The prime task of positivism, after all, is the elimination of crime —it does not therefore see the deviant as possessed of an incorrigible essence. It may, however, be that scientific knowledge is insufficient at the moment to solve the problem of successful therapy. This explains the pessimism of early positivists such as Lombroso (1913, p. 432): 'It would be a mistake to imagine that measures which have been shown successfully applied to born criminals: for these are, for the most part, refractory to all treatment, even to the most affectionate care begun at the very cradle.'

There can be little doubt that even Lombroso, who, after all, saw most crime as remediable, would have altered his views in the light of modern discoveries in genetic theory.

An embarrassment of riches

Positive criminology accounts for too much delinquency. Taken at their terms, delinquency theories seem to predicate far more delinquency than actually occurs. If delinquents were in fact radically differentiated from the rest of conventional youth in that their unseemly behaviour was constrained through compulsion or commitment, then involvement in delinquency would be more permanent and less transient, more pervasive and less intermittent than is apparently the case. Theories of delinquency yield an embarrassment of riches which seemingly go unmatched in the real world. (Matza, 1964, pp. 21–2.)

David Matza's conception of the positive criminal stems from his insistence that one of the fundamental assumptions of positivism is that (1964, pp. 11–12):

The delinquent was fundamentally different from the law-abiding. This conception too has persistently shaped the positivist image of delinquency. Differentiation is the favoured method of positivist explanation. Each school of positive criminology has pursued its own theory of differentiation between conventional and criminal persons. Each in turn has regularly tended to exaggerate these differences. At its inception positive criminology revolted against the assumption of the general similarity between criminal and conventional persons implicit in classical theory. In rejecting the obviously untenable classical conception of similarity, positive criminology characteristically proceeded to the other extreme—radical differentiation—and in a variety of guises has persisted in this caricature. From the born criminal to differential association, the explanation of delinquency has rested in the radically different circumstances experienced by delinquent and law-abiding alike. Each is constrained, but by a fundamentally different set of circumstances.

This conception of positivism is a fallacy. It is based on popularized versions of scientific criminology (for reasons we shall investigate in chapter 2), not on thoroughgoing positivism itself. Indeed precisely such an accusation could be levelled at popularized conceptions of classicist theory[14]—against which, as David Matza has correctly indicated, positivist theory emerged as a critique. For the essence of positivism is a quantitative, scientific approach to its subject matter. It does not envisage the world in terms of dualities but in terms of continuity. Thus, just as there are not merely tall and short people and nobody in between, there is no conception of the essentially criminal and non-criminal but rather an estimation of degrees of criminality or non-criminality. As Eysenck (1970, p. 74) plainly puts it:

Criminality is obviously a continuous trait of the same kind as intelligence, or height, or weight. We may artificially say that every person either is or is not a criminal, but this would be so grossly over-simplified as to be untrue. Criminals vary among themselves, from those who fall once and never again, to those who spend most of their life in prison. Clearly the latter have far more 'criminality' in their make-up than the former. Similarly, people who are not convicted of crimes may also differ widely in respect to moral character. Some may in fact have committed crimes for which they were never caught or, if they were caught, perhaps the court took a rather lenient view. Others have never given way to temptation at all. From a rational point of view, therefore, we cannot regard criminals as being completely distinct from the rest of the population. They simply represent the extreme end of a continuous distribution, very much as a mental defective represents the extreme end of a continuous distribution of intelligence, ranging upward, through the average to the very high I.Q. of the student or even the genius.

In this kind of positivist perspective, the person who commits a

25

crime may well be merely a fraction to the criminal side of the continuum. His future behaviour is therefore not necessarily likely to be consistently criminal—especially if some therapy has been attempted. Further, with the exception of very few genetic theorists, few positivists would argue against the possibility that increased age, maturity and changed circumstances could constitute new 'factors' which would impel the young criminal back into the ranks of normality. The embarrassment of riches is only a problem for a few positivists—sophisticated positivism, by its very nature, has little trouble in circumnavigating it.

The problem of insulation

For the positivist science to be objective is to be 'neutral'. The concern is to induce from the facts in a dispassionate manner, the laws of the social universe. This is a questionable objective and a questionable faith in two respects:

a   that it involves a misconception of the nature of natural science

b   that, further, the social world demands an alternative epistemology to that demanded by the 'natural' world.

Contemporary philosophers of science would dismiss the 'inductionism' of the positivists. As Thomas Kuhn (1970, p. 2) commented on his debate with Karl Popper '[we] are united in opposition to a number of classical positivism's most characteristic theses. We both emphasize, for example, the intimate and inevitable entanglement of scientific observation with scientific theory: we are correspondingly sceptical of efforts to produce any neutral observation language.'

Absolute objectivity becomes an impossible goal: facts do not speak for themselves. 'Facts' are a product of the work of those with the power to define what is to be taken to be 'factual' (cf. I. Taylor and Walton, 1970) and of the willingness of those without such power to accept the given definitions. The social scientist, it follows, makes choices from various paradigmatic universes: he chooses to exist in one 'factual' world or another. In criminology, or in areas of academic study and practice where reference is made to 'social' or 'political' problems, this essentially epistemological question presents itself more concretely as the problem of multiple realities.

The problem of multiple realities

Absolute objectivity depends on the existence of a consensus within society—a situation in which there is one widely-held conception of reality (as to what is 'factual'). In such a situation, alternative or deviant realities are not factual at all—they belong to the realm of the meaningless, the anomic, the disorganized, the irrational, and, in the final analysis, often to the criminal.[15] What, however, would a positivist make of Stokeley Carmichael's definition of reality when he writes (1968, p. 155):

> You see, because you've been able to lie about terms, you've been able to call people like Cecil Rhodes a philanthropist, when in fact he was a murderer, a rapist, a plunderer and a thief. But you call Cecil Rhodes a philanthropist because what he did was that after he stole our diamonds and our gold, he gave us some crumbs so that we can go to school and become just like you. And that was called philanthropy. But we are renaming it: the place is no longer called Rhodesia, it is called Zimbabwe, that's its proper name. And Cecil Rhodes is no longer a philanthropist, he's known to be a thief—you can keep your Rhodes Scholars, we don't want the money that came from the sweat of our people.

Or of Angela Davis who insists that: 'The real criminals in this society are not all the people who populate the prisons across the state, but those people who have stolen the wealth of the world from the people.' They might presumably answer that these quotations are political and that they therefore merit some peculiar exception. But these same problems arise if we ask marijuana-smokers, Jehovah's Witnesses, motoring offenders or professional criminals to describe the world from their own particular perspective. The positivist by appealing to law or to consensus ignores the manner in which power determines these 'obvious' sources of objectivity. As Richard Lichtman argues (1970, pp. 78–9, our emphasis):

> How many true descriptions of a social act are available? An indefinitely large number. What is it that I do when I lecture? Amuse students, undermine the university, rationalize the pretended liberality of American society, satisfy parental expectations, earn a living, remove my efforts from an indefinitely large number of alternatives, etc.? The list is endless. The same situation holds for any action. Why does one conception come to dominate the social perspective of the agents in a given community? How is the meaningful interpretation of action constituted? Democratically? Hardly. *The channelling of interpreted meaning is class structured. It is formed through lived engagement in the predominant class-controlled institutions of the society.* What of the character of those institutions which more specifically pattern the development of socially shared meaning . . . mass media, schools, etc.? They too are under the predominant control of that class of men who exercise hegemony over the means of production,

27

distribution, exchange and consumption upon which society vitally depends. The definition of activity, the shared description of an act and the very meaning of the function of acting, are largely shaped through the nature of productive power.

In his search for true definitions of reality, then: 'the social inquirer cannot dispense with the recognition that he faces a choice in the selection of his basic concepts, and that in exercising this choice he is to some degree supporting or subverting the system in power' (p. 79).

The non-problematic nature of social reaction

The scholar's or scientist's way of becoming partially blind is, inadvertently perhaps, to structure fields of enquiry in such a way as to obscure obvious connections or to take the connections for granted and leave the matter at that. The great task of disconnection—it was arduous and time-consuming—fell to the positive school of criminology. Among their most notable accomplishments, the criminological positivists succeeded in what would seem impossible. They separated the study of crime from the workings and theory of the state. That done, and the lesson extended to deviation generally, the agenda for research and scholarship for the next half-century was relatively clear, especially with regard to what would *not* be studied. Scientists of various persuasion thereafter wandered aimfully, leaving just a few possibilities uncovered, considering how deviation was produced. Throughout, a main producer remained obscure, off-stage due to the fortunate manner in which fields of enquiry were divided. The role of the sovereign, and by extension, instituted authority was hardly considered in the study of deviant behaviour. That lofty subject, unrelated to so seamy a matter as deviation, was to be studied in *political* science. There, as in the curriculum in government or political sociology, Leviathan had little bearing on ordinary criminals. And in criminology, the process of becoming an ordinary criminal was unrelated to the workings of the state. It was, it must be granted, a pretty neat division (Matza, 1969a, pp. 143–4).

'Social reaction' in the positivist model is not seen to be a problem: both the *causes* of the reaction against the deviant, and his perception and interpretation of the stigmatization and exclusion accompanying reaction are ignored. Ignoring these elements in a fully social theory of deviance, positivism lacks both scope and symmetry. It suffers in *scope* because it omits the reasons for reaction (the conflict of interests, the nature of the morality which informs reaction against deviance, the theories of deviancy held to by those with the power to act against the deviant); it ignores or debases the deviant's own reasons for engaging in deviant action, and it holds out no explanation at all of the deviant's interpretation of the reaction against him. It suffers in symmetry in that it divides up the social world into two totally disparate theories of human behaviour. No social explanation —in positivism's own terms—is offered of the behaviour of the 'reactors' themselves.

Contemporary positivism, like the positivist traditions before it, remains, in the final analysis, an assertion about the determinate nature of deviancy. Social reaction against deviancy, however much it is seen to vary historically and culturally, remains at the level of an (uninvestigated) mysterious automatic response. And, in this fashion, the structure of power, wealth and morality which patterns the reaction against deviancy, and sustains the authority of existing social arrangements, is given the stamp of approval by 'science': all that requires to be explained in the realm of social structure and its associated cultural elements is behaviour that deviates from it.

This conception of the role of a science of society relates to the final problem area, namely that of creativity.

The problem of creativity

Matza (1969a, pp. 92–3) captures the final, and critical, weakness of positivist endeavours in the following passage:

The existence of subjects is not quite exhausted by the arduous natural processes of reactivity and adaptation. Capable of creating and assigning meaning, able to contemplate his surroundings and even his own condition, given to anticipation, planning and projecting man—the subject—stands in a different and more complex relation to circumstance. This distinctively human capacity in no way denies that human existence frequently displays itself in ways characteristic of lower levels. Frequently man is wholly adaptable, *as if* he were just organic being. And sometimes though very rarely, he is wholly reactive, *as if* a mere object. But mere reactivity or adaptation should not be confused with the distinctively human condition. They are better seen as an alienation or exhaustion of that condition. A subject actively addresses or encounters his circumstance; accordingly, his distinctive capacity is to reshape, strive toward creating, and actually transcend circumstance. Such a distinctly human project is not always feasible, but the capacity always exists.

If man is merely an adaptive or reactive thing, a creature entirely of social or physical circumstance, how are we to explain the rise of new modes of social arrangements and new ways of defining the world? How do we explain the existing modes of arrangements themselves? Can we explain the new except as a necessary, natural evolution—predicated by the old social arrangements themselves? Can explanations of this kind exhaust and even describe the range of human creativity and social change?

We shall attempt, as the argument in this book evolves, to show that a fully social theory of deviance would be rather more demanding and comprehensive an explanation than that which is required in positivism. In the next chapter, however, we turn our attention to the specific attempts of biological and pyschological varieties of positivism to explain (and eradicate) deviancy. In other words, we shall be attempting to chart, by way of a warning, the continuing successes and advances of the positivist 'revolution' in contemporary criminology.

2 The appeal of positivism

Two types of questions can be asked of any theory: what is its explanatory power and what is its appeal? We wish to remove ourselves from that comfortable school of thought which believes that theories compete with each other in some scholarly limbo, heuristic facility being the only test of survival. We need to explain why certain theories, despite their manifest inability to come to terms with their subject-matter, survive—and indeed, as in the case of positivism, flourish. In the last chapter we criticized the capacity of positivism to explain deviancy. In this chapter we will, first of all, discuss the appeal of positivism. What benefits does this manner of viewing the social universe have as an ideology for protecting the interests inherent in the *status quo* and distorting the information perceived by its adherents?

We intend, therefore, to elucidate the ideological strengths of the central aspects of positivist thought.

The consensus world view

To insist that there is a consensus in society obviates all discussion of the possibility of fundamental conflicts of value and interest. There is only one reality and deviancy is envisaged as a lack of socialization into it. It is a meaningless phenomenon, the only proper response to which can be therapeutic. In one stroke, ethical questions concerning the present order and the reaction against the deviant are removed, for the humanitarian task of the expert becomes that of bringing the miscreant back into the consensual fold.

The determinism of behaviour

To argue that there is a consensus in society and a determination of behaviour allows the positivist to present an absolute situation

31

(uncomplicated by the exercise of choice) for both normals and deviants. The 'normal man in the street' has no option but to conform, for he is, given his adequate socialization, impelled to do so and as there is only one monolithic reality, no 'choices' exist outside of the consensus. Similarly, the deviant does not choose an alternative mode of life: he is propelled by factors beyond his control. The possible attractiveness of deviant realities is thus subtly defused: for no one could possibly freely choose them. The inevitable deduction from this, that punishment is inappropriate, merely serves to fill the positivist with the sense of his own rationality and humanitarianism.

The science of society

The evocation of natural science presents the positivist with a powerful mode of argument. For the system of thought which produces miracles of technology and medicine is a prestigious banner under which to fight. It grants the positivist the gift of 'objectivity'; it bestows on his pronouncements the mantle of 'truth'; it endows his suggestions of therapy, however threatening to individual rights and dignity, with the air of the inevitable. Thus Eysenck counters criticisms that his behaviourist techniques smack of brainwashing, in the following fashion (1969, p. 690):

> I think the major objection to the proposals I have outlined is that they smack of treating human beings as if they were nothing but biological organisms subject to strictly deterministic rules; this Pavlovian revolution, coming on top of the Copernican and Darwinian ones, is too much for the self-esteem of many people. Undesirable the fact may be, but that is not sufficient reason for rejecting it as a fact, one would need better reasons to change one's scientific judgement. And where there is (1) a recognised social need, and (2) a recognised body of scientific knowledge which looks likely to be able to create a technology to cope with that need, it needs little in the way of precognitive ability to forecast that in the course society will use this knowledge and create this technology.

The meshing of interests

All three of these strands: consensus, determinism and scientism, give weight to positivist rhetoric. What is necessary, at this juncture, is to explain why this mode of thought is taken up by the positivist and how the interests of the practitioner and the politician mesh together. It is important, at the outset, to realize that at the simplest level the positivist, by placing himself in the middle of the posited consensus, defends the reality of his own world. For example, Dr R. Cockett (Regional Psychologist to the Home Office Prison Department) writes of working-class drug-takers in the Ashford Remand Centre (1971, p. 142): '[they] were shown to be rather more suspicious and withdrawn than non-drugtakers, more emotionally tense and excitable, and more radical or less conservative in temperament, but to have relatively poor self-sentiment formation—persistence, will-power, social effectiveness and leadership'. This was coupled with: 'less emotional maturity and tolerance of frustration', 'intrapunitive-ness' and 'a tendency towards paranoid feeling'.

Such 'discoveries' are commonplace in the literature of all forms of deviant behaviour. But behind the neutral language lies, in Cockett's own words, 'what is popularly understood by "inadequacy" and "weakness of character" ' (p. 144). It is a simple translation to interpret hedonistic and expressive subcultures as not cultures at all but merely as aggregates of inadequate individuals who are excitable, have a low tolerance of frustration, maturity, etc. Moreover, it is sleight of hand which can conjure what some would term repression into a 'tendency towards paranoid feeling'. All of this reinforces the middle-class professional world of the expert; his stable employment and marriage, deferred gratification and planning are all indices of his own 'strong' personality and social 'adequacy'. By making statements about the deviant he is, inevitably, making valuations about his own world.

Further, the social universe of the expert, like so many others in a complex industrial society, is extremely segregated. He is, therefore, blinkered from receiving information at odds with his world view. As one of the present authors put it (Young, 1971b, pp. 72–3):

The [experts] must explain what is perceived as unusual in terms of the values associated by their audience as usual. In this process, utilising the theoretical ploys listed, they circumscribe and negate the reality of values different from their own. They do not explain, they merely *explain away*. They are well-trained men, but the rigour of their training has enabled them to view the world only from the narrow-blinkered perspective of their own discipline. The fragmentation of knowledge concomitant with specialisation has encouraged the strict compartmentalisation of analysis. . . . As a result such experts can, from the vantage of their cloistered chauvinism, scarcely grasp the totality of the social world even in terms of their own values let alone take a critical stance outside of these values. We are producing what Lucien Goldmann has described as the specialist who is simultaneously illiterate and a graduate of a university.

33

But ideas do not exist in a vacuum; if there are retailers of ideas there are also buyers; and we must now examine the nexus existing between expert, bureaucrat and politician. The emergence of large-scale bureaucracies in every sphere of social activity has given rise to the demand for co-ordination and predictability within enterprises and the precise determination of consumer and public responses. The 'normal' man must be understood in terms of his roles as consumer and voter. At the same time the emergence of alternative realities outside of the official consensus must be defused of their potential to deny consciously, or unconsciously, the ends of the system they threaten to disrupt.[1] The deviant himself is in a more powerful position in a tightly co-ordinated system. Hans Eysenck recognizes this well, for in an article urging the greater need for social conditioning (1969, p. 688), he backs up his argument by noting a trend which is so 'important and serious . . . that our whole future may rest on our ability to expedite it.' Namely:

> What seems to be happening is that society is getting more and more closely knitted together, due to our advancing technology: production is nearing the point where it is nation-wide, particularly in consumer goods like motor cars and such like, and distribution too is getting organized in larger and larger complexes. In other words, there is greater and greater dependence on cooperation between very large groups of people—which do not need to be in close proximity to each other, or even to know of each other's existence. Yet if even a small section within one of the coordinated complexes fails— the tally clerks at the docks, say, or the women sewing covers at Ford's, the whole nexus breaks down, and far-reaching consequences are experienced over a wide area. . . . It is hardly necessary to belabour the main point here made; it is too obvious to require much documentation. The problem to be discussed is: how can we engineer a social consent which will make people behave in a socially adapted, law-abiding fashion, which will not lead to a break-down of the intricately interwoven fabric of social life? Clearly we are failing to do this: the ever-increasing number of unofficial strikes, the ever-increasing statistics of crime of all sorts, the general alienation on which so many writers have commented are voluble witnesses to this statement. The psychologist would answer that what was clearly required was a technology of consent— that is, a generally applicable method of inculcating suitable habits of socialised conduct into the citizens (and particularly the future citizens) of the country in question—or preferably the whole world.

For the politician and the planner, positivism provides a model of human nature which, in its consensual aspects, allows the world 'as it is' to remain unquestioned and, in its determinist notion of human action, offers the possibility of rational planning and control. Thus Jack Douglas (1970b, p. 269) writes:

Positivistic social science provides the administrator of the official organisations with a completely deterministic metaphysics of man and his actions in society. If he chooses to practise the willing suspension of disbelief—to have faith—in the specific theories of this positivistic social science, it also provides him with specific explanations of behaviour which, in combination with deterministic metaphysics, give him a belief that he can *control* the public responses which will be used to judge his own adequacy as an official. At the same time, use of the positivistic social sciences, which always make maximum use of the very prestigious mathematical forms of the natural sciences, provides the official with the very powerful rhetoric of science in justifying his complex ways to the suspicious public. And, if the 'right' effects are not forthcoming from the operations of his agency, he will be well covered by the 'scientific' justifications for the actions with such unfortunate consequences.

The expertise of the positivist comes to be used as scientific justification for political and commercial action and he himself, in line with his own edicts, is bereft of any role in questioning the aims of such activities (Douglas, 1970b, p. 267):

Insofar as social scientists do not initiate and become personally involved in the practical action aimed at solving problems but, rather, await the summons to involvement from men of practical affairs, they not only allow but force the men of practical affairs to define the problems, define the relevance of the social scientists, *define which social scientists* are to be consulted, define the structure of the advising situation, and then, most importantly, force them to pick and choose from that advice those parts which they can interpret in some way which 'helps' them, as they see it, to construct their intended course of practical action. Because of this, it is actually the metaphysics of everyday life or practical affairs which determines most of the impact of the social sciences on everyday life. What has normally happened so far, and what threatens to become even more prevalent, is that the men of practical affairs make use through this consulting process of the prestige of expert scientific knowledge in our society to achieve the goals which

35

they set by the means which they determine: they use the social sciences as a front which helps them to control public opinions and, hence, public responses to what they intend to do.

In other words, during the course of the late nineteenth and early twentieth century, positivism has become institutionalized. Alex Comfort (1967) has pointed out how the growth of the medical profession has been accompanied by intervention in moral and personal spheres which are beyond the jurisdiction of the medical practitioner. C. Wright Mills (1943) has shown how the growth of the social work profession, sustained and infused with the terminology of psychoanalysis and other deterministic ideologies, has resulted in the translation of public issues into private problems. It is of no small significance that psychoanalysis, one of the major ideologies of an institutionalized positivism, was produced as a direct outgrowth of the medical profession, specifically as a result of the dissatisfaction of thinkers trained in the medical tradition (like Freud himself): since psychoanalysis, for all that it is a break with simple medical thought, remains impregnated with biological and physiological assumptions.

Thus, Freud's aim was to reduce explanations of pathology to explanations of neurophysiology. He believed, for instance, that schizophrenia was genetically determined; whilst even the more radical Reich, who combined his medical and psychoanalytical training with some grounding in a Marxist humanism, refused to treat homosexuals on similar grounds. Gouldner, in a recent attack on 'welfare state sociology' (1968), has argued that American sociology—whether traditionally positivist or 'sceptical'—serves the important social and political function of displacing, in the process of making amenable for research and policy, the structures of power, domination and control.

The positivist's epistemological split between facts and values thus corresponds to his institutional role in society (cf. I. Taylor and Walton, 1970). In this his interests are well served, for, as Dennis Chapman astutely notes (1968, p. 23), to challenge the consensual definitions of crime and deviancy is to invite heavy penalties. . . . 'The penalties are: To be isolated from the mainstream of professional activity, to be denied resources for research, and to be denied official patronage with its rewards in material and status.'

Yet if such a philosophy has its uses for the politicians, this does not mean it is accepted wholeheartedly by them. Rather, it is used to back up arguments and proposals, it is selected for quotation at the appropriate, strategic time and place. For there is a fundamental conflict between the free will classicist's models held to by the legal profession and the determinist notions of the psychiatrist and the social worker. Total determinism palpably contradicts the 'feel' of human existence. More importantly, from the perspective of those in control, it is in contradiction with democratic ideology—given its implicit assumptions of moral choice, free selection of employment and rational voting for political candidates, etc. Determinism is, in the last analysis, from the social control point of view, a dangerous doctrine, for it removes from individuals the sense of striving towards the 'good' beavhiour. As we shall see later, it tends to obliterate the distinction between what is (behavioural norms) and what should be (prescriptive norms). Other people (the therapist and the expert) can change 'what is' in the direction of what they perceive as 'what should be'. But the individual is not accountable for his actions and he is not likely on his own accord to change his behaviour without parallel change in significant determining factors (environmental or genetic). The resolution of the conflict between free will and determinism is achieved by the adoption of what we have termed neo-classicism. Namely, a qualitative distinction is made between the majority who are seen as capable of free choice and the minority of deviants who are determined.

We wish to turn, now, to the evolution of positivism and to the reasons for the emergence and continuing appeal of biological positivism in particular. The first attempts to tackle the problem of crime scientifically were social rather than biological. The transition between classicism and positivism was largely effected by the 'moral statisticians', Quetelet and Guerry, and is well exemplified in Guerry's assertion, made in 1863 (p. lvii), that:

> The time has gone by when we could claim to regulate society
> by laws established solely on metaphysical theories and a sort of
> ideal type which was thought to conform to absolute justice.
> Laws are not made for men in the abstract, for humanity in
> general, but for real men, placed in precisely determined
> circumstances.

Quetelet (a Belgian mathematician of wide intellectual concerns) and Guerry (a French lawyer) working independently, but almost simultaneously, had drawn very similar conclusions from the publication from 1827 onwards, of the first sets of national criminal statistics (in France). As the figures continued to be published, on an annual basis, it became more and more clear to Quetelet and Guerry, first, that the annual totals of recorded crime remained extraordinarily constant, and, second, that the contribution of the various types of crime to the annual total fluctuated hardly at all.

Such a discovery carried with it the clear implication that (officially-recorded) crime was a regular feature of social activity, as distinct from being the product of individual (and therefore arbitrary) propensities to asocial activity. There was, then, some fundamental feature of the existing social arrangements that gave rise to regular outcomes; so that it must be possible, theoretically, to specify the causes with a view to eliminating the outcome. Quetelet's 'social physics' and Guerry's 'moral statistical analysis' were concerned, above all, therefore, with specifying the relationship between different features of the social arrangements and different (especially criminal) outcomes. In this respect, they have been said to have provided the groundwork for the much more thoroughgoing revolution in theory undertaken by Emile Durkheim some few years later.[2]

The work of Quetelet and Guerry stemmed from the publication of social statistics, these in turn being a reflection of concern with social unrest (cf. Morris, 1957, ch. 3). For the next half-century, the analysis of crime was in a sociological vein, ranging from the work of Mayhew to Bonger[3] and the audience was concerned with reform. Then, in 1876, Cesare Lombroso published *L'Uomo Delinquente* and the whole focus of analysis drastically changed from the social to the individual. As Lindesmith and Levin (1937, p. 661) put it:

> What Lombroso did was to reverse the method of explanation
> that had been current since the time of Guerry and Quetelet
> and, instead of maintaining that institutions and traditions
> determined that nature of the criminal, he held that the
> nature of the criminal determined the character of institutions
> and traditions.

Indeed Terence Morris (1957, p. 41) has argued that:

> The founding of a school of 'criminal anthropology' seems to
> have resulted in the total or near total eclipse of the work of
> sociologists in the criminological field. The genetic theories
> of crime which have been subsequently replaced by psycho-
> logical theories of crimes seem to have excited so much interest
> that sociological theories, particularly in Europe, have been of
> secondary importance.

What caused this phenomenon? Lindesmith and Levin note how the genetic theories of Lombroso fitted in well with the rise of Darwinism. *The Origin of the Species* had been published in 1859 and Darwinian concepts had been applied in a wholesale manner throughout the social sciences. But, fundamentally, it involved the movement of the medical man into the field of crime with the corresponding ousting of the sociologically inclined (Lindesmith and Levin, 1937, pp. 668–9):

> The growth of the Lombrosian myth is to be accounted for,
> basically, not so much in terms of the acceptance or rejection

of theories or methods of research as in terms of a changing personnel. After Lombroso's attempt to appropriate criminology to biology and medicine had attracted wide publicity in Europe, physicians and psychiatrists were attracted to the problem in greater numbers and gradually displaced in public attention and prestige the magistrates, prison authorities, lawyers, philanthropists, journalists, and social scientists who had previously dominated the field, although it should be noted that physical factors in crime had been noted and studied long before Lombroso made his abortive attempt to make them the sole or the chief causes. The Lombrosian myth arose, therefore, as a result of the 'seizure of power', so to speak, by the medical profession. Medical men compiled medical bibliographies and traced the history of criminology as a branch of medicine through the works of Gall, Lavater, Pinel, Morel, Esquirol, Maudsley, etc., ignoring the voluminous sociological literature. Sociologists have uncritically accepted this medical conception of the history of criminology, and they too have ignored the older sociological tradition of Guerry and Quetelet.

This would seem to be an accurate appraisal of events with the proviso that, as we have argued, the positivist movement was severely curtailed by the classicist positions of both lawyers and politicians. It was sociological positivism (not magistrates, lawyers and prison authorities) which was ousted. Lindesmith and Levin (1937, p. 670) proceed to answer a more fundamental question: why was support for such a seizure so forthcoming:

> For more than a century before criminal anthropology came into existence society's responsibility for its criminal classes had been recognised and embodied in the legislation of all civilised countries. It may be that the theory of the born criminal offered a convenient rationalisation of the failure of preventive effort and an escape from the implications of the dangerous doctrine that crime is an essential product of our social organisation. It may well be that a public, which had been nagged for centuries by reformers, welcomed the opportunity to slough off its responsibilities for this vexing problem.

Leon Radzinowicz (1966, pp. 38–9) concurs with this and clearly indicates the superior ideological efficacy of biological positivism:

> This way of looking at crime as the product of society was hardly likely to be welcome, however, at a time when a major concern was to hold down the 'dangerous classes'. The concept

39

of the dangerous classes as the main source of crime and dis-order was very much to the fore at the beginning of the nineteenth century. They were made up of those who had so miserable a share in the accumulating wealth of the industrial revolution that they might at any time break out in political revolt as in France. At their lowest level was the hard core of parasites to be found in any society, ancient or modern. And closely related to this, often indistinguishable from it, were the 'criminal classes'.

It served the interests and relieved the conscience of those at the top to look upon the dangerous classes as an indepen-dent category, detached from the prevailing social conditions. They were portrayed as a race apart, morally depraved and vicious, living by violating the fundamental law of orderly society, which was that a man should maintain himself by honest, steady work. In France they were commonly described as nomads, barbarians, savages, strangers to the customs of the country. English terminology was, perhaps, less strong and colourful, but the meaning was fundamentally similar.

Biological determinism, then, has a greater appeal than sociological positivism in that it removes any suggestion that crime may be the result of social inequalities. It is something essential in the nature of the criminal and not a malfunctioning of society. In addition, it achieves the utter decimation of the possibility of alternative realities. For the biologically inferior is used synonymously with the asocial. The analysis focuses on the individual who is unable to be social; thus atomized, he poses no threat to the monolithic reality central to positivism. For no individual alone can create an alternative reality and his asocial nature ensures that he is a mere blemish on con-ventional reality.

We need to examine briefly several examples of biological posi-tivism in brief before turning to a fuller discussion of the work of Hans Eysenck and the derivative theory of Gordon Trasler. Eysenck will be dealt with in detail, and his theory used as the exemplar of biological positivism—its most developed formulation. We shall be concerned there to examine both the ideological appeal and the explanatory sufficiency of the most sophisticated statement in this whole tradition. It is our contention that Eysenck's breadth of approach and complexity of argument make him the most worthy twentieth-century successor to Lombroso. First, then, let us turn to Lombroso, and to the minor theorists working in his tradition.

Lombroso

Cesare Lombroso, the founding father of the biological positivist
school, is best known for his notion of the atavistic criminal. These
born crininals were seen to be reversions to earlier evolutionary
periods, and to earlier levels of organic development. Atavism was
suggested first by Darwin (1881, p. 137) when he wrote: 'With
mankind some of the worst dispositions which occasionally without
any assignable cause make their appearance in families, may perhaps
be reversions to a savage state, from which we are not removed by
many generations.'

Lombroso first claimed to have discovered the 'secret' of criminality
when he was examining the skull of the famous brigand Vihella. He
described his flash of inspiration in the following terms (1911,
p. xiv):

> This was not merely an idea, but a flash of inspiration. At the
> sight of that skull, I seemed to see all of a sudden, lighted up
> as a vast plain under a flaming sky, the problem of the nature
> of the criminal—an atavistic being who reproduces in his
> person the ferocious instincts of primitive humanity and the
> inferior animals. Thus were explained anatomically the enormous
> jaws, high cheek bones, prominent superciliary arches, solitary
> lines in the palms, extreme size of the orbits, handle-shaped
> or sensile ears found in criminals, savages and apes, insensi-
> bility to pain, extremely acute sight, tattooing, excessive idleness,
> love of orgies, and the irresistible craving for evil for its own
> sake, the desire not only to extinguish life in the victim, but to
> mutilate the corpse, tear its flesh and drink its blood.

Atavistic man could be recongized by a series of physical stigmata:
abnormal dentition, asymmetry of face, supernumerary nipples, toes,
fingers, large ears, eye defects, inverted sex characteristics, tattooing,
etc. Lombroso compared criminals to control groups of soldiers
and found significant differences in the incidence of such stigmata.
In a later investigation of the anatomical characteristics of anarchists,
he found that 31 per cent of his sample in Paris, 40 per cent in
Chicago, and 34 per cent in Turin had stigmata whereas in the ranks
of other 'extremist' political movements under 12 per cent were found
to have such 'blemishes'.

His theory was first spelt out in *L'Uomo Delinquente* in 1876 but
by the time of the publication in 1897 of the fifth edition, he, in the
face of criticism, was insisting less strongly on the atavistic nature of
all criminality. The born criminal as such was in the minority: to
this atavistic type were now to be added:

    a   the epileptic criminal

   b   the insane criminal

   c   a large corps of occasional criminals who may have a trace of atavism and degeneration, may be precipitated into crime by association with criminal elements, or may have poor education, or may be inspired by patriotism, love, honour or political ideals.

In the face of criticism, Lombroso hinted at (and sometimes expanded on) a large number of 'environmental influences'. Moreover, like all thoroughgoing positivists, he was willing to see the influence of atavism or degeneracy as a matter of degree. As we argued in chapter 1, the sharp distinction between criminal and non-criminal (the idea of differentiation that Matza alleges to be characteristic of criminological positivism) is often ruled out in relatively sophisticated positivist accounts—largely as a result of their concern for quantification.

The major shortcomings of Lombrosian theory can be summarized as follows:

Technical

Lombroso's statistical techniques (reflecting the level of development in the mathematics of his time) were totally inadequate. His results have been shown, repeatedly, to be statistically insignificant (cf. Goring, 1913).

Physical stigmata

It has been often remarked, and demonstrated, that physical stigmatization is often the direct result of social environment, for example, of poor nutrition. Tattooing, which is perhaps Lombroso's most laughable example, is clearly the result of cultural fashions which have tended to have been concentrated in the lower classes (i.e. amongst those most 'at risk' of criminal apprehension).

Genetic theory

Modern genetic theory has totally ruled out the possibility of an evolutionary throwback to earlier more primitive species.

Social evaluation

Individuals with pronounced physical stigmata may be evaluated differently from those without such visible markings by others in the course of ongoing social interaction. A self-fulfilling prophecy, therefore, in which the individual carries out the other's expectations of him, is entirely possible (Goffman, 1968, ch. 4). Further, as one recent English study has shown (Walsh, 1969), individuals who are generally socially stigmatized in this fashion tend to be more likely to be arrested.

Crime rates

Biological variation alone cannot begin to explain the variation in crime rates (e.g. across cultures, time and class) and has nothing to offer in the explanation of how (and why) law arises.

Body types in biological positivism

A direct derivative of Lombroso's work is the investigation of the relationship between criminality and body shape. Pioneers in this field were Ernst Kretschmer (1921) and William Sheldon (1940).

Building on Kretschmer's endeavours, Sheldon differentiated between three body types: the endomorphic (soft and round), the mesomorphic (hard and round) and the ectomorphic (fragile and thin). He argued that a particular temperament corresponded to each of these individual types: the endomorph being predominantly slow, comfort-loving and extraverted; the mesomorph aggressive and active; and the ectomorph self-restrained and introverted.[4] A statistically significant application of Sheldon's typology by the Gluecks (1950; 1956) found that there were twice as many mesomorphs amongst delinquents than could have occurred by chance, and half as many ectomorphs. In Germany a more recent development of this kind of theory by Klaus Conrad (1963) studied the percentage changes in body build as a child grows up. He calculated head to body length against age, and found that, on average, children were more mesomorphic and adults more ectomorphic.[5] Thus, adult mesomorphs were said to resemble children of a mean age of eight years whereas ectomorphs more resembled adults. Conrad concluded that mesomorphs are on a lower level of 'ontogenetic development' than ectomorphs. This notion of level of ontogenetic development is reminiscent of Lombrosian 'atavism'. Conrad further suggested that mesomorphs are more immature psychologically—and, in this, his theory goes close to that of Eysenck who also utilizes the notion of body shape and quotes Conrad's results approvingly.[6]

The criticisms of this school centre around the social origins of body type: the ways in which a particular somatype is to be explained. It may well be that lower-working-class children, who are more likely to be found in the criminal statistics, are also by virtue of diet, continual manual labour, physical fitness and strength, more likely to be mesomorphic than ectomorphic. Further, it is probably also

43

the case that admission to delinquent subcultures is dependent on bodily appearance. As Don Gibbons (1968, p. 134) puts it:

It could be argued that delinquent subcultures recruit new members selectively, placing a premium upon agile, muscular boys . . . excessively fat or overtly thin and sickly youngsters make poor candidates for the rough and tumble world of delinquent behaviour, so they are excluded. . . . If so, this is a social process, not a biologically determined pattern of behaviour.

The fact that many of the studies in this tradition have used inmates as subjects (and come up with significant results) may, of course, reflect only a tendency for mesomorphs to be incarcerated more than ectomorphs.[7]

The XYY chromosome theory[8]

A recent and well-publicized genetic theory of crime attempts to establish a connection between the possession of an XYY set chromosome complement and criminality.

The normal complement of chromosomes for the female is XX and for the male XY. However, in rare cases, a chromosome may be absent, or there may be additional chromosomes. For example, the combination XXY occurs 1·3 times per 1,000 male babies and XYY, 1·0 times per 1,000 male babies. In a very few instances, the combinations XYYY, XXYY and XXXYY occur.[9]

The first sex chromosome abnormality to be investigated was that of XXY males. Termed 'Klinefelter's Syndrome', this complement was found to be associated with the degeneration of testes during adolescence, with low intelligence and to be over-represented amongst inmates of institutions for the subnormal.

It was generally believed that because XXYY cases appeared to manifest traits similar to Klinefelter's Syndrome (i.e. XXY), and that, because XYY cases had mild mental defects, the extra Y chromosome was of very little significance. Then, in 1962, Court Brown found that the rate of delinquency amongst his patients who had sex chromosomal abnormalities was significantly high (p. 508). In Sheffield, Casey *et al.* (1966), following up this suggestion, searched for sex chromosome abnormalities amongst mentally abnormal patients, institutionalized in special security conditions and thought to be potentially criminal. They found twice as many sex chromosome abnormalities amongst this population as amongst 'normal defectives', and ten times as many as in the 'normal' population. But, most significantly, a large proportion had XXYY chromosomes. Now since the excess of sex chromosome abnormalities in these institutions could almost wholly be accounted for by the XXYY cases, it seemed that such patients had a special tendency to be delinquent. It was also noted that they were unusually tall.

Since in these respects these patients had the features of the more common XXY Klinefelter's Syndrome, it could be deduced that the extra height and the greater delinquency involvement was a product of the extra Y chromosome (which constituted the difference between XXY abnormality and XXYY aberrations of these particular patients).

On this assumption, Price *et al.* (1966, p. 565)[10] undertook chromosome counts on all available male patients in a special security institution in Scotland and found that XYY males were (a) not physically exceptional except in terms of height, (b) that their genitalia appeared to be well developed (in contrast to Klinefelter's Syndrome), and (c) that there was some evidence of slight mental deficiency. Since there was evidence of abnormal height amongst XXX females, it was concluded that the *extra Y* chromosome was responsible for increasing an individual's height.

In a subsequent investigation (1967, pp. 533-6), Price's team found that those patients with an extra Y chromosome tended, first, to be severe psychopaths; second, to be convicted at a younger age than other psychopaths; third, to commit crimes against property rather than against the person; and, finally, to come from backgrounds where there was no real evidence of crime. The extra Y chromosome, therefore, seemed to be positively linked to increased height and psychopathy.

The XYY sex chromosome theory is extraordinary in that it makes the remarkable claim to be able to pinpoint the precise genetic basis for a particular criminal disposition. In all other respects it is manifestly a very crude theory which (unlike the version of biological positivism expounded by Eysenck) does not even attempt to explain or even to indicate the mechanisms whereby these genetic differences are translated into behavioural differences (i.e. into different orientations to social action). The theory is also very restrictive in that its explanations—such as they are—apply only to a tiny proportion of all offenders.[11]

The limitations of sex chromosome abnormality theory are similar to the limitations of theories of body-type. As Hunter astutely pointed out in a letter to the *Lancet* (1966, p. 984):

Even if their behaviour was no more aggressive than XXY males, it might be that because of their great height and build they would present such a frightening picture that the courts and psychiatrists would be biased to direct them to special hospitals for community safety. The bias might be further aggravated by the associated intellectual abnormality. This factor might find expression in the raised incidence of XYY (and XXYY) males in special hospital groups.

Sarbin and Miller (1970) have pointed to the failure of the 'chromosomal theorists' to distinguish between the *efficient* causes of crime (the antecedents of the individual's performance of the illegal act) and the *formal* cause (the reasons for particular acts being stamped as illegal in the first place). As Lemert has argued elsewhere (1967, ch. 5), these two types of cause are only transitively related—the reasons for a person committing a criminal act may be entirely different in order and significance from the reasons for a particular law-breaker being arrested.

Sarbin and Miller point to the widespread occurrence of criminality throughout the population—and to the fact that one of the central concerns in contemporary criminology is an investigation of the processes of selection and sifting which result in only a small proportion of law-breakers being apprehended as such. It just is not possible to tell whether XYY chromosome males commit more illegal acts than XY (i.e. 'normal') males, until we are able to specify whether sex chromosome abnormalities are a part of the efficient or the formal 'causes' of crime. In fact, sex chromosomal theorists leave the formal causes of crime unexamined: and the formal causes may include what the police perceive as 'dangerousness'[12]—and thus relate (as Hunter suggested) to excessive height and mental defectiveness. It could also be the case, Sarbin and Miller suggest, that the number of XYY males located in the working class is disproportionately high (for reasons no one has explained):[13] if this is the case, then the fact that there is a disproportionate representation of XYY males in institutions may merely reflect the tendency of the police to apprehend working-class males (and the class-based nature of the law itself).

But this type of analysis alone, pertinent as it is, is essentially static. The bizarre appearance and behaviour of XYY males may be inextricably involved, in dialectical fashion, with the social labelling and stigmatization they experience; and their exclusion from 'normal' social interaction may (along with material deprivation associated with such handicaps) make it more likely that they will be attracted to illegitimate or illegal alternatives. That is, stigmatization of XYY individuals (the formal causes of *deviancy*) eventually engenders crime (the efficient causes of *deviancy*)—which, because of their unusual appearance, makes them more likely than other law-breakers to be arrested (the formal causes of *crime*). In short, biological abnormality is interpreted in such a fashion that is likely to result in the stigmatized person reacting to those who are responsible for interpreting his abnormality in a deviant fashion. Biological factors enter into crime only in an indirect respect: the crucial mediation which goes unexamined in positivistic accounts is the interpretation placed on biological characteristics.

We turn now to a biological theory which is a considerable advance on the theories just discussed. Both in analysing the mechanisms by which genetic potentialities are translated into criminal behaviour in particular, and social action in general, and in fully acknowledging the interplay of environmental factors, Hans Eysenck's formulations have a distinct advantage over other biological interpretations of society. Eysenck has extended his attention over a wide range of issues, and, in so doing, has allowed us the opportunity of discussing the fundamental attributes of biological positivism in its most developed form, namely its conception of human nature, social order, deviant behaviour and scientific method.

Conception of human nature

Man's primary motivation is the pursuit of pleasure and the avoidance of pain; to this extent Eysenck is in agreement with the classicist philosophers. He differs, however, in his dismissal of free will and rationality in human actors. For the stumbling block to this utilitarian notion of motivation is that the punishment of crime—by the inflicting of pain proportional to its consequences (as we have seen in Beccaria)—does not, in fact, eliminate criminality. The task of modern psychology, according to Eysenck, is to refurbish classical hedonism with positivistic refinements. First, he notes what he terms the principle of immediacy (1969, p. 689):

> To talk about a balance between pain and pleasure, as far as the consequences of a particular act are concerned, is similar to talking about two weights at opposite sides of a fulcrum; we need to consider not only the weights themselves but also the distance from the fulcrum at which they are suspended. A light weight far from the fulcrum may pull down a heavy one near it. In the case of pain and pleasure, what we have to consider is the temporal contiguity of these two resultant states to the action which produces them; the nearer in point of time the consequences are to the action, the more powerfully will they determine future actions. Thus an action followed by a small but immediate gratification will tend to be repeated, even though it is followed by a large but delayed painful consequence.

'Thus the negative effects of punishment are very much attenuated by the long period of time elapsing between crime and retribution. Furthermore, while the positive consequences of crime are fairly certain, the negative ones are very much less so' (Eysenck, 1965, p. 259). After all, as Eysenck points out, only a small proportion of crimes are cleared up and the chances of avoiding detection are often considerable. Man is seen here as a short-term hedonist; live today and enjoy yourself for you never know what tomorrow will bring.

What, then, can the positivist offer as a reasonable alternative in the control of crime? For punishment, because of its distance from the criminal deed and its probabilistic nature, has been manifestly ineffective. Eysenck (1965, pp. 260–1) turns to a concept of a distinctly non-utilitarian kind: the conscience. But he defuses it of any connotation of a striving towards values which are pursued for their own sake. Rather:

How does conscience originate? Our contention will be that conscience is simply a conditioned reflex. . . . What happens is that the young child, as he grows up, is required to learn a number of actions which are not, in themselves, pleasant or pleasurable and which in fact go counter to his desires and wishes. He has to learn to be clean and not to defecate and urinate whenever and wherever he pleases; he has to suppress the overt expression of his sexual and aggressive urges; he must not beat other children when they do things he does not like; he must learn not to take things which do not belong to him. In every society there is a long list of prohibitions of acts which are declared to be bad, naughty, and immoral, and which, although they are attractive to him and are self-rewarding, he must nevertheless desist from carrying out. As we have pointed out before, this is not likely to be achieved by any formal process of long-delayed punishment, because what is required to offset the immediate pleasure derived from the activity must be an immediate punishment which is greater than the pleasure and, if possible, occurs in closer proximity to the crime. In childhood it is possible for parents, teachers and other children to administer such punishment at the right moment of time; the child who does something wrong is immediately slapped, told off, sent upstairs, or whatever the punishment may be. Thus we may regard the evil act itself as the conditioned stimulus and we may regard the punishment—the slap, the moral shaming, or whatever the punishment may be—as the unconditioned stimulus which produces pain or, at any rate, some form of suffering and, therefore, of sympathetic response. On the principle of conditioning, we would now expect that after a number of repetitions of this kind, the act itself would produce the conditioned response; in other words, when the child is going to carry out one of the many activities which have been prohibited and punished in the past, then the conditioned autonomic response would immediately occur and produce a strong deterrent, being, as it were, unpleasant in itself. Thus the child would be faced with a choice between carrying on, obtaining the desired object but, at the same time (and perhaps even earlier), suffering from the unpleasant punishment administered by its conditioned autonomic system, or desisting from carrying out the act and thus avoiding this punishment. Provided that the conditioning process had been carried out efficiently and well, it is predictable, on psychological principles, that the choice would lie in the direction of desisting rather than carrying out the act. Thus the child acquires, as it were, an 'inner policeman' to help in controlling his atavistic impulses and to supplement the ordinary police force which is likely to be much less efficient and much less omnipresent.

This conception of conscience allows for the inbuilt punishments of the autonomic nervous system: anxiety and alarm, of which the classicists and criminologists were unaware. Thus behaviour is seen to be acquired in two ways:

a *learning* which is based on simple hedonism and involves the central nervous system. Problems are solved rationally through reinforcement: that which leads to pleasure is positively reinforced and those activities which give rise to pain are reinforced negatively. (This corresponds to *instrumental or operant conditioning*.) As we have seen the propinquity of pleasure is a major determinant of positive reinforcement.

b *conditioning*. *Classical conditioning* operates not by direct reinforcement but by contiguity, and involves the autonomic nervous system. As we see from the last quotation, activities pleasurable in themselves are associated in a reflex fashion with unpleasurable autonomic experience.[14]

Therefore man's voluntary, rational activity comes to be seen as being solely concerned with the satisfaction of his individual and pre-social desires. The implementation of such impulses is learnt in a trial and error fashion, success bringing forth the positive reinforcement of the behaviour, and failure the negative (the so-called 'law of effect'). The model of learning is Darwinian in its mindlessness. The reason is the seat of striving for pleasure, as it were, a cunning which schemes to maximize its immediate satisfactions and minimize its pains. The conscience is a passive reflex which unthinkingly checks these hedonistic impulses by virtue of autonomic distress. A strange model of man, this, where reason has become the seat of the passions and conscience relegated to the viscera!

The ideological nature of this model is immediately apparent.

What is pleasurable (the good) is unquestioned: it is a biological given which the organism will attempt to maximize. What restrictions occur are not created by the actors themselves but derive mysteriously from the normative order as it is. Man does not generate his own rules and oppose the rules of others, he is active only in that he attempts to reduce the tensions of displeasure and his desires for satisfaction.

Thus as far as the specific individual is concerned, his desires are not formulated by him, neither is the ability to curb them under his own control. His cathectic focus on certain objects is a function of 'rational learning', his inability to avoid 'anti-social' activities a result of lack of conditioning. The degree to which a person has been conditioned to avoid 'anti-social' behaviour is central to Eysenck's explanation of criminality. The measure of this conditioning is dependent on two variables:

a   the sensitivity of the autonomic nervous system which he has inherited.

b   the quality of the conditioning that he has received within his family in terms of their efficiency in utilizing adequate conditioning techniques.

Thus on top of the genetic potential of the person to become fully social is *added* the environmental variable of family of origin. It is noteworthy that both of these factors are sited in the early life of the individual. The ideological leverage of this is to deflect criticisms aimed at the origins of deviancy away from the present to the past history of the person or group concerned.

The differences in the autonomic nervous system give rise to variations in the individual's ability to be conditioned. That is, individuals range between those in whom it is easy to *excite* conditioned reflexes and whose reflexes are difficult to *inhibit*, to those whose reflexes are difficult to condition and easy to extinguish. This corresponds to Eysenck's major personality dimension of introversion to extraversion.[15] Once formed, by the end of early childhood, a biological potentiality is set up, measurable as a point on the introversion-extraversion continuum, which will determine the individual's propensity to crime.

In contrast to this, we wish to argue that man's action is not a mere attempt at reducing the tension between socialized desires and conditioned prohibitions: that an essential human characteristic is that man is both the product and the producer of society. At times he accepts, at times he reinterprets, at times he transcends and resists existing values. Much of his action in fact may be seen as tension-heightening rather than tension-reducing, in that he may find it necessary to act against social disapproval and early conditioning (negative reinforcement) in order to fulfil his ideals.[16]

The central and autonomic nervous systems are undoubtedly involved in the learning process—to deny this would be to deny that man has a body. But reason is not merely a set of deterministic reflexes—rather it is a consciousness of the world, an ability of the individual to give meaning to his universe, both to interpret and to creatively change the existing moral order. Man's reason, rather than being a conditioned amorality, is a conscious optimizing of choices. Similarly, autonomic responses of a conditioned nature doubtless occur but their meaning is dictated to by consciousness. A man may well feel autonomic anxiety when faced with the opportunity to steal and this may have been a product of early socialization but his action will take various courses—not necessarily of a tension-reducing nature. Thus he may:

a   feel anxiety and consciously agree that such an action is amoral, and, therefore, refuse to steal;

b   feel anxiety and consciously decide that despite all, stealing in this case is justified and, therefore, go ahead and steal despite autonomic distress;

c   feel anxiety and consciously (over time) resocialize himself into ridding himself of the 'hangovers' from his initial socialization.

As Gordon Allport (1955, pp. 34–5) suggests:

> The truth of the matter . . . is that the moral sense and life-styles of most people reach far beyond the confines of domestic and community mores in which they were first fashioned. If we look into ourselves we observe that our tribal morality seems to us somehow peripheral to our personal integrity. True, we obey conventions of modesty, decorum, and self-control, and have many habits that fashion us in part as mirror-images of our home, class, and cultural ways of living. But we know that we have selected, reshaped, and transcended these ways to a marked degree.

and again (p. 71):

> While applicable to the early stages of the growth of conscience, this theory is not convicing for later stages. For one thing, it is not often the violation of tribal taboos or of parental prohibitions that makes us as adults feel most guilty. We now have our private codes of virtue and sin; and what we feel guilty about may have little relation to the habits of obedience we once learned. If conscience were merely a matter of self-punishment for breaking an established habit taught with authority, then we could not account for the fact that we do often discard codes imposed by parents and by culture, and devise codes of our own.

It is a failing in sociological theory that it has rarely examined concepts such as guilt and conscience. For this reason it exposes a weak flank both to behaviourist and Freudian critiques. It is therefore urgently necessary to distinguish between the reflexive guilt of an autonomic nature and the guilt arising from conflict of consciously embraced values and expedient behaviour.

Lastly, the phenomenon of expediency must be seen in the light, not of the failure of internal prohibitions learnt in the past, but as the avoidance of sanctions of a present and external nature. That is, the social reaction of the powerful bent on protecting their interests by the manipulation of material and social rewards. 'Positive and negative reinforcements' are not the autonomic response of a 'taken-for-granted' universe to conformity or deviation but meaningful attempts of the powerful to maintain and justify the *status quo* of wealth and interest.

Social order

Eysenck is faced with the problem of where the rules of society come from and how is it that society manages not to degenerate into a 'war of all against all'. Translated into his own terms: Who decides what is to be positively and negatively reinforced? This is the Achilles Heel of all individualistic utilitarian theory. Eysenck would not maintain that the pleasurable and the painful is derivative from innate biological drives. He is only too aware of the relative nature of human desires and likes.[17] They differ from society to society (1953, p. 179):

> The tendency to regard certain forms of conduct as natural and biologically innate is not logically absurd. It seems to be based in many cases, however, on an erroneous identification of that which is natural with that which is current in our society. This tendency to regard as natural (instinctively · innate) that with which we are familiar is brought out very clearly in certain animal studies. We regard as instinctive and natural, for instance, the behaviour of cats who catch and kill mice and rats and feed on them. We may not regard this as ideal behaviour—in many cases we disapprove of a well-fed cat killing birds and other animals for no apparent purpose— but we regard this behaviour as innate and therefore natural and normal. Yet the evidence is fairly conclusive that it is nothing of the kind.

If values vary, then, presumably they must relate to the nature of the society within which they have evolved. A strict biological determinism would relate this either to racial characteristics or to a social Darwinian position concerned with the potentiality for human survival. But Eysenck is more sophisticated than this, for in 'The technology of consent' (1969, p. 690) (which we examined earlier in this chapter), he was willing to give social factors their due, arguing that human behaviour must be patterned around the technological imperatives of a society with a high division of labour: 'I think these developments are essential however, if society is to survive under the technological conditions created by physical and chemical science.'

Society, he constantly argues, is failing to adapt in a rational manner to the problems which face it. It is too permissive in its child-rearing practices (he is very critical of Dr Spock) and above all, it will not implement the conclusions of a scientific psychology. Thus he writes (1953, p. 175):

> Not so many have realised that a whole new approach to social and political problems may be in the making, an approach based on factual knowledge of human nature rather than on hypothetical beliefs and preconceived notions. Political parties generally seem to have exhausted the dynamic which once motivated them, and are looking around for new ideas and new conceptions. Might it not be that these new ideas and conceptions are to be found in a realistic appraisal of the potentialities, abilities, attitudes, and motives of the human beings who make up society? Where there is so much agreement among all parties about the *aims* of society, should not the disputes about *means* be handed over to scientific investigation? The solution of social problems can in principle at least be found in the same way as the solution to physical and chemical problems; we do not determine the atomic weight of gold, or the size of the moon, or the spectral colour of hydrogen by a counting of heads, and there appears no ground for assuming such a method to be any more effective in arriving at correct decisions about industrial productivity, or motivation, or other psychological problems.

Thus, for Eysenck in particular, and biological positivists in general, there is a general consensus in society and an élite which is capable of understanding the 'real' nature of human motivation.

Eysenck is critical of the *laissez-faire* nature of the social order and the pursuit of immediate satisfactions rather than their scientifically planned solution. His quarrel, it would seem, is with the very characteristics of human nature that he has empirically discovered. But he is a constant pessimist in that he believes untold blunders have been made in planning enterprises which did not conform to the basic 'facts' of human nature. Man will always pursue immediate pleasure unless he is conditioned to do otherwise. But who, then, are to be the far-seeing, 'unnatural' men who are able to transcend their narrow utilitarian natures and plan rationally for society in general? Presumably the psychologists—but, if this is true, it would demand that Eysenck's paradigm of behaviour does not apply to all men. Some, by virtue of their foresight, are able to create new norms more applicable to changed times. But behaviourism can only explain creativity by positive reinforcement. Thus Koestler (1964), in a brilliant demolition of behaviourist metaphysics, cites the following attempt at the explanation of creativity by the father of the behaviourist school, John Broadus Watson (1928, pp. 198ff):

> One natural question often raised is, how do we ever get new verbal creations such as poems or a brilliant essay? The answer is that we get them by manipulating words, shifting them about until a new pattern is hit upon. . . . How do you suppose Patou builds a new gown? Has he any 'picture in his mind' of what the gown is to look like when it is finished? He has not. . . . He calls his model in, picks up a new piece of silk, throws it around her, he pulls it in here, he pulls it out there. . . . He manipulates the material until it takes on the semblance of a dress. . . . Not until the new creation aroused admiration and commendation, both his own and others, would manipulation be complete—the equivalent of the rat's finding food . . . the painter plies his trade in the same way, nor can the poet boast of any other method.

But who is to supply such positive reinforcements if the innovation violates existing values? Eysenck himself cites incessantly the resistance and scorn poured on his own conclusions. It is difficult to understand how psychology managed to evolve in the context of political and public apathy. The creation of new norms, the innovation of scientific theories and artistic projects, the dynamics of social change are all inexplicable in terms of positivist theory. For, in reality, what will act as reinforcer for men is given by their purposive response to their situation, and the salience of a reinforcer for a human actor must therefore be explicable in terms of choices made freely but within conditions of material and social restraint. The valuation of what ought to be cannot be derived either from the imperatives of technology or the existing configuration of values.

Eysenck's insistence on following the 'facts' of human existence—whether technological necessity, the existing dominant values, or the essential psychological nature of man—places him in a contradictory position, for he is so often forced to recognize that these 'facts' can fall out of phase. Doggedly, however, he continues to deny human creativity and purpose, in deducing 'what ought to be' from 'what is'. He sees himself always in a different realm of being from the subjects he studies, he alone being able to criticize the existing order. It was precisely this kind of self-deceit that Marx was moved, in 1845, to describe in the following terms (Marx, 1968, p. 28):

> The materialist doctrine that men are products of circumstances and changed upbringing, forgets that it is men that change circumstances and that the educator himself needs educating. Hence this doctrine necessarily arrives at dividing society into two parts, of which one is superior to society.

Deviant behaviour

Eysenck views the description of an act as deviant as largely non-problematic—the consensus defines behaviour as normal or deviant, it being the psychologist's task merely to provide efficient means of treatment.[18] He does not fall into the trap of the biological determinists before him in suggesting that deviant behaviour is intrinsic in the biological nature of an individual. Thus he writes (1970, pp. 74–5):

> Nothing that has been said so far should lead the reader to imagine that environment plays no part at all in the causation of crime. . . . The very notion of criminality or crime would be meaningless without a context of learning or social experience and, quite generally, of human interaction. What the figures have demonstrated is that heredity is a very strong predisposing factor as far as committing crimes is concerned. But the actual way in which the crime is carried out, and whether or not the culprit is found and punished—these are obviously subject to the changing vicissitudes of everyday life. It would be meaningless to talk about the criminality or otherwise of a Robinson Crusoe, brought up and always confined by himself on a desert island. It is only in relation to society that the notion of criminality and of predisposition to crime has any meaning. While recognizing therefore, the tremendous power of heredity, we would by no means wish to suggest that environmental influences cannot also be very powerful and important indeed.

Society defines what is criminal and non-criminal, and the social environment plays a large part in determining the degree of socialization a person has experienced. This answers well the critique of environmentalists that biological variation is insufficient to explain changes in the rate of crime.[19] We wish to argue that Eysenck's analysis is misguided not because of his omission of social factors but because he constructs a false notion of the interplay between biology and society. For Eysenck the interaction between society and the individual potential for deviance is *additive*. He has a *steady state* notion of biological potential—it is something which is fixed and measurable and follows a man throughout his life. Rather, we wish to suggest that man's consciousness is not a product of what society makes of his biological attributes. The distinctively human trait is to be able to stand back and interpret bodily constitution and social circumstances. Raw biological drives and passive acceptance of socially imposed labels is true only at birth and diminishes thereafter. His definitions of himself evolve not as a determinate result of the addition of social factors on to a biological substratum but rather as *praxis*, as the meaningful attempt by the actor to construct and develop his own self-conception.

Eysenck, in contrast, characterizes deviant behaviour as meaningless: it is behaviour outside of a monolithic consensus. It is perceived independently of any social context as the pathology of the isolated individual. Ronald Laing (1967, p. 17), writing about mental illness, has noted how such a procedure can make any behaviour seem unintelligible:

> Someone is gibbering away on his knees, talking to someone
> who is not there. Yes, he is praying. If one does not accord him
> the social intelligibility of his behaviour, he can only be seen
> as mad. Out of social context, his behaviour can only be the
> outcome of an unintelligible 'psychological' and/or 'physical'
> process, for which he requires treatment. This metaphor
> sanctions a massive ignorance of the social context within
> which the person was interacting.

In contrast to Eysenck, we wish to suggest that instead of seeing extraversion as a discrete trait characterized by absolute undersocialization, we should take it to represent meaningful behaviour by individuals which is judged by others, in this case the psychological testers, to be undesirable. It is under-socialization with respect to certain values: it is not absolute lack of values. Thus, if we examine Eysenck's characterization of extraverts and introverts (1970, p. 50) we are struck by the social valuations which lie just beneath the surface of his 'objective' descriptions:

> The typical extravert is sociable, likes parties, has many friends,
> needs to have people to talk to, and does not like reading or
> studying by himself. He craves excitement, takes chances, acts
> on the spur of the moment, and is generally an impulsive
> individual. He is fond of practical jokes, always has a ready
> answers, and generally likes change; he is care-free, easy-
> going, optimistic, and likes to 'laugh and be merry'. He prefers
> to keep moving and doing things, tends to be aggressive and

loses his temper quickly; his feelings are not kept under tight control and he is not always a reliable person.

The typical introvert is a quiet, retiring sort of person, introspective, fond of books rather than people: he is reserved and reticent except with intimate friends. He tends to plan ahead, 'looks before he leaps', and distrusts the impulse of the moment. He does not like excitement, takes matters of everyday life with proper seriousness, and likes a well-ordered mode of life. He keeps his feelings under close control, seldom behaves in an aggressive manner, and does not lose his temper easily. He is reliable, somewhat pessimistic, and places great value on ethical standards.

It is extraordinary how similar such a list is to Matza and Sykes's depiction of the difference between formal and subterranean values (1961):

Formal values: deferred gratification, planning, continuity to bureaucratic rules, routine, predictability, non-aggressive, self-centred.

Introversion: 'introspective', 'reserved', 'tends to plan ahead', 'distrusts impulse', 'does not like excitement', 'likes a well-ordered mode of life', 'keeps feelings under control', 'seldom behaves aggressively', 'reliable'.

Subterranean values: short-term hedonism, spontaneity, ego-expressivity, new experience, excitement, aggressive masculine role, peer-centred.

Extraversion: 'sociable', 'has many friends', 'craves excitement', 'takes chances', 'acts on spur of moment', 'impulsive', 'carefree', 'easygoing', 'likes change', 'aggressive'.

Matza and Sykes suggest that the subterranean values are held throughout society and usually find expression in leisure time and play. Further, they note how certain groups such as juvenile delinquents tend to accentuate these values at the expense of the formal values of work.

One of the authors of this present study has suggested that the accentuation of subterranean values is associated with the structural position and problems faced by certain social groups (Young, 1971a). Important amongst these are the lower working-class, represented minority groups and deviant youth cultures. These are also the groups most prone to contribute to the criminal statistics. Thus the existence of values which are contracultural and closely related to purposive criminal activities is interpreted by Eysenck as a reflection of psychological propensities (i.e. high extraversion) denoting the absence of social values. This extraversion-introversion scale may, in fact, in certain instances be accurately yet unwittingly gauging

57

such value differences. However, crime is only related in certain instances to the subterranean values. The business criminal of the Mafia, the professional thief, the corporate criminal, the bank clerk embezzler are hardly likely to embrace the same values as the ghetto Negro and the juvenile vandal. Thus, the enterprise is doomed to failure: inconsistent results abound and 'significant' correlations where they occur merely result in false imputations of causality.

Scientific method

There has been a plenitude of critiques of Eysenck from within the ranks of positivism. Thus Hoghughi and Forrest (1970) point to the frequent finding that persistent young offenders are significantly more introverted than control groups (see also Little, 1963). Further, his research techniques have come under vehement criticism. As Richard Christie (1956, p. 450) put it:

> Errors of computation, uniquely biased samples which forbid any generalisations, scales with built-in biases which do not measure what they purport to measure, unexplained inconsistencies within the data, misinterpretations and contradictions of the relevant research of others, and unjustifiable manipulation of the data. Any one of Eysenck's many errors is sufficient to raise serious questions about the validity of his conclusions. *In toto*, absurdity is compounded upon absurdity, so that where the truth lies is impossible to determine.

It is not, however, our intention to enter into technical criticisms of Eysenck. For our argument would be, as we have outlined in the last section, that even if in some instances reliable correlations were found between extraversion and crime, these would be based on a causality of a social nature *not* of a theory based on the autonomic nervous system. This is not to deny the falsifiability of his theory— for if our argument is correct successful correlations will only be found to occur amongst a minority of criminals. Eysenck meanwhile, in order to keep pace with his critics, must desperately invoke new 'sophistications' of factor analysis and involve added complications and dimensions to his theory (e.g. Eysenck and Eysenck, 1970). Like a Ptolemaic astronomer, he must add epicycle after epicycle to keep the theory in line with the facts, until all parsimony is lost and the last vestige of scientific open-mindedness vanishes.

Our aim in this text is to concentrate on the criticisms of Eysenck's theory rather than to enter the internecine squabbles of positivism. For this reason we turn to his underlying notion of reductionism (1970, p. 75):

What will be suggested rather is that without an understanding of the way in which the innate criminality, the predisposition of the person to commit a crime, is translated into reality, it will be very difficult, if not impossible, to carry out investigations into the environmental influences which determine criminality or lack of criminality in a given person. It will be argued that purely statistical studies, such as those which have customarily been carried out by sociologists and others, in an attempt to correlate such items as absence of the father, absence of the mother, poor conditions of upbringing, lack of home life, and so forth, with criminality, while interesting, lack any great causal importance because it is difficult to see just precisely how these various factors exert their influence. It is hoped that, by relating these factors to a general theory which also accounts for the way in which the hereditary causes work, we shall be able to produce a more satisfactory picture of the whole complex of causes which produce criminal behaviour in our modern world.

Eysenck's belief is that there are psychological and physiological laws which will explain social behaviour. Such reductionism supposedly increases the scientific validity of the analysis. Eysenck attempts to relate such measurable psychological and physiological states to 'objective' behaviour (1965, pp. 13–14, our emphasis):

The 'mind', or the 'soul', or the 'psyche', are a little too immaterial to be investigated as such by any scientific procedures; what the psychologist deals with, in fact, is *behaviour* which is palpable enough to be observed, recorded, and analysed. The hard-headed view is often criticized by people who say that this way of looking at things leaves out important qualities and aspects of humanity. Such an objection may or may not be true in the long run; this becomes almost a philosophical, rather than a scientific question, and there would be little point in arguing it here.

The 'meaning' of behaviour is thus somehow seen as obvious to the psychologist and valuable information can legitimately be obtained from animal studies where deviancy can be seen as a behavioural deviation subject to simple statistical calculation (Eysenck, 1965, p. 228):

Too many similarities in conditioning and learning behaviour have been shown to exist when animals and human beings are compared, to deny a biological basis of considerable similarity for these various types of organisms, and if we maintain, as I think we must, that social behaviour is learned

59

and conditioned very much as are other types of behaviour, then it is difficult to deny that a knowledge of these laws, whether derived from animal work or from human work, is an essential pre-requisite for an understanding of such behaviour.

Eysenck's assumption is that the meaning of an item of behaviour is non-problematic, and that to explain the physical basis of it is to explain it as a social phenomenon. But as Alasdair MacIntyre (1962) has succinctly put it:

> The same physical movements may constitute in different contexts quite different actions. So a man may go through the same physical movements involved in signing his name and be concluding a treaty or paying a bill, which are quite different actions. But is not the man performing the same action in each case, namely signing his name? To this the answer is that writing one's name is never merely by itself an action: one is either signing a document or giving information or perhaps just doodling. All these are actions, but writing one's name is not. Equally, the same action may be constituted by quite different physical movements. Writing on paper, passing a coin, even saying words may all constitute the same action of paying a bill. When we talk about 'explaining human behaviour', we sometimes blur this distinction. Because there is no human action which does not involve physical movement we may suppose that to explain the movement is to explain the action.

Even if it were true that the physical basis of behaviour lay in the reflexes of the autonomic nervous system, it would not explain the nature of deviant action. To explain social phenomena demands social analysis involving the meaning that the behaviour has to the actor. The man who breaks the window of the British Embassy in Dublin might well have a poor autonomic response but both his lack of reflex and violent behaviour can only be understood in terms of the meanings he gave to the situation and the social context of the movement for a united Ireland. Indeed, as MacIntyre argues, causality in the social sciences is different from causality in the natural sciences in so far as the connection between mere behaviour and social action is to be found at the level of beliefs. Thus, the relationship between beliefs and action is 'inner and conceptual'. If, as with Eysenck, it is to be believed that one can reduce explanation of action to explanations in terms of the acquisition of conditioned reflexes which in their turn could be explained in terms of genetics, then the situation in which an act occurs and the meaning which an actor gives to his physical behaviour would be irrelevant. There is, however, a crucial epistemological break between biological and social explanation (and not a continuum of reductions). For *in social explanations causes are 'inner and conceptual'*—that is to say, the connection between physical movement and the outside world is in terms of what men believe (the purposes to which they hold). Thus men rob banks because they believe they may enrich themselves, not because something biologically propels them through the door of a bank. The fact that people may have different chromosomal configurations or are different biophysiological types may be of interest in accounting for constitutional differences between men, but it goes no way towards explaining deviancy as social action. The epistemology of social science is of a different order to that of a natural science: a social theory must have reference to men's teleology—their purposes, their beliefs and the contexts in which they act out these purposes and beliefs.

Behaviourist and positivist analyses contain no such epistemology. Indeed, their very appeal is to be explained in terms of their having a view of man as malleable and conditionable. The positivists refuse to question beliefs, since this would involve consideration of values, an area which they would see to be irrelevant to science. The appeal is made to the scientificity of physical explanation—the more physical the explanation, the more scientific it is. The positivist conception of science as exemplified in the work of Eysenck, is a conception of science which denies meaning to any action taken outside the consensus and thereby the established social order itself.

Trasler

One of the theorists influenced by Eysenck and yet at the same time, apparently more respectable amongst English sociologists, psychologists and social workers because of his supposedly 'balanced' views of the relationship between environment and genetics, and the aetiology of crime, is Gordon Trasler.

As a derivative theorist his work is far less comprehensive than Eysenck's—its contribution is in its different emphasis rather than in any radical innovation. In particular, by stressing the importance of child-rearing practices based on well-articulated moral principles, he has produced a theory which, at least at first sight, appears to correct the undue emphasis placed by Eysenck on genetic factors. We want to argue, however, that he merely compounds the failings of biological positivism with the defects of positivist studies of child-rearing.

We can best provide a usefully concise summary of Trasler's social learning theory by quoting his own nine propositions (1962, pp. 63, 71, 74):

    I.   The acquisition of values and attitudes of respect for

property and persons of others is mediated to a considerable extent by conditioning reactions of an autonomic kind (anxiety).

II.   The anxiety reaction, so conditioned, acts as a learned drive, having the effect of inhibiting or motivating kinds of behaviour. *Corollary from* II: It follows that learned inhibition of specific kinds of behaviour (theft, violence), being motivated by a conditioned anxiety reaction, will be strongly resistant to extinction, because it is constantly reinforced by anxiety reduction.

III.   Extraverts are resistant to conditioning; introverts are readily conditioned. *Derivation from* I *and* III: It follows that in a given pattern of environmental circumstances, introverts will tend to acquire more effective values of attitude and respect for the property and persons of others (i.e. become more thoroughly 'socialized') than extraverts.

IV.   An individual's position upon the introversion-extraversion continuum is partly determined by genetic factors.

V.   The effectiveness of social conditioning will depend upon the strength of the unconditioned reaction (anxiety) with which it is associated.

VI.   Where there is a strong dependent relationship between a child and his parents, the sanction of withdrawal of approval will evoke intense anxiety.

VII.   The relationship between a child and his parents is likely to be one of dependence if it is (i) exclusive, (ii) affectionate and (iii) reliable.

VIII.   Social conditioning will be most effective where sanctions are applied consistently and reliably.

IX.   Social conditioning will be most effective when it is presented in terms of a few well-defined principles.

Like Eysenck, therefore, Trasler utilizes two basic variables (although with more equal stress), namely, *differential ability to be conditioned* (which is linked to extraversion-introversion and is genetically inherited) and *differential quality of conditioning*. The latter centres on the efficiency of child-rearing practices.

The middle class because of their use of 'love-withdrawal' rather than 'primitive' techniques of child-rearing and because they base their moral discipline on well-defined principles, are superior to the working class in the quality of conditioning that they impart to their children. The prevalence of crime amongst the lower classes is thus seen as a product of permissive, erratic, punitive, 'unprincipled' child-rearing. Extraversion (because of its genetic basis) is evenly distributed throughout the population and, therefore, cannot be the cause of differential crime rates between the classes—it is variation in socialization practices which must therefore be the explanatory variable. Extraversion is utilized to explain who within a class is likely to be criminal. Because of this Trasler argues that middle-class criminals have a greater tendency to be extraverts than those in the working class. For as they have the advantage of efficient social training those who fall into crime are more likely to be relatively unconditionable.

Trasler's emphasis on the articulation of moral principles in socialization is an advance on the behaviourist notion that each prohibition must be specifically inculcated. He asserts precisely the opposite: that the learning of general principles to which specific acts are referred is a more efficacious technique.

The appeal of Trasler is that he provides a rationale for social agencies which wish to evolve 'scientific' yet humanitarian means of minimizing delinquent behaviour. Those who would balk at behaviour therapy sometimes welcome the notion of training programmes based on principled conditioning involving the manipulation of affection and a theoretical position which emphasizes the importance of the family as the bulwark against delinquency.

Criticisms of Trasler, as a result of his theoretical premises, parallel many of the points already covered in our examination of Eysenck. Certain defects are, however, highlighted in his work.

The steady state notion of biological potential

The degree to which a person is susceptible to conditioning is seen as a relatively fixed constant on to which the actual quality of conditioning is an added factor. The autonomic nervous system fixed by heredity represents a steady state of biological predisposition for conformity or deviancy. No change in this predisposition is seen as possible. In fact it would seem to be more plausible to assume that there is an ongoing interaction between conditioning and biological base, so that a person's rating on an extraversion-introversion scale represents a product of both inherited physiological structures and subsequent learnt responses. If physiologists such as Hebb are correct in assuming that there is a cellular base to learnt responses, and that this lies in the nervous system, then one would expect the structure of the autonomic nervous system to change over time with what has been acquired through the process of social interaction. In addition, we would argue that rational learning in the form of creative attempts to make meaningful and workable individual projects generate a situation where the individual's social environment is not merely an external facticity imposed upon a passive individual, but one where responses are often purposefully learnt

63

and earlier conditioning intentionally discarded. This is not to deny the irrational resistance of autonomic conditioning to purposeful action, but to insist that such reflexes vary throughout the individual's life-span and are frequently superseded, controlled and supplanted.

Lower working-class disorganization

Trasler contends that parents in lower working-class districts have the same goals as middle-class parents, but that their techniques of inculcating these goals are less efficacious. He cites as confirmations of this assertion the ecological studies of Mays, Kerr, Jephcott and Carter, and Morris. As David Downes has rightly pointed out (1966a, p. 112), these sources in fact show the opposite—the deviant nature of values in these areas. As Terence Morris (1957, p. 177) puts it, a working-class child is adequately socialized, but into a 'subculture unambiguously defined and in some aspects blatantly at variance with widely accepted middle class norms'.

Thus, as one of the present authors has noted elsewhere (Young, 1971a, p. 56):

The apparent social disorganisation of slum areas is often merely organisation centring around different ends than those of respectable society. And what is perceived as the faulty childrearing practices of individual families is more easily understood as *differential* socialisation occurring in different groups and utilising different techniques. To grow up as a mature adult in the East End demands the inculcation of different norms, by different means, than does that needed to produce a well-balanced inhabitant of Knightsbridge.

The high crime rate amongst the lower working class may be seen as either: (a) a product of the deprivations faced in their everyday life, or (b) a function of their vulnerability as far as arrest and detention are concerned, or (c) (most likely) a combination of the above two influences. To ascribe it to isolated psychological weaknesses is a convenient ideology—a defusion of the authenticity of alternative and threatening values and, ultimately, a scholarly yet convoluted justification of the *status quo*.

Moral principles

It is correct that man's behaviour is oriented towards moral principles. But Trasler's principles seem to appear out of thin air. There is no explanation of how these moral generalizations are created nor of human reflection and striving towards values. As Laurie Taylor (1971, p. 81) has put it:

64

Genetic notions or concepts surely require by their very nature some sort of act of categorisation before events or situations can be assigned to them. This means that conscious reflection precedes their application to distinctive situations. How can one then have an immediate autonomic response (for such is the nature of the conditioned response) conceptually related to the original conditioning situation?

Conclusion

Biological positivism has, in the work of psychological positivists such as Eysenck and Trasler, reached a higher level of sophistication than in the work of simple genetic or physical type theorists. Social factors are taken into account, moral relativism mooted, and precise postulations of the manner in which genetic influences manifest themselves in behaviour is elaborated upon. No claim is made to explain the formal causes of crime (i.e. the reasons why certain acts are deviant and particular deviant actors are apprehended); the focus is exclusively placed on the efficient causes. Positivism as a doctrine is wedded to the position of taking social reaction for granted. Yet, as we have seen, Eysenck in a critical vein stumbles on the problem of social order. The explanation of the creation of value and thus the meaningful nature of both deviant action and social reaction, eludes a theory which utilizes a model of human nature where man is a passive actor. We would not deny the influence of autonomic responses in human behaviour but we would argue that their role must be seen in the context of human creativity and purpose. As Matza (1969a, pp. 92-3) says:

Capable of creating and assigning meaning, able to contemplate his surroundings and even his own condition, given to anticipating, planning and projecting man—the subject—stands in a different and more complex relation to circumstance. This distinctively human capacity in no way denies that human existence frequently displays itself in ways characteristic of lower levels. Frequently man is wholly adaptive, *as if* he were just an organic being. And sometimes, though very rarely, he is wholly reactive, *as if* a mere object. But mere reactivity or adaptation should not be confused with the distinctively human condition. They are better seen as an alienation or exhaustion of that condition. A subject actively addresses or encounters his circumstance; accordingly, his distinctive capacity is to reshape, strive towards creating, and actually to *transcend* circumstance. Such a distinctly human project is not always feasible, but the capacity always exists.

65

Our position in this critique is not one in which psychology is totally excluded or denied. But, as our argument evolves, it will become clear that the most pressing need is for a social psychology which is capable of situating the actions of men acting according to beliefs and values in their historical and structural contexts. Martin Nicolaus (1969) has said of social science: 'What kind of science is this, which holds true only when men hold still?' A social theory of deviance must attempt to deal with men who move.

3 Durkheim and the break with 'analytical individualism'

Durkheim's central achievement was to spell out the elements of social explanation at a time when political and ethical philosophy, the 'science' of political economy, and the positive schools were united under the banners of individualism. Taking up the temporarily eclipsed work of the moral statisticians, Durkheim (1964a, pp. 144–5) urged a confrontation between sociologists, concerned with social facts, and those who would engage in individualistic reductionism:

> If we consider social facts as things, we consider them as
> *social things* . . . It has often appeared that these phenomena,
> because of their extreme complexity, were either inhospitable
> to science or could be subject to it only when reduced to their
> elemental conditions, either psychic or organic, that is, only
> when stripped of their proper nature. . . . We have even refused
> to identify the immateriality which characterizes [social facts]
> with the complex immateriality of psychological phenomena;
> we have, furthermore, refused to absorb it, with the Italian
> school, into the general properties of matter.

Psychology and biology were not alone in being unable to explain the social determination of action. 'Analytical individualism' found expression, in particular, in the traditional political philosophies of liberalism: the classical philosophies of a social contract freely entered into by atomized individuals, renouncing a degree of that freedom in exchange for protection by the society. This kind of analytical individualism, for Durkheim, had no relationship to the realities of industrial society. A society divided into different interest groups, on an inequitable basis, was not a society in which 'just contracts' between individuals and society could be struck. He writes 1964b, p. 202) that:

The conception of a social contract is today very difficult to defend, for it has no relation to the facts. The observer does not meet it along his road, so to speak. Not only are there no societies which have such an origin, but there are none whose structure presents the least trace of a contractual organisation. It is neither a fact acquired through history nor a tendency which grows out of historical development. Hence, to rejuvenate this doctrine and accredit it, it would be necessary to qualify as a contract the adhesion which each individual, as adult, gave to the society when he was born, solely by reason of which he continues to live. But then we would have to term contractual every action of man which is not determined by constraint.

The attack on utilitarian political philosophy was also, necessarily, an attack on the view of economic life depicted in the work of Herbert Spencer and the *laissez-faire* political economists. Where these thinkers tended to see economic relations as a confrontation and an exchange between social interests of supply and demand, resulting in the satisfaction of both, Durkheim (1964b, p. 204) had a less sanguine view of 'interests' in the industrial society of his time: 'There is nothing less constant than interest. Today, it unites me to you: tomorrow, it makes me your enemy.'

The ethical and economic 'sciences' of his day, seemed to Durkheim to proceed as if conditions of individual equality of interest, just contracts, and the like, did in reality obtain. Durkheim (1964a, p. 26) denied this and decried the fact that

No experiment or systematic comparison has ever been undertaken for the purpose of establishing that, *in fact*, economic relations *do* conform to this law [i.e. of supply and demand]. All that these [utilitarian] economists could do was to demonstrate by dialectics that, in order to promote their interests, individuals ought to proceed according to this law. . . . But this quite logical necessity resembles in no way the necessity that the true laws of nature represent. The latter express the regulations according to which facts are really connected, not the way in which it is good that they should be interconnected.

In asserting that social order was not so automatic as the utilitarians would have it, Durkheim was concerned to spell out the conditions in which order would be possible. But this importance does not lie simply in the fact that he attempted (especially in *The Division of Labour* and in *Socialism and Saint-Simon*) to isolate and describe the determinants of social order and cohesion, but also in the fact that he explained why no such order existed in the industrial society of his time.

The break with analytical individualism, most clearly stated in *The Rules of Sociological Method*, published in 1895, finds expression in the concept of the 'social fact'. Durkheim had come to realize that the world was not simply the result of individual action. Unlike the utilitarians and the classical liberals, Durkheim (1964a, p. 2) believed that society was not the direct reflection of the characteristics of its individual members. Individuals could not always choose.

> The system of signs I use to express my thought, the system of currency I employ to pay my debts, the instruments of credit I utilize in my commercial relations, the practices followed in my profession, etc., function independently of my own use of them. . . . [They are] . . . ways of acting, thinking, and feeling that present the noteworthy property of existing outside the individual consciousness.

Moreover, these characteristics of a society's system of commerce, communication, morality and, indeed, its general functioning, were not only external but also constraining. The coercion might be formal, by means of law, or informal and indirect, by means of ridicule, for example, but it is none the less effective. Much of Durkheim's later work was concerned with the explanation of the precise form assumed by the external, coercive social facts as they obtained in nineteenth-century industrial society. In *The Rules*, however, the concern is largely polemical, and the polemic is concerned to identify utilitarianism as methodologically inadequate, and, in particular, as being unable to conceive of social facts as *things* (existing outside of the individual consciousness) and exercising constraint over men (1964a, p. 14):

> Man cannot live in an environment without forming some ideas about it according to which he regulates his behaviour. But, because these ideas are nearer to us and more within our mental reach than the realities to which they correspond, we tend naturally to substitute them for the latter and to make them the very subject of our speculations. . . . Instead of a science concerned with realities, we produce no more than an ideological analysis.

The break with analytical individualism, then, was also a break with an idealistic ideology, and turned Durkheim, like the positivists, towards the investigations of the concrete, as distinct from the ideal, possibilities dictated by the social facts of industrial society.

Durkheim's break with positivism

It has frequently been pointed out that Durkheim's whole life-work can be interpreted as a response to his own personal marginality, and, associated with this, his fear of the disorganization engendered by industrialization (in particular, his aversion to the revolutionary 'mobs' of 1789 and 1870).[2]

The common stress in Durkheim, the early positivists (in particular, Comte) and the 'moral statisticians', on the search for order has often led commentators to see these thinkers as pursuing also a common methodology. For example, Douglas (1967, p. 15) has argued that Durkheim's *Suicide* is 'primarily an attempt to synthesize the better principles, methods of analysis, and empirical findings of the moral statisticians in such a way as to demonstrate the need for an independent discipline concerned with human society'.

The view of society as external, and characterized by a constraining morality, is alleged to be taken from Esquirol's *Des Maladies mentales*, published in 1839, and from Quetelet's *Treatise on Man*, published in 1842. Durkheim is also said, by Douglas, to have drawn the methods of statistical compilation and aetiological comparison used in *Suicide* from the pioneering work of Brierre Brosmont (1856). And, at the most general level of all, Douglas (1967, p. 21) asserts (at least as far as *Suicide* is concerned) that: 'Durkheim's sociologistic approach to suicide was seen by Durkheim and others as fundamentally analogous to the basic ideas of the science of thermodynamics, which was greatly advanced and systematised in the nineteenth century.'

It is precisely this view of Durkheim's method as mechanistic, (involving similar techniques to those of thermodynamics and positivistic statistical analysis), and the implicit suggestion that Durkheim operated with a simple organic model of society (adhered to by Comte and the moral statisticians) with which we wish to quarrel. Certainly it is the case that, for Durkheim, society can usefully be understood as an organism (and, thus, understood to some extent in terms of models derived from the natural sciences), but is also the case that Durkheim attempted to spell out the social, i.e. the historical and structural, conditions for health (order) and disease in a society. In this latter enterprise, his work was not informed by a natural science methodology so much as by a grasp of the dialectics between the needs of men (having the ability to interpret social arrangements as appropriate and/or meaningful) and the arrangements in the structure itself. In short, he had a political sociology of the state, of productive relations, and of social facts in general—none of which is reducible to a simple social biologism.[3]

It is worth emphasizing this point here, prior to full discussion of

Durkheim's understanding of the division of labour, inasmuch as it is the view of Durkheim as mechanistic, biologistic and deterministic in a simple sense which has been assimilated as an orthodoxy into the sociologies of crime and social control, which go under the names of systems theory, functionalism, and, most recently, cybernetic 'theory'. We shall argue later that this 'translation' of Durkheim was affected, with good and bad consequences, on the one hand by Talcott Parsons and (to a greater extent, so far as criminology and the sociology of deviance are concerned) by Robert Merton, and, on the other, much less obviously, by the applied sociologists in Chicago who were interested in the ecology of social structure and organization. It is this latter tradition—of Durkheim as social ecologist and a theorist of culture—that leads into contemporary subcultural theory, in particular in relation to juvenile delinquency. Our concern here is to stress the peculiar way in which Durkheim's sociology, for all that has been said by later commentators, *is* a break with positivism (and thus with the static, and unelaborated theories of man involved in the work of Comte) and the way in which his sociology is underpinned not only by a radical critique of industrialization but also by a complex (non-positivistic) image of man in an ordered society.

Much of what is said (incorrectly) about Durkheim's theoretical concerns, is very much more applicable to the work of Auguste Comte—by acclamation, the founder of positive science. Comte, like Durkheim lived most of his early life in a divided France, and, also like Durkheim, was associated with Saint-Simonian circles in Paris that wrestled with the problem of social reformation in a period of apparent social collapse. Comte's concerns (encapsulated in the catch-phrase so often associated with the mention of his name: *savoir pour prevoir*) were to ensure that:

> The coming of sociology itself was part of a determinate
> pattern of historical change. Once the sociologist had discovered
> the laws of such change it was his task to use the discovery to
> mastermind the political course of 'social regeneration'. What
> is more, this insight possessed by the sociologist was an insight
> into ethically valuable policies and purposes—that is, those
> policies which will advance 'progress'. Comte slips, in other
> words, very gently from the indicative into the imperative
> mood (Gould, 1969, p. 40).

Imperative and polemical Comte's writings often were, for there was little doubt in his mind as to the seriousness of the contemporary crisis, posed, as he saw it, by the rapid differentiation of men into different occupational groups for the purpose of industrial production. He writes (1854, Book IV, p. 429): 'the extension of general society threatens . . . to decompose it into a multitude of incoherent corporations which almost seem not to be of the same species.'

Fundamentally, Comte's argument is that the differentiation of men from men into separate places of work and residence (a progress to a higher stage of material civilization) has subverted the moral authority of a previously united society. Men will rob, struggle and conflict not necessarily—or primarily—because it is in their material interests to do so, but basically because there is no higher authority which would influence men to do otherwise. The creation of this higher authority is the historic task of positive science.

Comte's attempt to do this, in the name of positive science, is variously called (by Durkheim) 'metaphysical' and 'utopian'. The difference between Durkheim and Comte has to do with their views of the social—in the most general sense—and, more particularly, their respective images of man. For Comte, the task of creating a legitimate moral authority which will ensure social order is simply the task of creating a moral authority which will encourage humanity in its natural progress through the stages of civilization. Man has a natural, inbuilt desire to perfect himself; and thus a perfect and ordered society is guaranteed by the erection, by positive scientists, of a moral authority which legitimates rather than obstructs progress. The explanation of disorder, then, really centres on 'cultural lag'—the failure of a moral authority to keep pace with men's productive and progressive structural initiatives.

Durkheim, quite simply, disagrees with Comte on the nature of man. For Comte, in Durkheim's words (1964a, p. 99), 'the relation between the fundamental laws of human nature and the ultimate products of human nature [never] ceases to be intimate. The most complex forms of civilisation are only a development of the psychological life of the individual.' For Durkheim (pp. 103–4), however:

> Individual minds, forming groups by mingling and fusing, give birth to a being, psychological if you will, but constituting a psychic reality of a new sort. It is, then, in the nature of this collective individuality, not in that of the associated units, that we must seek the immediate and determining causes of the facts appearing therein. . . . In a word, there is between psychology and sociology the same break in continuity as between biology and physiochemical sciences. Consequently, every time that a social phenomenon is directly explained by a psychological phenomenon, we may be sure that the explanation is false.

In the same way as Durkheim, contrary to the view of many commentators, quite specifically rejected Thomas Hobbes's view of man as 'naturally' refractory (p. 121), so he denied Comte's psychologistic view of the perfectability of man. Both were a-historical, assuming that man is unaffected by the new moral currents of a changing society, and both tended to assume that there is a break in continuity between man and society. In his emphasis on the dialectical exchange taking place between humanity (or human nature) and society (in particular, the forms assumed by the division of labour), Durkheim made a fundamental break not only with the utilitarians (for whom society was merely a sum of its parts) but also with positivism (with its static view of the relationships between men and society).

Durkheim's view of human nature

If, as Durkheim argued against Comte, it was utopian and idealistic to argue that some kind of moral authority was universally appropriate to the constraint of men's absolute nature in all periods, it was largely because of his 'dualistic' view of human nature. Durkheim's notion of human nature—which was, again, to be systematically deprived of its essential content in the American translation (Horton, 1964)—involved an appeal to 'the constitutional duality of human nature'—a duality of the body and its needs, on the one hand, and of the soul, on the other. His position here was never clearly formulated until he published *The Elementary Forms of the Religious Life* in 1912 and, even then, he felt compelled to repeat his position for critics in an Italian journal in 1914.

In this article he writes (Wolff, ed., 1960, p. 328):

> The old formula *homo duplex* is . . . verified by the facts. Far from being simple, our inner life has something like a double centre of gravity. On the one hand is our individuality—and, more particularly, our body in which it is based; on the other, is everything in us that expresses something other than ourselves. Not only are these two groups or states of consciousness different in their origins and their properties, but there is a true antagonism between them. They mutually contradict and deny each other. We cannot pursue moral ends without causing a split within ourselves, without offending the instincts and the penchants that are most deeply rooted in our bodies.

The instincts of men are organically given; and the control and constraint of men is the task of social sentiment acting through the 'soul'. 'It is evident that passions and egoistic tendencies derive from our individual constitutions, while our rational activity—whether theoretical or practical—is dependent on social causes' (Wolff, ed., p. 338).

The egoism of the constitution, however, has not to be confused with the individualism of the body politic. The institutionalization of 'individualism' as a social and political creed is, for Durkheim, the product of a long period of social evolution, and, in particular, the development of relationships of organic rather than mechanical solidarity.[4] But there is no natural, or Comtian, coincidence of these features of social progress and change. 'There is no doubt', Durkheim concluded (ibid., p. 338) in reply to his critics (our emphasis):

> that if society were only the natural and spontaneous develop-
> ment of the individual, these two parts of ourselves would
> harmonize and adjust to each other without clashing. . . . In
> fact, however, society has its own nature, and, consequently, its
> requirements are different from those of our own nature as
> individuals: *the interests of the whole are not necessarily those
> of the parts.* Therefore, society cannot be formed without our
> being required to make perpetual and costly sacrifices.

Among the perpetual and costly sacrifices to be demanded of Durkheim's *homo duplex*—in the name of the advancement of moral regulation, and, thereby, of civilization—was a constant submission to the constraints of the *collective conscience* (the general, *social* morality of the time)—and this submission, it was alleged, was a part of the route to freedom (ibid., p. 339).

> Since the role of the social being in our single selves will grow
> ever more important as history moves ahead, it is wholly
> probable that there will be an era in which man is required to
> resist himself to a lesser degree, an era in which he can live a
> life that is easier and less full of tension.

The similarity between this position and that of Freud—in seeing increased repression of the individual conscience as necessary to civilizing advances—has been widely noted (cf. Coser, 1960). The difference in assumptions, however, has not. Man has to be repressed not only because he has certain constitutional (or biological) needs and predispositions (the position taken by the biological reductionists) but also because the failure to repress this part of man's constitutional duality can lead to an anomic, i.e. asocial, situation of normlessness. Man's body and soul would be out of phase.

Durkheim on anomie and the division of labour

Durkheim's attack on the utilitarians was motivated, most im-
portantly, by a concern to understand society as it is, rather than as it ought to be: his view, fundamentally, was that the utilitarians were engaged in ethical philosophy rather than social science.

In sum, Durkheim differed both from the biological positivists in his attempt to explain the existence of social norms, and from the

classicists in his attempt to see the social norms constraining individuals, not as freely-willed but rather as a product of the dialectic
of the individual and society, the body and the soul. A 'social
science . . . needs concepts that adequately express things as they
actually are, and not as everyday life finds it useful to conceive them
to be' (Durkheim, 1964a, p. 43).

The science of 'social facts', elaborated in *The Rules of Sociological
Method*, highlighted above all else the fact that men are living, not in
a universe of choice and freedom (troubled only by the absence of an
appropriate moral authority), but that rather they were living under
conditions in which their natural faculties were not being utilized.
They were, in short, living under a 'forced' division of labour.

This insight, above all else, is at the basis of Durkheim's conception of anomie, and the conditions conducive to crime, deviance
and disorder. Informed perhaps to some extent by his immersion in
the 'socialism' of Saint-Simon (a tradition which Comte had,
arguably, misunderstood), Durkheim realized that moral authority
was acceptable to men only to the extent that that authority was
relevant to men's real, material situation. Moral authority was no
authority at all unless it was meaningful to men caught in unfamiliar,
rapidly changing, or, most importantly, *forced* social positions. In a
situation where men were not performing occupational and social
tasks concomitant with their natural talents, moral authority would
have no power at all—unless it had relevance to the task of social
reform. Where Comte's 'positive science' (and many contemporary
sociologies of social control) proceed only in fear of the 'decomposi-
tion [of society] into a multitude of incoherent corporations', a
position which indicts them as ideologies of social reaction and retrenchment, Durkheim's 'sociology' is concerned with the springs of
social change, and, in particular, the destruction of the forced
division of labour. He writes (1964b, p. 387):

> The task of the advanced societies is . . . a work of justice. ˙
> That they, in fact, feel the necessity of orienting themselves in
> this direction is what we have already shown and what every-
> day experience proves to us. Just as the ideal of the lower
> societies was to create or maintain as intense a common life
> as possible, in which the individual was absorbed, so our
> ideal is to make social relations more equitable, so as to assure
> the free development of all our socially useful forces.

Giddens (1971b, p. 494, our emphasis) sees Durkheim's 'radicalism' in the following terms:

> There is in Durkheim's writings no yearning for a former age,
> no wistful search for the revitalisation of the stability of the

past. There can be no reversion to the social forms of earlier types of society, and neither, in Durkheim's eyes, would this be a desirable prospect if it were possible. In traditional society men are subject to the tyranny of the group; individuality is subordinated to the pressure of the *conscience collective.* The expansion of the division of labour, and the weakening of the *conscience collective*, are the agencies of escape from this tyranny; but the dissolution of the old moral order threatens the individual with another tyranny, that of his own inexhaustible desires. An individual can only be free if he is an autonomous actor, capable of mastering and realising his impulses.

'Traditional' society was, for Durkheim, characterized by relationships of mechanical solidarity, that is, 'a social structure of determined nature' associated with 'a system of segments homogenous and similar to each other' (Durkheim, 1964b, p. 181), or, as Giddens (1971a, p. 76) puts it, 'juxtaposed politico-familial groups [clan groups] which are very similar to each other in their internal organisation'. These relationships correspond to the systems of social control—the means whereby the overweening moral authority (or *conscience collective*) is enforced—and, in particular, the law. The law is the objective, rather than the ethical, index of the progress of the division of labour, in developing societies: the absence of such an objective index in alternative theories of society being their fundamental flaw (Durkheim, 1964b, pp. 39–46). 'Repressive law' is the law of traditional societies, and is characterized by the existence of general moral agreement on the nature of sanctionable behaviour (crime). There is, in other words, a strong *conscience collective* underpinning the enforcement of repressive law, and there is general agreement on the nature of punishment (involving, for example, the deprivation of liberty, loss of honour and inflicting of pain). These punishments, importantly, do not specify any moral obligations to obey the law, for example, by stressing 'rehabilitation' or 'reform', because everyone is very well aware of the obligations anyway: they are already specified in the existence of a strong *conscience collective*, in which individual obligations as well as individual rights are enshrined.

As soon as laws are written down and codified, says Durkheim (1964b, p. 75), this must be because: 'questions of litigation demand a more definite solution. If the custom continues to function silently, without raising any discussion or difficulties, there is no reason for transforming it.'

This situation, in turn, can only arise when relationships of mechanical solidarity are weakened, by the development of what Durkheim (1964b, p. 11) calls 'specialised functions' in the advancing division of labour: 'The very nature of the restitutive sanction suffices to show that the social solidarity to which this type of law corresponds is of a totally different kind.'

The development of restitutive law, which is characterized by the fact that it does enforce sanctions and does demand expiation, and is institutionalized in the growth of specialized courts and tribunals which had not existed (and do not exist) in societies of mechanical solidarity, is testimony to the collapse of the hold of the *conscience collective*, and to the growth of individuality of interest, function and identity encouraged and developed by the specialization of task in the division of labour. Under these conditions, of *organic solidarity*, the tension between the interests of the *conscience collective* and those of men with individual interests—the source of anomie—is opened up (Durkheim, 1964b, p. 131):

> Whereas [mechanical solidarity] implies that individuals resemble each other, [organic solidarity] presumes their difference. The first is possible only in so far as the individual personality is absorbed into the collective personality: the second is possible only if each one has a sphere of action which is peculiar to him, i.e. a personality. It is necessary, then, that the collective conscience leave open a part of the individual conscience in order that special functions may be established there, functions which it cannot regulate.

The situation under conditions of organic solidarity, then, is one in which 'individualism' is actually strengthened by the collective conscience, whereas under conditions of mechanical solidary collectivism is institutionalized under the collective conscience. In other terms, under *mechanical solidarity*—where roles are less specialized and differentiated—there is a close proximity between inherited faculties and social activity, where in an *organic* society, with a specialized division of labour, it is necessary that the inherited faculties are socially developed, and hence the importance of norms which actually encourage individuation.

Anomie has its source in this dissociation of individuality from the collective conscience. It can find expression in two interrelated ways. Either the collective conscience is unable to regulate man's appetites and anomie results, or the 'cult of the individual' is encouraged beyond that sufficient and necessary to man the roles, and perform the specialized functions, of a differentiated society. In the latter case, norms occur which actively encourage the development of unregulated aspirations and 'egoism' ensues.

The anomic-egoistic situation was seen by Durkheim to be a pathological phase in the development of society. Like the positivists,

Durkheim did have an ethical alternative; unlike the positivists, he thought that the alternative would develop, not out of the moral activities of men of science,[6] but, via the formation of occupational associations and the abolition of inheritance, as a result of the progress of the development of the division of labour itself. Anomie, egoism and the disorder of his times would be removed with the development of the 'spontaneous' over the 'forced' division of labour (Durkheim, 1964b, p. 377, our emphasis):

> We may say that the division of labour produces solidarity only if it is spontaneous and in proportion as it is spontaneous. But by spontaneity we must understand not only the absence of all express violence, but also of everything that can even indirectly shackle the free unfolding of the social force that each carries in himself. It supposes, not only that individuals are not relegated to determinate functions by force, but also that no obstacle, of whatever nature, prevents them from occupying the place in the social framework which is compatible with their faculties. *In short, labour is divided spontaneously only if society is constituted in such a way that social inequalities exactly express natural inequalities.* But, for that, it is necessary and sufficient that the latter be neither enhanced nor lowered by some external cause. Perfect spontaneity is, then, only a consequence and another form of this other fact,—absolute equality in the external conditions of this conflict. It consists, not in a state of anarchy which would permit men to satisfy all their good or bad tendencies, but in a subtle organisation in which each social value, being neither overestimated nor underestimated by anything foreign to it, would be judged at its true worth.

Durkheim on 'the Normal and the Pathological'

Durkheim spent a considerable amount of space and time in discussing the question of crime, usually by way of illustrating his methodological approach in general (in *Rules*), his understanding of the development of individualism (in *The Division of Labour*), or the decline of the collective conscience (in *Professional Ethics and Civic Morals*). Conventional criminological textbooks have taken these illustrations from out of their context in order to describe 'the Durkheimian position on crime'. We want briefly to describe this caricature, with a view to re-locating it in Durkheim's overall social theory.

Crime, for Durkheim, is a 'social fact': it is 'normal'. Usually, in the textbooks, this is intended primarily as a statistical and cultural observation. Commenting on Durkheim in *Ideology and Crime*, Radzinowicz (1966, p. 72) writes:

> Undeniably crime was a general phenomenon. It occurred not merely in all advanced societies but in all societies of whatever type, at all stages in their development. There was no sign that it was on the decline. It must therefore be accepted as a social fact, as a normal part of society which could not be eradicated at will.

In the next section, we attempt to show that Durkheim's position was rather more complex than this; that, in particular, he did operate with a view of a certain kind of society in which crime would not be normal in the sense of being a social fact, and that the general notion of crime in textbook interpretations of Durkheim disguises the different senses in which he intended it to be used. The conventional interpretations are, however, quite correct in pointing to the fact that Durkheim, even more than the moral statisticians, was convinced that crime was a regular and normal social fact in so far as it performed some kind of social function. There was a reason for its persistence—over and above the existence of any number of biological and physiological throwbacks distributed through the society. He writes (1964a, p. 67):

> Let us make no mistake. To classify crime among the phenomena of normal sociology is not merely to say that it is an inevitable, although regrettable, phenomenon, due to the incorrigible wickedness of men; it is to affirm that it is a factor in public health, an integral part of all societies.

For Durkheim, public health has to be defined—appropriate forms of behaviour have to be identified. Thus, the collective conscience is inextricably bound up with the fact of crime. Crime marks the boundaries of morality (1964a, p. 68):

> Robbery and simple bad taste injure the same altruistic sentiment, the respect for that which is another's. However, this same sentiment is less grievously offended by bad taste than by robbery; and since, in addition, the average consciousness has not sufficient intensity to react keenly to the bad taste, it is treated with greater tolerance. That is why the person guilty of bad taste is merely to blame, whereas the thief is punished.

The evolution of public morality, however, is the creation of changes in social, and, in particular, occupational relationships. The advance of the division of labour, and the creation of new occupational specializations, is to some considerable extent in the hands of 'the idealist whose dreams transcend his century' (Durkheim, 1964a,

p. 71) and, for this idealist to have freedom, under the law and within the general moral norms of society, to express these dreams, it is essential that 'the collective sentiments at the basis of morality must not be hostile to change' (p. 70) in general.

It is not only that crime keeps 'open the path to necessary changes', however; it is also that crime can under certain circumstances directly prepare these changes. Crime's 'functionality' in this respect has lost out in the later American translation, involving as it does some recognition of the purposive nature of illegitimate activity, but it is crucial to the original Durkheimian formulation. Yesterday's criminal is tomorrow's philosopher, and, for Durkheim (1964a, p. 71), Socrates was the prime example.

> How many times, indeed [is crime] . . . only an anticipation of
> future morality—a step towards what will be! According to
> Athenian law, Socrates was a criminal, and his condemnation
> no more than just. However, his crime, namely, the indepen-
> dence of his thought, rendered a service not only to humanity
> but to his country. It served to prepare a new morality and faith
> which the Athenians needed, since the traditions by which they
> had lived until then were no longer in harmony with the current
> conditions of life.

Crime, then, is persistent precisely because it is the work of men with ideas defined as illegitimate within the existing collective conscience. A flourishing crime rate, then, is an indication of the anachronistic nature of systems and ideas of social control. And more than anything else to be feared is the stagnation of a society—reflecting, as it must, an obstruction in the struggle of men to develop productive relationships (in the division of labour) and to master material nature. 'Crime . . . must no longer be conceived as an evil that cannot be too much suppressed. There is no occasion for self-congratulation when the crime-rate drops noticeably below the average level, for we may be certain that this apparent progress is associated with some social disorder' (Durkheim, 1964a, p. 72).

Most of these ideas have, as we shall see, been later wrenched from their overall context (the theoretical elaboration of Durkheim's concept of the relationship between man—as a creature with body and soul—and society, structured into different divisions of labour). This decontextualization of Durkheim on 'the normal and the pathological' is a serious distortion of Durkheim himself, and, more importantly for our purposes, stands in the way of a fully social theory of conformity and deviance. The emasculation of classical social theory is symptomatic of the insulation of applied criminology from social theory at large; the reconciliation of the two requires that their respective substance is not reduced in the translation into textbook knowledge.

Durkheim as a biological meritocrat

In the situation of a forced division of labour, occupational choice is not, Durkheim argues, a matter of biological determination (1964b, p. 315):

> The son of a great philologist does not inherit one word; the son of a great traveller can be surpassed in geography in school by the son of a miner. That is not to say that heredity is without influence, but that it transmits very general faculties and not a particular aptitude for this or that science. What a child receives from his parents is some power of attention, a capacity for perseverance, a wholesome judgement, imagination, etc. But each of these faculites can be suitable to a multitude of different specialities, and assure the success of each.

It follows that the kind of biological determinism used by Lombroso in the explanation of crime must similarly be inadequate (ibid., p. 317):

> All that one can conclude . . . is that the propensity toward evil in general is often hereditary, but can deduce nothing relative to the particular forms of crime and delict. We know . . . that this pretended criminal type has, in reality, nothing specific about it. A great many traits constituting it are found elsewhere. All one sees is that it resembles that of degenerates and neurasthenics. But, if this fact is a proof that among criminals there are a great many neurasthenics, it does not follow that neurasthenia inevitably and always leads to crime.

Similarly, with suicide (Durkheim, 1952, p. 81):

> no psychopathic state bears a regular and indisputable relation to suicide. A society does not depend for its number of suicides on having more or fewer neuropaths. . . . Although the different forms of degeneration are an eminently suitable psychological field for the action of the causes which may lead a man to suicide, degeneration itself is not one of these causes. Admittedly, under similar circumstances, the degenerate is more apt to commit suicide than the well man; but he does not necessarily do so because of his condition. The potentiality of his becomes effective only through the action of other (i.e. social) factors.

81

Durkheim's reference to the hereditary predisposition to evil echoes the assumptions of Eysenck's psychological and biological determinism—with the important difference that Durkheim is able to spell out the overwhelmingly social influences that will intervene between heredity and action. The degenerate can be an honest man in the appropriate social circumstances: he is, however, more likely to be deviant in anomic social circumstances.

Durkheim also resembles Eysenck in his excursions into the problem of order, and the conditions conducive to the orderly society. Eysenck, like Durkheim, is very much taken up with the way in which—in an organic, integrated division of labour—it is all the more necessary that individuals be adequately socialized into their ascribed roles. Failure on the part of society to socialize its members will threaten the existence of that form of society; but for Eysenck a specialized society is all the more threatened by the problem of people's differential ability (and differential organic constitution) to be socialized.

For Durkheim, in contrast, the relative importance of heredity and the organic constitution has diminished with the advancement of the division of labour.[7] Where, in mechanical society, simple roles demanded only the playing out of inherited aptitudes, the specialized roles of an organic society demand the learning of specific social skills. 'To make the hereditary legacy valuable, a great deal more must be added than formerly. In effect, in so far as functions are more specialized, simply general aptitudes are no longer enough' (Durkheim, 1964b, pp. 319–20).

Socialization in an advanced society must exalt the 'soul', in Durkheim's terms, at the expense of its dependency on the attributes of the 'body' (ibid., p. 321): 'In short, civilization can be fixed in the organism only through the most general foundations on which it rests. The more elevated it is, the more, consequently, it is free of the body. It becomes less and less an organic thing, more and more a social thing.'

But it is the conflict between general social aptitudes and social roles which, under conditions of a forced division of labour, gives rise to anomie and hence to deviance. Durkheim (op. cit., pp. 374–5) argues that there is:

a greater distance between the hereditary dispositions of the individual and the function he will fill [in societies as compared with in organisms]. The first does not imply the second with such immediate necessity. This space, open to striving and deliberation, is also at the mercy of a multitude of causes which can make individual nature deviate from its normal direction and create a pathological state. . . . Doubtless, we are not, from birth, predestined to some special position; but we do have tastes and aptitudes which limit our choice. If no care is taken of them, if they are ceaselessly disturbed by our daily occupations, we shall suffer and seek a way of putting an end to our suffering. But there is no other way out than to change the established order and to set up a new one. For the division of labour to produce solidarity, it is not sufficient, then, that each have his task; it is still necessary that this task be fitting to him.

Essentially, then, in a perfect social order (a 'spontaneous division of labour'), occupational arrangements would be in accord with individual aptitudes. Discontent with the present social order arises from the *forced* nature of the division of labour. In these conditions, an abnormal degree of constraint is, therefore, unavoidable and necessary (Durkheim, 1964a, p. 123n):

> all constraint is not normal . . . only that constraint which corresponds to some social superiority *i.e.* intellectual or moral . . . merits the name. . . . That which one individual exercises over the other because he is stronger or wealthier, especially if this wealth does not express his social value, is abnormal and can only be maintained by violence.

Durkheim (1964b, p. 375) specifically argues against the thesis that the lower classes are discontented because they desire to 'imitate' their social superiors. For, he says: 'imitation can by itself explain nothing, since it supposes something other than itself. It is possible only between beings who already resemble each other and only in proportion to their resemblance.' Discontent occurs, then, when (p. 375) 'through changes produced in society, some must have become apt at functions which were at first beyond them, while the others have lost their original superiority'. Man finds happiness in realizing his true nature; he does not covet what he cannot aspire to.

In a society where roles were distributed in accordance with biological merit, discontent would not exist. The contrast between this position and that adopted by Merton is worth stressing at this point, since, although Merton is accused of 'dehumanising' Durkheim, especially on the question of 'anomie', Merton's notion of social deprivation is in no way biological in foundation. So, for example, Durkheim's position on the relative deprivation of women is that, in a spontaneous division of labour, women would be 'separate but equal' (1952, p. 385n):

> Woman would not be officially excluded from certain functions and relegated to others. She could choose more freely, but as

her choice would be determined by her aptitudes it would generally bear on the same sort of occupations. It would be perceptibly uniform, though not obligatory.

The correspondence of social roles and biological aptitudes in the hypothetical healthy society is underpinned by the collective conscience; social control, that is, is the control of the biologically inferior by the biologically meritorious.

Our contention, here, is that Durkheim's notion of deviancy can be fully understood only in the light of his assumptions about the 'dualism of human nature' and the tensions that arise under the forced division of labour when occupational and social arrangements are out of accord with the demands of men's nature and needs. Conventional discussions of Durkheim on conformity and deviance, in a word, have suffered from their inability to comprehend the interconnectedness of Durkheim's biological anthropology and his political sociology of production and the state.

There appear, in fact, to be three different types of deviant in Durkheim's writings.

1 The biological deviant

Even in an organic society where there is a spontaneous division of labour, deviancy will occur as a normal phenomenon. *Individual* consciences will still vary widely, because of genetic inheritance and situational factors, and this, together with the existence of a workable collective conscience, will give rise to deviant actions. In this situation, as commentators have noted, the deviancy could still be functional to the collectivity, defining the boundaries of appropriate behaviour (Erikson, 1962).

In a perfect Durkheimian society, deviancy would be universally attributable to genetic and psychological malfunctioning. The biopsychological misfit would be the lone example of the individual conscience at odds with the collective conscience.

2 The functional rebel

The functional rebel acts out the 'true' collective conscience as it is in the process of emerging. In particular, the functional rebel is responsible for a revolt against the forced division of labour (and the unmerited social inequalities associated with it).

The rebellion he instigates is functional to the extent that it illuminates and challenges the lack of correspondence between the allocation of social role and the distribution of biological faculties. So, at various places, Durkheim indulges in polemic (Richter, 1960, p. 183): 'Resistance may be justified when an individual compre-

84

hends the reality of his society better than most of its other members' and 'Socrates expressed more clearly than his judges the morality suited to his time' (Durkheim, 1953, pp. 64–5), and, again, 'The morality of one's society may be resisted only in the name of that morality properly expressed' (Richter, 1960, p. 183).

The functional rebel, thus, is not an absolute (biological) deviant: he is branded a deviant because the existing institutions of power and influence do not represent the appropriate (and the true) collective conscience.

3 The skewed deviant

Whereas the functional rebel is a normal person reacting to a pathological society, the skewed deviant is an inappropriately socialized individual in a sick society.

This is seen as having two related sources: anomie and egoism. *Anomie* involves lack of regulation and weakness of the collective conscience, where *egoism* represents the (institutionalized) 'cult of the individual'. Both circumstances allow the appetites of the individual free rein, the first by default, the second by active normative encouragement. In such circumstances, individuals strive to achieve their egoistic desires in a way that is incompatible with social order and incommensurate with their biologically given abilities.

The three types of deviant can be located (along with the normal conformist) on two 'typologies': the 'altruistic' actor discussed by Durkheim in *Suicide* can be either a functional or a skewed deviant, depending on one's conceptualization of the society in which he is placed (as either normal or pathological) (see Tables 1 and 2).

TABLE 1 *Durkheim's types of deviants*

Society	Individual	
Normal division of labour	(Conformist)	Type 1 Biological or psychological deviant
Pathological division of labour	Type 2 Functional rebel	Type 3 Skewed deviant (anomie or egoism)

Most textbook discussions, of course, deal only with what we have called the 'skewed deviant'—and even then they fail to realize

85

that, for Durkheim, this type arises only in abnormal, or 'pathological' situations (situations remediable, for Durkheim, only through
social reform). Textbook discussions of Durkheim's view of crime
and deviance tend also to confuse the relative importance given by
Durkheim to biological givens and social facts—largely because
they have no conception of Durkheim's political sociology.

TABLE 2 *Propensity of societies to produce deviant types*

Normal division of labour	Pathological division of labour
Type 1 Biological-psychological deviant	*Type 1* Biological-psychological deviant
Some likelihood of *Type 2* Functional rebel	*Type 2* Functional rebel
	Type 3 Skewed deviant (under anomic or egoistic conditions)

Our contention (in contrast with these conventional interpretations) is that, for Durkheim, biological positivism would be the
prime explanation of deviant motivation only in a perfectly regulated,
organic society. In such a situation, anomie, egoism and the need for
functional rebellion would not obtain. But, importantly, even in the
case of a perfectly organic society, some kind of social explanation
would be required—specifically, in order to understand the nature
of the transactions occurring between the inadequate individual (the
biological-psychological deviant) and the regulating normative order.
In the imperfect industrial society (characterized, that is, by the
forced division of labour), however, explanations of deviant behaviour would be almost exclusively and predominantly social. That
is, a social explanation would be required of the forces that made
for the lack of regulation characterizing the anomic situation. The
rise of asocial individualistic norms—the egoistic situation—would
also require social explanation. And so functional rebellion would
demand explanation in terms of the inappropriateness of the means—
the level of social constraint in operation in particular social structures
(the anachronistic nature, that is, of the collective conscience). The
last two types, it is worth emphasizing, would imply a critique of
existing social arrangements (the abnormal society).

Several levels of analysis and several fine distinctions in terminology and concepts are involved in the social explanations advanced
by Durkheim himself. They have been systematically confused in
existing literature.

86

At the psychological level of analysis, Durkheim is concerned with the fact that individuals vary in their ability to be regulated. At the societal level, he sees that societies vary in their ability to impose regulation. And at the level of values, he sees that social values vary in their ability to achieve social integration (that is, to represent effectively the collective conscience).

Durkheim distinguishes the concepts of egoism and anomie, on the one hand, and individualism on the other, with considerable precision. *Anomie* involves lack of social regulation, and a situation in which the unrestricted appetites of the individual conscience are no longer held in check. *Egoism*, however, is a normative phenomenon—a situation in which a value has been placed on the unrestricted pursuit of individual desires—in Durkheim's view, a false freedom. In contrast, *individualism* is seen by Durkheim, following Rousseau, as a healthy development, involving as it does the freedom to take up the differentiated roles in the division of labour. Anomie and egoism, therefore, are antagonistic to individualism in the sense that a forced division of labour is antagonistic to spontaneity in the division of labour.

Several misconceptions about Durkheim—particularly in the criminological literature—stem from an ignorance of these dimensions of his thought. He does not, for instance, suggest that all deviance is a product of 'normlessness'[8] (that is, arising out of an ability to be regulated or a lack of effective social regulation). On the contrary, he suggests that certain social values—in particular, egoism—are the direct precursor of deviance. Furthermore, he does not suggest that there is one set of values to which people either conform or from which they deviate. Rather, he suggests that certain deviants may be functional in that they attempt to realize the true collective conscience against the prevailing moral climate (the false collective conscience). Far from having a simple organic model of a society dominated by value-agreement, Durkheim was at pains to emphasize the coexistence and ongoing conflict of different sets of values and interests in societies with abnormal or pathological divisions of labour. Any sociology of deviance which fails to recognize and to remain faithful to these complexities in Durkheim stands indicted of distortion and simplification.

Durkheim and a social theory of deviance

The most serious consequence of the emasculation of Durkheim's social theory in the work of many criminologists has been the depoliticization of criminology. Durkheim himself is unambiguously radical in his approach to social order. He holds that the existence of inherited wealth is at the root of the problem, making for 'unjust contracts' between men, unjust in being based on power and wealth rather than on natural aptitude and abilities. The collective conscience in a forced division of labour, far from being an idealization of social order, is a principle of 'justice' in which wealth is apportioned to men on a fundamentally inequitable basis. Quite simply, says Durkheim (1964b, p. 384) 'there cannot be rich and poor at birth without there being unjust contracts. This was still more the case when social status itself was hereditary and law sanctioned all sorts of inequalities.'

Durkheim believed that the abolition of inheritance and all those external constraints would allow the development of situations in which free contracts were possible and for him this was an essential and unavoidable political conclusion; it flowed from his theory. Only in such a situation could men be satisfied.

Indeed, Durkheim's politics—his belief in the need for a free and thoroughgoing meritocracy—do not stop short of appearing to justify the continuation of the conflict of classes, in situations where such warfare might serve purpose in restoring justice within an abnormal society. He writes (1964b, pp. 375–6):

> When the plebeians aimed to dispute the right to religious and administrative functions with the patricians, it was not only in imitation of the latter, but it was also because they had become more intelligent, richer, more numerous, and their tastes and ambitions had in consequence been modified. In accordance with these transformations, the agreement between the aptitudes of individuals and the kind of activity assigned to them is found to be broken in every region of society; constraint alone, more or less violent and more or less direct, links them to their functions. Consequently, only an imperfect and troubled solidarity is possible.

The plebeians, then, were 'functional rebels', concerned with realizing a true and just consensus, and a society in which constraint would be just in itself and not a mystification (Durkheim, 1964a, p. 123, our emphasis):

> *Constraint [must] not result from more or less learned machinations, destined to conceal from men the traps in which they have caught themselves.* It is due simply to the fact that the individual finds himself in the presence of a force which is superior to him, and before which he bows; but this force is an entirely natural one. It is not derived from a conventional arrangement which human will has added bodily to natural reality, it issues from innermost reality, it is the necessary product of given causes.

The politicality of these, and other sections in Durkheim's sociology of deviance, is quite unambiguous; and it is precisely this radical politicality which has been lost in the varieties of functionalist thought which claim a Durkheimian tradition. We are at one with Durkheim in maintaining that there can be no break between theoretical investigation and practical action (and, indeed, we agree with his specific proposal for the abolition of inheritance). However, it is on the question of Durkheim's ideal society—deriving, as it does, from his image of man's nature—that we differ. For Durkheim, natural reality (to which justice must, and will, correspond) derives quite directly from his conception of man's natural 'duplexity'. Man's nature is constituted, on the one hand, by biological givens (of aptitude and merit) and, on the other, through social processes (and, in particular, the advance of inequitable structures in the division of labour). So functional rebellion would constitute an attempt to match aptitudes to an ideal social reality, pathological deviancy occurring when appetites extend beyond natural aptitudes and reality. There is a crucial contradiction here, and one which we hope to resolve in later chapters.

Durkheim is not unaware that aspirations are socially induced and that aptitudes are shaped by the social milieu of the individual. He is aware, also, that men collectively can achieve a degree of consciousness about the total society and demand a more equitable distribution of wealth and function. Again and again, he refers to these developments as socially explicable—most notably in the polemics against analytical individualists in the early works, and later in his discussion of socialism. Yet, repeatedly, deviancy is described merely as an expression of biological impulses, aspirations are seen as egoistic and not as collective sentiments, and biological aptitude is seen as fixed. In short, although Durkheim's analytical approach often involves a dialectical version of the relationship between the individual and society, he more frequently retreats to a static description of *homo duplex*, caught between the imperatives of individual appetite and social necessity. He attempts to resolve this contradiction in suggesting that the rational, constructive deviancy of the 'functional rebel' is the work of the reason in man (the collective conscience internalized in the individual), this reason being pitted against the libidinous tendencies of his nature. But all other deviancy is necessarily condemned: far from being a rational appraisal of social needs, deviancy in general is seen either as the expression of a meaningless, given impulse or as a manifestation of a skewed situation between the individual and the social (in an abnormal or pathological society).[9]

In this book as a whole, we are concerned to show the way in which human action is social—however inarticulate, capricious or falsely conscious it might sometimes appear in practice. Durkheim's crucial and impressive break with analytical individualism, therefore, is achieved, for us, at the expense of erecting an incomplete picture of sociality, and, in particular at the expense of ambiguity over the questions of rationality, purposiveness and socialization in divided societies. In functionalism, and in the work of Robert Merton, to whom we now turn, there is a similarly narrow and limited view of the kind of purpose and meaning at the back of deviant and conforming social action.

4 The early sociologies of crime

In the last chapter, we were concerned to identify Durkheim's work as an important break with analytical individualism, and, also, as a polemic against the classicist notion of unfettered individualism. Utilitarian ideology (and practice) could be seen, on the one hand (in the *egoistic* case) to encourage the desires of the individual conscience, and, on the other (in the *anomic* situation) to provide insufficient restraint on the individual conscience. The discussion of norms, therefore, was double-edged. Norms did not merely inhibit deviant behaviour (anomie); they could also encourage and sustain it (egoism).

These two perspectives on the significance of norms were taken up later by American sociologists claiming a Durkheimian inspiration. The first position, characterized by Kai Erikson (1962) as a 'leakage' conception of deviancy, was a feature of the ecological tradition of the Chicago school, operating, to some extent, within the traditions of biological positivism. Writing in 1938, Robert Merton noted (p. 672) that:

> There persists a notable tendency in sociological theory to attribute the malfunctioning of social structure primarily to those of man's imperious biological drives which are not adequately restrained by social control. In this view, the social order is solely a device for 'impulse management' and the 'social processing' of tensions. These impulses which break through social control, be it noted, are held to be biologically derived. Nonconformity is assumed to be rooted in original nature. Conformity is by implication the result of an utilitarian calculus or unreasoned conditioning. This point of view, whatever its other deficiencies, clearly begs one question. It provides no basis for determining the non-biological conditions which induce deviations from prescribed patterns of conduct.

In this passage, and in this influential paper as a whole, Merton began to make a *partial* break with Durkheim's original formulations.[1] Although Merton is at one with Durkheim in his emphasis on and denunciation of the normative inflamation of aspirations (egoism), he begins to discard the notion of normative control (and its absence) as leading to anomie or normlessness. As we shall see, the latter emphasis did find a place in American sociology—but in the writings of the ecologists and the theorists of 'social disorganization'. Merton himself comes to see deviance as a normal adaptation to an egoistic environment rather than simply as biological 'leakage' resulting from lack of social control.

Merton and the American Dream

In his pioneering work, Merton separates out two central elements in what he calls the 'cultural structure' of a society: the culturally defined goals, and the institutionalized means by which these goals are achieved.

In the well-regulated society, goals and means are harmoniously integrated: both are accepted by, and available to, the population of the society as a whole. Malintegration occurs when there is a disproportionate emphasis on either ends or means. Thus, Merton (1957, p. 134) argues, certain societies develop

a very heavy, at times a virtually exclusive, stress upon the value of particular goals, involving comparatively little concern with the institutionally prescribed means of striving toward these goals. . . . A second polar type is found in groups where activities originally conceived as instrumental are transmitted into self-contained practices. . . . The original purposes are forgotten and close adherence to institutionally prescribed conduct becomes a matter of ritual.

In the integrated society, Merton argues, the individual obtains satisfaction via his acceptance of both the means and the goals (p. 134, our emphasis):

Thus, continuing satisfactions must derive from sheer participation in a competitive order as well as from eclipsing one's competitors if the order itself is to be sustained. If concern shifts exclusively to the outcome of competition, then those who perenially suffer defeat may, understandably enough, work for a change in the rules of the game. The sacrifices occasionally— not, as Freud assumed, invariably—entailed by conformity to institutional norms must be compensated by socialized rewards. The distribution of statuses though must be so organised that positive incentives for adherence to status obligations are provided *for every position* within the distributive order.

The perfect society inculcates into its members the joys of competition, the justice of making sacrifices and the value of rewards. The perfect society would be like a gigantic game, where everyone would be encouraged to obey the rules, and where *everyone* would be rewarded with prizes they judged to be appropriate rather than tawdry.

American society, however, for Merton, has in practice placed undue emphasis on the goals behind the game, and has neglected, in utilitarian fashion, the necessity for making appropriate means universally available. More specifically, Merton argued that normatively legitimate means have been replaced by (and confused with) technically efficient means, and, in particular, money has been consecrated as a value in itself, over and above its use simply for necessary consumption. The desire to make money, without regard to the means in which one sets about doing it, is symptomatic of the malintegration at the heart of American society.

Moreover, this malintegration is in a sense inevitable. Success, defined in monetary terms, is 'indefinite and relative'. 'In the American Dream there is no final stopping point' (Merton, 1957, p. 136). A vast amount of exhortational literature (deriving from the advertising agencies, and from the media in general) keeps an intense pressure on individuals to strive for further income in the interest of conspicuous consumption and the possession of additional status symbols. There is no attempt to question the relationship between *success*, defined in these terms, and the nature of *satisfaction*: and the system's capacity for encouraging the continuing pursuit of monetary income and consumption is limitless. In Merton's own words (1957, p. 157, our emphasis):

> The cultural emphasis shifts from the *satisfactions* deriving from competition itself to an almost exclusive concern with the *outcome*, the resultant stress makes for the breakdown of the regulatory structure. With this attenuation of institutional controls, there occurs an approximation to the situation erroneously held by the utilitarian philosophers to be typical of society, a situation in which calculations of personal advantage and fear of punishment are the only regulatory agencies.

The important problem for Merton is that these strains are occurring—and could only occur—against the background of an overall social ideology of egalitarianism. Since not all people are

93

equally well placed to partake of the joys of competition, it makes no sense to hold out a set of social goals which depend exclusively for their acceptance on their relevance to the population at large. The disjunction between the goals of success (specifically money; more generally, 'the joy of competition') and the means for their achievement (unequal opportunity) is a disjunction that is created, sustained and amplified by the populist myth of American society: the idea that the road from the log cabin to the White House is open to all. In a society which did not adhere so obviously to an egalitarian ideology, the disjunction between ends and means would not be so disruptive. As it is, American society produces effort on the one hand—amongst those well placed in the pursuit of success goals—and strain on the other, amongst the lower classes in general, and in particular, amongst those whose access to legitimate means is blocked.

The ideology of the American Dream, however, insists that everyone should pursue the same monetary goals of success: the idea that everyone should be ambitious and that success comes to those who exert sufficient effort, and who possess the sufficient merit. Failure, therefore, is seen ideologically as an individual rather than a social phenomenon, Merton himself noting the utility of this in detracting from criticism of the existing structural arrangements. Merton was concerned to erect a limited (but, importantly, a sociological) critique of those arrangements. His critique can be summarized as centering around:

a   the lack of attention paid *to the availability of institutionalized means*. At certain points in the social structure, that is, the rules governing the playing of the game are unclear, absent or simply inappropriate.

b   the existence of an *overweening social ideology of egalitarianism* in an unequally structured society. The diminution of disruption in the social structure requires either the opening up of opportunity with a view to giving the general social morality a reality it does not possess or the replacement of the egalitarian ideology with a more appropriate modified ideology which recognized the inequality of individual positions.

c   *the fetishism of money*. The rewards of the competition have taken on an exclusively monetary form: success, therefore, has become a relative and indefinite experience. It is never made clear to an individual when he has finally succeeded.

d   *the continuing and disruptive exhortation of individuals*: unless and until this is replaced by more appropriate distribution and circularization of goods, disorder and normlessness will continue.

We shall organize our exposition and critique around these themes in Merton's critique. A crucial argument, however, revolves around

94

the relationship of Mertonian and Durkheimian formulations of order and deviance. John Horton, in a widely quoted critique of Mertonian theory (1964, pp. 294–5), has claimed that Merton has shifted the meaning of anomie away from the more radical implications of the term as used by Durkheim. He claims that:

> Merton's anomie differs from that of Durkheim's in one crucial respect—in its identification with the very groups and values which Durkheim saw as the prime source of anomie in industrial societies. For Durkheim, anomie was endemic in such societies not only because of inequality in the conditions of competition, but more importantly, because self-interested striving (the status and success goals) had been raised to social ends. The institutionalization of self-interest meant the legitimization of anarchy and amorality. Morality requires, according to Durkheim . . . social goals obeyed out of disinterest and altruism, not self-interest and egoism. To maximize opportunities for achieving success would in no way end anomie. —showing diff. Merton & Durkheim.

In the last chapter, we showed that Durkheim, contrary to many interpreters, had a very clear conception of social justice: that, for him, altruism and disinterest would flourish when there was an equitable division of labour based on biological merit. Merton, in fact, follows very closely in Durkheim's tradition: opportunities, in a just society, would, for Merton, be commensurate with social possibilities and ability. Durkheim would have been in complete accord with Merton when he decries the 'artificial' restriction of opportunities: and neither Durkheim nor Merton would have called, without qualification, for the maximization of opportunities for all. Merton (1964, p. 225) is only too aware of the dangers of unrestricted aspiration:

> The anomia of the disadvantaged develops from a disjunction between aspirations which even when relatively limited, cannot be approximated, owing in part to socially patterned limitations of access to opportunity. The anomia of the successful arises from another kind of seemingly futile pursuit, when progressively heightened aspirations are fostered by each temporary success and by the enlarged aspirations visited on them by associates.

Merton's ideal or perfect society would be one in which there was an accord between merit and its consequences. The means for achieving success would be respected, and the opportunities open to all those of sufficient merit. The motivation to compete and the opportunities to succeed would be in proportion to the degree of individual stratification necessary for the society to function. The

95

competition for success, furthermore, would be enjoyed as an end in itself, and the cultural goals would be substantial and definite—rather than fetishistic and relativistic. In all these respects, Merton's ideal society is very similar to Durkheim's—except that the meritocratic emphasis is elaborated in terms of opportunity structures and socially engendered motivations.

The great change in emphasis is that Merton does not operate with a Durkheimian conception of merit. Merton never insists that merit is biologically based; neither does he have a conception of raw biological drives unrestrained by social regulation (as does Durkheim in the case of the 'biological-psychological deviant'). Merton attempts to explore the social derivations of egoism; and he rejects the notion of anomie (in its limited sense as a feeling of 'normlessness') as the result of the society's failure to prevent the 'leakage' of biological impulse. In these senses, at least, Merton's initial statements are an attempt to break with the biological assumptions in Durkheim; they are much more fully social in content, and they do attempt to advance a social explanation of egoism and anomie.

The typology of adaptations

Merton evolves a typology of responses—individual adaptations, in his terms—to the imperfect American society, specifically to the disjunction between the ends held out as universally desirable and the means made available for their achievement. The typology is radically sociological in two distinct respects. First, it is opposed to those theorists operating with a biologically derived model of deviant action as 'leakage', the result of the failure of an organic society properly to inculcate its values (leaving the field open for the free play of pathological and egoistic desires). Merton intends his typology to depict the actions of men making meaningful choices, accepting or rejecting cultural goals, accepting or rejecting institutionalized means. Second, however, although the typology is called

TABLE 3 *Merton's typology of modes of individual adaptation*

Modes of adaptation	Cultural goals	Institutionalized means
I Conformity	+	+
II Innovation	+	−
III Ritualism	−	+
IV Retreatism	−	−
V Rebellion	±	±

a typology of individual adaptations, it is clearly intended to refer to the kinds of choices that are made by people occupying speci- fiable positions in the social structure (cf. A. K. Cohen, 1966, p. 77). Initially, at least, the typology holds out the promise of being able to specify the relationship between an actor's position in a social structure, the kind of strain experienced in that position, and the kind of (conforming or deviant) outcome or adaptation.

Four of these adaptations are categorized as 'deviant' adaptations:

Innovation

Innovation is by far the most important deviant adaptation in Merton's typology, as it is his individual equivalent to the total society (as he sees that society). The utilitarianism of America places an all-encompassing stress on success and yet sees the question of means as relatively inconsequential. The 'American Dream' urges all citizens to succeed whilst distributing the opportunity to succeed unequally: the result of this social and moral climate, inevitably, is innovation by the citizenry—the adoption of illegitimate means to pursue and obtain success.

Ritualism

Ritualism 'involves the abandoning or scaling down of the lofty cultural goals of great pecuniary success and rapid social mobility to the point where one's aspirations can be satisfied. But ... one draws in one's horizons, one continues to abide almost compulsively by institutional norms' (Merton, 1957, pp. 149–50).

Where innovation is seen to be a typically working-class adapta- tion, ritualism is typically lower middle class in location: 'It is the perspective of the frightened employee, the zealously conformist bureaucrat in the teller's cage of the private banking enterprise ...' (Merton, 1957, pp. 150–1).

This is to be explained, according to Merton, in terms of the strict patterns of socialization in this class, and by the limited opportunities for advancement offered out to its members.

Retreatism

This adaptation is the least common. The retreatist is *in* society but not *of* it, in the sense that he does not share the consensus of societal values. Into this category, therefore, fall: 'psychotics, autists, pariahs, outcasts, vagrants, vagabonds, tramps, chronic drunkards and drug addicts' (Merton, 1957, p. 153). The retreatist has rejected both institutionalized means and the goals of the system. He is seen as having internalized objections to innovative (illegitimate) means

97

which might have helped him to achieve the goals, and also as lacking the opportunity to utilize legitimate means (ibid., pp. 153-4, our emphasis).

> It is thus an expedient which arises from continued failure to near the goal by legitimate measures and from the inability to use the legitimate route because of internalized prohibitions, *this process occurring while the supreme value of the success-goal has not yet been renounced.* The conflict is resolved by abandoning *both* precipitating elements, the goals and the means. The escape is complete, the conflict is eliminated and the individual is asocialized.

Retreatism is a highly individualized, or, more properly, a privatized adaptation. The social element in the explanation offered out is ambiguous and minimal.

Rebellion

Rebellion does not involve, for Merton, what Max Scheler has elsewhere called 'ressentiment'—that is, the condemnation of that which one secretly craves. For Merton (1957, p. 155) the condemnation is actually of the craving itself—both for the success goals themselves and for adherence to the institutionalized means. Rebellion as an adaptation aims: 'to introduce a social structure in which the cultural standards of success would be sharply modified and provision would be made for a closer correspondence between merit, effort and reward'.

The lack of attention paid by Merton, and his interpreters, to the conformist adaptation is not altogether surprising. Apart from the fact that it might be difficult to specify empirical examples of the totally conformist in American society[2]—since, almost by definition, anyone who conforms to the goals of that society will be something of an innovator, continually searching out new means for the achievement of success—a detailed examination of the sources of conformity would involve Merton in an altogether more difficult enterprise: that of explaining the legitimacy of authority in an imperfect society. It might also confront Merton with the awkward social fact that conforming individuals are few and far between even in those positions in the social structure where, according to his own formulations, structural strain is at its most minimal. To confront this possibility would involve Merton in something more than a marginal critique of the anomie experienced exclusively in the 'margins' of society. Merton's discussion of the modes of adaptation does however contain a relatively explicit critique of society. The

98

fundamental flaw in the social order, for Merton, is that aspirations and opportunities are out of accord with one another. The innovator is deviant and disruptive because he does not adhere to legitimate means, but he is also to be understood as a product of socially induced aspirations and the objective inequality in the distribution of opportunity. He is akin to Durkheim's 'functional rebel'. The *ritualist* is to be pitied for continuing to play the game without hope of reward. The *retreatist* is an asocial product of social disorganization: he finds himself in certain social situations because of personal failings. If Merton sees himself as taking up any one of these adaptations for himself, it is that of the *rebel*—whose ideal is a society 'where cultural standards of success would be sharply modified and provision would be made for a closer correspondence between merit, effort and reward.'

This ideal, as we have noted before, is a characteristically utilitarian dream: but it is not utilitarianism in its individualistic guise. Merton's view of social structure is a polemic against Benthamite utilitarianism: an attempt, like Durkheim's, to integrate the value of individualization with the demands of social order. He takes the most radical strand of Durkehim's thought—the critique of egoism —and clearly makes it the centre of his own theory. Like Durkheim he is aware of the way in which the 'functional rebel' may have a clearer understanding of the needs of the system than the understanding enshrined in the ethics prevailing at a particular time (Merton, 1966, p. 823):

In the history of society, one supposes some of its culture heroes eventually come to be regarded as heroic in part because they are held to have the courage and the vision to challenge the beliefs and routines of their society. The rebel, revolutionary, non-conformist, heretic or renegade of an earlier day is often the culture hero of today. Moreover, the accumulation of dysfunctions in a social system is often the prelude to concerted social change that may bring the system closer to the values that enjoy the respect of members of the society.

But what are the real needs of the system, that the functional rebel can highlight by his actions, and are commensurate with the just reward and encouragement through competition of individual merit? For Merton, the 'system needs' are not identical with those of the existing consensus—the American Dream—and indeed Merton is highly critical of the tendency to disequilibrium (and disorder) built into that consensus. Rather, system needs are to be discovered (ibid., p. 801, our emphasis) by:

[what] amounts to *a technical judgement about the workings of a*

99

social system. And each case requires the sociological judge to supply competent evidence that the actual organization of social life can, under attainable conditions, be technically improved to make for the more substantial realization of collective and individual purposes.

Evidence of disorganization is apparent where inadequacies occur (ibid., p. 801):

in meeting one or more functional requirements of the system. Social patterns of behavior fail to be maintained . . . possibly as a result of inadequate socialization. Or, personal tensions generated by life within the system are insufficiently controlled, canalized, or siphoned off by social processes. . . . Or, the social system is inadequately related to its environment, neither controlling it nor adapted to it. Or, the structure of the system does not allow sufficiently for its members to attain the goals that are its *raison d'être*. Or, finally in this list of functional imperatives of a social system, the relations between its members do not maintain the indispensable minimum of social cohesion needed to carry on both instrumental and intrinsically valued activities.

Merton is not, as many would have him, a believer in an all-embracing consensus (ibid., p. 819):

People occupying different positions in the social structure tend to have distinctive interests and values (as well as sharing some interests and values with others). As a result, not all social standards are evenly distributed amongst diverse social positions. It follows logically and is found empirically that to the extent that these standards differ among social positions and groups within a society, the same circumstances will be variously evaluated as being at odds with the standards held by others. Thus, one group's problem will be another group's asset.

Further (ibid., p. 785): 'the same social pattern can be dysfunctional for some parts of a social system and functional for other parts'.

Merton, however, refuses to lapse into a form of social and moral relativism. There is an objectivity lodged in the total system and its functioning. Merton opts neither for a wholesale acceptance of 'what is' (he is critical of such tendencies in functionalist theory) nor for a thoroughgoing critique of the fundamentals of the system. The dysfunctions in the system are peripheral rather than basic.

Merton is aware of contradictions within the system: and, as Gouldner puts it, in this respect he can be said to use Marx to prise open Durkheim. However, the contradictions highlighted by Merton are non-material and they are a part of the social fabric—there *is* an inequality of opportunity and this is underpinned, in contradictory fashion, by the cultural exhortations enshrined in the American Dream; but we are offered no structural (or other explanation) of why there should be such inequality or such a cultural and moral climate. As Laurie Taylor (1971, p. 148) nicely puts it:

It is as though individuals in society are playing a gigantic fruit machine, but the machine is rigged and only some players are consistently rewarded. The deprived ones then either resort to using foreign coins or magnets to increase their chances of winning (innovation) or play on mindlessly (ritualism), give up the game (retreatism) or propose a new game altogether (rebellion). But in the analysis nobody appeared to ask who put the machine there in the first place and who takes the profits. Criticism of the game is confined to changing the pay-out sequences so that the deprived can get a better deal. ... What at first sight looks like a major critique of society ends up by taking the existing society for granted. The necessity of standing outside the present structural/cultural configurations is not just the job of those categorized in the rebellion mode of adaptation—it is also the task of the sociologist.

Merton—the cautious rebel

The pity of it is that, contrary to the impression given by the preceding quotation, Merton does take on the role of the rebel in the substantive analysis. He does stand outside the system and make criticisms, which, if taken to their logical conclusion, would necessitate radical social change. But he never follows the criticisms through to that point. He is constrained by his belief that the people best fitted to make scientific comments on the system are the functionalist sociologists who 'objectively' pronounce on the real needs of the system and its members. These are limited to the refurbishing of the *status quo*, to changing the payout sequence; and they never extend to changing the nature of the game itself.

In fact, of course, the contradiction identified by Merton—as having to do with the disjunction between a set of cultural exhortations (encapsulated in the American Dream) and a situation of inequality of opportunity is not only a cultural problem to be resolved by the specification of appropriate and functional system values. It does not merely exist in the realm of ideas: it has a real basis in the inequitable distribution of property and power in American (and capitalist) society. In a society of this kind, as Durkheim realized in his discussion of the forced division of labour, reward is partly distributed *ascriptively*: it is not, and it cannot be, a result of *achievement* by effort. People are not equally placed at birth in the competition for success. It was just such a contradiction that infused the work of the classical utilitarian theorists: the structurally given contradiction between the existence of property and the possibility of a liberal equality. Gouldner (1971, p. 324) has put this well:

> Values will be conformed with to the extent that men are given gratifications for doing so. But under these conditions only a part of the gratificational resources of society may be utilized to foster conformity with its moral values. Institutions which transmit possessions and wealth through the testamentary or hereditary succession of private individuals thus demoralize men and conduce to anomie; because of them a significant supply of the reinforcing gratifications is withdrawn from support of the society's value system, and is thus weakened. This is rather different from saying, as Robert Merton does, that anomie results from the mal-integration between means and ends, or arises when individuals lack institutional means to realize the cultural goals they have been taught to want. For here, men who attempt to live by the value system are demoralized not simply by their *own* lack of means and their own *failures*, but also by witnessing that *others* may *succeed* even though they lack valued qualities.

There are no good reasons for assuming, that is, with Merton and the functionalists, that men born into different social positions and in widely different relationships to the structure of opportunity, will want or be able to internalize the dominant social goals. On the contrary, there is every good reason to postulate the existence of cultural diversity. Indeed, Merton himself recognizes the fact of cultural diversity at places—but only with a view to correcting it.

In his most recent well-known statement, Merton is quite clear about the fact of cultural diversity and its correctional implications. He writes (1966, pp. 819–20):

> The periodically popular notion of a society in which everything works together for good is literally utopian, and describes an engaging utopia at that. But to forgo this image of society entirely free of imperfections does not require us to assume that nothing can be done, through deliberate plan, to reduce the extent to which obsolescent institutions and disorganization work against the realization of values that men respect.

The problem of identifying the 'values that men respect', the conditions deserving of the name 'disorganized' or 'obsolescent' is a task for those who direct the society, who, despite earlier critiques, now emerge as the guardians of 'system needs'. Indeed, Merton invests the meritocratic ideology of American society with the power to hasten the progress of the division of labour, and of individualization of function, fixing men to the positions appropriate to their aptitude.

His position is well abbreviated by two of his most rigorous disciples, Richard Cloward and Lloyd Ohlin (1960, p. 81), when they write that:

> A crucial problem in the industrial world is to locate and train the most talented persons in every generation irrespective of the vicissitudes of birth, to occupy technical work roles. Whether he is born into wealth or poverty, each individual, depending upon his ability and diligence, must be encouraged to find his 'natural level' in the social order. The problem is one of tremendous proportions. Since we cannot know in advance who can best fulfil the requirements of various occupational roles, the matter is presumably settled through the process of competition. But how can men throughout the social order be motivated to participate in this competition . . .? One of the ways in which the industrial society attempts to solve this problem is by defining success goals as potentially accessible to all, regardless of race, creed or socioeconomic position.

But is not this ideology, also, whatever its direct 'functions' to the system, a very convenient ideology which serves to mask the advantage of property under the rubric of a fair race between meritocrats? Indeed, is this not the central significance of recent excursions by positivists, operating with an ideology which is similar in its essentials to that of functionalism, into the field of educational research and into ethnic and racial relations with a view to administering IQ tests?[3] Merton himself peripherally touches on this when he points to the 'self-blaming' rather than 'society-blaming' nature of 'failure' in those who embrace this ideology yet are not successful in the race. The American Dream, in other words, serves to conceal inequality; it could only function in a society where hereditary wealth was abolished. Innovation, then, is not so much failure of socialization in the abstract as the partial demystification of the game by the underprivileged.

Merton in his later more policy-orientated work would solve the problem of anomie by two strategies: first, success must be based on merit and second (in order to implement this) there must be ample opportunities. But this assumes that there is a consensual criterion of merit and that the central dictum should be 'from those according

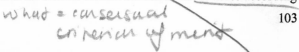
what = consensual
criterion of merit

103

to their merit to each according to his merit' rather than 'to each according to his need'. Further, an implementation of such a programme would considerably bulwark the existing ideology. For it could be said that we are judging merit objectively by virtue of psychological testing and we are providing the outlets for each according to his measured ability. That there is a social and inequitable basis to 'objective' testing and that the provision of sufficient jobs, of an instrumentally and expressively satisfying nature, is beyond the possibilities of the social system as we now know it, is the bitter reality of the matter. The liberal plans of sociologists such as Merton serve merely to attempt to contain and obscure this reality.

A pluralistic society

The utilitarian calculus to which Merton subscribes (and to which he accords a central place in his explanation of deviant motivation) may well be an important factor in the moral climate in which we all live—but it may just be one of many. Merton himself points to a considerable array of heterogeneous values and of 'counter-cultures' (ranging in ideology and structure from the extremely inarticulate to the most developed). He references, for example:

1. the craftsmen's stress on 'expressivity' over and above the monetary consequences of their work.

2. the lower middle-class preference for security rather than competition, born of that class's knowledge of their low potential for success. This 'realism' is caught in Merton's 'ritualist' adaptation.

3. the 'psychedelic' revolt against utilitarianism by the 'bohemian' young.

4. the rebel himself—in Merton, for all his bows to the positive scientist as 'rebel', a residual category.

5. the monopoly of certain ethnic groups (e.g. the Italians) over certain sets of illegitimate means. Such a monopolization is seen, by Merton himself, to involve a clear understanding on the part of these groups that the cards are stacked against them in legitimate competition.

However, despite these references, Merton's central typology assumes that all men initially embrace the American Dream, and then adapt in an anomic and antisocial fashion. Our suggestion here is that the heterogeneity of values (overlaid but not to the point of suffocation by a dominant meritocratic ideology) is the initial normative configuration of modern capitalist society. The dominant social values are, as Matza has put it, 'guides for action' rather than 'categorical imperatives', and in a society riven by differences of interest, the guides for action are unlikely to be universally appropriate.

Further, in a society of diverse interests, 'deviation' is unlikely to be individual or positional in the sense implied by Merton. Rather, faced by similar cultural problems, interest groups are likely to form ongoing and developing subcultural adaptations—appropriate to the problems they experience in the place they occupy in the overall social structure. In this respect, the adaptations are (analytically, and, increasingly, in practice) collective resolutions. Merton, for example, demonstrates the banality of his own individualistic emphasis in his discussion of the 'retreatist' adaptation, wherein the bohemian is portrayed as 'asocial'. This clearly points to Merton's inability to view any cultural adaptation outside his monolithic consensus as anything but an individual and reactive object.[4]

It may very well be the case, as Merton argues, that society's value-consensus (and thus the domination of a utilitarian calculus) is underpinned by the fetishistic pursuit of money. But this is to describe only one of the aspects of contemporary culture: namely, the social fact that all men must (to different extents) engage in activities necessary for their sustenance and material comfort. Money, however, is an abstract symbol: it can be used to purchase a wide variety of commodities and to support a catholic range of life-styles. To say that all men require money is not to show that all men have the same cultural goals. Men differ widely in their use of this and other symbols. And these differences tend to be patterned collectively and structurally, rather than in terms of highly idiosyncratic or asocial pathologies:

a   men will differ in the uses to which they will put the money they amass. The businessman and the street heroin addict both require and seek after money: are we therefore to argue that they have common cultural goals? Indeed, should we not be seeing money as a means to other ends rather than as an end in itself?

b   men differ in the amount of money they want, as well as in the extent to which they pursue other ends. Much of social behaviour can be viewed as an attempt to create an 'optimum balance' between instrumental and expressive ends.[5]

c   there is obvious political dispute amongst men as to how the money (as a symbol of success) should be distributed, and by what criteria it should be earned. That is, men conflict rather than agree over the goals in a quite fundamental fashion; over the ordering of the rewards for which the competition is played.

Mertonian anomie theory and a social theory of deviance

Merton's original formulation of anomie theory as a middle-range theory, a bridge between the abstractions of grand theory and the 'real' problems of empirical research, has given rise to a considerable secondary literature. The crucial development, however, has been the attempt to investigate the 'individual adaptations' as *subcultural* adaptations. This development of Mertonian anomie theory has been informed by two distinct intellectual traditions: the *anthropological* emphasis on the responses available to men faced by a culture in which certain values, goals and symbols are accorded a paramount importance, and the *ecological* tradition with its concern for the ways in which cultural responses to problem situations are patterned within spatially-bounded areas of interaction. We shall turn later in this chapter, by way of a discussion of the Chicago school and the subcultural theorists, to an examination of this extended form of anomie theory. For the moment, however, we need to anticipate these later remarks in order to highlight what we see to be the major weaknesses in the classical Mertonian form of anomie theory (which still retains its adherents among sociologists and social reformers alike).

a We have already indicated, for example, in pointing to Merton's highly truncated discussion of the conformist adaptation, that Merton is never really able to specify the causes of strain that give rise to the disjunctions in the first place. The assertion is that disjunctions arise out of a maldistribution of opportunity in a situation where equality of opportunity is ideologically stressed. This obviously implies that deviance is concentrated in those situations where structural strain of the kind specified by Merton is most likely to occur, i.e. in the sections of society where opportunity is limited. There is considerable evidence to suggest, however, that 'deviance' is far more widely distributed than Merton would allow, and that in particular the law-breaking activity of the well-to-do (those with no blockage on their opportunity) is much more widespread and persistent than Merton's theory would predict (Gold, 1970). In this sense, because Merton restricts his concept of strain to the strain experienced by lower-class individuals, he predicts too little of the law-breaking that is actually occurring. This would be forgivable if Merton's anomie were intended only to apply to apprehended law-breaking, i.e. crime: for there is no doubt at all that lower-class individuals (who could feasibly be experiencing something like an anomic frustration of the Mertonian variety) are over-represented in the official criminal statistics. But this observation does not necessarily mean that lower-class individuals, experiencing the anomia that Merton sees as the psychic expression of structural strain, are more committed to delinquency and criminality than members of the higher social class. As we shall see, and as Albert Cohen (1966) has realized (by way of an attempt to save anomie theory from itself) the over-representation of the lower-class amongst apprehended offenders could equally well reflect the way in which police practice is organized, the class bias of the courts, and the ability of lower-class offenders to afford legal defence. It could also reflect the ways in which informal social processes of 'labelling' occur in societies that are unequally divided into classes and status groups. In any case, as Matza has indicated, if it really were the case that individuals experiencing the fact of structural strain were necessarily propelled into delinquency and criminality (into the pursuit of illegitimate means), then there really ought to be much more officially apprehended and committed delinquency and criminality than there actually is. If the American Dream really is pressurizing individuals in the way that Merton claims it is, then an explanation is required of the fact that only a relatively small proportion of those in positions of strain are actually involved in committed careers of deviance. Anomie theory stands accused of predicting too little bourgeois criminality and too much proletarian criminality.

b Merton presents no general rules whereby we can relate classes of strain to classes of outcome. We are presented only with a general concept of structural strain, which is differentially experienced, presumably, by the innovator, the ritualist, the retreatist and the rebel, and which results in these particular deviant outcomes. But we are given no causal explanation of the determinates of strain in each individual case. Does economic strain, for example (i.e. poverty), lead to rebellion or to retreatism? Does failure to achieve upward mobility, as Merton seems to imply, necessarily lead to ritualism? What criteria are we to use in building explanatory and causal links between a particular type of strain and a particular adaptation? Even a middle-range theory has to confront the problem of causal explanation.

c Anomie theory can, indeed, be seen to confuse cause and effect. How do we know, for example, whether revolutionaries are the cause of disjunction or the effect of it? The Weatherman branch of the SDS (Students for a Democratic Society) in contemporary America would certainly argue that their intentions are to bring about further disjunctions in that society, in order to polarize the social forces politically (Walton, 1973). How do we know that retreatism is caused by strain? Could it not be that long periods of excessive drinking or drug-taking can impair a person's social relations (by encouraging his exclusion and stigmatization)[6] and his ability to achieve certain goals? At the most fundamental level of all, of course, Merton's anomie theory confronts certain problems in developing causal explanation precisely because it assumes that there is every good reason for conforming unless one is caught in an anomic social position. A causal analysis of how conformity and acceptance of authority arises in a society might reveal that the obedience people give to existing social arrangements is not at all natural or automatic. It might indicate, that is, with Max Weber, that authority has to be seen as meaningful by individuals in society at large before it can emerge even to be statistically normal.[7]

d Although Merton devotes a considerable amount of attention to the ways in which the mass media and the agencies of social control sustain the urge to succeed and the desire to consume, he has little sense of the way in which these institutions carry out the important cultural task of typification and labelling. He does not accord the media much importance, that is, in developing stereotypes of the conformist and the deviant: the deviant presumably is self-evident, a conscious and committed adaptor who is pitied, condemned, or controlled (but is never actually identified inaccurately or spuriously). There is, in short, no real attempt to deal with the 'social reaction' against deviance and its determinates in classical Mertonian theory.

e Anomie theory has paid insufficient attention to the theory of roles in general sociology. In Mertonian formulations, the deviant is seen as failing to achieve and consequently becoming reactively committed to deviant roles. This simple exposition of the realities of social action under-emphasizes the ways in which conformist and deviant roles are something one automatically achieves or fails to achieve. Roles are learnt in interaction, there being a gradual change in self-concept as role requirements are internalized. The fact of being a failure or a success is an extremely ambiguous social fact: most actors are drifting, in Matza's terms between different sets of role requirements. They are not to be easily placed or located in a fixed role (or individual adaptation). There is, in other words, no sense of the sequences, contingencies and choices, involved in the drift into deviant (and into conformist) careers, which informs the work of the social reaction theorists.[8] In classical anomie theory, the typical actor is in a box, in a social position, and he is not to get out until social reformers have opened the opportunity chest in which are contained the curatives to anomic malaise.

f The individual actor—boxed into a fixed social position—is rarely seen to evolve a solution to his problem in his own terms. Although Merton references a whole series of counter-cultures and collective social groups he observes to exist in American society, he never attempts to see these groups as involved in collective sub-cultural adaptations. The actions taken by those in positions of structural strain are seen, in one-dimensional fashion, to be determined by the fact that these particular individuals are caught in these structural situations, and these situations result—presumably automatically—in the adaptations described. As we shall see, the sub-cultural theorists do advance on this, recognizing the need to explain how individuals react differentially, and collectively, to the experience of strain. The subcultural theorists do take rather more seriously than Merton himself the fact that the social structure of American society is underpinned by a set of cultural arrangements which can be used by the disadvantaged in attempting to solve the problems of structural inequality. In particular, as we shall see, Albert Cohen attempts to use subcultural analysis as a way of explaining the ways in which delinquent boys in America resolve the problems posed to adolescent self-esteem by a rejecting middle-class society.

Classical anomie theory, then, is riven with a set of unresolved and possibly irresolvable analytical problems. It is commonplace to point to the relative difficulty of identifying the dominant cultural goals in societies other than America (Downes, 1966a). More recently, some commentators have pointed to the problems posed for anomie theory by the existence of societies in which the dominant culture goals of capitalist societies have been rejected, perhaps, as in the case of Cuba, to be replaced by systems of moral, rather than tangible, material incentives (Loney, 1973). Attempts have been made, however, to rescue anomie theory from these problems, specifically via the various excursions into subcultural theory and into the social reaction perspective, and we shall turn to these subsequently to our discussion of the intellectual origins of this approach to the study of culture.

We have taken time to highlight some of the central problems of anomie theory as developed by its mentor, however, in order to indicate the intellectual inconsistencies in the theory as originally developed. These are never fully resolved in any theory operating with fundamentally similar assumptions about the relationship of structure and culture, or with a similarly ambiguous status as causal explanation. The fact that anomie theory retains its hold on many sociologies of social problems and deviance, can be explained, we suggest, not in terms of its theoretical adequacy, but rather in terms of the contemporary relevance of the ideological assumptions it shares with functionalism and positivism. Merton's critique of American society (with its initially substantial denunciations of the disruptive nature of the unfettered pursuit of success) is never fully carried through (and, indeed, is de-emphasized in his policy-oriented polemics) precisely because it would be ideologically inappropriate to do so. What commenced as an attempt to remove the biological assumptions in the Durkheimian critique of society, in conditions of optimism about the possibility of social reconstruction and the opening-up of individual opportunity, ends up as a more or less similar, though less explicitly biological, statement in support of a continuing meritocracy. The discussion of norms moves from a critique at one pole in the 'utilitarian' vision—the encouragement of

109

egoism—to an acceptance of the other polar-concern, the question of controlling individual desires. The potentially radical critique increasingly becomes a means of refurbishing the American Dream —of providing it with 'objective' justifications. Whilst the task of the contemporary positive scientist—the sociologist *qua* sociologist—is to act as an ally of social reformers within the set social goals, with some continuing but responsible attempt to open up opportunities within particular community areas. In a continuing anomic situation, the sociologist, acting correctly in the Mertonian tradition, is to act as an adviser to the powerful and as an agitator of 'public opinion'. He is the 'cautious rebel' *par excellence* (Merton, 1966, p. 799):

> Whereas deviant behaviour at once attracts the indignant
> notice of people whose norms and values have been violated
> by it, social disorganization tends not to. . . . Technical
> specialists, unattached intellectuals, and social critics play a
> central role in trying to alert greater numbers of people to what
> they take to be the greater immorality—living complacently
> under conditions of social disorganization that in principle
> can be brought under at least partial control. Under the
> progressive division of social labor, it becomes the office of
> these specialists to try and cope with social disorganization.

The Chicago school and the legacy of positivism

Several years before the appearance of Merton's *Social Structure and Anomie*, a group of sociologists in and around the University of Chicago had begun to evolve a specifically sociological critique of prevailing social conditions, and had already taken on for themselves the roles of advisers to the policy-makers and agitators of the public conscience. Indeed, prior to his appointment as lecturer in the Department of Sociology in 1914, Robert Ezra Park had spent some twenty-five years as a journalist using the methods of the reporter to obtain documentary information on social conditions in the city with a view to newspaper campaigns on housing issues in particular, and urban problems in general.

In the following twenty years, a mass of research was carried out by Park's colleagues and students into what they came to call the 'social ecology' of the city: research into the distribution of areas of work and residence, places of public interaction and private retreat, the extent of illness and health, and the urban concentrations of conformity and deviance. The Chicago School of Sociology, motivated by the journalist's campaigning and documentary concerns, was the example *par excellence* of determined and detailed empirical social research: a tradition which, for good or for ill, is extremely resilient still in most departments of sociology on the North American continent.

The resilience of this tradition in American sociology is partly explicable, but only partly, in terms of the convenience of ecological perspectives for an academic milieu antagonistic to theory and supportive of small-scale, methodologically-detailed dissertations.[9] But the ecological tradition is more than the tradition of certain research techniques and methods, and more than a simple empirical area for the careerist's research dissertation: our contention here is that the ecological tradition is the tradition most responsible for the continuing hold of positivistic assumptions in American sociology. The abstraction and anti-theoretical nature of much American sociology (and criminology) can best be explained, not as the legacy of Durkheim translated for home consumption by Merton, but as the legacy of the scientism of Comte translated into naturalistic observation for quantification and codification by technologists attached to the sociology departments.

It is usual to argue that Park and Burgess in particular, and the Chicago School in general, were most strongly influenced—in their concern with the shaping and structuring of interaction by the ecology of the material world—by the interactionist tradition of W. I. Thomas, Simmel and Cooley.[10] Indeed, in their 'Source Book for Social Origins', Park and Burgess (Chicago University, c. 1930) acknowledge their indebtedness to these thinkers in quite explicit a manner.

But this is only one of the intellectual sources from which the Chicagoans drew their inspiration and their methods. Like Quetelet and Guerry some seventy years before them, the Chicagoans, and in particular Clifford Shaw and Henry Mackay (1931) (who were to be the most prolific writers in the school on the subject of crime and deviance), were struck by the regularity of human activities within certain 'natural' boundaries. For the Chicagoans, however, these boundaries were the boundaries not of nation states but the boundaries of urban neighbourhoods; and, in a city of extremely rapid immigration commencing around 1860, the boundaries of ethnic group residence in particular.

Now it is true, as Terence Morris has indicated (1957, pp. 9–10), that there were differences amongst the Chicagoans as to the immediate origins of natural areas. Harvey Zorbaugh (1925), for example, conceived of natural areas as the immediate product of patterns of land utilization, modified by specific features of the geography of urban settlements; whilst for Robert McKenzie (1933), the natural area was the result of the recent mixing of population, race, income and occupation. It was, as Morris puts it, a 'cultural rather than physical isolate'. At the base of both conceptions of the

111

immediate origins of natural areas, however, was an implicitly biological conception of the fundamental causes of human groupings.

The argument is crucially bound up with the way in which the Chicagoans, and in particular, Park himself, built their explanations of what they observed in Chicago (patterns of immigration, the emergence of what seemed to be different types of residential zones, the relationship of areas of work to areas of living, etc.) around analogies taken from the study of the ecology of plant life. Much of the language they use is drawn directly from ecological studies, and notably from the pioneering work of the German philosopher-biologist, Ernst Haeckel. The most important term they derive, which is riven with the assumptions of continuity, equilibrium and balance which was to characterize the empirical investigations of the Chicagoans, is 'symbiosis'. *Symbiosis*, as Morris puts it (1957, p. 5), 'may be defined as the habitual living together of organisms of different species within the same habitat'. In plant communities, the perfect symbiosis is the *biotic balance*; a situation which obtains when all the processes involved in plant reproduction, in the relationships between plant life and the climate, the soil, etc., are in a state of equilibrium.

The task of the sociologist, according to Park, is to search out the mechanisms and processes whereby such a biotic balance can be achieved and sustained in social (and in particular, urban) life (cf. Park, 1936). For the argument is that the social problems facing the city of Chicago, as revealed to Park in his work as a journalist, stemmed from the unchecked patterns of migration and the creation of natural areas in which the inhabitants were insulated from the general culture of the society. As Park (1929, p. 36) says, 'it is assumed [that] people living in natural areas of the same general type and subject to the same social conditions will display, on the whole, the same characteristics'.

This similarity of cultural patterns with natural areas, however, is not explained in terms of the resilience with which, for example, immigrants from Italy or Eastern Europe hold on to their natural culture patterns. Rather it is due to the fact that, like plants that have been inefficiently tended or like plants that have been sown in bad soil, the inhabitants have been forced together by processes entirely beyond their control. In this sense, the similarity of cultural patterns is symbiotic in the biological sense, and an unhealthy symbiosis at that. But it is not explicable socially. The assumptions at the base of Chicago ecology are revealed, for, as Alihan put it, in a classic extrapolation of the ecological tradition (1938, p. 239, our emphasis):

if the relations between the individuals in an area are 'symbiotic rather than social', then by what manner do these complex cultural patterns become a common pattern? There remains only one interpretation of Park's words: namely, that *selection alone determines that the individuals in any area have similar traditions*, customs, conventions, standards of decency, and so forth; that these are not preserved by reciprocal communication of ideas, by social interrelationship, but rather in the social isolation of these selected individuals. . . .

Park is rather more explicit in his conception of the natural area than are the Chicagoans in general who, following in his footsteps, proceeded to examine the specific problems of delinquency, social disease, and social problems in general, within the various natural areas of the city. The same limitations, however, apply to the theoretical assumptions underpinning the numerous empirical variations: most importantly, the reliance on an organic analogy that owes more in inspiration to Comte and to the plant ecologists than it does to Durkheim or any other social theorist.

Park (1936, p. 4) argues that:

every community has something of the character of an organic unit. It has a more or less definite structure and it has a 'life history in which juveniles, adult and senile phases can be observed'. If it is an organism, it is one of the organs which are other organisms. It is . . . a superorganism.

This conception of the organic nature of natural areas allows Park and the Chicagoans to proceed as if the natural area is something more than a geographical or physical isolate. They are able to extend their discussion into a consideration of 'the environment' as a whole and, having a fundamentally organic model of the healthy symbiotic society as their operating goal, they are able to argue that certain environments—by virtue of their parasitical existence on the overweening social organism, and their insulation from its integrative culture—are pathologically disorganized.

Indeed, as Alihan has argued (1938, p. 246), the ecologists' use of the cultural (rather than geographical) version of ecological analysis, leads them out of ecology as such: 'if the environment includes such aspects as the social and the technological, the process of competition loses its ecological significance.'

One of the results of this extension of the terminology of natural science into the explanation of social processes has been that (ibid., p. 248):

'Succession', which refers in biology to the displacement of one species of animals or of one form of life-form of plants by another has been applied to the displacement of racial, age, economic and cultural groups, institutions, utilities, structures, cultural factors, architectural styles; to sequences of technological inventions, and cultural trends; and in short to anything and everything.

At base, then, the Chicago ecological perspective is an example of what Harold and Margaret Sprout (1965, p. 71) in another context, have called 'free-will environmentalism', a reaction historically against cruder forms of environmental determinism:

Those who speak in this idiom populate their universe with 'influences', derived in the main from the non-human environment, sometimes called 'geography' or 'nature'. But they avoid verbs that might cast doubt on volition. In this watered down version of environmental determinism, man is assumed to have a free-will. Nature gives him instructions, but he is capable of choosing, however unwisely, to disregard them.

The 'influences' which concern the ecologists are those of the continuing succession of new cultural tendencies (in immigration) impinging on the city and giving rise to zones of transition, and to socially problematic urban areas. Always, however, there is a tension in the description, since the journalistic imperative to remain faithful to the description of individual purpose in specific situations, careers and incidents is maintained. It is just this tension between 'naturalism' (with its attempt to allow the actors some freedom of action, especially in learning patterns which are favourable to the violation of law) and determinism (the segregation of natural areas from the symbiotic influences of the general environment) which infects the work of those who follow in the footsteps of the Chicago ecologists: and, in particular, Edwin Sutherland with his theory of differential association, Oscar Lewis and the theory of the culture of poverty, and, finally, the subcultural theorists who now occupy such a central place in criminological discussion. All of them have in common a simple and essentially positivistic view of the relationship between men and society: the external constraints are 'influences' on social action and yet men somehow assert an ambiguous free will (e.g. to become criminal or not). Free will is the added factor which may propel people into natural areas of criminal residence. There is no sense of men struggling against social arrangements as such; no sense of a social structure riven by inequalities and contradictions, and no sense of men acting to change the range of options.[11]

The city, social problems and capitalist society

The legacy of biological positivism in 'human' ecology is nowhere so clearly revealed as in the applications of the general perspectives to the specific study of the city.

Laurie Taylor (1971, pp. 124–5) has summarized this well:

There is then, a *struggle for space* [our emphasis] at the core of ecological theory, whether it is conceived in primarily economic or biological terms. As a result of this struggle certain distinctive patterns of urban growth become distinguishable, certain types of neighbourhoods emerge, a 'pecking order' is established. At the top of the hierarchy is the central business district; the head of the body (the biological analogies are not confined to the description of the struggle). This district was at first surrounded by a residential area inhabited by the respectable citizens of the town. Gradually, however, the business district began to expand and set its sights upon such property. The occupants moved further out, abandoning their threatened and increasingly less salubrious property to a group which had no ability to move elsewhere—the poor—in Chicago's case, the new immigrants. So the following pattern emerges; a central business district surrounded by crumbling residential property beyond which lie rows of working men's houses and an area containing flats and hotels. On the perimeter of the city lies respectable suburbia. It is the 'zone' next to the central business district which predominantly concerned the ecologists, for it was in this 'transitional' or 'insterstitial' zone that they claimed to find especial concentration of deviants.

The 'struggle for space' (dependent in the original ecological formulations on a sequence of movements of the population— invasion, dominance and succession—akin to those 'observable in the plant community when new species come in and oust existing ones' (Morris, 1957, p. 8) is at the base of contemporary sociological in- vestigations of city life and the relationships of the struggle for space in the city to the struggle for existence in general. Each of the three tendencies that we shall identify in these sociological investigations implies a different approach to the understanding and explanation of deviance.

The three central traditions are those of (a) the structurally informed critiques of urban sociology implicit in social ecology, (b) the phenomenologically influenced theories of social space and the relationships between spatial constraints on leisure, on work, and, in general on social and personal expression, and (c) social dis- organization, differential association and subcultural theory.

We shall deal with the first two traditions initially, although it is not chronological to do so—in that they both depart quite radically from the biological analogy underpinning the remaining tradition, in order to highlight more effectively the limitations of that tradition (which continues to dominate the existing literature on urban delinquency, especially subcultural theory, with its overweening insistence on a monolithic or absolutist culture).

The struggle for space and a sociology of the city

The most important implication of the use of biological analogies in explaining the development of housing zones in the city, and natural areas of delinquency, is the implication that the inhabitants of those zones and areas live where they do because of some personal characteristic they possess or because of some natural (and inevitable) feature of human selection. Indeed, many empirical studies of urban delinquency in both Britain and America are largely concerned with the demonstration of one or other position; though often it is difficult to move beyond the technical debates about the use of data (census tract material) with a view to isolating their theoretical assumptions.[12]

The reliance of urban sociology on a biological analogy has been thrown seriously into doubt by the publication, in 1967, of John Rex and Robert Moore's analysis of the structure of the city of Birmingham, and by its detailed account of how one part—the Sparkbrook area—emerged as a 'twilight zone' of multi-occupation for immigrants. Breaking entirely with the biologism of the Chicago School, whilst allowing for the importance empirically of understanding the differentiation of areas of residence, they argue (p. 273) that the central feature of the city is a 'class struggle for housing'. The classes involved in this struggle are understood in Weberian terms (ibid., pp. 273–8): 'class struggle [is] apt to emerge wherever people in a market situation enjoy differential access to property and ... such class struggles might therefore arise not merely around the use of the means of industrial production, but around the control of domestic property.'

Rex and Moore are primarily concerned to explain the form assumed by 'race relations' in Sparkbrook: and they argue that the Labour Party, as the organized representative of the established (white) working class is responsible for encouraging the development of a 'public suburbia' (on the council estates) for white workers. They argue that the Chicago theorization has to be modified to take account of the ways in which interest groups in the (Weberian) market situation can utilize political power to their advantage and to the disadvantage of other, less well-placed and less well-organized, groups. The substantive sections of *Race, Community and Conflict* are concerned with a description of the obstacles and constraints facing the new black immigrant entering Birmingham (the five-year waiting list for council houses, the selection processes operated by the council when immigrants do eventually qualify, the periodic symbolic prosecutions of immigrant landlords by an indifferent 'host' society, etc.). The formal modification of theorization, however, is the attempt to demonstrate that the processes of invasion, dominance and succession delineated by Park, Burgess and others are really descriptions of the ways in which very real social interests (housing classes) move into new areas and successfully achieve authoritative control: or, alternatively, the ways in which other real—and less powerful—interests lose out in the ongoing struggle in the accommodation market. A process which elsewhere might be as a kind of Darwinian selection of the naturally superior is translated and seen for what it really means in terms of social relationships: 'a process of discriminative and *de facto* segregation which compelled coloured immigrants to live in certain typical conditions and which of itself exacerbated racial ill-feeling' (Rex and Moore, 1967, p. 20).

John Lambert has applied the Rex and Moore modification of Chicago ecology to a study of race relations and crime in another part of Birmingham. He agrees that an ecological map of Birmingham makes it possible (1970, pp. 283–4)

> to describe a crescent-shaped zone, consisting largely of older
> and larger types of houses, mostly now in multi-occupation.
> This crescent encloses an area abutting the city centre, made up
> either of small terraced houses or of blocks of flats or houses
> of recent build as a result of redevelopment schemes. Within
> the crescent and area occurred the vast majority of crimes;
> there, too lived the majority of offenders, the majority of whom
> were not coloured immigrants. In these areas is found a
> significant measure of overcrowding and poor amenity. . . . A
> high rate of population change in the lodging-house zone
> further points to the transience and insecurity of life-styles in
> the area.

The processes which Rex and Moore have described as making for the concentration of black immigrants within zones of transition also make for the association of race and crime in a single *milieu*. Although, as Lambert has demonstrated, immigrants are not responsible for the high rates of crime that obtain in these areas, it is clear that in so far as assimilation occurs between the 'newcomer' and the 'host' society, it will be assimilation to 'something called a slum culture' (ibid., p. 284). 'Thus . . . it can be stated, almost as a law, that, so long as immigrant newcomers are forced to live in

117

certain high-crime areas, their rate of crime will in time increase to match that of the overall population in the area' (p. 285).

A similar process was observed in the West Stepney area of London earlier in the 1960s (Downes, 1966a, p. 217): 'Virtually barred from council flats, the "blacks' " inevitable resort is to . . . deteriorating [slum] property. Local white residents link the onset of deterioration with the arrival of the "blacks" and blame the newcomers for the deterioration.'

Indeed, in this particular part of London, where, it was argued, the black population was unrepresentative of the black population of the country as a whole 'lacking the skills to overcome the handicaps attached to finding employment and housing', there had already arisen 'a retreatist way of life sufficiently desperate to create a sub-group situation of anomie' (Downes, 1966a, p. 217). The criminality of the black retreatist, and of a section of the young white male population (akin to William F. Whyte's corner boys), is associated mainly with prostitution, gambling, drug-use, drinking and violence; all of these being an expression of the exclusion of these two sections of society from alternative areas of the cities, and their concentration in the zone of transition.

The important feature of these recent British excursions into the explanation and description of urban criminality and urban social problems is that they locate their naturalistic descriptions of the transitional zone in a formal sociology of the city. Where earlier writers (Mays, 1954; Carter and Jephcott, 1954; Scott, 1956; and Fyvel, 1961) have contented themselves with an essentially internal description of the organization, attitudes and needs of 'delinquent' or 'alienated' working-class youth, Lambert, following Rex and Moore, and Downes, in the radical Mertonian tradition, have located their description in an explanation of the market for jobs, for houses and for leisure. In so doing, they have shown that the delinquency of the criminal area is a function of the availability of opportunities and of gratification in particular urban contexts—rather than being a natural outgrowth of the 'demoralization' of the less able, the biologically inferior, or the individually pathological.[13]

One of the crucial contributions they have made, from the point of view of constructing a fully social theory of deviance, is to break with the static view of culture and of social stratification involved in Chicago positivism (cf. in particular, Taft, 1933). The definitions which are placed on certain urban areas and their residents, and the reaction that is evidenced whenever one of the residents, for example, appears in court, is seen to be ultimately explicable in terms of the struggle for space in the city. They have broken with the tendency to reduce what is in reality 'a number of overlapping and sometimes contradictory systems of social relations' (Rex and Moore, 1967,

118

p. 13)—i.e. urban society—to a monolithic culture where deviants are seen as pathological blemishes on an otherwise perfectible and integrated whole. This has opened out the possibility of a theory which can encompass change, conflict and struggle, whilst simultaneously holding true to the original Chicago tenet of remaining 'faithful' in one's description of men acting with purpose within a situation of constraint.

There is one danger, however, with the critique of social ecology which is informed only by the explanation of the struggle for space and for housing within the city, and that is the *reification of the city*. Just as the residents of delinquency areas are not immune from the culture of the wider society, so the struggle for space in the city is not independent of the struggle for power, prestige and material well-being in the society as a whole. The housing market is not independent of the labour market, and the fact is that men's ability to struggle for accommodation is in part a function of their success in the labour market. Rex and Moore (1967, p. 274) recognize this, but have stated, following Weber, that 'it is . . . the case that men in the same labour market situation may come to have differential access to housing and it is this which immediately determines the class conflicts of the city as distinct from those of the workplace.'

Of course it is the case that men who are similarly placed materially may have different access to housing (or, for that matter, to leisure opportunities, or to other crucial human needs or desires). The relationship between one's position in a labour market and one's position in these other 'market situations' is never simple or determined: and it is clear that one crucial mediation is the 'institutionalized racism' of a capitalist society in crisis (Rex, 1971a). A society which is unable or unwilling to provide a sufficient number of jobs for its population, for a space in which to live, is a society which needs to scapegoat and to label an increasing number and variety of individuals.[14] So the 'idle' member of the working class who is unable to find a job is to be forced from council houses (by the Fair Rents Bill) into temporary and less salubrious accommodation; the low-paid worker is to be labelled as an 'unfortunate'—implicitly, without skills, and, therefore, without much to contribute productively to a society in which unskilled jobs are disappearing—and to be deserving of special accommodation in low-rental accommodation (indeed, on 'problem housing estates', cf. R. Wilson, 1963). In the meantime, the conforming and the productive are being redefined—as no longer in need of subsidized housing—but as being able to contribute to the public purse by paying an 'economic' rent.

To maintain, therefore, that the class struggle for housing is distinct from the struggle for jobs, and that one's ability to obtain

119

accommodation in the city is independent of one's ability to contribute to a changing capitalist economy, is to focus on the cultural definitions (e.g. of racial groups) at the expense of an understanding of the imperatives underpinning those cultural definitions—in this case, we would argue, the deep crises being experienced in the British economy at large. Just as we shall later argue that a fully social theory of deviance cannot rest content with an explanation of the immediate (precipitating) reactions to deviant action, but must attempt to explain the wider origins of those reactions, so we would argue that a sociology of the city (with its important implications for an understanding of the etiology of delinquency and criminality) must be underpinned by a sociology of the overall political economy. Racism, delinquency, deviation and social problems are not simply the result of the activities and cultural predispositions of what Gouldner has called the 'mopping-up agencies'—they are intimately connected with the problems faced by the 'master institutions' of an inequitable society (Gouldner, 1968).

The struggle for space and the phenomenology of the ecological structure

It is a commonplace in critiques of industrial-urban society— particularly in those critiques which emphasize above all else the division of that society into bureaucracies—to talk of the segregation of individuals into relatively limited areas of interaction and communication. Various terms have been employed to describe the results of this bureaucratization of social life—'privatization', 'individuation', and even (inaccurately) 'alienation' and 'anomie'. The general theme, however, is one which stresses the decreasing amount of time being spent by inhabitants of contemporary industrial societies in affective (i.e. close, interpersonal) relationships with other members of the society.

One consequence of this, in general cultural terms, is the tendency for people to operate with stereotypical pictures of the other members of the society. Erving Goffman (1968) and Dennis Chapman (1968, ch. 3) have both described the ways in which individuals who fall foul of the law or informal expectations can be stigmatized or stereotyped in what are often entirely spurious and inaccurate ways.

Another consequence, however, which has received little attention until recently, is the increasing interpenetration of what have been called areas of 'public' and 'private' space (O'Neill, 1968). The fundamental argument is that the unchecked development of commercialism, or, more properly, capitalist modes of production and consumption, has destroyed what was one a basic feature of pre-industrial societies.

So, it is argued (O'Neill, 1968, p. 70):

In the Graeco-Roman world the boundary between the public
and private realms was clear and men were conscious of the
threshold between public and private life. Although the ancient
city state grew up at the expense of the family household and
kinship group, the boundary between the public and private
realms was never erased. Indeed, the definition of the public
realm as an area of freedom and equality presupposed the
recognition of 'necessity' in the household economy. . . . In
the modern period, this ancient boundary between public and
private realms was dissolved with the emergence of 'society'
and the liberal concept of mini-government. A whole new
world—the social universe—emerged between public and
private life.[15]

In this new social universe, individuals are subjected to the
ideologies of a consumer capitalism, in particular to the ethic of
individualism. There emerges what O'Neill calls a 'continuity of
psychic and socio-economic space' (ibid., p. 71).

This psychic and socio-economic space is reflected in new social
ideologies concerning the territorial (i.e. ecological) space in which
we move. At its most obvious level, the ideology tells us that we
cannot walk into other people's houses, that we cannot enter the
institutional buildings of the state (without authorization) and that
we all live and should continue to live (and interact) in certain areas
of the city. Less obviously, but rather more importantly for our
purposes, the ideology defines appropriate and deviant territorial
behaviour: there are, in other words, rules to be observed in moving
through the areas of 'space'. Lyman and Scott (1970) have delineated
four kinds of territories, and the rules associated with them, defiance
of which is likely to result in some act of social proscription. These
are:

a *Public territories*

These are 'Those areas where the individual has freedom of access,
but not necessarily of action, by virtue of his claim to citizenship.'
Examples are public parks, streets, and 'places of public resort' in the
conventional sense.

b *Home territories*

Here, 'the regular participants have a relative freedom of behaviour
and a sense of intimacy and control over the area'. Examples are

121

private clubs, ethnic enclaves, or the territories claimed by juvenile gangs.

c *Interactional territories*

These are more temporary in nature; referring to any area which is designated for a social gathering for a period of time. Examples include restaurants set aside for a party, a street corner conversation, or an office corner where people engage in gossip.

d *Body territories*

Literally, this is 'the space encompassed by the human body and the anatomical space of the body': but it is important, for Lyman and Scott, that even this area of territory is not absolute or inviolable. Norms governing apperance, presentation of the body, and the right to touch another person mean that even the territoriality of the body is problematic.

The rules governing appropriate behaviour in each of these four territories are often ambiguous, and sometimes they are not even known to people who are moving in these territories. The three important threats to the integrity of a territory that can occur are the threats of violation, invasion and contamination. Violators of a territory lay claim to possession or domination of territory (e.g. a private party, office discussion). Invaders wander unwittingly into the territory without necessarily making a claim to possess it. They nevertheless disrupt its social 'meaning'. Contaminators create ambiguity about the integrity of a territory by bringing unwanted characteristics (e.g. a skin colour, a sexual preference) into an otherwise unambiguous situation.

The point of such an analysis for our purposes is that these phenomenological dimensions of social space are, as O'Neill suggested, rooted in the individualistic ideology underpinning a capitalist social structure (in which our private lives and areas of interaction are continually violated, invaded and contaminated by a public morality of commercialism). It is not sufficient simply to assert that there are different types of territorial interaction: one has to ask why there are these types, and not others (e.g. the public realm of freedom granted the citizen of the Graeco-Roman civilizations); and one also has to ask how they are maintained.

In reality of course, territorial integrity is maintained not only by the existence of interpersonal expectations and informal sanctions (exclusion, segregation, or, as Lyman and Scott have it, by 'linguistic collusion')—they are also subject to enforcement by formal agencies of social control.

The most important aspect of the social control of territory is the official protection of the 'home territory' of the powerful. These particular home territories are the example *par excellence* of what Arthur Stinchcombe (1963) has called the 'institutions of privacy'. These institutions are those (predominantly middle-class) areas which are protected (by law and by convention) from invasion and violation by the police, in particular, and by the agencies of state in general. They obviously include the institutions of the state themselves—which are entirely *private* and not open to policing in the conventional sense at all. In a privatized society, where one is supposed to interact most often and most appropriately in a nuclear family situation (or in certain places of entertainment and leisure appropriate for the family man or the man in search of a spouse and a family), anyone who spends a lot of his time in *public space* (or, in Lyman and Scott's terms, in public or interactional territories) is open to suspicion. Public space is highly policed precisely because to move in public space is to be suspicious. To spend one's time in public space is to indicate that one is not tied into the cultural fabric of the society to the extent that is thought desirable, and it is thus to give the police, and others, a clue to one's potentially deviant identity.[16]

The development of these new ecological concerns—with territory and space—premises a significant contribution to the understanding of the patterns of policing, to the evolution of 'criminal areas', and to the causes of social reaction against certain kinds of deviance.[17] It could inform the study of the etiology of crime and deviance with a phenomenology of urban territories: where previously, the selection processes involved, for example, in placing individuals into different kinds of housing estates (Baldwin, Bottoms and Walker, 1973) or in the official (local council and police) designation of an area as criminal had always been seen (on the basis of a biological analogy) to be 'natural', and correct—in the sense that the inhabitants of that area were seen to be members of a pathogenic culture of the slum. It is to this latter tradition, the view of cities as containing areas of social disorganization, a view which has until recently almost exclusively dominated criminological discussion that we now turn. The limitations of this perspective can now be viewed against the background of the model of the 'struggle for space' in the city proposed by Rex and Moore, and the view of the phenomenology of social space that is involved in the 'new ecology'.

Society as an organism

Social disorganization

We have seen earlier how the Chicago school of ecology initially utilized what was in the final analysis a biological analogy; the

123

symbiotic relationship between various 'species' of humanity was seen to have fallen into a state of disequilibrium. Relationships within a community were perceived as being competitive *and* co-operative: 'co-operative in that by their interaction the organisms help to establish a state of equilibrium in which conflict is minimal, and competitive in that each organism struggles against each other for resources' (Morris, 1957, p. 11). Deviancy occurs when the competition becomes so harsh as to upset the biotic balance and this, in turn, is a product of speed of migration into, and turnover within, 'delinquent areas'.

When the biological analogy in ecology is translated into social terms, we are presented with a view of 'organization', the overall society, which is identifiable in positivistic fashion, and with a picture of social disorganization within certain residual or transitional areas —disorganization which is defined by reference to the organization that characterizes the dominant society. The Durkheimian notion of anomie is implicit here in the sense that the individuated competition of the delinquent areas gives rise to normlessness.

Matza has indicated that the Chicagoans faced a crucial dilemma: they were aware of the diversity of behaviour within American society and this diversity threatened their view of society as a consensual or organic monolith (Matza, 1969a, p. 45 *et seq.*). A simple solution would have been to ascribe such diverse deviant behaviour to the arbitrariness of individual pathologies. However both their natural-istic persuasions and their orientations towards social reform stood in the way of such reductionism. They had to insist that the causes of deviancy lay beyond the level of the individual psyche. They solved this dilemma by maintaining that diversity was a product of *social* pathology: social disorganization caused deviant behaviour in the sense that the normative guidelines necessary for 'normal' behaviour were not penetrating to every level of the body social: the society itself.

The empirical demonstration of this solution was accomplished, in the main, by Clifford Shaw and Henry Mackay (1929; 1931; 1942). They were able to demonstrate that high delinquency rates were associated with the 'natural' areas of transition (undergoing process of 'invasion, dominance and succession') and there were able to replicate these findings outside Chicago: in examining the dis-tribution of delinquency in Birmingham, Cleveland, Denver, Philadelphia and Richmond (Virginia). It was therefore possible to argue that areas of social disorganization were associated with a set of values and cultural patterns supportive of delinquency, and that social reform was necessary to bring the beneficent effects of the wider culture to bear on these transitional urban zones. Morris (1957, p. 78) puts it in this way: 'Under the pressure of disintegrative forces which are endemic in the process, the community ceases to function effectively as an agency of social control, and as resistance to criminal behaviour diminishes, it becomes not only tolerated but sometimes accepted.'

Shaw and Mackay reject the notion that any other feature of the transitional zones, like overcrowding or poor hygienic standards, are causal in themselves.[18] These features are symptoms only of what Morris calls the 'absence of a consistent set of cultural standards' in such areas.

'Social disorganization' theory, however much it continued on as a research tradition in American criminology, was nevertheless unsatisfactory in two important respects. Methodologically, the theory, at least as used by Shaw and Mackay was, as David Downes (1966a, p. 71) has pointed out, essentially descriptive and tautological: 'the rate of delinquency in an area [is] the chief criterion for its "social disorganisation" which in turn [is] held to account for the delinquency rate.'[19] Theoretically, social disorganization theory presented the Chicagoans with no real resolution to the problem they faced in reconciling their views of 'pathology' and 'diversity'. The Chicagoans' naturalistic stress on diversity was threatened by a view of the disorganized as lacking a 'coherent' set of dominant cultural standards. A more revolutionary resolution was required in order to maintain the integrity of the delinquent subject.

The resolution was found in rejecting the notion of society as a consensus, a view that was implicit in the work of Shaw and Mackay,[20] and its replacement with a view of society as a normative plurality. In one stroke, both the individual and the social pathological conception of deviance could be rejected, and yet the fundamental techniques and imaginative flow of the ecological perspective could be maintained. Each specific area could be seen to represent the territorial base of a differing tradition. Social disorganization was translated into *differential social organization*, and its associated theory of learning, the theory of *differential association*.

If a view of society as being differentially organized into different cultures is adopted, it is possible to recognize conflict—for conflict is not so much 'the absence of a consistent set of cultural standards' in particular areas, as it is the clash of different, and equally valid, sets of social and group relationships. If the yearning after a co-operative, and symbiotic balance of the species in the early ecologists (Park, Burgess, Shaw, and Mackay, etc.) is reminiscent of the vision of the existence of 'mutual aid' between the species in the writings of Kropotkin, then the pluralism that characterizes the work of the later ecologists comes closer to the popularized Darwinian view of the perpetual war of each species against each other. The architect of ecological pluralism was Edwin Sutherland, and it is to his view of social transmission of culture that we now turn.

Differential association and organization[21]

The twin concepts of differential association and organization may be seen, respectively, as arising out of the opposition, on the individual level, to notions of crime as a product of personal pathology, and on the social level, to crime as a product of social disorganization. Differential association theory maintains that: 'a person becomes delinquent because of an excess of definitions favourable to violation of law over definitions unfavourable to violation of law'. Further, that such definitions are learnt in a normal learning process. Crime is not a product of a lack of social training as theorists such as Hans Eysenck would have it—rather it is acquired in an identical fashion to non-criminal behaviour. This learning includes: '(a) techniques of committing the crime, which are sometimes very complicated, sometime very simple; (b) the specific direction of motives, drives, rationalizations, and attitudes' (Sutherland and Cressey, 1966, p. 81). This learning process occurs because of association with other persons—the principal part of which is in intimate personal groups. 'Negatively, this means the impersonal agencies of communication, such as movies and newspapers, play a relatively unimportant part in the genesis of criminal behaviour'. The efficacy of such a learning process is a function of the *frequency*, *duration*, *priority*, and *intensity* of differential association. Further (p. 85):

> The theory does not say that persons become criminals because of associations with criminal behavior patterns; it says that they become criminals because of an overabundance of such associations, in comparison with associations with anti-criminal behavior patterns. Accordingly, it is erroneous to state or imply that the theory is invalid because a category of persons— such as policemen, prison workers, or criminologists—have had extensive association with criminal behavior patterns but yet are not criminals.

Presumably, the numerical abundance of definitions presented to such individuals would favour non-criminality and the duration, priority and intensity of non-criminal associations would rule out criminal behaviour because of simple contact with many criminals.

The theory is not merely antagonistic to notions of individual pathology as causing crime; it is also, to its credit, critical of any notion that the motives behind crime are mere 'rationalizations' of unconscious processes or smoke-screens for deeply hidden biological drives (Cressey, 1962, pp. 452, 459):

> Motives are not inner, biological mainsprings of action but

126

linguistic constructs which organize acts in particular situations the use of which can be examined empirically. The key linguistic constructs which a person applies to his own conduct in a set of circumstances are motives; the complete process by which such verbalizations are used is motivation. . . . Motives are circumscribed by the actor's learned vocabulary.

Differential association theory involves the concept of 'vocabulary of motives' similar to that advocated by C. Wright Mills (1967).

Differential organization is a reversal of the disorganization theories of the early Chicago school. In complex industrial societies, there are said to be heterogeneous conflicting norms all involving their own particular organization, orientated towards different ends and utilizing alternative means. Differential organization attempts to explain the existence of criminal norms whereas differential association seeks to understand their transmission. Thus, whereas the former is concerned with the variation in the crime rate between groups, the latter is concerned with the likely criminal or non-criminal behaviour of individuals.

Criticisms of differential associations theory

Limitations of applicability

It has been suggested (e.g. Vold, 1958) that certain kinds of criminal behaviour are inexplicable in terms of differential association theory. Cressey, in a brilliant defence of the theory, takes one of the most extreme instances of such 'exceptions', viz. kleptomania, and attempts to show that his theoretical premises are valid even in this instance. Kleptomania, he insists (1962, p. 460), is a group product in which typical motives are learned in group interaction:

A person might in some situations identify himself as a kleptomaniac, since that construct is now popular in our culture, and a full commitment to such an identification includes the use of motives which, in turn, release the energy to perform a so-called compulsive act. The more positive the conviction that one is a kleptomaniac the more automatic his behaviour will appear. The subject's behaviour in particular situations, then, is organised by his identification of himself according to the linguistic construct 'kleptomania' or its equivalent. . . . The fact that the acts are recurrent does not mean they are prompted from within but only that certain linguistic symbols have become usual for the person in question.

Presumably, the definitions of psychiatrists and social workers would be of great importance in this process. So far so good, but no explanation is made why the individual adopts such a kleptomaniac role: what, in short, are the attractions of such automatic behaviour to the individual? In contrast, one of the present authors (Young, 1972a) has noted how the automatic role of the 'sick junkie' is learnt through interaction with the psychiatrists and is attractive because it involves a means of denying responsibility for, and thus avoiding, what is perceived as an impossible social predicament. As Aubert and Messinger put it (1958, p. 142): 'any situation in which an individual stands to gain from withdrawal is such as to render suspect his claim to illness'. Although it is correct that such motives are learnt and do propel behaviour, it should not be assumed that the actors' notion of their causes is valid nor that they should be taken uncritically, at their face value, by the theorist.

The learning process

The actor is regarded, in differential association theory, as a passive recipient of criminal and non-criminal motives: 'It subscribes to the image of man as a vessel. He is viewed as an object into which various definitions are poured, and the resultant mixture is something over which he has no control' (Box, 1971, p. 21). The individual does not choose a type of behaviour because it has meaning and purpose to him—he is merely 'templated' with the meanings prevalent in his social environment.

This model of human nature is, in part, the result of Sutherland's notion of differential organization and the heritage of the ecological school. For although differential social organization pointed to the competition between different social values and, therefore, the possibility of man choosing between alternatives, his picture of men living in their discrete ecological niches did not allow for the immediate availability in terms of personal interaction, of alternative value choices. Thus, in *Principles of Criminology* (Sutherland and Cressey, 1966), the chapter on social disorganization stresses the normative conflict which the individual faces, whilst that on differential association makes the choice seem more restricted and somewhat inevitable. The lack of balance between the two branches of the theory is concomitant with the eclectic undeveloped nature of differential organization theory and the systematic presentation of differential association. It is no accident that Sutherland is known as primarily the theorist of differential association. David Matza (1969a, p. 107) with characteristic astuteness has alerted us to Sutherland's predicament:

Though sensitive to pluralism . . . Sutherland was not always appreciative of the movement of ideas and persons between deviant and conventional realms. Partly obsessed by the idea of ecology Sutherland nearly made his subject a captive of the milieu. Like a tree or a fox, the subject was a creature of affiliational circumstances except that what Sutherland's milieu provided was meaning and definition of the situation. Sutherland's subject was a creature, but he was half a man. Had Sutherland appreciated the interpenetration of cultural worlds —the symbolic availability of various ways of life everywhere —and more important, had he appreciated that men, but not trees or foxes, intentionally move in search of meaning as well as nourishment . . . if, in other words he had rejected the notion of radical cultural separation along with an ecological theory of migration well suited for insects but not man, his creature would have been wholly human.

The theory of differential association omits a notion of human purpose and meaning. If it had encompassed this concept of human nature it would have been forced to turn to differential organization for its explanation, and this branch of theory would have become a developed and integral part of the theory instead of an added appendage. What is needed is aptly summed up by Glaser (1956, pp. 433–44):

What we have called differential identification reconceptualizes Sutherland's theory in role taking imagery, drawing heavily on Mead as well as later refinements of role theory. Most persons in our society are believed to identify themselves with both criminal and non-criminal persons in the course of their lives. Criminal identification may occur . . . during direct experience in delinquent membership groups, through positive reference to criminal roles portrayed in the mass media, or in a negative reaction to forces opposed to crime. The family probably is the principal non-criminal reference group, even for criminals. It is supplemented by many other groups of anti-criminal 'generalized others'.
   The theory of differential identification, in essence, is that a person pursues criminal behaviour to the extent that he identifies himself with real or imaginary persons from whose perspective his criminal behaviour seems acceptable. Such a theory focuses attention on the interaction in which choice models occurs including the individual's interaction with himself in rationalizing his conduct.

Differential identification allows for human choice, and stresses the importance of vocabularies of motives existing in the wider

129

culture independently of direct intimate association. That is, direct, social and symbolic support for deviance need not necessarily coexist before deviant action is undertaken (Box, 1971, p. 156). Once this step has been taken, differential association becomes important only to the extent that personal interaction is a considerable factor in criminality and the 'excess of definitions favourable over those un-favourable' is now seen to be involved with the relative weightings purposively given to these factors by the actor.

Differential organization

This, as we have suggested, is an eclectic and undeveloped part of the total theory. Egoism, anomie, cultural conflict are all added un-systematically by Sutherland and Cressey. What is necessary and missing is some notion of the causes of conflict between groups and the manner in which values are evolved in the process of conflict.

Behaviourist revisions to Sutherland's theory

Because of the conception of human nature as passive and the rudimentary taken-for-granted nature of differential organization, Sutherland's theory exposes itself to revisionist takeovers from behaviourism. The most notable example of this is Burgess and Akers's differential association—reinforcement theory. As outlined in chapter 2, behaviourism need not necessarily pursue a conception of crime as a lack of socialization (which is completely antipathetic to differential association theory)—it can focus on operant rather than classical conditioning and maintain that crime is rationally learnt by virtue of positive and negative reinforcements. Thus Burgess and Akers can blandly state that their 'urgent task' is: 'helping criminologists become aware of the advances in learning theory and research that are directly relevant to an explanation of criminal behaviour' (1966, p. 131). The positivist assumption is explicit, that behaviourist learning theory represents, without doubt, an advance in the understanding of social learning. Sutherland's statement of the learned nature of criminal behaviour is translated into 'Criminal behaviour is learned according to the principles of operant conditioning' (ibid., p. 137). They would extend, however, Sutherland's notion that crime is learnt exclusively in social inter-action, for the 'non-social situation' can also be reinforcing: 'stealing is reinforcing in and by itself whether other people know about it or not and reinforce it socially or not' (ibid., p. 138). They further acknowledge with Glaser (1956) the importance of socially distant reference groups as well as intimate primary groups in the learning process. But this is translated into behaviourist terminology: 'The principal part of the learning of criminal behaviour occurs in those groups which comprise the individual's major source of reinforcements' (Burgess and Ackers, 1966, p. 140).

But where do such reinforcements originate? They would argue that certain groups because of deprivation are starved of reinforcement for 'normal' behaviour and therefore develop alternative norms or 'reinforcers' (ibid., p. 145):

Structural factors such as the level of deprivation of particular group with regard to important social reinforcers and the lack of effective reinforcement of 'lawful' behaviour, lead to the concomitant failure to develop the appropriate behavioural repertoires to produce reinforcement legally . . . these behaviours which do result in reinforcement may, themselves, gain reinforcement value and be enforced by the members of the group through the manipulation of various forms of social reinforcement such as social approval and status, contingent upon such behaviours. In short, new norms may develop and these may be termed delinquent by the larger society.

Cultural pluralism is thus a result of the deprivation of certain members of society and provides its own criteria of reinforcement. In this fashion they explain the onset of opiate use, which initially is unpleasant to most people, by pairing it with the reinforcers of social approval and status (Akers, Burgess and Johnson, 1968, pp. 461, 463):

A subculture has emerged in which social reinforcers such as approval, status and prestige may be contingent upon the recurrence of deviant behaviour, including drug use. . . .
Whether the unconditioned stimulation provided by the drug is aversive or simply neutral it can be positively reinforcing through pairing with social approval, attention, and the granting of status.

In the first place, irrespective of the criticisms we would offer of both positions, it is worth emphasizing how this transplant of behaviourist learning theory on to the premises of differential association, although possible because of its theoretical inadequacies and vulnerability, is in the final analysis inimicable to Cressey and Sutherland's own position. Burgess and Akers's breathless ingenuity for papering over the cracks of old theories, with the 'scientific' formulae of the new positivism, is based on a fundamental theoretical illiteracy. For differential association is a theory concerned with the acquisition of motives in which an element of human choice and purpose is an essential ingredient. Criminal vocabularies of motive

131

are used to justify criminal action in the face of alternatives. Thus Cressey (1962, pp. 452–3) writes:

Using this conception of motivation, it is immediately apparent that not all behavior is equally motivated; there are differences in the degree in which behavior is linguistically controlled. Certainly some behavior is performed with almost no social referent, that is, with the use of no shared verbalization. For instance, behavior which is physiologically autonomous is clearly non-motivated since the release of energy appropriate to performing the behavior does not depend upon the application of a linguistic construct. Similarly, if one's behavior has been so conditioned by his past experiences that he behaves automatically, in the way that Pavlov's dogs behaved automatically at the sound of a bell, he is not motivated. Genuinely fetishistic behavior probably is of this kind. However, it is equally certain that other behavior cannot be enacted unless the actor has had rather elaborate and intimate contact with linguistic constructs which are, by definition, group products. Such behavior is motivated, and it may be distinguished from automatic behavior by the fact that it has reference to means and ends. If a person defines a situation as one in which there are alternatives, if there is evidence of planning, evidence of delaying small immediate gains for future larger gains, or evidence of anticipation of social consequences of acts, he is motivated.

The problem with differential association is that human choice is not adequately stressed and the resulting behaviour appears to be totally determined. Neither is the creation of alternative vocabularies of motive ever developed. Failing to deal with these questions, differential association exposes a weak flank to the imperialism of behaviourist theory. But again we emphasize that automatic behaviour, the tautological pursuit of that which is reinforced because it is reinforced, is fundamentally alien to its theoretical position. The addition by Burgess and Akers of non-social learning of criminal patterns is a travesty of Sutherland's position. Men do not seek goods unless the goods are socially defined as desirable—stealing is not reinforcing itself unless we assume that there are basic drives which lie behind the motive to steal. But this would not be the general position that Burgess and Akers would adopt, for they claim to be concerned with the social learning of motives (rather than with biologically given drives). Thus, opiates are learnt to be pleasurable because they are associated with status and approval in a deprived contracultural group. But why did such contracultural values arise in their given form and why are opiates of significance in such cultures?[22] Again and again, Burgess and Akers are forced back on to the tautology of stating that people pursue that which is reinforcing. For the purposeful evolution of value meaningfully related to perceived situation of deprivation cannot be explained in terms of automatons propelled through their lives like Skinnerian rats. It is a tragic testimony to the theoretical inconsistency of such American groups as the Society for the Study of Social Problems, which through their magazine *Social Problems* have done so much to develop interactionist theories of deviancy, that they can include, without comment, in their columns, work which seems to undermine all that is progressive in modern deviancy theory.

The theory of subcultures and beyond

We want to return now to the tradition we highlighted at the start of this chapter; the tradition of anomie theory, and to the developments that have occurred in it since Merton.

We have seen that the predominant emphasis amongst the theorists of social disorganization was on the absolute 'normlessness' existing in delinquent areas. The subculture theorists, following Merton, used the conception of disorganization in an altogether different fashion. For them, the existence of anomie implied that cultural goals were widely diffused and internalized, but there was no corresponding internalization (or institutionalization) of the means of achieving them. Social disorganization, therefore, refers, in subcultural theory, as in anomie theory at large, to the disjunction between culture and structure.

In moving from a discussion of the ecologists to the subcultural theorists, and in returning to the Mertonian tradition which focuses on the whole society, and does not reduce the society to an amalgam of territories, milieux and areas, we are turning, therefore, from the geography of human affairs to the politics of social relationships.

Cloward and Ohlin: Merton reasserted

Richard Cloward and Lloyd Ohlin have made important advances in Mertonian anomie theory. In fact, they may be regarded as the most significant representatives of the many subcultural theorists who based their initial premises on the work of Merton.

Cloward and Ohlin attempt to unite two strands of early sociologies of crime: anomie which is concerned with the origins of deviancy and differential association, which focuses on the transmission of deviant life-styles. They differ from Merton in several fundamental respects:

1. They represent deviancy for the most part (the one exception

133

being their discussion of 'retreatism') as a collective endeavour rather than an individual 'adaptation'.

2. They indicate the way in which self-blame may be avoided and the system may be identified as being responsible for the problems collectively forced, viz. that in certain situations the obstacles to success may be visible and collective adaptations ensue. For example, Negro adolescents may quickly become aware that it is their blackness, rather than any individual inadequacy shared by their peer group, which prevents them competing.

3. They point to the transmission of criminal cultures in the organized slum which provide what they call a structure of illegitimate opportunities of success. 'Subculture' does not merely crystallize out of the existing consensus, it already exists, and provides by differential association its own particular brand of opportunities and life-styles.

4. They point to the development of new subcultures completely outside of the consensus—resulting from the absence or the paucity of both legitimate and illegitimate opportunities—for example, the development of the conflict gang which springs up in the 'disorganized slum' basing its values on the manipulation of violence.

Men are envisaged, therefore, as being placed in cultures which they have learnt by differential association and in facing particular problems of anomie which are a function of the opportunities, legitimate or illegitimate, which such an association offers them. Out of this moral base, their culture of origin, men collectively evolve solutions to the problems of anomie which face them. But the diversity of subcultures in modern industrial societies is scarcely grasped by Cloward and Ohlin. They inherit the consensual legacy of Merton—there is one all-embracing cultural goal, monetary success, the only difference being that there are two types of institutionalized means available for its achievement: legitimate and illegitimate opportunity structures. The former is available in the organized respectable society, the latter in the organized slum. Two distinct social organizations exist each with their own ecological base but sharing eventually the same cultural goals. Outside of this utilitarian monolith there is only 'disorganization'. In the disorganized slum both legitimate and illegitimate opportunities and 'culture' are absent. It is here that the residue of the Chicago tradition of social disorganization survives. For the adolescent boys faced with 'normlessness' erect their own culture outside of utilitarian values. Here, alone, is the creativity of human praxis given full expression: amongst those who had no choice in the first place. The active rejection of playing the bourgeois values and ideology by those who have some access to institutional means (e.g. the skilled working class or the bohemian) is ignored. Nowhere is this better evidenced than in their treatment of bohemian subcultures. For their culture is not seen as 'a psychedelic revolt against utilitarianism' (Gouldner, 1971) but as an asocial phenomenon. Cloward and Ohlin's only concession is that a minimal structure must occur in order that the illicit market for drugs can exist.

At no time is the cultural diversity of goals and means, and the multitude of graduations of acceptance and rejection of utilitarianism, existing in modern industrial societies, fully encompassed. It would be amusing, for instance, to conjecture what Cloward and Ohlin would have made of the Black Panthers or the hippies, in their typology of subcultures.

Albert K. Cohen: the non-utilitarian culture

Albert K. Cohen in *Deliquent Boys: The Culture of the Gang* (1955), utilizes what at first sight may seem a version of anomie theory. He argues that delinquent subcultures are a product of the conflict between working- and middle-class culture. The working-class pupil finds himself in a school where he is judged by the middle-class standards of self-reliance, good manners, deferred gratification, respect for property, etc. His own working-class values make him ill-equipped for competition in this situation; yet he has to some extent internalized the middle-class norms of success As a result of the 'status frustration' the adolescents collectively react against the standards which they are unable to measure up to. In a process of 'reaction formation', they invert middle-class values and form a culture which is malicious, short-term hedonistic, non-utilitarian, and negativistic. Cohen (1955) denies that his theory, despite its parallels with Merton, is an application of anomie. For whereas the latter is (p. 36): 'highly plausible as an explanation for adult professional crime and for the property delinquency of some older and semi-professional thieves', its non-utilitarian nature; 'the destructiveness, the versatility, the zest and the wholesale negativism which characterizes this delinquent subculture are beyond the purview of this theory'.

Cohen's theory, by characterizing the delinquent subculture merely as the negation of middle-class culture, fails to point to its close relationship with adult working-class culture. There is a world of a difference between a culture which is normative in its own right and antagonistic to the middle class and one which is mere inversion of the culture it opposes. Rather, it should be seen as an accentuation of adult working-class culture (Miller, 1958). It is revealing that Cohen depicts anomie theory as capable only of dealing with utilitarian situations, but non-utilitarian cultures as somehow lacking in normative status. In fact, as Merton himself indicates, anomie

135

theory could be applied to any thwarting of aspirations because of restricted opportunities (e.g. in sex, or athletics). His focus on the utilitarian quest for money arises out of his characterization of American society. It might be useful, therefore, to separate out the concept of anomie from consensual theory and to suggest that a fundamental cause of deviant behaviour can be seen to lie in any situation where the aspirations of the actors (which may be of myriad kinds) are thwarted by the social restriction of their fulfilment. In the case of Cohen's adolescents it is more likely that what has occurred is a realistic disengagement from the success goals of school because of a lack of tangible opportunities and inappropriate cultural skills and a focus of their expressive aspirations on leisure pursuits. Here, in the leisure field, restrictions on expressive opportunities (because of tight social control and lack of money) lead to the evolution of a subculture which manufactures its own sources of excitement and satisfies its dislike of middle-class restrictions and control. This suggests that the motivation for delinquency is 'expressive anomie' and that instrumental aspirations (and therefore anomie) have been realistically discarded.[23] What we are suggesting is an expansion and reinstatement of the concept to allow for cultural diversity and the complexity of motivation.

Albert K. Cohen: anomie theory and beyond

Albert K. Cohen in 1965 produced what is one of the most significant articles in recent criminological theory. We shall deal with its major contributions point by point:

1   The genesis of deviant behaviour

Although Merton's aim is to create a fully sociological theory of deviant behaviour, he focuses largely on the individual actor's adaptations (Cohen, 1965, p. 6):

> The bearings of others' experience—their strains, their con-
> formity and deviance, their success and failure—an ego's
> strain and consequent adaptations is comparatively neglected.
> [For] how imperious must the goals be, how uncertain their
> attainment, how complete their fulfilment, to generate strain?
> ... One thing that is clear is that level of goal attainment that
> will seem just and reasonable to concrete actors, and therefore
> the sufficiency of available means, will be relative to the attain-
> ment of others who serve as reference objects.

The irony, as Cohen points out, is that a major strand in Merton's work is his consideration of reference group theory. But the two strands are never really brought together. Cohen indicates that the success of like others, and of the wicked who infringe the codes, are important pointers in the degree of concern and anomie of the actor. But he does not expand on this in any macro-sociological way. At this juncture we note that some of the important reference points would be:

a   those who because of wealth have an unfair advantage. As Gouldner (1971) suggests they obtain rewards independently of their merit. The likelihood of strain depends on the efficacy of the meritocratic ideology in legitimizing (i.e. mystifying) the existing system of property relations.

b   'like others': if a few are successful, then this can be attributed to their special grace; if none is successful, then a caste-like situation of comparative content will ensue; but if a moderate proportion are successful, then the barriers are likely to be more visible.

c   the wicked must be seen to suffer—if they do not, mass defection to the illegitimate is likely. The meritocratic myth must have as its reverse, the punishment of the rule-breakers and the comparative poverty of the unsuccessful.[24]

2   The immediate solution

Cohen notes how Merton assumes that the solution to the problem of anomie is regarded by Merton as an individual project. Cloward and Ohlin, and Cohen himself, have shown how such a subcultural solution is in reality a collective and collaborative endeavour. Individuals with like problems create a solution together which relates to their culture of origin and, specifically in Cloward and Ohlin, to the illegitimate opportunity structure available. As we have noted earlier such a division between legitimate and illegitimate opportunity both with the same utilitarian consensual goals scarcely caters for the diversity of subcultures within the population.

3   The assumption of discontinuity

Anomie theory, like biological positivism, regards deviance as if it were an abrupt, sudden product of anomie or strain. In contrast Cohen (1965, p. 8) insists that: 'human action deviant or otherwise, is something that typically develops and groups in a tentative, groping, advancing, back-tracking, sounding out process', but until now: 'the dominant bias ... has been towards formulating theory in terms of variables that describe initial states, on the one hand, and outcomes, on the other, rather than in terms of process whereby acts and complex structures of action are built, elaborated and transformed' (p. 9). The reference is, of course, to what Howard Becker

137

(1963) called 'sequential' rather than 'simultaneous' models of deviancy.

4 *Interaction*

The history of a deviant act is a history of an interaction process. The antecedents of the act are an unfolding sequence of acts contributed by a set of actors. A makes a move, possibly in a deviant direction; B responds; A responds to B's responses, etc. In the course of the interaction, movement in a deviant direction may become more explicit, elaborated, definitive—or it may not. Although the act may be socially ascribed to only one of them, both ego and alter help to shape it (Cohen, 1965, p. 9).

Anomie theory assumed the social reaction against deviant behaviour and it accorded little recognition to the interaction between deviant and society.

Here Cohen makes his distinctive contribution to anomie theory, for he attempts to fuse the interactionist and anomie schools. He asserts that alter's response to ego's deviancy (a product of anomie) may be either to close or to open up the illegitimate or legitimate opportunities of the actor. This in turn will change the degree of anomie of the actor, i.e. he may be presented with more possibilities the less his aspirations are thwarted, and vice versa. Moreover, this may well be a continuous interaction process, with changes on the part of alter resulting in changes in the activities of ego, and so on.

It is significant that such a use of anomie almost inevitably shifts this kind of theory away from a consensual model of society, in that reaction becomes problematic—dependent on the various agencies of control, each with its own particular views of deviancy; and the aspirations and blocked possibilities of the actors can potentially be viewed in terms of a plentitude of social values (rather than simply in those of a given 'system' of dominant values).

In the following chapter, we shall be concerned to show, however, that even this attempt to fuse anomie theory with the social reaction perspective, sophisticated as it is, is unable (by virtue of being imprisoned within the assumptions of both) to grasp the full implications of seeing man as the creator as well as the creation of structures of power, authority and control.

5 Social reaction, deviant commitment and career

The act of injecting heroin into a vein is not inherently deviant.
If a nurse gives a patient drugs under a doctor's orders, it is
perfectly proper. It is when it is done in a way that is not
publicly defined as proper that it becomes deviant. The act's
deviant character lies in the way it is defined in the public
mind. H. S. Becker (1971, p. 341).

This is a large turn away from older sociology which tended
to rest heavily upon the idea that deviance leads to social
control. I have come to believe that the reverse idea, i.e., social
control leads to deviance, is equally tenable and the potentially
richer premise for studying deviance in modern society. E. M.
Lemert (1967, p. v).

In this chapter we shall be critically assessing the work of a group of
theorists (largely American) who share several assumptions in
common; they have been variously called social control theorists,
social reaction theorists, transactionalists, or labelling theorists.
These names are unimportant; but their assumptions are not, for
although our assessment of their work is highly critical, the social
reaction approach to deviance (as we shall call it) is a remarkable
advance towards a fully social theory of deviance. Whilst we shall be
mainly looking at the work of Howard Becker and Edwin Lemert,[1]
the criticisms we offer of their salient assumptions can be applied
with little modification to other writers who share a similar perspective, amongst whom K. Erikson, J. Kitsuse and E. M. Schur are
better known.

    This chapter is doubly difficult. Not only does it engage in
critical exposition of the social reaction approach, but also it encompasses a variety of theorists who, although they share many
assumptions, hold to these assumptions with differing degrees of

subtlety, sensitivity and sophistication. Indeed, it is perhaps unfair to single out such a set of assumptions, and then criticize diverse theorists for not seeing the limitations of their common position. On the other hand, it is precisely one of our basic criticisms of the social reaction position held to by Lemert, Becker, Erikson, Kitsuse and others, that the degree to which these assumptions are systematically worked through in their studies is ambiguous and inconsistent.

Indeed, whilst at times the social reaction approach is presented as a full-blown theory, it is also often presented, when criticized, merely as a necessary re-orientation in criminology and the sociology of deviance. Edwin Schur (1971, p. 158), who is perhaps one of its most sophisticated defenders, has suggested that, 'from the point of view of causal theory, labeling processes [as they have been broadly conceived in this study] represent perhaps a necessary condition of certain deviant outcomes, but labelling analysis does not concern itself basically with the specification of necessary and sufficient conditions'. Schur's statement is rather tendentious, for the work of the social reaction or labelling theorists suffers precisely because whilst it avoids full causal or etiological analysis, on the one hand, it has also come to form a coherent body of thought serving to correct absolutist theories of deviance, and providing a processual account of the creation and maintenance of deviance, which concentrates its attention on the reaction to rule-breaking behaviour.

What is the social reaction or labelling approach to deviance?

The approach is part of a larger move in criminology and sociology against the legacy of positivistic or absolutist notions of crime, deviance and social problems. The approach rejects those genetic, psychological or multi-factoral accounts of crime and deviance which stress the absolute nature of the causes of criminality or deviation. It usually, but not necessarily, rejects the standard sociological structure-functional approach to such questions, and in its examination of the social processes giving rise to deviation it asks 'deviant to whom?' or 'deviant from what?' (Schur, 1971, p. 29).[2]

Their emphasis is on the nature of social rules and the labels or social reaction aimed at individuals who contravene such rules. They are, therefore, sociological relativists, insisting that what is deviant for one person may not be deviant for another, and perhaps more importantly, what is treated as deviant at one time and in one context, may not necessarily always be treated as deviant.

At its simplest, the suggestion is that the attempt to deter, punish and prevent deviation can actually create deviation itself. The statement that social control leads to deviance, or social control creates deviance can mean at least three different things:

140

a It can simply mean that whilst massive amounts of rule-breaking goes on in our society, this is not really deviant behaviour, or is not to be regarded as deviant behaviour until some social audience labels it deviant.

b It can be the possibility that an actor will become deviant as a result of experiencing the social reaction to an initial rule-infraction. In short, reaction by 'social control agencies' to an initial deviant act is so powerful in its implications for self that an individual comes to see himself as deviant and becomes increasingly committed to deviation.

c It can mean that the everyday existence of social control agencies produces given rates of deviance. In this sense it is obvious that actual indices of crime or deviation are produced as a result of the everyday workings of the police, courts, social workers, etc., which probably do not reflect actual amounts of deviance, but are merely indices of the deviance which is processed or handled by the social control agencies themselves.

Now whilst social reaction can mean three different things, the theorists under consideration in this chapter are primarily concerned with (a) and (b), and it is mainly ethnomethodologists who are concerned with the analysis of (c). We shall treat ethnomethodology separately in the next chapter.

It has been suggested that what makes comprehension of the social reaction perspective difficult is its cynical realism. Lemert himself suggests that 'it starts with a jaundiced eye on collective efforts of societies to solve problems of deviance' (1967, p. 59). The ultimate preoccupation of this group of theorists is with the way in which being labelled deviant by a social audience, or by an agency of social control, can change one's conception of self, and possibly lead to a situation where, even if there was no initial commitment to deviation, there may be a progressive turn to such commitment. Thus they suggest that the very processes of social control can often lead to a 'negative self image' (Erikson) or to a symbolic reorganization of self (Lemert)—where one comes to see one's self as deviant and progressively to act out such deviancy. This social psychological assumption is utilized by many of the theorists to explain commitment to deviancy. A processual account is offered of the way in which individuals (a) come to be called deviant, and (b) come to be committed to a deviant career. Part of this distinction is shown in the work of Becker (1963) when he refers to the difference between rule-breaking and deviance. As he states (p. 14):

In short, whether a given act is deviant or not depends in part on the nature of the act (that is, whether or not it violates some rule) and in part on what other people do about it.

141

Some people may object that this is merely a terminological quibble, that one can, after all, define terms any way he wants to and that if some people want to speak of rule-breaking behavior as deviant without reference to the reactions of others they are free to do so. This, of course, is true. Yet it might be worthwhile to refer to such behavior as rule-breaking behavior and reserve the term deviant for those labeled as deviant by some segment of society. I do not insist that this usage be followed. But it should be clear that insofar as a scientist uses 'deviant' to refer to any rule-breaking behavior and takes as his subject of study only those who have been labeled deviant, he will be hampered by the disparities between the two categories.

In fact, Becker is confused, for we are not dealing here with two categories but two separate social processes, that is, how a piece of behaviour comes to be labelled deviant, and what happens to a person once the label is applied. Becker's confusion stems from his desire to preserve the category deviant for those people who are labelled deviant, but, to do this, is to imply at the outset that rule-breakers, and rule-breakers who are labelled (i.e. deviants), are fundamentally different from each other in their self-perceptions. As we shall see, this leads to an over-concentration by Becker and other social reaction theorists on the importance of the application of a label in creating a self-conscious commitment to deviant acts.

Let us return for the moment, however, to the advances made by the social reaction approach. They have concentrated on demonstrating that being defined or labelled as deviant can be an important stage in a larger process. Following the tradition of George Herbert Mead, they stress that the self is a social construct, that the way in which we come to act and see ourselves as individuals is in part the result of the way in which other people act towards us. Now it is apparent that if people see us as somewhat strange or different from other people, then we are liable to begin to conceive of ourselves as different. It is the case that someone seen as different may well be treated differently. We may treat people differently out of ignorance or prejudice, but the result is the same as if the supposed differences were real. Studies have shown that school children seen as liable to be educationally backward become educationally backward and that, vice versa, children seen as educationally capable become educationally capable (Rosenthal, 1968). If we define ourselves as incapable as a result of others' definitions, we begin to act as if we are incapable. In part, what we are describing follows from a dictum erected by W. I. Thomas that a situation is real if it is real in its consequences.

Albert Cohen (1966, p. 24) has discussed the question of the application of deviant definitions and has pointed out that:

> It is one thing to commit a deviant act—e.g. acts of lying, stealing, homosexual intercourse, narcotics' use, drinking to excess, unfair competition. It is quite another thing to be charged and invested with a deviant character, i.e. to be socially defined as a liar, a thief, a homosexual, a dope fiend, a drunk, a chiseler, a brown-noser, a hoodlum, a sneak, a scab, and so on. It is to be assigned to a role, to a special type or category of persons. The label—the name of the role—does more than signify one who has committed such-and-such a deviant act. Each label evokes a characteristic imagery. It suggests someone who is *normally* or *habitually* given to certain kinds of deviance; who may be expected to behave in this way; who is literally a bundle of odious or sinister qualities. It activates sentiments and calls out responses in others: rejection, contempt, suspicion, withdrawal, fear, hatred.

Of course, the acceptance of a label is not inevitable. We have all experienced the kind of situation in which someone has in anger called us a thief or called us ugly. Just because a person defines a situation as real does not mean that we always act out their definitions. Mere definitions of reality are *not* always real in their consequences. But, despite its problematic character, the social self is firmly rooted in interactions with others, and it is this social fact which is so important in the consideration of an individual career.

If someone has been caught and publicly identified as deviant, the public labelling may begin to affect a person's self-image (his social self). His personal identity may undergo transformation and, as a consequence, he *may* well come to view himself as a committed deviant. In Becker's terms (1963, p. 32): 'He [the rule-breaker] has been revealed as a different kind of person from the kind he was supposed to be. He is labeled a "fairy", "dope fiend", "nut", or "lunatic" and treated accordingly.' Once one is labelled as a certain kind of person one is liable to be treated in a different kind of way from those who commit similar actions but have not been labelled. Attention is then directed towards the institutions of social control because, as the social reaction theorists correctly argue, the control of crime and deviance frequently engenders in the criminal or deviant exactly those psychological self-perceptions which can hasten him along the road to a deviant career. Mead (1918, p. 592) had recognized this paradox early in his work and stated, in a famous essay on the psychology of punitive justice, that:

> The two attitudes, that of control of crime by the hostile

procedure of the law and that of control through comprehension of social and psychological conditions, cannot be combined. To understand is to forgive and the social procedure seems to deny the very responsibility which the law affirms, and on the other hand the pursuit by criminal justice inevitably awakens the hostile attitude in the offender and renders the attitude of mutual comprehension practically impossible.

It is not surprising therefore that social reaction theorists, concerned as they are with processual explanations of deviancy, should have anchored their work in a social psychology derived from Mead. We shall later, however, find these premises to be an insufficient and a limited assumption. As our exposition unfolds, we hope to demonstrate that the social reactions theorists' reliance upon social psychological assumptions (even where critical of Mead's work) useful and necessary as they are in combating absolutist criminology, often lead either to a one-sided determinism or an avoidance of structural considerations relevant to their own position.

Perhaps the best conclusion to this section lies in a reference to Lemert's critical précis of Mead's position; for with all their modification of Mead's 'taken-for-granted' determinism, the social reaction theorists do themselves sometimes lapse into the very same error (Lemert, 1967, pp. 42–3):

Mead's conclusion . . . was that a system of deterrent punishments not only fails to repress crime but also 'preserves a criminal class' . . .

Mead held that impartiality, maximization, and the consistent application of punishment, expressed in the 'fixed attitude towards the jailbird', provoked intransigence and hostility in the criminal. He seemed to take it for granted that such reactive antagonism led to further crime.

Deviance, behaviour and action

Forms of behavior per se do not differentiate deviants from non-deviants; it is the responses of the conventional and conforming members of the society which identify and interpret behavior as deviant which sociologically transform persons into deviants (John I. Kitsuse, 1962).

Deviance is not a property inherent in certain forms of behavior; it is a property conferred upon these forms by the audiences which directly or indirectly witness them (Kai T. Erikson, 1962).

The theoretical advance of the social reaction approach lies in its ability to demystify cruder structural approaches which lost sight of the importance of social control as an independent variable in the creation of deviancy. Yet, despite this notable advance, much of the pioneering work nevertheless lapses into a relativistic idealism, where it is almost as if without labels there would be no deviance. Now in the broadest sense of the term (label or social reaction) this is obviously the case. A society without any rules or norms cannot have deviance—for 'anything goes'. A society that describes all behaviour in neutral rather than pejorative terms is presumably a society free of variable social reaction. But this reliance upon a conceptual relativism in their work often leads to ambiguity and confusion.

The social reaction theorists assert that deviance or criminality is not to be seen as an inherent property of the act. Rather, for an act to be regarded as deviant, a deviant label has to be conferred upon it by society. Thus, for Becker and for others, deviant behaviour is to be seen as 'the product of a transaction which takes place between some social group and one that is viewed by that group as a rule breaker'. Now there is a sense in which this perspective is both true and untrue. A couple of examples will illustrate the sense in which it is true. In wartime, for instance, the taking of life (murder, homicide, etc.) may be defined as one's patriotic duty. In other particular circumstances, it may be seen as understandable and indeed perhaps a normal, if regrettable, response, as in the case of *crimes passionelles* or euthanasia. In the case of premeditated killing for personal gain, however, there is, of course, almost universal agreement on the deviant label. A few further examples here should clarify. With the introduction in the United Kingdom of the breathalyser test a few years ago, it suddenly became illegal to drive with a certain amount of alcohol in the blood. Similarly, the popular psychotropic drug LSD was legal in the UK and in the United States until comparatively recently. Again, it was entirely legal for a long period to raise the rents charged to tenants in private houses without restriction. The introduction of legal sanctions against all these forms of behaviour resulted in an increase in 'deviance' and, indeed, some of these instances, of criminality. What had happened is that society, or, more precisely, the rule-creators in society, extended their definitions and constraints to include previously non-deviant groups. Thus, there are a number of senses in which the same piece of physical action can be treated as either deviant or non-deviant depending upon the label applied to it, or, and importantly, upon the social context in which it occurs.

However, there is also a sense in which the social reaction perspective is untrue. Whilst the social reaction theorists are, of course, correct in distinguishing physical from social acts, in insisting that

145

meanings are not constant, and that a definition is something endowed on the action rather than the action itself, there is a sense in which this is only true once a social context is taken for granted. Whilst the act of killing can be seen as patriotism or murder— according to the social context—it is only within the existence of certain social contexts that labels are acceptable. Thus, it is unlikely that an individual found to have killed another individual in England in 1972 could claim to have committed an act of patriotism, since patriotism is a social definition used largely in periods of war.[3]

If it is true that certain social meanings are only acceptable in certain social contexts, *then* the social meanings of acts and the choice to commit them are not as variable or arbitrary as many of these theorists would have them to be.

This leads us to confront the weakness of one *assumption* of the 'theory', namely, the statement of Howard Becker (1963, p. 9) that:

> Social groups create deviance by making the rules whose infraction constitutes deviance, and by applying those rules to particular people and labeling them as outsiders. From this point of view, deviance is *not* a quality of the act the person commits, but rather a consequence of the application by others or rules and sanctions to an 'offender'. The deviant is one to whom that label has been successfully applied; deviant behavior is behavior that people so label.

In the light of our earlier argument, this position seems clearly to be in need of stringent re-examination. Becker's statement can only be true of physical action, that is an action to which social meaning has not yet been given. We would follow Max Weber in suggesting that deviants, like all other actors, often endow their acts with meaning; and that, furthermore, this meaning is not re-invented on each occasion that individuals engage in physical action. Rather, is it derived from a fairly constant stock of social meanings which exist to describe physical acts, It is only by crudely opposing physical to social action that the social reaction approach can claim that an action is only deviant when so defined by others. This approach rests on the variability of the social processes giving rise to its being labelled. But most deviant, and especially criminal, acts are physical acts which have quite clear social meanings. Where is the criminal who engages in the robbing of banks and who is unaware that he is engaged in the social act of stealing? Taking an object (a physical act) without the owner's permission will always be described as stealing in those societies where the institution of private property exists.

Our objection, then, to one assumption of the social reaction position, is this: that we do not act in a world free of social meaning. With the exception of entirely new behaviour, it is clear to most people which actions are deviant and which are not deviant. That is, whilst marijuana-smokers might regard their smoking as acceptable normal behaviour in the company they move in, they are fully aware that this behaviour is regarded as deviant by the wider society.

In contrast to these theorists, we would assert that *most deviant behaviour is a quality of the act*, since the way in which we distinguish between *behaviour* and *action* is that behaviour is merely physical and action has meaning that is socially given. In the case of the marijuana-smoker, it is obvious that his action is motivated by hedonistic reasons, but there is a fundamental difference between engaging in an universally approved pleasurable act and engaging in a pleasurable act which is regarded by large numbers of people as deviant and, in this case, as illegal. The awareness that an action is deviant fundamentally alters the nature of the choices being made.

In part, the confusion of the social reaction theorists stems from the often unanalysed sense in which they use the term social reaction or label. It is important to distinguish between the effects of social reaction, the variable or arbitrary nature of social reaction, and the perceived legitimacy of social reaction. The extent to which social reaction influences a deviant may in part depend on whether the deviant sees social reaction as 'legitimate'.

We have here shifted the focus away from the view of the deviant as a passive, ineffectual, stigmatized individual (what Gouldner has called 'man on his back') to that of a decision-maker who often actively violates the moral and legal codes of society.

Whilst advancing these criticisms of the social reaction perspective, we are not intent upon dismissing it. But we are insisting that, in elevating one assumption almost to a slogan for their whole orientation, they have been led into confusion and ambiguity with regard to their propositions. It is obviously the case that deviant acts and reactions to those acts are different analytically and may in fact be the result of two different social processes. However, there is a difference between viewing deviance as a normative or rule-breaking act, and insisting that deviance is simply to be defined in terms of reaction to such action. Much of the work of the social reaction theorists moves uneasily between these two conceptions. What we must do is to develop a clear view of deviance which allows that further commitment to deviancy can sometimes be explained or partly explained by the reaction, whilst at other times a sufficient explanation would be simply in terms of initial motives (independently of social reaction). A full explanation of deviance requires both possibilities. Jack Gibbs (1966) has drawn attention to the inconsistencies in the social reaction approach in similar manner (p. 13):

> The failure of Becker, Erikson and Kitsuse to specify the kind of reactions which identify deviance is further complicated by the contradictions in their own position. The contradictions stem from the fact that a deviant act can be defined as behaviour which is contrary to a norm or rule . . .
> But this is not so from the viewpoint of Becker, Erikson and Kitsuse, because deviant behavior for them is defined in terms of reactions to it. On the one hand, while advocates of the new perspective do recognise the 'norm' conception of deviation, they do not consistently reject it.

This shift between the 'norm or rule-breaking' conception of deviance and the 'reaction approach' constantly leads to difficulties: for instance, Becker who, as we have shown earlier is aware (even if confused by) this distinction, actually attempts to lay out a typology of deviant behaviour which embodies these problems. He suggests we should see deviancy as follows (1963, p. 20):

	Obedient behavior	Rule-breaking behavior
Perceived as deviant	Falsely accused	Pure deviant
Not perceived as deviant	Conforming	Secret deviant

Here Becker is arguing that at any given point in time, with the one exception of the pure 'conforming' type (who is not deviant and is not perceived as deviant) the rest of us may be deviant or be seen as deviant. This, Becker insists, may even be the case when we are falsely accused, or, as he puts it, when we are in receipt of a 'bum rap'.

The problem with this typology is that it collapses and confuses all the issues which have correctly been raised by the social reaction theorists themselves. For if deviancy is given by public reaction, how can we have a secret deviant? It is apparent that the typology only makes sense if we allow both the rule-breaking conception of deviance and the reaction approach to coexist, for whilst these are analytically separable they are also connected in the sense that without rule-breaking there could be no deviants at all, except for the 'falsely accused'. Gibbs (1966, p. 13) is one of the few deviancy theorists to have drawn attention to this question and highlights the social reaction theorists' inconsistency on this question when he states:

> Thus, if deviant behavior is defined in terms of reactions to it, then Becker cannot speak properly of 'secret deviance'. If

behavior defined as deviant by sociologists in reference to the prevailing social norms is 'real', then in what sense can one maintain, as Kitsuse does elsewhere, that behavior is deviant if and only if there is a certain kind of reaction to it? Finally, in the case of Erikson, how can the behaviour of 'large groups of persons' be identified as deviant when they have been given 'license' to engage in it? To be consistent, Becker, Kitsuse and Erikson would have to insist that behavior which is contrary to a norm is not deviant unless it is discovered and there is a particular kind of reaction to it.

For us, these problems are *not* semantic quibbles which occur in a vacuum: they have very real consequences for the way in which social processes are studied, examined and explained.

Edwin Schur (1971, p. 14) seems to see the social reaction theorists' reaction against absolutism as the strength of their whole position:

It is a central tenet of the labeling perspective that neither acts nor individuals are 'deviant' in the sense of immutable, 'objective' reality without reference to processes of social definition. Gibbs is, in fact, not far off the mark in his allegation that the approach is 'relativistic in the extreme', yet this relativism may be viewed as a major strength, rather than as a weakness.

But it is not merely the relativism of the approach that Gibbs or we are objecting to. The objection is to the tendency to insist that deviancy is only to be grasped in terms of social reaction. It is the confusion over definitions and conceptions of behaviour, action, and deviancy to which we object. We are not suggesting that the social reaction approach is wrong, or false, but that it lacks systematic development and that it is frequently and inconsistently polemically one-sided in its contributions to a fully social theory of deviance. We can best conclude this section of our examination of this perspective with a picturesque quotation from a highly perceptive critic of their position (Akers, 1967, p. 46):

Rather, although those of this school come dangerously close to saying that the actual behavior is unimportant, their contribution to the study of deviancy comes precisely in their conception of the impact of labeling on behavior. One sometimes gets the impression from reading this literature that people go about minding their own business, and then— 'wham'—bad society comes along and slaps them with a stigmatized label. Forced into the role of deviant the individual has little choice but to be deviant. This is an exaggeration of course, but such an image can be gained easily from an over-

149

emphasis on the impact of labeling. However, it is exactly this image, toned down and made reasonable, which is the central contribution of the labeling school to the sociology of deviance.

Primary and secondary deviance and the notion of sequence or career

It is Lemert, furthermore, who developed the distinction between primary and secondary deviation, a distinction that has been central to the work of recent labeling analysts (E. M. Schur, 1971, p. 10).

Etiology was never as important a question as Sutherland felt it to be; we can, however, understand his concern by recognising the almost exclusive emphasis put on this problem by earlier criminologists (H. Becker, 1971, p. 337).

In this section we shall examine the way in which one of the 'central' distinctions in the social reaction perspective proves, on closer examination, either to be over-deterministic or to be so general as to prove faulty. Our concern is to point to several inadequacies in the way in which the social reaction theorists deal with the manner in which actors become committed to continued deviancy. We shall argue that the notion of career deviancy is of doubtful value, and that moreover, despite much work of their own which testifies to the contrary, the picture which the social reaction theorists give of 'commitment to deviancy' plays down the degree of choice and consciousness which they themselves would wish to grant deviant actors.

In a very important series of essays in this tradition, 'Human deviance, social problems and social control', Lemert (1966, p. 16) confronts the whole question of a self-commitment to deviation by pointing to the inadequacies of the structural approach advanced by Merton. He suggests that there are two kinds of research problems in the study of deviation, the second of which he sees to be untouched by Merton. These two problems are (Lemert, 1967, p. 17): '(1) how deviant behavior originates; (2) how deviant acts are symbolically attached to persons and the effective consequences of such attachment for subsequent deviation on the part of the person.' In his work, Lemert utilizes this important distinction between what he terms primary and secondary deviation. For Lemert, primary deviation is (ibid., p. 17): 'assumed to arise in a wide variety of social, cultural and psychological contexts, and at best to have only marginal implications for the psychic structure of the individual: it does not lead to symbolic reorganization at the level of self-regarding attitudes and social roles.' Whereas secondary deviation is conceived as (ibid., p. 17): 'deviant behavior, or social roles based upon it, which becomes a means of defense, attack or adaptation to the overt and covert problems created by the societal reaction to primary deviation.' The significance of this distinction is its concern to give some description of the process of commitment. Primary deviation has to be explained in different terms from secondary deviation. The causes of primary deviation for Lemert are wide and varied, or as Becker puts it (1963, p. 26): 'There is no reason to assume that only those who commit a deviant act actually have the impulse to do so. It is much more likely that most people experience deviant impulses frequently.' But secondary deviation is different (Lemert, 1967, p. 17): 'In effect, the original causes of the deviation recede and give way to the central importance of the disapproving, degradational and labeling reactions of society.'

The affixing of some kind of deviant label—be it a mild, disapproving glance or a full-blown stigmatization of one variety or another—is crucial, in the work of the social reaction theorists in explaining the progressive commitment of an individual to a deviant mode of life. For instance, Lemert points to the possibility that the roles and relationships made available to the individual subsequent to stigmatization and labelling will be used to *sustain* a deviant identity. Lemert cites the example of girls labelled prostitutes, noting that their need to resolve conflicts between their roles and identities may result in closer relationships with pimps, or with other girls in a lesbian relationship, each of which relationships will sustain a continuing definition of self as deviant, and also act as a cushion from the exclusion of society.

These stratagems are seen by Lemert as essentially defensive: that is, they are used as a means of sustaining a 'social self' in the face of exclusion and stigmatization. As Lemert points out, however, a person labelled as deviant may have problems, resulting from the ascription of his new identity, which will require a more positive response. For example, the individual who is overtly labelled a homosexual may need not only to defend himself against the possibility of losing his job, and the ensuing loss of income and material security: he may need also to attach the problem of relationships (e.g. within a family) which are incompatible with his label. He may then use his label aggressively to fend off the painful involvements with heterosexual society.

We can add a more recent example of aggressive reaction to labelling—the reaction of political radicals to attempts to apply spurious labels to their activities. During the May 'events' in France in 1968, students reacted to the accusation that they were under the influence of the 'German Jew', Daniel Cohn-Bendit, by parading through Paris under banners emblazoned with the slogan 'We are all German Jews'. This embrace of the deviant label served not only to highlight the spurious (in this case, irrelevant) nature of the label; it also helped to solidify the movement in the face of attempts at a stereotypical dismissal.

In any case, whatever the reaction to labelling may be, it is Lemert's contention (1967), p. 18 that 'the distinction between primary and secondary deviation is deemed indispensable to a complete understanding of deviation in modern pluralistic society. Furthermore, it is held that the second research problem is pragmatically more pertinent for sociology than the first.'

This distinction has led to an over-concentration on the assumed differences between primary and secondary deviation to the exclusion of any fully social explanation of 'how deviant behavior originates'. For the social reaction theorists are asserting that the secondary deviant is committed to deviancy for reasons different from his original action. Now this kind of analysis of commitment to deviancy seems to us to be unproven and ridden with unjustified psychological assumptions. As a recent British critic of this approach has stated (Box, 1971, p. 218, our emphasis):

> To see the full irony of this possibility—that social control can lead to deviance—interactionist analysis has been directed towards examining the *social-psychological implications* of official registration. Unfortunately, the *theoretical* links between social control and further deviant behaviour have never been completely forged, yet alone subjected to adequate empirical testing.

Moreover, as the same critic suggests (p. 219):

> The distinction between the two [primary and secondary deviation] is either in terms of etiology or the extent to which the offender has a deviant identity. Thus Lemert suggests that secondary deviation refers to a 'special class of socially defined responses which people make to problems located by societal reactions to their [primary] deviance', and it is committed by people 'whose life and identity are organised around the facts of deviance.'

These distinctions are often unworkable in theory and unproven in practice. If we take political deviancy as an example it is clear that the 'original causes of the deviation' may in no way 'recede' simply because of social reaction. Indeed, it may be argued with more justification that social reaction to radical ideas, in the form of what Gouldner (1971, p. 297) has called 'normalized repression', is the cause of initial commitment to political deviation. Furthermore it is by no means clear except in the case of political deviants and organized criminals that there are many deviants 'whose life and identity are organised around the facts of deviance' (cf. Walton, 1973).

Much of this approach *avoids the question of initial deviation* and drives it towards a dubious stress on the psychological impact of social reaction. Yet it is perfectly possible to conceive of deviants who never experience the kind of social reaction that Lemert and Becker are talking about, but are constantly committing deviant acts, for example, smoking pot, stealing, agitating, engaging in sexually deviant acts, etc. Implicit in the social reaction approach is some peculiar fascination with the attempt to erect *a priori* explanations of why some people become 'hard core' criminals and deviants and others do not. Explanations of this kind will only be revealed by looking at social contexts and beliefs. In any case the search for hard as against soft deviation seems to be based on an assumption that deviants (and especially the 'hard-core' deviants) are radically different from 'conformists'. We have indicted the social reaction approach as unsocial and psychological; the claim is not being made that social psychology is unnecessary but rather if we are to have such explanations they must in no way be a-historical. If we substituted the terms socialization for deviation it would become immediately apparent that contextually embedded beliefs and experiences may be primary determinants of commitment. But what would primary as opposed to secondary socialization mean unless we had some theory which clearly differentiated between them? The social reaction theorists have no developed theory to explain why secondary deviation is more important in commitment to deviancy than is initial deviation.

As Milton Mankoff has argued (1971, pp. 211–12):

The most salient theoretical difficulty is in the conception of initial rule-breaking and the nature of the sources which bring it into being. There is a premise in the writing of the labeling theorists that whatever the causes of initial rule-breaking, they assume minimal importance or entirely cease operation after initial rule-breaking (Scheff 1966 50–54; Lemert 1967 40). Without such a premise, one might attribute career deviance and its consequences not to societal reaction but to the continued effects of social structural strains, psychological stress, or disease states which produce initial rule-breaking.

In this connection, the labeling model fails to seriously consider the possibility that deviant behavior may be persisted in even when the rule-breaker has every opportunity to return to the status of non-deviant (Becker 1963 37), because of a positive attachment to rule-breaking.

The rigid and often unexplored assumption, that career deviance or continued commitment deviance are to be explained in terms which are significantly different from the reasons for initial deviance, stands in the way of a fully social explanation. Insufficient attention is paid to developing social accounts of initial deviation which are not absolutist, but which could be as sensitive in their considerations of initial deviance as the social reaction theorists are with respect to secondary deviation. Indeed not only are explanations of initial deviancy not necessarily incompatible with explanations of secondary deviance, but these are not two separate phenomena. Why people commit and continue to commit deviant acts, requires explanation in terms of the totality of social processes in operation within society. 'Action-social reaction-deviant reaction' are, of course, all analytically separable, but empirically they are linked. Akers (1967, p. 463) is correct when he suggests that: 'the label does not create the behavior in the first place. People can and do commit deviant acts because of the particular contingencies and circumstances in their lives, quite apart from or in combination with the labels others apply to them.'

We are saying with Akers, Mankoff and others that the contingencies and circumstances of everybody's lives entail a study of society at large. It makes necessary the study of social conflicts, power and interest, and the way in which the social processes have constraining effects upon the shape of law and social reactions.

By direct implication, we are led to examine the causes of deviancy as lying ultimately in the larger social inequalities of power and authority. In other terms, we come to see larger parts of deviant behaviour as actions often consciously evolved by individuals in order to meet problems generated in and by a society over which they have very little control. An explanation of initial deviance (rule-breaking) as the result of random impulses in which there are no primary causes tends to deny that these deviant solutions can have real meaning for the individual. The adolescent, for example, steals 'on a whim'; he becomes a delinquent on being labelled. His stealing is not really seen as a meaningful act, perhaps as an attempt to resolve inequalities, or a means of obtaining excitement or goods which he cannot obtain legitimately in the course of his everyday life. We want to argue that many people commit deviant acts as a result of making choices.

The making of choices was precisely the emphasis intended in many social reaction theorists' accounts of deviant action. However, because of their over-concentration on the distinction between primary and secondary deviation, rational calculation or any degree of self-consciousness about deviant action is usually dealt with only in the case of secondary deviation. A clear example of this is Lemert's discussion of what he calls the 'law of effect' (1967, p. 54):

> Restated and applied to deviance, the law of effect is a simple idea that people beset with problems posed for them by society will choose lines of action they expect to be satisfactory solutions to the problems. If the consequences are those expected, the likelihood that the action or generically similar action will be repeated is increased.

One might think from this that Lemert's 'law of effect' would apply to all human behaviour. But here again the over-reliance on one particular social process leads the social reaction theorists in general, and Lemert in particular, to view initial deviants as passive recipients of the kind of stigmatization, which then opens up choices but choices within the confines of a deviant career. Thus, Lemert, although he refers at points to the possibility of 'hedonistic' or 'calculative' deviance, actually contradicts his own 'law of effect' by reserving it for secondary deviants. Lemert (1967, p. 53, our emphasis) writes:

> Thus far I have offered a sociological brief for some form of neo-hedonistic theory of secondary deviance. Baldly reduced, it says that persons become secondary deviants because they manage to find more satisfactory solutions to their problems through deviance than through non-deviance: *the nature of their problem solving differs because degradation and newly perceived contingencies change their conceptions of what is satisfying.*

If Lemert and the social reaction theorists were to be consistent and thoroughgoing in their belief in man's ability to choose, they would not reserve their remarks for those situations in which men confront the problems posed by secondary deviation: it would pervade their analysis of initial infractions too.

Actually, Lemert does endow his deviant actors with a considerable powers to choose, but the choices are of a kind that is not available to non-deviant individuals. He writes (1967, p. 17):

> There is a processual aspect to deviation, whose acknowledgement is forced on us by the fact that with repetitive, persistent deviation or invidious differentiation, something happens 'inside the skin' of the deviating person. Something gets built into the psyche or nervous system as a result of social penalties, or degradation ceremonies, or as a consequence of having

155

been made the subject of 'treatment' or 'rehabilitation'. The individual's perception of values, means, and estimates of their costs undergoes revision in such ways that symbols which serve to limit the choices of most people produce little or no response in him, or else engender responses contrary to those sought by others.

The deviant seems here to be endowed with *more* choice than the non-deviant. He is a fundamentally different person for having experienced the fact of secondary deviation. He is, in Lemert's terms, a 'degraded individual' (ibid., p. 54). Contrary to many interpretations, the social reaction theorists, operating with a distinction between inseparable social processes (action and reaction), do on occasion differentiate the deviant from the non-deviant person: they do indulge in what Matza (1964, ch. 1) has called the fallacy of positive differentiation. The 'degraded individual' is accorded a morally *inferior* range of choices. His rationality is seen as different from that of the apparent conformist. And, as Mankoff (1971, p. 216) has pungently observed, 'the implicit notions of human passivity [in the social reaction theorists], so characteristic of behaviorism, seem out of place in a sociological tradition that has been founded upon penetrating observations of the creative potential of human beings.' For us, in one sense at least, deviants are always rational creatures; like any other persons, they engage in choice and evaluation.

It is, of course, the case that being deviant means that the actor's ends and purposes are frequently opposed to those of other groups: given that the attempt rationally to isolate any one particular end involves us in a consideration of the actor's other ends, purposes and values, rationality may be defined operationally as the optimum balance between all these factors (cf. I. Taylor and Walton, 1970). However distasteful we find the ends of particular deviants, and by whatever processes (including the process of social reaction) we see them arriving at these ends, it is still the case that their actions are based on the same process of achieving an 'optimum balance' as anyone else's. Lemert, working in the Meadian tradition, has attempted to avoid the logic of his own liberal position by suggesting that the symbolic change in self actually results in deviants evaluating ends and purposes in some fundamentally different fashion.

Lemert's work is important for the questions it poses of absolutist and positivistic conceptions of deviance. However, it suffers from exactly those problems that C. Wright Mills has identified in the tradition of American pragmatism. In a brilliant piece entitled 'Social psychology for liberals' (1966, p. 447), Wright Mills argued that:

Now there were two features of the general instinctivist view which liberals wished to overcome or to replace: they wanted to give mind, rationality, a place in nature and in the psychology of human affairs; and they wanted to see human nature as modifiable through the reconstruction of the social 'environment'. They wanted substantive rationality to prevail and to be diffused by mass education, but they wanted to deny the political implications of historical individualism. It is between these two poles that the social psychological tradition of pragmatism is worked out.

If we were to allow that individuals are both determined and determining, then we would have to build a consistent processual model which allows for this conception of man and situates it in a total analysis of social processes rather than merely in one aspect of them. As we shall see later, one of the implications of taking up a fully social analysis of the reasons for initial deviation is that it would lead us beyond liberalism: and to develop a structural analysis involving a radical critique of power and inequality.

It is not simply that Lemert's distinction between primary and secondary deviation is untenable in a rigid form[4] but that Lemert himself contradicts many of his own symbolic and social psychological assumptions when he criticizes the concept of the deviant career (advanced by Becker (1963, p. 24) and others). Some theorists have argued that the concept of career is important in drawing sequential models of deviant behaviour. Lemert, as with us, recognizes the difficulties (which he does not acknowledge elsewhere) of drawing such models for, as he suggests (1967, p. 51): 'A career denotes a course to be run, but the delineation of fixed sequences or stages through which persons move from less to more serious deviance is difficult or impossible to reconcile with an interactional theory.'

But this is precisely our objection to the insistence by the social reaction theorists upon sequences leading from primary to secondary deviation: that it is not fully reconcilable with an interactional position, laying emphasis as it does on only one side of social processes, the determinants of which have to be assessed and not assumed.

Becker reveals similar contradictions. In arguing for a modified version of the career concept, Becker is led to a position which is either definitional or unproven (1963, p. 39): 'Thus the deviant who enters an organized and institutionalized deviant group is more likely than ever before to continue in his ways. He has learned, on the one hand, how to avoid trouble and on the other hand, a rationale for continuing.'

Here, Becker is reiterating what he believes to be the difference between 'rule-breakers' and 'deviants'; that is, a distinction between the mere infringers of norms on the one hand and people labelled deviant and therefore committed to deviancy on the other. Thus Lemert, Becker and others have often argued that commitment is to be explained in terms of social reaction. But Becker, like Lemert, abandons this position in more clear-thinking moments. In his 'Notes on the concept of commitment' Becker (1960, pp. 32–40) argues the position that we have been insisting on throughout this chapter. He writes (p. 36):

> Whenever we propose commitment as an explanation of consistency in behavior, we must have independent observations of the major components in such a proposition: (1) *prior actions of the person staking some originally extraneous interest on his following a consistent line of activity*; (2) a recognition by him of the involvement of this originally extraneous interest in his present activity; and (3) the resulting consistent line of activity [our emphasis].

We hear little or nothing of the 'prior actions' of the person and his 'extraneous interest' in Becker's own theoretical writings on deviance. Time and time again, Becker, Lemert and others' contributions to the theory of deviance are contradicted in their own work. Essentially, this seems to us to be bound up with their refusal to allow deviant actors the kind of choices allowed to men in general.

Sometimes, however, a bridge is built between the deviant and the non-deviant set of choices. It is possible, Lemert argues, for deviants to 'normalize' their deviant acts. The deviant's strategy is to persuade the social audience to accept his rule of behaviour. Lemert argues that acceptance is most easily achieved within 'primary groups', but unlikely in the wider society. Indeed, in perceptive moments, Lemert allows that, even when fully affected by social reaction, deviants may escape entry into a determinate sequential career.[5] Flexible as he might be about the choices open to deviants here, Lemert does not see these choices operating at other points. We are, inevitably, led to ask, therefore, whether we are being presented with a theory (a consistent and interrelated set of hypothetical concepts) or whether we are merely being offered a catholic and unconnected perspective. More specifically, we must wonder whether the so-called social reaction literature, sometimes called 'transactionalism', is in fact transactional enough, or whether the transactions considered exhaust the possibilities of social control and deviant action.

Social reaction: theory or perspective?

For the present, it suffices to note that Gibbs' characterization is probably correct; by itself the labeling approach (with its lack of clear-cut definition, failure so far to produce a coherent set of inter-related propositions, testable hypotheses, and so on) ought not at least at this stage, to be considered a theory in any formal sense. Formal theoretical status, however, should not be the major criterion in assessing its value (Schur, 1971, p. 35).

But the new conception has left at least four crucial questions unanswered. First, what elements in the scheme are intended to be definitions rather than substantive theory? Second, is the ultimate goal to explain deviant behavior or to explain reactions to deviation? Third, is deviant behavior to be identified exclusively in terms of reaction to it? Fourth, exactly what kind of reaction identifies behavior as deviant? (Gibbs, 1966, pp. 9–14).

For us, the social reaction literature does not contain a theory as such. Rather, it represents an attempt to demystify one side of a continuous dialectic of human activity. But this activity has determinants which cannot be encompassed by any approach which relegates the etiological questions concerning the causes of deviation to an ambiguous location subsidiary to social reaction. We regard it as a pity that Lemert and others lost sight of a valuable understanding he himself expressed in one of his earlier papers (Lemert, 1948, p. 27). Here he wrote:

Interaction is not a theory or explanation at all. It does little more than set down a condition of inquiry, telling us that dynamic analysis must supplement structural analysis, and is best understood as a necessary reaction to the metaphysical explanations of human behavior current among nineteenth century writers. Further reason for rejecting interaction as a theory *per se* is that it results in a directionless inquiry ending in a morass of dog-in-the-mangerish variables, none of which have priority or provide a formula for prediction.

The same may be said of the 'social reaction' literature, except that it does have a direction. The direction, however, is one-sided. Lemert's own dismissal of primary deviation as 'polygenetic, arising out of a variety of social, cultural, psychological, and physiological factors' smacks of just such a formula for 'directionless enquiry' into the causes of initial deviation itself.

159

But if the social reaction approach is not a theory, what is it? For us, it is a *description*, in analytical language, of agreed-upon concepts of various (previously under-described) aspects of social reality.

There are inevitable weaknesses in this approach: for when it comes to the task of *explanation*, there is a tendency amongst all the 'social reaction' writers to operate with an essentially linear rather than a transactional view of the determinants of human action. Thus, it is often difficult to know whether the social reaction theorists, at any particular point in their analysis, are engaged in *causal analysis* or whether they are merely offering out a description. Lemert, for instance, in arguing that social control must be taken as an independent variable worthy of study in itself (rather than something derived from the fact of deviance), does assert that (1967, p. 18): 'Thus conceived, social control becomes a "cause" rather than an effect of the magnitude and variable forms of deviation.' Elsewhere, however, he appears to deny it (p. 52): 'Whether the imputation of self-characteristics, or "labeling" in itself initiates or causes deviant acts is something of a moot point.' Lemert attempts to resolve the problem of whether social control is in fact causal by turning towards the concept of 'process'. Indeed, the social reaction approach can be said to depend on their claim to be engaged in the sequential analysis of social processes. Writing on the relationship between law and addiction, Lemert has it that (p. 50):

it remains to be shown that the laws themselves cause addiction. . . . In this and other forms of deviance, there remains a knotty problem of assigning relative weights to the factors assumed relevant, determining their mutual effects and the order in which they occur. The solution for this methodological problem traditionally has been held by many sociologists to lie in the concept of 'process'.

The concept of process is erected, and given considerable emphasis in social reaction literature, as an alternative to the static analysis indulged in by positivistic criminologists. The sequential emphasis has been enshrined as a new mythology, involving an assumed relationship, in itself asserted rather ambiguously to be causal, between action, reaction and amplification in deviant processing. If the claim is being made that the social reaction perspective encompasses a formal model, the claim is false.

A crucial part of the social reaction mythology is the idea that social reaction necessarily amplifies the character of the initial deviation: that is, that the initial causes of deviation recede and new problems emerge for the deviant confronted by social reaction and control. In terms of any formal model, this question must be left open: it is an empirical question. It may be that, in certain periods and under certain social conditions, the 'abuse of drugs' will be stigmatized and dramatized by the social audience: under others it may not (cf. Young, 1971a). The fact of social control, as classical theorists of punishment have always understood, is always problematic: it may deter some, it may also propel others into action to change the nature of control, or it may engender self-conceptions in those affected by social control in such a way that 'amplification' does in fact occur. Whilst the effects of social control cannot be assumed to be determinate, but must be left open to study in individual cases, the interests underlying the fact of social control are indeed determinate. Thus, we would argue, the attribution of a label to an individual or a behaviour can be effective or ineffective (and is therefore not deterministic), but the question of who is labelled and why they are labelled is determined extraneously.

Interpreters of the social reaction perspective, admitting that the perspective falls short of being a formal theory, and allowing also that it has erected some ideas which may in practice be mythological, assert that it is, more or less, a paradigm, or alternatively that it is a 'sensitizing' perspective, which, if accepted, provides a fruitful redirection for research (cf. Trice and Roman, 1970; Schur, 1971). However, whether social reaction writers are engaged in paradigmatic representations or in a practice of sensitization, we still need to know with what status they want their writings and researches to be endowed. Are they intended as a contribution to the construction of a formal, social theory of deviance or not? If they are so intended, how are we expected to move from the 'paradigms' to the formal theoretical model of deviancy?

Two writers attempted seriously to deal with these issues. DeLamater, for example (1968, pp. 445–55), argues that it is essential to separate out the different levels of the analysis of deviant behaviour. He argues that there are four distinct questions to be answered in the explanation of deviance.[6] These are, first, the genesis of a deviant act or role (a structural question); second, the maintenance of a role (again, a structural question); third, the reasons for an actor engaging in a deviant act (a social-psychological question) and, finally, what maintains the actor's commitment to deviant activity (once more, a social-psychological question). DeLamater's contribution is important in demonstrating, in a formal analytical exercise, that there are structural and social-psychological questions which need to be answered in a fully social and comprehensive theory of deviance. The social reaction writers pay lip-service to such necessities: they tend always in practice to fall short of explanations encompassing these separate questions.

DeLamater highlights also the problem of distinguishing between the activities of *formal* and *informal* agencies of social control. The

161

social reaction theorists, are of course, fully aware of this distinction (Lemert, 1967; Wheeler, 1968)[7] but they tend to see it as an empirical rather than a theoretical problem. They are engaged in spelling out the interrelationships of formal control agencies (e.g. the courts and the mental hospitals) with informal agencies (e.g. 'significant others') in actual social processes. Again, it is never clear whether these empirical accounts are to be taken as a contribution to a theory of formal and informal social control, and, if so, in what way.

The most developed criticism, however, of social reaction theorists, is a recent paper by Milton Mankoff (1971, pp. 204–18). Although he is aware that the social reaction writers are reticent about the 'generalisability' or the theoretical status of their work, Mankoff is concerned to consider the limits of the social reaction 'model' for explaining career deviance. Specifically, he intends to provide tentative answers to the following three queries (Mankoff, 1971, p. 205):

(1) Is social reaction to rule-breaking a necessary and sufficient condition for career deviance?

(2) Is societal reaction to rule-breaking equally significant in the determination of career deviance for all kinds of rule-breaking phenomena, or is it best applied to a limited number of rule-breaking phenomena?

(3) What are the most serious obstacles to an adequate assessment of the theory?

The argument is that the social reaction theorists have failed to distinguish between two types of rule-breaking: *ascribed* and *achieved* rule-breaking. *Ascribed rule-breaking* is characterized, for Mankoff, by a particular physical or visible impairment. The ascribed rule-breaker acquires his deviant status irrespective of his particular actions or wishes. Thus (p. 205) 'the very beautiful and the very ugly can be considered ascriptive rule-breakers.' By contrast, *achieved rule-breaking* involves '*activity* on the part of the rule-breaker regardless of his positive attachment to a deviant way of life' (our emphasis). 'The embezzler who attempts to conceal his rule-breaking behavior, no less than the regular marijuana user, who freely admits his transgression, has had to achieve rule-breaking status, at least to some extent, on the strength of his own actions' (ibid., p. 205). Mankoff uses these distinctions in order to demonstrate the 'severe limitations of labelling theory as a general theory of career deviance' (p. 206). He points out that many of the social reaction or labelling theorists have been concerned with effects of social reaction on the physically or visibly handicapped and that, in such cases of ascriptive deviance, it is obvious that social reaction is a *necessary* condition for deviant careers, involving people 'who would not normally interfere with conventional role-playing: for example, dwarfs, the extremely ugly and blacks'. However, as he indicates, whilst it might be a *necessary* condition, it is not necessarily a *sufficient* condition. The question hinges on whether social reaction itself represents a *sufficient* condition for *ascriptive rule-breaking*: that is, as he suggests, it can always be argued that severe social reactions can be successful in preventing ascribed rule-breakers from taking up normal roles, and thus in forcing them inexorably into deviant careers. But, as he insists, one could not argue this unless one was able to spell out the differential effects of differences in the severity of social reaction, something which their formal model clearly fails to do. Thus, the assertion that severe social reaction forces ascribed rule-breakers into career deviance is untestable. Whilst it may be that social reaction 'theory' is valid, in the abstract, it cannot link the severity of social reaction to handicaps in different historical periods and under different social arrangements to any process which *necessarily* forces them into a deviant career. Yet *ascribed deviance* fulfils (more than *achieved deviance*) the basic requirements of rule-breaking phenomena to which the labelling paradigm is typically applied. That is, it is highly visible rule-breaking that is totally dependent on social reaction whilst being totally independent of the intentions of the rule-breaker. If labelling or social reaction theory falls short of providing an explanation of the *necessary* and *sufficient* conditions for this form of deviance, it must necessarily fail rather more seriously with the more complex forms of rule-breaking in the cases of *achieved deviance*.

Achieved rule-breaking, for Mankoff, actually requires the 'commission of a norm-violating act by the rule-breaker'. The research work of the social reaction theorists themselves can be used to question whether social reaction to rule-breaking is a *necessary* condition for achieved rule-breaking. Indeed, Becker's own study of marijuana-users appears to be an illustration of career deviance primarily determined by hedonism, unaffected by the fact of a social audience. In one of the author's own studies, into industrial sabotage, it was revealed that a number of motivations informed the continued use of sabotage on the shop-floor, some of which related to men's instrumentality and some of which were merely responses to given structural conditions (L. Taylor and Walton, 1971). It was clear in this study that men continued to use sabotage for a variety of reasons which has nothing whatever to do with social reaction. These examples and others (Cressey, 1953; Schwendinger, 1961) illustrate the possibility of consistently *achieved rule-breaking*, unmediated by the intervention of social reaction.

Is then the social reaction approach a sufficient condition in the explanation of *achieved rule-breaking*? Just as the severity of social reaction to *ascribed rule-breaking* is problematic, so (it follows) is

163

the question of reaction to *achieved rule-breaking* insufficient in itself. Indeed, even in the extreme case of incarceration, the empirical data on the extent to which people's self-images alter and the extent to which they accept the values of other institutionalized career deviants is open to various interpretations (Box, 1971, pp. 230–51 and Irwin and Cressey, 1962). Thus, in the real world, *achieved rule-breaking* can be taken up and dropped; the rule-breaker is not automatically propelled by the nature of social reaction into a permanent deviant career.

One of the tenets of the social reaction perspective which, as we said earlier, has achieved a mythological status in some writings and some sociological circles, is that social reaction to rule-breaking necessarily *amplifies* the nature and characteristics of the deviant act. Great emphasis is placed on the possibility of deviant actors adjusting and reacting to the ascription of labels to their behaviour, no matter how spurious the labels (Simmons, 1969). However, in the real world, the reverse can occur. *Achieved rule-breakers* are frequently deterred by the possibility of social control. And *ascribed rule-breakers* can organize to change societal values and/or social structure and to rid themselves of the stigma ascribed to their particular handicap. But even here social reaction would be neither a necessary nor sufficient explanation of how people are, on the one hand, deterred by the fact of social reaction, or how they are moved to attempt to change it (Walton, 1973). If we follow Mankoff in his distinction between ascribed and achieved rule-breaking, it is apparent that 'deviancy amplification' is *not* an inevitable result of involvement in rule-breaking, and that, therefore, in many cases, 'social reaction' is *neither* a necessary *nor* a sufficient explanation (nor indeed a description) of career deviance (Wilkins, 1964).[8]

Mankoff concludes his excellent examination of the theory of social reaction and its relationship to emprical evidence in the following terms. In so doing, he points to many of the problems with which we have been concerned in this section: the social reaction perspective's status as a 'theory' (or otherwise) (1971, p. 216):

> Among the theoretical problems are the previously stated failure to consider the *continuing* effects of the social structural and psychological sources of initial rule-breaking in the development of career deviance, the lack of sources of concern with the vulnerability of certain rule-breakers to self-labeling processes which may reduce the significance of *objective* labeling practices in determining deviant careers, and the related omission of any serious analysis of the types and severity of actual social sanction which facilitate 'successful' labeling. Ultimately, students of deviance will have to reconsider the mechanistic

assumptions of labeling theory when applied to achieved and to a lesser degree ascribed rule-breaking.

For us, then, the social reaction perspective cannot be seen as a full-blown theory: it stands as a one-sided exercise in the demystification of some of the faults of earlier positivistic sociologies of crime and deviance. A fully-social theory of deviance would require extension far beyond these limits. We have indicted the social reaction perspective for its inability to spell out the formal requirements of a model. An adequate model of all the processes involved in the evolution of deviant action, if laid out formally, would look something like the following:

1. *Wider origins.* Underlying and societal determinants of deviant action. These are to be sought in structural, cultural and social-psychological conflicts existing in the wider society.

2. *Immediate origins.* The situated background of deviant action. General problems pertaining to that particular type of deviancy.

3. *The actual act.* Set against the background of (1) and (2), an attempt to examine the nature of the action: is it problem-solving? Is it instrumental? Is it expressive? Is it individual or is it collective? What attempts at an 'optimum balance' of rationality are consciously made by the deviant?

4. *The immediate origins of social reaction.* What form does the social reaction take? Is it variable in severity and degree? Is it informal or formal? Is it widespread or is it specific?

5. *Wider origin of social reaction.* Structural contexts of social reaction. Are there vested interests? How is social reaction maintained? Is it variable or is it constant?

6. *The outcome of social reaction on the deviant's further action or commitment.* Is the content of social reaction internalized or resisted by the deviant? Does amplification occur? Or does it deter? Does social reaction circumscribe deviant choices or change the range of choices?

7. *Persistence and change of action.* The content, direction and persistence of deviant action must be constantly reassessed in the light of 1–6. Particular attention should be paid here to shifts in the structure of opportunity for types of deviants and whether they vary coterminously with, or independently of, shifts in social reaction.

We shall return to further discussion of this formal model in the conclusion. Simply to state such requirements, however, is to illuminate the limited nature of what is probably the most popular form of so-called contemporary deviancy theory: for it can easily be seen that its concentration is on the elements (3), (4), and (6) to the almost total exclusion of the other three.

Power and politics

Earlier, following C. Wright Mills, we argued that social reaction 'theory' suffered from the same political and epistemological short-comings that characterized early American pragmatism: namely, its liberal character. More recently, two English writers (L. Taylor and I. Taylor, 1968) have said the same of most criminological schools of thought. Identifying Mertonian and functional approaches as being underpinned by a conservative theory of values, they also suggested that (p. 30):

> Much the same can be said about labelling (or transactional) theory which also attracts its share of radical adherents. This concentrates on the way in which those who accidentally or unintentionally break the rules governing the playing of the machine are dealt with by society, by describing the way in which people are defined by others (by societal reaction) as delinquents, drug addicts or mental patients. In other words, what starts out as an attack upon the official or unofficial power-holders in society (e.g. probation officers, teachers and policemen) emerges as a complex theoretical edifice with arguable psychological assumptions and considerable political ambiguity. Of course there are definers and defined but what do the definers represent? What interests are they defending? How do their actions reinforce the existing nature of capitalist society? No answers to such questions are provided: the definers are a group of free-floating 'baddies'.

In the same way as the social reaction theorists attempted to endow the deviant with the power and ability to exercise choice, and failed (relegating choice to the experience of secondary deviation), so the social reaction theorists attempted to infuse their analysis of deviance with a sense of powerful interest groups and individuals enforcing a deviant label on to subordinate groups. Indeed, Howard Becker (1967) is so convinced of the division of society into interests that he argues that deviancy theorists have to take sides with one interest or another. Again, however, the promise (in this case, of a structural analysis) is not fulfilled.

Becker's own attempt to discuss the creation of laws relies heavily upon his notion of 'moral enterprise'. He distinguishes between two sets of individuals or entrepreneurs: the crusading reformers (e.g. prohibitionists and abolitionists) who are responsible for the creation or destruction of law, and the rule-enforcers, who are responsible for the application of any new law once it has become statutory (1963, ch. 8). This division leads Becker into a rather cursory discussion of the role of interest. Whereas the rather 'moral' rule-creators may well believe that 'their mission is a holy one', the rule-enforcer 'may not be interested in the content of the rule itself, but only in the fact that the existence of the rule provides him with a job, a profession, and a raison d'être' (p. 156). However, this very important distinction, which highlights the different kinds of interests informing rule-creation and rule-enforcement, is never fully utilized in Becker, in explaining, for instance, his own illustrative case of the Marijuana Tax Act (pp. 135–46). Becker has been correctly criticized by Dickson (1968, pp. 143–56) for not noting that:

> Similar to the earlier expansion of narcotics legislation, the Marihuana Tax Act was the result of a bureaucratic response to environmental pressure—that the Narcotics Bureau, faced with a *non-supportive environment* and a *decreasing budgetary expropriation* [our emphasis] that threatened its survival, generated a crusade against marihuana use which resulted in the passage of the act and the alteration of a societal value.

It is not that structural analysis (whether of the variety advocated by Dickson or some other variety) is precluded in the social reaction perspective, but rather that it remains consistently under-applied. Gouldner has suggested, in a well-known article (1968, p. 107) that the under-application of any structural analysis

> is inherent in the very conception of the processes by means of which deviance is conceived of as being generated. For the emphasis in Becker's theory is on the deviant as the product of society rather than as the rebel against it. If this is a liberal conception of deviance that wins sympathy and tolerance for the deviant, it has the paradoxical consequence of inviting us to view the deviant as a passive nonentity who is responsible neither for his suffering nor its alleviation—who is more 'sinned against than sinning'. Consistent with this view of the underdog as victim, is the more modern conception of him as someone who has to be managed, and should be managed better, by a bureaucratic apparatus of official care-takers. In short, it conceives of the underdog as someone maltreated by a bureaucratic establishment whose remedial efforts are ineffectual, whose custodial efforts are brutal, and whose rule enforcement techniques are self-interested. While it sees deviance as generated by a process of social interaction, as emerging out of the matrix of an unanalysed society, it does not see deviance as deriving from the specific master institutions of this larger society, or as expressing an active opposition to them.

Liberal values are no substitute for clear-headed sociological analysis. In the 1970s, indeed, liberalism as a political creed—which

manifests itself in a theoretical ambiguity (the recognition of structure, but the absence of structural *analysis*)—has been rapidly out-
paced by the progress of events in the world it claims to explain. As
Milton Mankoff (1971, p. 215) has put it:

> Liberal sociologists may not be able to have their cake and
> eat it; either certain 'subversive' forms of rule-breaking may
> have to be suppressed by police-state methods, or social life
> may have to be reorganized around values other than profit,
> productivity and puritanism.[9]

It is surprising that the social reaction theorists, arguing as they
do for the analysis of social control, have made no explicit reference
to recent contribution by sociologists working in the 'interest-group'
tradition to the analysis of law. Chambliss, for example, in a well-
known paper on the vagrancy laws in medieval England (1964, pp.
67–77) has argued that

> the . . . laws emerged in order to provide the powerful land-
> owners with a ready supply of cheap labour. When this was no
> longer necessary and particularly when the landowners were
> no longer dependent upon cheap labour nor were they a
> powerful interest group in the society the laws became dormant
> . . . a new interest group emerged and was seen as being of
> great importance to the society and the laws were altered so as
> to afford some protection to this group.

The failure of the social reaction theorists, concerned not only
with the content and nature of social control but also, by declaration,
with the reconciliation of criminological and social thought, to build
a bridge with the sociology of law, and the traditions of grand
sociology from which this area of study has grown, is an outstanding
omission. Marx and Durkheim, as we show in this book, were both
taken up with the relationship between social control (whether to
be seen as the law of the propertied or as the collective conscience
associated with a particular division of labour) and individual
human action: they were both concerned, in a sense, to delineate
the areas of freedom and constraint made possible by particular
social arrangements of 'order', and, thus, the particular form that
the law and everyday rules for action could assume. Like the prag-
matists before them, the social reaction theorists, operating within
the confines of liberal ideologies, fail to lay bare the structured
inequalities in power and interest which underpin the processes
whereby the laws are created and enforced (the processes referred to
in individualistic fashion by Becker in his discussion of moral
enterprise). Our position here attempts to confront the way in which
authority and interests enforce and maintain sets of laws, rules and

norms which in themselves are part and parcel of the creation of deviancy. It is unfortunate that, in examining the problematics of societal consensus, the social reaction theorists choose to ignore the way in which deviancy and criminality are shaped by society's larger structure of power and institutions.

As Gouldner states (1971, p. 295): 'legitimacy and authority never eliminate power—they merely defocalize it, make it latent. How could authority eliminate power when it becomes, in short, "normalized repression"?'

Our contention is that much deviancy must be viewed as a struggle, or reaction, against such 'normalized repression', a breaking-through, as it were, of accepted, taken-for-granted, power-invested commonsense rules.

The outcome—the everyday conception of what is right, the common-sense world in which both normals and deviants live, is then fully seen as having been shaped by entrenched positions of power and interest. In so far as it is legitimate to view deviance as a challenge to authority at either the instrumental or oppositional level, it must also be viewed as ultimately predetermined by structural inequalities and ideologically enforced consensus, *no matter how complex the mediatory variables.* From this viewpoint, structured inequalities, preserved and protected by the powerful, act as causal forces *preventing* the realization of actors' interests by means other than deviant ones. Our view of this repression follows Gouldner's statement in *The Coming Crisis of Western Sociology* (1971, p. 297) that:

> The powerful are both ready and able to institutionalize compliance with the moral code at levels congenial to themselves. *Power is* amongst other things this ability to enforce one's moral claims. The powerful can thus conventionalize their moral defaults. As their moral failures become customary and expected, this itself becomes another justification for giving the subordinate group less than it might theoretically claim under the group's common values. It becomes, in short, *normalized repression.*

Following Gouldner, we are suggesting that it is useful to view deviancy as a break from the moral bind involved in ongoing 'normalized' repression. Whether deviants merely neutralize this moral code in order to justify their breakthrough, or whether they develop an ideological opposition to the code, is not at stake here (though it will be fully discussed in chapter 6). What is clear is that this view of deviancy deals with what we can now isolate as *the missing element of power in the creation of deviancy.* For whilst the social reaction perspective deals with the power of public pressure and differential rule-enforcement in the creation of deviancy, it does not deal with the larger processes which form the governing framework for the smaller processes and transactions.

When we single out these theorists as being guilty of this omission, it is not because it is any more guilty than any other variety of sociological theorizing in criminology but because it held out the promise of a fully sociological account, and failed to deliver.

We have suggested that the social reaction perspective falls far short of a 'theory' of deviancy. In trying to correct the limitations of the structural approach of Merton and others, it has ignored the structure of power and interest. But a relevant theory of deviancy must treat the causal variables—motivation and reaction—as determinate and as part of a total structure of social relationships. If we examine the creation of deviancy and reaction in this way, we do not end up with a completely indeterminate picture: we see that the institution of private property, in a stratified and inequitable society, divides men from men as owners and non-owners. It is in the light of this division that the activities of thieves, police, magistrates and property-owners become explicable. Again, in a sharply competitive industrial society with a high premium set on technological innovation, big business creates, fosters and cynically condemns industrial espionage. A society which expands its higher educational system at a phenomenal rate and is unable to provide interesting or materially rewarding jobs is likely to be faced with a problem of student militancy on an ever-increasing scale. In all these cases of deviance—thieves, industrial spies and student rebels—no explanation is possible without a detailed social history of the constraints, aspirations and meanings which inform and activate the actors. And in all of these above respects, social reaction 'theory' must be found to be lacking.

Conclusions

Throughout our discussion of the various approaches to the explanations of crime and deviancy, we have been concerned to identify the ability of each 'theory' to meet certain formal, substantive and theoretical requirements, implicit in a general social theory of deviance.

Whilst recognizing the substantial contribution made by social reaction approach to the illumination of the processes of societal reaction, the ways in which different acts and actors are more or less likely to be apprehended, labelled, and stigmatized, we have developed a critique which is intended to highlight the failure of this approach to deal with the wider or indeed the immediate origins of deviancy, its avoidance of a discussion of the causes of the societal reaction and its narrowing down on to a focus upon the important, but limited, questions of the outcome of societal reaction on a deviant's further behaviour.

It is in this process that the motives and interests of the deviant actors have been befogged in the social reaction approach. What is necessary is that, having rejected the assertion that deviancy 'is not a property of the act', we should be able to move towards a structural sociology on the one hand (a sociology competent to deal with power and interests) and a sociology of motivation on the other (a sociology that can account for the way in which individuals give meaning to their acts).

It is this latter concern—the concern with how social meanings are constituted—that has become the chief prerogative of a group of theorists which we shall call the ethnomethodologists. As we shall see, their concern has been the creation and destruction of meaning at the micro-level. This is the problem to which we turn in chapter 6.

In sum, the social reaction revolt against the structuralism of the Mertonian anomie theorists, and the subcultural critics is, for us, an over-reaction. In the study of deviancy as in the study of society at large, what is required is a sociology that combines structure, process and culture in a continuous dialectic.

6   American naturalism and phenomenology

The work of David Matza

> My purpose in writing a book of this sort is that the pictures of
> delinquency that thus far have been drawn do not remind me
> and many others of the real things which they purport to
> explain. It is not that they distort reality, for all pictures do that,
> but that rather, in distorting reality, current pictures seem to
> lose what is essential in the character of the deviant enterprise
> (Matza, 1964, p. 2).

> Each digression was allegedly justified by my implicit claim
> that the process of becoming deviant made little human sense
> without understanding the philosophical inner life of the subject
> as he bestows meaning upon the events and materials that
> beset him (Matza, 1969a, p. 176).

The major theme in Matza's work (around which several variations
are developed) is *naturalism*: the constant attempt to remain true
to the phenomenon one is studying. His objection to other theories
of deviance is that they distort the essence of deviant reality—that
in the process of explaining deviancy they provide accounts of
deviance that just do not tally with what the deviants themselves
would recognize or give as motivational accounts for their own
actions. In one important sense, then, Matza's work is an attempt to
re-address and redirect criminologists and sociologists to the central
question of the relationship between beliefs and action. He correctly
argues that, 'Delinquency is fundamentally the translation of beliefs
to action. There are many variants of this formulation and there are
many disputes. But the disputes centre on the process by which
delinquents come to have such peculiar commitments' (1964, p. 19).
    Matza's resolution of the relationship between beliefs and actions

172

is at once both theoretical and methodological: his methodological prescription (like that of the ethnomethodologists whom we shall examine later in this chapter) is deceptively simple: 'Tell it like it is'. Matza's theoretical pronouncements ultimately tie in well with this slogan, for he suggests that if we 'tell it like it is' consistently, we will discover that there is no antagonistic disjunction between deviant or subterranean values and the values of larger society. Rather deviant values are held to only intermittently and are an extension of pre-existing societal beliefs, attitudes and predispositions. Thus Matza's latest book, *Becoming Deviant*, shares a concern with other American phenomenologists (the ethnomethodologists in particular) to show how beliefs and actions are related in the mind of social actors via the process of constructing meaning. In describing the 'philosophical inner life of the subject as he bestows meaning upon events', Matza recommends to his readers what he terms the *naturalistic perspective*. This is the attempt to give an accurate and truthful description of phenomena in their own right rather than to describe or explain them in order to correct, reform or eradicate them (the *correctional perspective*).

It is at this very general level that we shall discover our disagreements with Matza—for, whilst we see the importance and necessity of a social theory of deviancy which 'strives to remain true to the phenomena under study' (Matza, 1969a, p. 5), we do not agree with his theoretical explanation of how these phenomena are constituted or created. For instance, Matza's work is importantly concerned to attack rigid or hard deterministic views of deviant action, to abolish notions of the pathology of deviant phenomena and to stress its similarity with any other piece of action by insisting that deviants exhibit choice. So Matza offers us a view of deviants which is indeed a considerable advance upon the social reaction theorists who frequently hold to a one-sided determinism. But in attempting (correctly) to rid us of any commitment to any correctional view of deviancy, Matza himself often slips into an avoidance of larger etiological questions. Yet it is precisely these questions which have led us into a radical approach to criminology. As one otherwise highly favourable reviewer wrote of Matza's last book (L. Taylor, 1970, p. 6): 'The disagreement between philosophers is not about how faithful they should be to the nature of the phenomenon but about what exactly is the real nature of the phenomenon.' Unless we are careful, therefore, the naturalistic perspective can lead (as it does with many ethnomethodologists) into a position where the only true account of how the deviant phenomena come into being, and what its real nature is, can be given by the deviants themselves. This position is paradoxically (and Matza thrives on paradoxes) both true and untrue. It is clearly true that what deviants believe must be the

173

motor force behind their actions, since beliefs and action are not separate phenomena. But it is also the case that what they believe may be false, even when it is regarded by them as true. There will obviously be important etiological differences in our accounts of those deviants whose action we believe is informed by false beliefs and those deviants whose beliefs we believe to be true. But the overall danger here is to deny the theorist any right to question the validity of the deviant beliefs in his assessment of the actor's social situation. A white-collar worker who joins a fascist organization may believe that his financial predicament is a function of the Jewish control of the economy. He has a set of beliefs about the causes of his social situation and also a set of directives as to how to ameliorate it. Although, by definition, we must take into consideration these beliefs in our account of his behaviour, we may be able to show that his causal assessment of the problem and the means of solving it are both palpably false. We may be able to show that his explanation of his position and its resolution are the products of the dissemination of false beliefs about the underlying social structure. Concepts are used as much to mystify as to clarify social reality. False beliefs may motivate men but their causal and predictive efficacy must be challenged by the social theorist.

Matza sometimes over-extends his humanistic antagonism to the correctional perspective and suggests that to appreciate the deviant enterprise is to deny oneself the right to disagree or to condemn. Thus we can understand or condemn deviants, but are not able to do both. He goes so far as to suggest that (1969a, p. 15): 'The goal of ridding ourselves of the deviant phenomenon, however utopian, stands in sharp contrast to an appreciative perspective and may be referred to as correctional.' But this juxtaposition is false, for it blurs the distinction between individual and society, and like much subjective phenomenology slips into false dichotomies. For instance, we may wish to rid society of thieving by abolishing the precondition for theft—namely private property. It is perfectly possible to wish to be rid of a certain deviant phenomenon whilst appreciating and grasping its significance within present society. Indeed Matza's own work on the disreputable poor does exactly this (1967; 1971a). Whilst wishing for poverty to be abolished in a process which would give 'all power to the people', he gives an illuminating description of how the 'disreputable poor' are demoralized, and how that demoralization helps to sustain their deviant position. In short, there is a difference between wanting the correction of individuals, and wanting the correction of beliefs which are false (i.e. demoralization) and which sustain an unequal repressive and criminal-producing society. One can attack the correctional component as an ideology whilst avoiding the kind of subjective relativism which treats both true and false beliefs as having the same causal efficacy in the creation of deviancy. A considerable amount of deviant action is falsely-conscious in the sense that it is not fully conscious of its own constitution. The false view of society encouraged and propagated by the powerful is one of the constitutive features in the causal chain which encourages acceptance of a set of constraints which are not in fact necessarily eternal or unchangeable. Thus, the 'disreputable poor' are demoralized and their false consciousness helps to sustain a fundamentally inequitable system. Our argument is, then, that Matza's final inability to link his illuminating sociology of motivation with its larger structural determinates often leads him to lapse into the kind of subjectivism for which we shall later criticize the ethnomethodologists. In fact, Matza's work is ultimately saved from this unambiguous fate by his sensitive (if rather covert) recognition of these problems. He is *not* unaware of the possibility of the kind of critique offered here and in a recent interview had this to say of his own work: 'I decided that though *Delinquency and Drift* and *Becoming Deviant* were defensible, each missed a key point the relation between property and the state . . .' (Weis, interview, 1971 p. 42); and he went on to add that

> Actually, my first book was a critique of the juvenile courts mainly, at least that's the way I intended it. My second book, especially in the final part, is a critique of the state. So I think they partially coopted me but not completely, because I looked at the criminal, which is what you're saying they wanted me to do, but I looked at him in a way that I don't think they especially wanted me to do.

Let us return now to Matza's examination of the deviant and the criminal. The picture he gives us involves a subtle grasp of the dialectics of deviant motivation that goes a long way to obliterating many of the obstacles which stand in the way of a fully social theory of deviance.

Subterranean values, neutralization and drift

Matza's earlier work is largely taken up with explicit rejection and criticism of subcultural theory. Writing with Gresham Sykes he rejected the standard sociological descriptions of delinquent subcultures on the grounds that they characterized delinquents as holding to a system of values which were 'an inversion of the values held by respectable society' (Sykes and Matza, 1957). Sykes and Matza insisted that these descriptions represented an over-antagonistic view of the relationship between delinquent values and those of larger society. They pointed out that if delinquents really held values

175

which were antagonistic they would tend to view their illegal behaviour as morally correct. Because of such a commitment they would exhibit no sense of guilt or shame when detected, apprehended or confined. In reality, Matza argued, delinquents in such situations are often ashamed and guilty. Moreover, he asserts, it would be incorrect to see such expressions merely as a cynical attempt to win appeasement with those in authority. In reality, delinquents do seem to be committed to values which are ultimately linked to those of the wider society. Their deviancy is like much conformity to moral standards—a flexible affair. Sykes and Matza thus suggest that the adolescent is not involved in a rejection of conventional morality—rather the adolescent neutralizes the normative bind of society's legal order by 'extending' the justifications for deviance which are often implicit in either social values or legal pleas of innocence. 'Techniques of neutralization' are similar to C. Wright Mills's 'vocabularies of motives' (1943). They are phrases or linguistic utterances used by the deviant to justify his action. Their importance lies in the fact that they are not merely *ex post facto* excuses or rationalizations invented for the authorities' ears, but rather phrases which actually facilitate or motivate the commission of deviant actions by neutralizing a pre-existing normative constraint. Thus, a well-known neutralization for stealing from a company or corporation is that 'nobody suffers' or 'the insurance will pay' (cf. L. Taylor, 1972). The importance of this argument is that it is possible to conceive of deviants who are both motivated by special circumstances to commit crime but who would nevertheless agree (if asked) that they are doing 'wrong'. Their morality is not so much one which is opposed to that of larger society but is nevertheless one which definitely weakens the moral bind of that society. This leads Sykes and Matza (1957, p. 668) to suggest that:

in this sense the delinquent both has his cake and eats it too, for he remains committed to the dominant normative system and yet so qualifies its imperatives that violations are 'acceptable' if not 'right'. Thus the delinquent represents not a radical opposition to law abiding society but something more like an apologetic failure, often more sinned against than sinning in his own eyes. We call these justifications of deviance behaviour techniques of neutralization; and we believe these techniques make up a crucial component of Sutherland's 'definitions favourable to the violation of law'. It is by learning these techniques that the juveniles become delinquent, rather than by learning moral imperatives, values or attitudes standing in direct contradiction to those of the dominant society.

They list five major types of techniques of neutralization:
(1) *denial of responsibility*, e.g. 'I'm sick!'; (2) *denial of injury*, e.g. 'they can afford it'; (3) *denial of victim*, e.g. 'we weren't hurting anyone', or even, 'they had it coming to them' (cf. the discussion of blackmailers in Hepworth, 1971); (4) *condemnation of the condemners*, e.g. 'everybody is crooked', or 'everybody uses some form of drugs'; (5) *appeal to higher loyalties*, 'I didn't do it for myself' or 'I couldn't leave my mates'. The importance of Sykes and Matza's early statement is not that it claims to be correct or exhaustive (there may be six or seven types of techniques, and as they admit, some delinquents may be so isolated from the world of conformity that they have no need of such techniques.) Rather, it is important for its illumination of the way in which the effectiveness of social control can be lessened by 'neutralization'—and the previously unexamined possibility that this availability of 'techniques for neutralizing' the moral bind may lie behind a large amount of deviant behaviour.

The stress on the similarity of delinquent values and those of larger society later led Sykes and Matza to replace the notion of a *delinquent subculture* with the idea of a *subculture* of delinquency which exists in a subterranean fashion in normal society. In an article entitled 'Juvenile delinquency and subterranean values' (1961), they criticize those subcultural theories which place a great stress on the differences between delinquent and non-delinquent values. They suggest that this faulty picture is bound up with an erroneous view of the middle-class value system. If we look closely at this value system, they argue, we will find that a 'number of supposedly delinquent values are closely akin to those embodied in the leisure activities of the dominant society' (p. 712).

They go on to say that, whilst their techniques of neutralization theory could explain evasion or weakening of social control, it could not really account for the initial attractiveness of deviance. They begin by suggesting that the leisure activities of those who dominate society are not so different, in value terms, from the pursuits of the delinquents at the bottom end of the same society. They quote Thorstein Veblen's sardonic illustration of the dominant leisure class with its concept of 'machismo', its thirst for daring and adventure, the taste for conspicuous consumption. The assertion is that in 'our haste to create a standard from which deviance can be measured, we have reduced the value system of the whole society to that of the middle class. We have ignored both the fact that society is not composed exclusively of the middle class and that the middle class is far from homogenous' (ibid., p. 715). Further, society is not only split normatively into strata: contradictions occur *within* the dominant values. For coexisting alongside the overt or official values of society are a series of *subterranean* values. One of these,

177

for example, is the search for excitement: for new 'kicks'. Society, they argue, tends to provide institutionalized periods in which these subterranean values are allowed to emerge and to take precedence. Thus they write (p. 716): 'the search for adventure, excitement and thrill is a subterranean value that . . . often exists side by side with the values of security, routinization and the rest. It is not a deviant value, in any full sense, but must be held in abeyance until the proper moment and circumstances for its expression arrive.' The delinquent, far from deviating, conforms to these commonly held values yet accentuates them and is no respecter of the 'proper moment and circumstances'. Sykes and Matza summarize their position by arguing (p. 717):

> that the delinquent may not stand as an alien in the body of society but may represent instead a disturbing reflection or caricature. His vocabulary is different, to be sure, but kicks, big time spending and rep have immediate counterparts in the value system of the law abiding. The delinquent has picked up and emphasized one part of the subterranean values that coexist with other, publicly proclaimed values possessing a more respectable air.

So the motivation informing delinquent action derives from an accentuation of dominant values—coupled with the techniques of neutralization which release the individual from the vectors of social control. At no point is the motivational thrust abnormal: indeed it derives directly from conventional morality.

This insistence on the similarity of larger societal values and the values embodied in 'delinquent ideology' lies at the basis of all of Matza's work. The assertion is that deviant beliefs have to be seen as arising out of the beliefs of the wider society as well as in opposition to them. There is, in this sense, a dialectic at play which goes unrecognized in more static versions of subcultural theory.

In an article entitled 'Subterranean traditions of youth', Matza (1961) applied this dialectic to that section of American society thought to be potentially most oppositional in values: youth. He argued that young people in America had been subjected to three major deviant patterns: delinquency, radicalism and bohemianism. The central theme in this essay is that whilst it is possible to trace differences in the vulnerability of youth to modes of rebelliousness (in terms of these three patterns)[1] it is also the case that most youth are fairly conventional. Matza explains the relationship between conventional and subterranean traditions as one of modification (1961, p. 105): 'The notion of subterranean implies that there is an ongoing dialectic between conventional and deviant traditions and that, in the process of exchange, both are modified.'

178

INSTITUTIONAL / STRUCTURAL
MORALITY &
CRIME

At the back of this argument, there seems to lie a crude model of consensus, conflict and integration. The attack on subcultural theory, interesting for other reasons, stops short of the crucial question: are the value differences between delinquents and non-delinquents (because of 'extension') ever so great as to prevent integration with more conventional traditions? For Matza, delinquents neutralize the moral code of society. But it is just as possible to argue that the accounts offered out by delinquents (and not just by bohemian and/or radical youth) represent oppositional accounts. It is possible to argue that the techniques which Matza calls techniques of neutralization are in reality an 'implicit critique' of society, which is often quite well understood by other delinquents. In attacking a crude antagonistic model of delinquency, Matza seems to fall into the trap of withdrawing any possibility of self-conscious and oppositional meaning from deviant action.

We shall attempt to deal rather discursively with three major levels of analysis implicit in Matza's work: the *motivational*, the *cultural* and the *structural* levels of analysis, by way of illustrating the continuing tendency to deny the possibility of authentic or alternative delinquent accounts.

Matza's conception of motivation in the construction of delinquency is questionable in two distinct respects. On the one hand, as we have indicated briefly, it is possible that the vocabulary of motives utilized by the actor could be a form of false consciousness. That is, the explanations offered out by an actor may represent a false account of the realities of his predicament, and an inaccurate directive—inadequate to the resolution of his predicament (i.e. to *praxis*).[2] Second, Matza's refusal to allow the possibility of alternative and qualitatively different systems of motivation rests, we would argue, on a peculiar conception of what a *different* motivational construction would really look like.

To place these critiques in a context, it is necessary to understand Matza's view of the causation of delinquency as embodied in his concept of *drift*. Matza (1964, p. 28) defines it as follows:

Drift stands midway between freedom and control. Its basis is an area in the social structure in which control has been loosened, coupled with the abortiveness of adolescent endeavour to organize an autonomous subculture, and thus an important source of control, around illegal action. The delinquent *transiently* exists in a limbo between convention and crime, responding in turn to the demands of each, flirting now with one, now the other, but postponing commitment, evading decision. Thus he drifts between criminal and conventional action.

179

The development of a contraculture, Matza argues, is impossible because of adult surveillance and adolescent dependence; periodically, intermittently and without commitment, the adolescent drifts into delinquency motivated by a pursuit of subterranean values and uncontrolled by virtue of having neutralized the conventional values.[3]

Now, this notion (of drift)—like the conception of neutralization techniques—is heavily anti-deterministic in rhetoric. Drift is not compulsion. But neither is it freedom, because, for Matza, 'freedom is self-control . . . the delinquent clearly has not achieved that state' (p. 29). Drift, like neutralization, seems to exist in Matza's linear-type theory at some point between determinism and freedom. That point is the point of 'soft determinism': a determinism which still allows of the exercise of free will. There is a great tension in the conceptualization here, for whilst Matza is concerned to stress the role of choice, he still seems intent on minimizing deviant consciousness. The theory is mainly a theory in which the drift into delinquency is precipitated by 'accidental' and 'unpredictable' circumstances. Thus, he states (Matza, 1964, p. 29):

Drift is a gradual process of movement, unperceived by the actor, in which the first stage may be accidental or unpredictable from the point of view of any theoretic frame of reference, and deflection from the delinquent path may be similarly accidental or unpredictable. This does not preclude a general theory of delinquency. However, the major purpose of such a theory is a description of the conditions that make delinquent drift possible and probable, and not a specification of invariant conditions of delinquency.

Here Matza confuses the formal requirements of a general theory with concrete instances—nobody but tight positivistic theorists really believe that it is possible to construct a general theory which specifies 'invariant' conditions. Moreover, and more importantly, it is now clear that Matza's notion of 'delinquent drift' like his 'techniques of neutralization' is not an explanation of delinquency—for in denying the 'drifters' an ability to perceive the processes they are involved in (in the same way as he earlier denied the ability of any delinquent to sustain a critique of morality) Matza has to develop the idea of a 'mundane' delinquent who is somehow different from the hard-core delinquent. His critique of deterministic theories is revealed to be contradictory at its very roots. For the non-mundane delinquents are revealed as the 'minority' of juvenile delinquents who go on to become adult criminals. Matza suggests that the 'mundane delinquent is the exemplary delinquent in that he personifies, more fully than the compulsive or the committed' the delinquent actor. But if this is true, Matza is not offering us a general theory of delinquency but a description of the conditions that make mundane delinquency possible. Indeed, Matza can be seen to abandon his own attempt to explode positivistic invariants and to be guilty of 'differentiating' the mundane delinquent from other delinquent types. Somehow, 'the mundane delinquent is the exemplary delinquent'—he is invariantly different from the minority. The minority—some of whom, Matza argues, are 'neurotically compulsive'—are *different* from mere drifters.

Matza avoids the full implications of his sociology of motivation. We can accept that there is some variation in commitment to delinquent beliefs (which needs explaining in itself) but we do not have to resort to distinctions which artificially separate 'mundane delinquents' from others. Indeed, Matza's own discussion of the techniques of neutralization allows, in its implications, that 'what is reason for one man is rationalization for another' (Wright Mills, 1967, p. 448). It follows therefore that it must allow that the 'differing reasons men give for their actions are not themselves without reason' (p. 439); and that these reasons must involve historical understanding rather than abstract analysis. In short, Matza's mundane delinquents, drifting in a limbo, associating with deviants who are somehow different, is a restrictive *description* of a situation which requires *explanation* in terms of the highly varied reasons for which people move from occasional to frequent delinquency.

Matza does offer an explanation of why people continue to commit delinquency. They find themselves in the company of people who have the *will* to commit delinquency; and all that is then required is the learning of techniques which are common knowledge in that particular 'situation of company' (Matza, 1964, p. 184): 'The will to repeat old infractions requires nothing very dramatic or forceful. Once the bind of the law has been neutralized and the delinquent put in drift, all that seems necessary to provide the will to repeat old infractions is preparation.'

Techniques of neutralization render the offence feasible on a moral basis; and the acquisition of the requisite skills completes the preparatory process. But, importantly, for Matza, drifting boys must learn to overcome their fear if they are to have the will to commit the infraction: boys who remember the fear that accompanied previous infractions are unlikely to be involved in further action. 'Drift is unlikely to culminate in new or previously inexperienced infraction unless the will to crime receives massive activation. Such activation may be provided by desperation' (ibid., p. 188).

Matza is compelled here to assign motives to the drifting delinquent in a fundamentally idealistic fashion. Boys might actually want money, sex, excitement, without having to be desperately activated to go about obtaining them. But Matza goes on to see the drift into delinquency as encouraged in the final analysis by an attempt to transcend the 'mood of fatalism'. For Matza (p. 188):

> one variety of neutralization—the mood of fatalism—is of central importance because of the variety of functions it may simultaneously serve. The mood of fatalism neutralizes the legal bind since it renders subcultural adherents irresponsible: it elicits or is itself provoked by the situation of company because it exacerbates the feeling of dependency on peers who unlike others can be presumed to provide similar moods; and, finally, it provides a sense of desperation.

Now there is considerable evidence to support Matza's contention that working-class boys are fatalistic—or, more properly, that they are realistic about their life-chances (Veness, 1962; Downes, 1966a; Hargreaves, 1967; L. Taylor, 1968a).[4] But there are no good grounds for the assumption that fatalism (or realism) is primarily the child of the existential mood of desperation. We believe that it is true that delinquency is in part the result of an external situation of inequality, poverty and powerlessness and can be seen as an attempt to assert control and thereby to re-establish some sense of self. But this is very different from Matza's description of the active delinquent—moving out of desperation in search of a mood (of humanism)—a shift in which the delinquent is propelled from one pole to another not by a consciousness of self and of external situation but by existential forces beyond his command.

Matza extends the argument to say that a person is propelled into action because he wants to 'make things happen'. He goes on to say that delinquency does not have the same risks of failure as more conventional pursuits like 'athletics, scholastics, or heterosexual prowess'. So delinquency is convenient. Matza (1964, p. 190) believes that delinquent involvement, whether successful or not, encourages the delinquent that he has made things happen because 'they have, by their infraction, put the criminal process in motion.'

He thus believes that delinquents—whether or not they fail or succeed—restore the mood of humanism. In this it is unlike other possible alternatives where to fail would be to fail absolutely—it would not make things happen. Thus, the schema for the explanation of subcultural recruitment in Matza involves three necessary elements: (a) the moral neutralization of the law; (b) the learning of delinquent techniques in the 'situation of company'; and (c) the will to commit infraction—arising out of desperation and propelled to restore the mood of humanism.

We should remind ourselves that Matza is aware that he is not describing a definite, or inevitable process. People can be diverted. However, he does insist in his closing sentence in *Delinquency and*

Drift (1964, p. 191) that this is 'the process by which the potential for crime implicit in drift is realized'.

It is commonplace now to remark on the evidential problems that Matza denies. All of the evidence about the guilty demeanour and the techniques of neutralization is derived, we are told, from the situation of apprehension, and Matza merely asserts that apprehended delinquents could have no reason to give strategical (apologetic) answers to the questions he (or others) might have asked him. In contrast, a recent empirical study (Hindelang, 1970, p. 508) has suggested that 'individuals may engage in delinquent behaviour not because of episodic release from moral constraint, but perhaps because those engaging in delinquent activities do not generally subscribe to the moral codes which prohibit such activities.' Hindelang's data is open to objections, as he himself admits, and, in any case, is not entirely relevant to an immanent critique of Matza. A more important argument however is that of Travis Hirschi (1969) derived from his own data, which takes issue with Matza's assertion that *most* delinquency is the product of drift. Hirschi suggests that most delinquents may perhaps not concur in conventional assessment of delinquency because (p. 26) 'the less a person believes he should obey the rules, the more likely he is to violate them'. David Downes in *The Delinquent Solution*—as we noted earlier—has argued that much delinquency is explicable as a reaffirmation of working-class values which is 'dissociated' from middle-class values. Whether or not one accepts Hirschi's version of 'control theory' or whether one accepts Downes's view of adolescents in conflict over opportunities at the point of leisure consumption, there is a considerable literature which denies the systematically integrated view of culture to which Matza, in almost Parsonian fashion, attributes to contemporary society. In sum, the empirical evidence to support Matza's view of the neutralization of the moral bind of law is thin and ambiguous.

Rather more importantly, if one were to accept with Matza that every kind of statement made by delinquents about the morality of law (whether in the situation of apprehension or elsewhere) is a neutralization, then it would be difficult to conceive of any kind of statement that could be anything else. How, then, could one begin to explain the statements of political deviants in court? Was Jonathan Jackson neutralizing the moral bind of Californian law when he took a gun to court, and told them 'OK, gentlemen, this is where we take over'? Matza would allow this exception, arguing that Jonathan Jackson was a radical, and that bohemians too may make oppositional statements in the situation of apprehension. Juvenile delinquents, on the other hand, are juveniles and they are held in check by the moral bind of the family. However, as Hirschi (1969, pp. 199–200) has astutely noted: 'the more strongly the child is tied to the conventional order, the less likely he is to be able to invent and use techniques of neutralization.'

We do not accept, with Hirschi, that delinquency may result from differential attachment to parents, and learning processes which result in children being differentially attached to moral authority in general—especially at a time when the hold of the nuclear family is, by all accounts, being weakened. However, we do accept Hirschi's argument that large numbers of delinquents have a limited code of discourse which takes the form of restricted codes of communication prevalent throughout the working class (Bernstein, 1972). There is no warrant for assuming, with Matza, that because these codes enable only a non-critical and inarticulate response that therefore their 'implicit critique' is not a critique at all but a neutralization. Indeed, even in the most extreme cases of verbal disorder where linguistic utterances are hardly possible by the deviant (e.g. schizophrenia), it has been strongly argued by Laing and others that non-communication itself can be understood as political attack upon the double-bind concentration camp of the nuclear family. Moreover, Matza seems to assume that all his techniques of neutralization are on the same level, that is that they are all techniques which neutralize the moral bind of society in the same kind of way. Of course, he does allow that there are various degrees of freedom in using different techniques. For example, he allows that disclaiming responsibility because one is sick is altogether different from denying one's responsibility by 'condemning the condemners'. The problem with this convolution of different types is that even a full-blown ideology could be made to look like a neutralization. Moreover, the list of types is posed in a unilinear fashion: all of the techniques, or any one of them, is seen to neutralize conventional morality. However, it is perfectly apparent that they make different sense depending on what deviant action is being contemplated and upon what kind of morality is being 'extended'. A homosexual who says he cannot help being a homosexual because he is sick is very different from the homosexual who denies the fact of harm to the victim, who declares that 'gay is good' and that his partner agrees. Of course, deviants do switch from one position to another, but this is contingent upon the dialectical relationship between their deviant action and (not just the conventional morality) and the structure of power, the changes in cultural options, the opportunity to act and the likelihood of apprehension.

We are claiming, as against Matza, that deviant motivations run the whole gamut from total acceptance of social morality (coupled with an absolute need to break that morality, e.g. theft in order to feed, killing in self-defence) through to those cases where deviants are in total opposition to conventional morality and are in large part motivated by their desire to alter or destroy it (e.g. total cultural nihilists). In sum, Matza's schema of 'moral neutralization', underpinned by a simple notion of the relationship of the individual to his culture, must be seen to be what it is: an ambiguous construction of highly articulate assertions.[5] If, however, Matza had been operating with a rather more explicit view of the relationship of men to structures of power and authority he might have become aware that the cultural options available to the majority of citizens in an inequitable capitalist society are designed to make opposition look like neutralizations rather than the critique of the frustrated and the deprived.

Paradoxically (and Matza is a man of paradoxes), Matza almost realizes this himself when he observes that (Sykes and Matza, 1957, p. 251): 'The normative system of a society . . . is marked by . . . flexibility; . . . the individual can avoid moral culpability for his criminal action—and thus avoid the negative sanctions of society— if he can prove that criminal intent was lacking.'

Most of the cultural options available to those who are oppressed in a divided class society serve to minimize the possibility of their choosing an alternative system of culture. Of course, Matza knows this, but, by refusing to commit himself to a clear analysis of the structure of power and authority and thus to a view of the total society, he proceeds—in undialectical fashion—to split culture off from the rest of society. In an interview (Weis, 1971, p. 48) Matza has stated that:

I think that *Delinquency and Drift* is a confused jumbling of conservative, liberal, and radical views. Different chapters have different philosophic and political implications. I think *Becoming Deviant* is sort of liberal and radical, maybe a little conservative too; but I think somewhat more consistent than *Delinquency and Drift*. So the view of society that I had, if I had one, in *those* books . . . what in hell *did* I think when writing those two books? Actually, my view of society is much more evident in something I wrote called 'Poverty and Disrepute' and an essay on poverty that I'm working on now. I'm not sure I have a view of society.

It is difficult to see how Matza could have held to the firm views on the cultural imprisonment of individual men if, when he wrote about neutralization, he had 'no clear view of society'. Matza is an honest man and admits in this recent interview to other significant changes of view. The point is, however, that a view of society—of one kind or another—is implicit, and changing, in every thing he writes.

One theme, however, seems to remain relatively constant, and that

185

is his view of the poor. Both in 'Poverty and disrepute' (in 1967 and in 1971) and a polemic with Charles Valentine, the author of *Culture and Poverty*, Matza adheres to what he sees to be the orthodox Marxist position: a position on which we shall dwell at some length in our discussion of Marx, Engels and Bonger. Of Valentine's view of the poor, Matza (1969b, p. 193) writes:

> Far from seeing the poor as stupified or disorganized until they have mobilized and achieved consciousness—the classic view of writers since Marx—Valentine follows the romantic tradition in which the poor are merely different in their culture and arrangements. . . . Being poor does not lead to a degradation and debasement of the potentialities of human potential; this is just something that is wrongly construed in that way by ethnocentric outsiders.

This is the view of the poor as the *Lumpenproletariat*—the unproductive, unorganized and the parasitical sections of the unemployed and the unemployable. Whilst Matza correctly sees the 'disreputable poor' as a permanent feature of an inequitable society, it does not follow, as his several articles suggest, that disreputability or 'lumpen-ness' is immutable, for demoralization can be overcome by organizing in the ghettos, the slums and the back alleys which we know to be so productive of delinquency.[6]

In fact, the view of society here, though there may be a shift from *Delinquency and Drift*, is still a very static picture. Matza sees false-consciousness and disreputability as immutable: but for us it is precisely because they are not that societies change. His view of the poor in society, like his view of the delinquent in his subculture, tends to be one-dimensional. The weight of oppression tends to bind people in. Of course it does this: but it can also thrust them out. Matza's sociology of poverty (and his criminology too) tends to be pitched at the level of describing false-consciousness: but false-consciousness is a one-dimensional ideology and, since Matza has no notion of contradiction (that the same forces that produce false-consciousness may produce its opposite), he is unable to move beyond this recitation of cultural statics.

In the final analysis, then, in the early Matza, we are presented with a picture of criminal consciousness, rather like that of the lack of consciousness among the disreputable poor: a consciousness that, for all Matza's strictures about the reintroduction of will into the explanation of subcultural recruitment, is in reality a consciousness that is propelled. The deviant has no choice but to move between the two poles of desperation and humanism: between a despairing and a less despairing (celebration) of false-consciousness. In Matza's own words (1964, p. 191):

The mood of fatalism neutralizes the bind of law, elicits the situation of company, and fosters a sense of desperation, which in turn provides the will or thrust to commit new infraction. Such desperation does not necessitate the commission of a previously inexperienced infraction. It merely provides the will or the impetus for it.

Thus, Matza's critique of the positive delinquent amounts in effect to an indeterminate picture of a variant process—a picture that is not only unconvincing about how people become deviant but also one which is totally taken up with a mood of fatalism that seems to arise directly out of Matza's own pessimism. Like Marcuse's critique of social positivism (to which Marcuse can only pessimistically put as an alternative a one-dimensional man in one-dimensional society), Matza's critique of criminological positivism leaves us with the picture of a totally one-dimensional delinquent.[7] Matza's delinquent, moreover, is largely concerned to negate his society in a neutral fashion: a peculiar observation to make about delinquency in societies where the mass of delinquents are literally involved in the practice of redistributing private property.

Pluralism

Matza's insistence on the interpenetration of values is correct in that the notion of isolated normative ghettos held to by the early sociological theorists are patently incorrect. Values coexist, interpenetrate and are dialectically related, as Matza insists. But his notion of subterranean values would seem to deny the possibility of genuinely deviant values. For 'deviancy' becomes merely a display of unofficial commonly held values derived from accentuation and neutralization. The confusion becomes merely semantic: for surely, if we extend and accentuate any values sufficiently they must at some juncture become different values? And if we 'neutralize' sufficiently do we not eventually recast 'normal' justification of action? Matza's delinquent abhors work, he accentuates subterranean values, he displays them in the wrong time and place, he indulges in a series of involved techniques of neutralization (one of which includes a sense of injustice); he is regarded by the mass of the population as deviant. Is this not sufficient to term him deviant or do we merely have David Matza's word for it, that he is just like us? (See Young, 1973a.) Further, Matza's notion of the relationship between subterranean and official values demands a material underpinning. For (Young, 1971a, p. 128):

the world of leisure and work are intimately related. The money earned by work is spent in one's leisure time. . . .

Leisure is concerned with consumption and work with production; a keynote of our bifurcated society, there, is that individuals within it must constantly consume in order to keep pace with the productive capacity of the economy. They must produce in order to consume, and consume in order to produce. The interrelationship between formal and subterranean values is therefore seen in a new light: hedonism, for instance, is closely tied to productivity. Matza and Sykes have over-simplified our picture of the value systems of modern industrial societies: true, there is a bifurcation between formal and subterranean values, but they are not isolated moral regions; subterranean values are subsumed under the ethos of productivity. This states that a man is justified in expressing subterranean values if, and only if, he has earned the right to do so by working hard and being productive. Pleasure can only be legitimately purchased by the credit card of work.

The bifurcation of values is understandable in terms of a neo-Keynsian economic system—but Matza does not attempt at any point to deal with the system as a whole. The violent social reaction against the undisciplined hedonist is understandable in this light: for it is palpably deviant in terms of the ethos of productivity. It is really only in the pursuit of what Bennet Berger has called 'bohemian business' ('record industry', 'head shops', etc.) that extreme subterranean accentuations are conventionalized in the manner that Matza suggests (Berger, 1963).

The late Matza: becoming deviant?

I take a subjective approach in *Becoming Deviant* but it's not a subjective approach which denies that there are realities in the world (Matza in Weis interview, 1971, p. 39).

In this last section, we shall be examining Matza's latest criminological work, *Becoming Deviant*, which, as Weis pointed out in the interview quoted above, could more accurately have been entitled *Becoming Criminal*.

We have already given a considerable amount of space in this book to Matza's plea for a return to *naturalism*, namely the attempt to remain faithful to the deviant phenomena under study. Here we are concerned to compare and contrast *Becoming Deviant* and *Delinquency and Drift*, to see how far the later position deviates from the position we have criticized so far.

In fact, we shall not be discussing *Becoming Deviant* in full: the book is divided into two distinct halves, and to the first of these we have no marked objection. This first part is largely concerned, in

Matza's words (1969a, p. 1), 'to develop the perspective of naturalism and to trace its main themes through the Chicago School, the functionalists and the contemporary neo-Chicagoan approach'. His demonstration of the development of the appreciation of deviance through these three schools is unobjectionable; and his rigid opposition to the pathologizing of deviant phenomena and/or correctional stances in the study of these phenomena is exemplary. Indeed, a large part of what he says in these earlier pages is paralleled in our treatment of these same theorists earlier in this book.

However, there *is* one aspect of the first half of *Becoming Deviant* that cannot remain undiscussed; and that is related to the book as a whole. Throughout the book, Matza generates new concepts and linguistic terms which—depending upon one's own predilections— are to be seen as innovation or hurdles to be overcome in understanding Matza's concern (in Part 2) with the process of becoming deviant. Steven Box (1971b, p. 403) provides a more than adequate précis of the first part of the book when he writes that 'Matza argues that the perspective has shifted from one which viewed it as *simple pathology* in need of *correction*, to another which views it as *complex diversity* we should *appreciate*.'

In Part 2 of *Becoming Deviant*, Matza discusses the etiology of deviance within a naturalistic perspective. Simply put, the deviant is seen to become deviant as a result of exercising certain choices. Matza argues that one key question in the study of deviance is the way in which delinquents become delinquents as a result of their circumstances, and he suggests that people have an affinity to deviancy because it is 'an attractive force'. He argues that the notion of favoured affinity—that is, the choice to commit infractions—can be explained in terms of the ideas of the context of *affiliation* and *signification*. For Matza (1969a, p. 100) there is 'in the context of affiliation and signification the human meaning of affinity'.

Affiliation, Matza suggests, has two meanings. From the correctional perspective, affiliation is really contagion, but humanized it means conversion. Matza, utilizing the latter conception, goes on to say that 'the consequence of affinity is being willing to do a thing, no more no less' (ibid, p. 112) and thus people are converted to a sense of an option. In Matza's terms, when the actor experiences affinity, he encounters the invitational edge of deviant behaviour. As he correctly suggests (ibid., p. 112), 'the ordinary consequence of having been exposed to the "causes" of deviant phenomena is not in reality doing the thing. Instead, it is picturing or seeing oneself literally, as the kind of person who might possibly do the thing.' He illustrates the problematics of this situation with a long discussion and re-evaluation of Becker's by now classic essay on 'Becoming a marihuana user' (1963). In a sense, what Matza is doing here is to use

189

the phenomenology of the new convert to marijuana as a way of illustrating various inner processes or stages in the process of becoming deviant.

Now, standing inbetween Matza's discussion of affiliation and signification is the notion of ban. It is at this point that the 'realities in the world' referred to by Matza in his interview intrude into an account that is otherwise merely phenomenologically based. Ban alters the nature of the activity being engaged in: it is the force of the state criminalizing an activity, proscribing it specifically as beyond the bounds of law. This affects the subjective phenomenology of affiliation, or, as Matza argues rather deterministically, 'it virtually guarantees that further disaffiliation with convention will be a concomitant of affiliation with deviation; but slightly differently, that the scope or range of disaffiliation will surpass or go beyond the amount implicit in the deviation itself' (1969a, p. 148). Matza seems to slip here into a kind of determined amplification process in which he sees the phenomenology of the deviant increasing his affiliation with deviation by virtue of the need to hide one's initial deviation from the law and society. He puts it that (ibid., p. 148):

> In its effect on the wrong-minded, ban compounds disaffiliation and thus contributes to the process of becoming deviant—unless, of course, the subject reconsiders the entire matter and returns to a righteous path. Ban hardly makes commitment to a deviant path inevitable; it only assures the compounding of deviation as long as the path is maintained.

The assertion is that committing a deviant act which is also a criminal act forces one into secrecy. But secrets can only be kept if one can prevent one's secret self from becoming transparent. Conscious of the possibility of his transparency, the subject becomes more highly attuned to his own deviancy, and, thus, in a phenomenological sense, one's deviance is compounded.

The final stage in the process of becoming deviant is signification. To signify 'is to *stand for* in the sense of representing or exemplifying ... thus signifying makes its object more significant. ... To be signified a thief is to lose the blissful identity of one who amongst others happens to have committed a theft. It is a movement, however gradual, towards being a thief and representing theft' (p. 156). It can lead to exclusion and displays of authority. Indeed, it is not until the subject is signified that he understands the nature of the state or of organized authority. For Matza, Part 2 of *Becoming Deviant* is an inner philosophical exploration. That is, it is tracing through the phenomenology of changing identity. But whilst we are given a highly subjective account of Matza's view of the phenomenology of mind involved in deviation, we are not presented with the matter. In other words, *Becoming Deviant* is phenomenological supposition.

Matza, however, claims that the book is really about the state. We are entitled to ask 'What kind of state?'—and we are told Leviathan. But if Leviathan is to be anything more than a state of mind we need a description of the structure (or 'realities') as well as phenomenology. Indeed, Matza himself suggests (1969a, p. 178), 'in all likelihood, the circumstantial context of the subject has remained nearly constant during the entire period being considered; it is his [the deviant's] philosophical situation that has undergone radical alteration. Thus, the main shift has been in the subject's definition of a situation he *may* find himself in.'

Becoming Deviant concludes with the observation that (p. 196):

> Even at the conclusion of the signification process—imprison-
> ment and parole—the process of becoming deviant remains
> open. Reconsideration continues; remission remains an
> observable reality. Nonetheless, signification implies a closure
> or a finality; at least, in the minds of conventional members of
> society and empowered officials, though not in the lives of
> deviant persons.

Matza provides a plausible if unprovable answer to those theorists who see deviancy as an inevitable process. However, this pheno-menological ghost has no substance: the deviant has no material basis. We are not given any account as to why individuals should find affiliation to deviation attractive. Matza's phenomenology, like that of the ethnomethodologists, avoids the question of etiology which it presumes to resolve. Any etiological factors outside of the constitutive in the mind are not discussed—with the one exception of Leviathan. Even in phenomenological terms, the project is not complete, for despite his assertion that he is following the subject who discovers his deviant identity, Matza never discusses the phenomenology of imprisonment. In any case, the level of abstraction precludes social refutation, for all that Matza has done is to describe one possible phenomenological reaction. But there are a number of possible phenomenological trips. The existence of ban, for instance, may increase the attraction of an infraction. As Carl Werthman (1969, p. 628), a writer much concerned with the phenomenology of delinquent character, has put it in relation to apprehended de-linquents:

> Although the consequences of taking risks become more serious
> as arrest records get longer, a boy who knows that the
> California Youth Authority awaits him if he is caught for

theft or joyriding one more time can demonstrate possession of more courage than the boys who have never been caught.

Alternatively, it may be the case that ban does not always have the same effect upon the subject because the subject is aware of the differential possibility of apprehension inherent in the structured nature of any real state activity.

The only value of the above imaginary phenomenological process is that it sensitizes us to the role of consciousness in the process of becoming deviant, in a way that Matza himself had avoided in *Delinquency and Drift*. However, the choice and awareness accorded the subject is peculiarly presented. We are never given accounts of collective choice. In dealing with the 'inner' man, the 'outer' man got lost. If ever Marx's plea that social analysis involves, at a minimum, the anatomy of society was relevant as a critique, it is with Matza's processes of becoming deviant. In building deviancy upon affinity, Matza gives us an individualistic phenomenology which loses sight of affinity completely. In this sense, the book is essentially disconnected; the brilliant critique of correctional criminology reduces into a criminology that itself requires correction.

In explaining the process of becoming deviant as being based upon anxiety—about the worry of transparency, about the inevitability amplication in the face of ban—Matza's phenomenologically anxious deviant is merely an abstracted version of the fatalistic drifter. Both have in common an inevitability of fate. *Becoming Deviant*, like *Delinquency and Drift*, presents us with an essentialist view of deviation. The essence of deviation is its base in an unanalysed and unanalysable existential *Angst*, and it is precisely this in Matza which despite brilliant work to the contrary, removes his wilful deviant from the social to the transcendental world.

American phenomenology and the study of deviance: ethnomethodology

'Well in our country' said Alice, still panting a little, 'you'd generally get to somewhere else—if you ran very fast for a long time, as we've been doing'. 'A slow sort of country' said the Queen, 'Now here, you see it takes all the running you can do to keep in the same place' (Lewis Carroll, *Alice in Wonderland*).

Here I have been arguing that if all we propose to do is handle common-sense matters, only better than they are common-sensically handled, there are no guarantees that we can claim superiority. If, alternatively, we claim to be doing a different job, then it seems quite unclear that the satisfaction of that claim can be warranted (H. Sacks, 'Sociological Description', *Berkeley Journal of Sociology*, vol. 8, 1963, p. 15).

Ethnomethodology and the phenomenological project[8]

In this section, we take a brief look at the rise of a phenomenologically orientated sociology and its implications for social theory in general and a social theory of deviance in particular. Earlier we indicated how Matza's 'naturalism' was a turn to phenomenology in its 'back to the phenomena' insistence on 'telling how it is'. That is, it insisted upon remaining accurate in its representation of the phenomena under study. Now, generally, there are two related methodological imperatives built into a phenomenological orientation. One imperative is to give a correct representation of the phenomenon under study; the other is to show how the phenomenon is constituted or built up. Michael Phillipson and Maurice Roche in an unpublished paper on phenomenological sociology and the study of deviance (1971, p. 2) point out that:

> The basic themes of phenomenological philosophy have a reputation for being difficult to excavate from its notoriously verbose literature. But, once excavated, they can be seen to cluster around two methodological imperatives. These imperatives, in spite of their complex context and complex implications are themselves simple enough to state. The first is contained in the slogan—'back to the phenomenon', and the second is contained in the slogan 'show how the phenomenon is built up'. The former can be called *descriptive imperative* and the latter a *constitutive imperative* [our emphasis]. The meaning of these two imperatives can best be explained by considering the concept phenomenon. This concept refers to that which is given in perception or in consciousness, for the perceiving and conscious subject.

Phenomenology, then, stresses that mind is a conscious active process. Activity is to be studied via a subject's intentionality. To suggest this, is to turn the focus of social investigation away from crude deterministic theories and to orientate attention to the study of intentional action. As we shall see the underlying assumption of the American brand of phenomenology, ethnomethodology, is that general explanations are impossible—or, anyone claiming to have erected an explanation is engaged in unwarranted abstractions. For the ethnomethodological approach to deviance not only eschews any causal or etiological approach to deviance but raises the classical sociological question of how subjective understanding or *verstehen* is scientifically possible. The stress in this approach is not on the

193

constraints which men labour under, rather the attempt is to show the active constitutive side of man's activity. Man is seen as engaging in the production and construction of social structure. The American phenomenological heritage takes off from Schutz's criticisms of the Weberian approach to the question of subjective understanding, and how it was possible.[9] Schutz believed that whilst Weber had correctly stressed the importance of the role of subjective understanding in any constructing of an account of an actor's motive and reasons for engaging in an activity, he had not gone far enough. Interpretative sociology must go beyond Weber to the phenomenological project (Schutz, 1967, p. 6):

> Never before had the project of reducing the 'world of objective mind' to the behaviour of individuals been so radically carried out as it was in Max Weber's initial statement of the goal of interpretative sociology. This science is to study social behaviour by interpreting its subjective meaning as found in the intentions of individuals. The aim, then, is to interpret the actions of individuals in the social world and the ways in which individuals give meaning to social phenomena.

Schutz (ibid., pp. 7–8) says of Weber that:

> He breaks off his analysis of the social world when he arrives at what he assumes to be the basic and irreducible elements of social phenomena. But he is wrong in this assumption. His concept of the meaningful act of the individual—the key idea of interpretative sociology—by no means defines a primitive, as he thinks it does. It is, on the contrary, a mere label for a highly complex and ramified area that calls for much further study.

Schutz's answer to the problem bequeathed by Weber was to insist that we turn to a 'constitutive phenomenology of the natural attitude.' Whereas both Weber and Durkheim saw social action as some kind of orientation to a normative external constraint, it was necessary to go beyond this and enquire into the common sense world of everyday life by showing how social realities are experienced and constructed by interacting subjects. Thus, Schutz is engaged in the phenomenology of intersubjectivity. He suggests that the reciprocity of perspectives upon which agreement is based has to be analysed rather than taken for granted, and that, furthermore, a basic feature of everyday life is that we assume the 'interchangeability of standpoints'. That is, we operate in such a way as to suggest that if we changed places with other people then they would experience objects and phenomena in the same way as we do. This position is based on another assumption (similar to the notion of shared purposes) namely the 'congruency of relevances'. Here it is assumed, that for everyday purposes, other people with whom we are involved in some practical activity share—until we are given evidence to the contrary—a given common situation.

The constant problem is to demonstrate that given actors have constructed the same taken-for-granted rules which are necessary for the maintenance of their ongoing practical problems. Thus, as Phillipson and Roche suggest (1971, pp. 19–20),

> Schutz allows sociology only a tentative status, a qualified validity and a suspect authenticity. Much conventional sociology remains, on this view, a documentation of commonsense, undertaken according to unclarified rules of commonsense. Substantive documentation and research in any field, including that of deviance, is almost premature until the rules which societal members (including sociologists) follow in constructing their realities and meanings have been revealed and clarified. But of course research will not and cannot wait upon such clarification. That being the case, the requirements of the phenomenological critique of conventional sociology would be met to some extent in the following way. The investigation of substantive areas should give primacy to the revealing of the shared meanings people attach to their situation, and the rules in terms of which they interpret their situation. This at least would ensure some continuity between the more formal level of the constitutive phenomenology of the natural attitude, and the more substantive level of mundane sociology. In the absence of clarification on the formal level, mundane sociology can respect the principle of intentionality, and of the meaning-fulness of actors' thoughts and actions, by documenting the actual commonsense meanings men give to their acts.

They go on to add that (p. 20):

> An interpretation must be compatible with and translatable back into the terms of members' commonsense (postulate of adequacy); validity can never be fully established because an interpretation is always a reflection on a past project and past projects can theoretically be the subject of an infinite number of accounts. However, sociologists can establish validity (for all practical sociological purposes) by demonstrating the continuity between their typifications and the typifications of the members studied. A demonstration that interpretations are compatible with members' experiences establishes adequate validity at the level of intentionality.

195

Thus, one central problem with such a phenomenological sociology is that it is always uncertain whether the sociologist can, in fact, articulate theories which are capable of coming to terms with, and explaining, all the active aspects of human subjectivity. It is unclear from this perspective whether there are any universal basic pre-requisites to interaction other than some kind of reciprocity of perspectives. An actor's interpretations of what he is about, or why he did something, are always, as Phillipson and Roche suggest, reflections on past projects, and past projects can obviously be subject to an infinite number of possible accounts. Any account that the sociologist might give is simply a typified account, and there is then the further problem of establishing isomorphism or continuity between their account and the actor's accounts. Schutz attempts to resolve this problem by suggesting that all we can do is demonstrate that our accounts are compatible with members' accounts at the level of intentionality. In part, we have faced this problem before, for one of our criticisms of Matza's naturalism was that his techniques of neutralization might not square with the deviant's accounts of his purposes or intentions, because although inarticulate he may well be expressing active opposition to a society's culture or values.

Further, alongside this compatibility question, we are led to a further question: 'phenomenological bracketing'. This is simply a methodological device in all phenomenological enquiry which sets aside all judgments about ontology (i.e. the nature, or *reality* of things) and puts them into brackets. This makes the central subject matter of phenomenology an account of how members' common-sense interpretations of what they were about (their intentions) is constituted. Now from the viewpoint of maintaining continuity between our accounts and members' accounts at the level of *intentionality*: our explanations of how members constitute or accomplish their activity cannot be explained in terms which are superior of radically different from members' own typifications. Thus, from the vantage point of the phenomenologists, the 'reality' or 'truthfulness' of a member's account is not open to study; it is a question which is 'bracketed' away. The Marxist theoretician, Georg Lukacs (1966b, pp. 137–8), noted this many years ago, and in a humorous yet critical vein had this to say:

> Even when the phenomenologists dealt with crucial questions of social actuality, they put off the theory of knowledge and *asserted that the phenomenological method suspends or 'brackets' the qestion whether the intentional objects are real* [our emphasis]. The method was thus freed from any knowledge of reality. Once during the First World War Scheler visited me in Heidelberg, and we had an informing

conversation on this subject. Scheler maintained that phenomenology was a universal method which could have anything for its intentional object. For example, he explained, phenomenological researches could be made about the devil; only the question of the devil's reality would first have to be 'bracketed'. 'Certainly', I answered, 'and when you are finished with the phenomenological picture of the devil, you open the brackets—and the devil in person is standing before you.' Scheler laughed, shrugged his shoulders, and made no reply.

The arbitrariness of the method is seen especially when the question is raised: *Is what phenomenological intuition finds actually real?* What right does that intuition have to speak of the reality of its object? ... *The intuition of essence takes the immediate givenness of inner experience as its starting point, which it regards as unconditioned and primary,* never looking into its character and preconditions, and proceeds thence to its final abstract 'vision', divorced from reality. Such intuitions, under the social conditions of the time, could easily abstract from all social actuality while keeping the appearance of utter objectivity and rigor. In this way there arose the logical myth of a world (in splendid accord with the attitude of bourgeois intellectuals) independent of consciousness, *although its structure and characteristics are said to be determined by the* individual consciousness.

Thus phenomenologists assume that experience and perception is 'unconditioned' and 'primary'. It follows from this that actors' accounts and actions are to be explained in terms which must be phenomenologically reducible to the actors' meanings and intentions. Now this is a problem common to all phenomenological enquiry, namely that our objectives in studying deviance are not the same as those members or actors whose actions constitute deviance. Yet we have seen that the only possible critieria for the validity of a phenomenological account is that our interpretation shares the same common-sense intentionality with the members accounts. For Schutz, and the ethnomethodologists, most of the theoretical concepts of sociology, terms like class, deviance, alienation, anomie, etc., are second-order constructs. That is to say, they are constructions at one order removed from any phenomenological typification, for they do not have reference to, neither are they reducible to, everyday taken-for-granted, practically constituted, intentionally created phenomena. Thus there is no guarantee that in extracting these second-order analytical constructs from the totality of social phenomena that they are in any sense homologous or isophorhic with the concrete reality of social existence. In one important sense, then, the process of phenomenological investigation is a radical attack upon the possibility of the very foundations of an etiological social theory itself. For it insists that sociology deals in *decontextualized* meanings and that there is no guarantee that actors in concrete settings construct their lives and the rules which govern them in a similar fashion.[10]

But our problems do not end here, for it is apparent that if we follow the two methodological imperatives of phenomenology (the 'descriptive imperative', and 'constitutive imperative') that we are caught up in a relativistic regress that only ends when we accept the actors' or members' phenomenological bracketing-off of their own accounts. One leading ethnomethodologist has called this 'The etcetera problem', for it is the case that no matter how hard we try to *describe* a phenomenon, the only limit to possible descriptions are the purposes or intentions of the members who have constituted the phenomena. Moreover, even in such cases they could, of course, go on describing why they did what they did endlessly. Actors stop giving such accounts because they regard as sensible the accounts that they have given, they have given accounts which are plausible in terms of 'what everybody knows', or what everybody for all practical purposes 'would want to know'. Sacks (1963) argues that the difference between science and common-sense can be accounted for in terms of the sociologist's concern with the etcetera problem. He states that this problem can be phrased as follows (p. 10):

> How is the scientific requirement of literal description to be achieved in the face of the fact, widely recognized by researchers, that a description even of a particular 'concrete object' can never be complete? That is, how is a description to be warranted when, however long or intensive it be, it may nonetheless be indefinitely extended? We call this 'the etcetera problem' to note: To any description of a concrete object (or event, or course of action, or etc.), however long, the researcher must add an etcetera clause to permit the description to be brought to a close.

It is upon this difference between sociological and 'any man' accounts of society that ethnomethodology builds its attack and this leads Sacks to state that 'if all that is claimed is that our "abstract" objects contain typical features of the collection of particular objects, then while the statement is safe, no advantage over common-sense "generalized description" can be claimed'. It is precisely this assertion of ethnomethodology which we shall examine and challenge in our next section. For in insisting that there is an unwarranted and unjustified gap between sociological theory and everyday life they abandon idiographic possibilities and force upon us—indexicality: the study of communication and understanding in concrete practical settings. This move has resulted in both good and bad consequences in the study of deviance, and it is to a consideration of ethnomethodology's accomplishments here to which we now turn.

The ethnomethodological critique[11]

In essence the ethnomethodological critique of sociology, and especially the sociology of deviance, is that our shorthand concepts like alienation, class, deviance, etc., are either meaningless or if they do have meaning, they are no more meaningful than the generalizations made by members. As Phillipson and Roche (1971, p. 28) remark in their discussion of the ethnomethodological perspective on deviance:

> The most intractable problem raised for conventional sociology
> by the ethnomethodological critique of Cicourel, Garfinkel
> and others is the nature of the fit between abstract sociological
> concepts, which turn out to be convenient short-hand for
> subsuming 'large masses of unintelligible data' and the inter-
> action sequences to which they purport to refer. In the event
> the fit is managed by fiat; correspondence is forced or is merely
> assumed. The concepts typically used by sociologists to
> describe assumed underlying patterns (e.g. class, status, role,
> norm, value, structure, institution, etc.) bear an unknown
> relationship to the procedures used by members to accomplish
> events in the social world, such concepts are of 'limited utility
> for specifying how the actor or observer negotiates everyday
> behaviour'.

It should be apparent then that the phenomenological basis of ethnomethodology is not merely an extension of sociology to everyday life; rather it insists that it wishes to study society from a viewpoint which will show how members erect procedures to accomplish events, and that in going beyond this sociology has no advantages whatsoever over common-sense. Harold Garfinkel can be said to be the father of ethnomethodology, not in the sense of being its initial practitioner, for Garfinkel's argument is that we are all engaged in practical accomplishments, but rather in the sense that he has defined the term and it is to his work that we turn to examine its advantages and limitations. Garfinkel (1968a, p. vii) defines his field of activity as follows: 'Ethnomethodological studies analyse everyday activities as members' methods for making these same activities visibly-rational-and-reportable-for-all-practical-purposes, i.e. 'accountable' as organizations of commonplace everyday

199

activities.' In *Studies in Ethnomethodology*, Garfinkel argues that the notion of 'following a rule' or 'rule governed action' enables us to understand the problem of how everyday social life is accomplished, to understand routinely produced order requires an analysis of the stated and unstated conditions of order in everyday life. For Garfinkel, the existence of normative order is always to be regarded as problematic, it is an achievement of everyday life, not an internalized pre-given. Thus, Garfinkel argues that all so-called structural phenomena are, in fact, the emergent constituted products of a large amount of perceptual and judgmental work by members. The basic task of ethnomethodology therefore is to demonstrate that the structure and process of everyday life is reducible to and, in fact, is the same thing as: 'members' methods for making these same activities visibly-rational-and-reportable-for-all-practical-purposes.' Elsewhere (1968b, p. 10) Garfinkel puts his position more cogently: 'That is what ethnomethodology is concerned with. It is an organizational study of a member's knowledge of his ordinary affairs, of his own organised enterprises, where that knowledge is treated by us as part of the same setting that it also makes orderable'. Garfinkel (1968a, p. 4) is thus following the phenomenological attitude through to its logical conclusion and is insisting that:

> In short, recognisable sense, or fact, or methodic character,
> or impersonality, or objectivity of accounts are not independent
> of the socially organised occasions of their use. Their rational
> features consist of what members do with, what they 'make of'
> the accounts in the socially organized occasion of their use.
> Members' accounts are reflexively and essentially tied for their
> rational features to the socially organized occasions of their use.

Garfinkel's position is that sociological study of indexicality will show that knowledge or rather accounts so gained whilst establishing the essential reflexity of members reveals that the 'objectivity' of the account is only 'objective' within the acceptability of the purposes for which the account is given. Moreover as accounts are tied to the 'socially organised occasions for their use' we are stuck in social science with either indexical expressions or some unwarranted and unexplained theoretical leap. He states that in this sense sociology is no different from any other member's account of a setting (Garfinkel, 1968a, p. 6):

> Wherever practical actions are topics of study the promised
> distinction and substitutability of objective for indexical
> expressions remains programmatic in every practical case and
> in every actual occasion in which the distinction or sub-
> stitutability must be demonstrated. In every actual case without

exception, conditions will be cited that a competent investigator will be required to recognise, such that in that particular case the terms of the demonstration be counted an adequate one.

His position amounts to the statement that *objectivity* in the human sciences (involving as it does intentional reflexive active subjects) is accomplished only for practical purposes, but, in fact, is not really established at all. Thus, Garfinkel insists upon the phenomenological bracketing of the reality of members' accomplishments, for they are accomplishments achieved for specific practical purposes, and sociological theory cannot ignore this fundamental feature. For Garfinkel, reflexivity is possessed by members (people or organizations) and consists of the fact that organizations or people do things and at the same time give accounts of what they do. Garfinkel is worried by the whole question of correspondence between theory and reality. He is interested in the social organization of talk or accounts. For Garfinkel, Sacks and others, accounts are to be assessed in terms of the property of accounts themselves. Accounts are simply sensible or not, in terms of 'what everyone knows' about the job in hand. The most obvious examples of this reappear time and again in the work of the ethnomethodologists: they point out that any person has an infinite number of memberships. Sex, age, social class, religion, etc., are the more obvious ones; but they point out that as the list of membership properties is indefinite, categories must be selected, the selection of criteria for categorization is a practical task which whilst theoretically endless is accomplished in terms of what any member would regard as sensible. As Garfinkel puts it (1968b, p. 225):

> Whenever a member is required to demonstrate that an account analyses a setting, can be used as a guide to action, or can be used to locate comparable activities, he uses invariably and without remedy, these practices of etc., unless, let it pass, the pretence of agreement, this retrospective-prospective reconstruction of the present state of affairs, sanctioned vagueness ... and so on, with which he achieves the demonstration as an adequate-demonstration-for-all-practical purposes.

The ethnomethodological critique then is very much bound up with how procedural rules are generated, sustained, and maintained. Their criticism of conventional sociology is that it assumes that norms give rules, and that these rules will (except in the case of deviance) be clearly followed. But as the above categorization example was meant to show, the rules of everyday life are not immutable and unambiguous. The ethnomethodologists argue that conventional sociology endows actors with some internalized attitudes[12] and

201

assumes that norms are relatively automatic guides to role-playing. But this fails to distinguish between interpretive procedures, (deep structure) and norms (surface rules).[13] Peter Lassman (1970a) in an unpublished paper succinctly summarized the position of the ethnomethodologists when he argued:

> The conventional way of suggesting the existence of inter-
> pretative procedures is to refer to the notion of 'denifition of the
> situation', but no attempt is made to specify the structure of
> norms and attitudes, nor indicate how internalized norms and
> attitudes enable the actor to assign meaning to his environment,
> or how such norms are developmently acquired and assume
> regulated usage. . . . The internalisation of norms is assumed to
> lead to an automatic application of rules on appropriate
> occasions. Appropriateness is not explained nor viewed as
> developmentally and situationally constrained. When deviance
> is said to arise, it is deviance in terms of the surface rules as
> conceived by actors and/or sociologists but norms or surface
> rules presuppose interpretative procedures and can only be
> consulted after the fact of revealing the detection and labelling
> of deviance.

This distinction is an important contribution to the analysis of everyday life, and as we shall see, a distinction which lies at the basis of any contribution ethnomethodology may be said to have made to the study of deviancy. Cicourel (1970, p. 29), whose work has had most to contribute so far, has argued that:

> Basic or interpretive rules provide the actor with a develop-
> mentally changing sense of social structure that enables him
> to assign meaning or relevance to an environment of objects.
> Normative surface rules enable the actor to link his view of
> the world to that of others in concerted social action and to
> presume that consensus or shared agreement governs interaction.

Thus, the main contribution of ethnomethodology is a sustained critique of models or images of men that collapse these two types of rules, and utilize crude notions of role-playing. For terms like role, status, deviant, etc., are not unproblematic—it must be shown that members or actors actually exhibit the characteristics which are imputed to them when such ascriptions are made; and further that such ascriptions are organized and constituted by the members themselves. Applying this perspective to deviance leads Cicourel (1968, p. 331) to comment that:

> Recent advances recognising the problem of how members of

a group come to be labelled as 'deviant', 'strange', 'odd', and the like, have not explicated terms like 'societal reaction' and 'the point of view of the actor', while also ignoring the practical reasoning integral to how members and researchers know what they claim to know. Sociologists have been slow to recognise the basic empirical issues that problems involving language and meaning pose for all research.

Cicourel's own work on the *Social Organization of Juvenile Justice* is the best example of the contribution ethnomethodology can make to the study of deviancy. His study of social control agencies is different in substance from studies in the perspective we criticized in chapter 5. His work attempts to specify the 'observable and tacit properties making up the practical decision making both lay and law enforcement officials utilize when deciding some act or sequence is wrong' (Cicourel, 1968, p. 55). It demonstrates that the everyday existence of social control agencies produces given rates of deviance. In this sense it is revealed that actual indices of crime or deviation are produced as a result of the everyday contingencies faced and produced by the police, courts, social workers, etc. Moreover, it is thus demonstrated that these do not reflect any actual or real amounts of deviation (whatever they would be); rather they are indices of the 'deviance' which is processed, handled, or accomplished by the workings of the social organization of the control agencies. In other words, his study illustrates how the 'tacit unanalysed properties' which lie behind practical decisions go to produce given 'rates' of 'deviation' as an organizational accomplishment. Cicourel, like other ethnomethodologists, claims that the sensitivity of his studies to the practical accomplishments of everyday life rests upon the superior model of action, derived from the earlier mentioned distinction between interpretive (or basic) rules and surface (or normative) rules. In a later work (1970, pp. 30–1) he lays out the paradigmatic model of the ethnomethodologists as follows:

> Unlike the rather static notion of internalised attitudes as dispositions to act in a certain way, the idea of basic or interpretative rules must specify how the actor negotiates and constructs *possible* action and evaluates the results of *completed* action. Our model of the actor (1) specify how general rules or norms are invoked to justify or evaluate a course of action; and (2) how innovative constructions in context-bound scenes alter general rules or norms, and thus provide the basis for change. Hence the learning and use of general rules or norms, and their long term storage, always require more basic interpretive rules for recognising the relevance of actual, changing scenes, orientating the actor to

possible courses of action, the organisation of behavioural displays, and the reflective evaluation by the actor.

All this is, of course, correct as a demystification of the kind of reified sociology utilizing what Dennis Wrong (1961) has called an 'oversocialised conception of man'. However, what are these interpretive rules? Norms or surface rules are easy to see, but what are the *basic* interpretive rules? One critic of Cicourel's writing from an ethnomethodological vantage point argued that (Coulter, 1972, p. 18):

> There are a number of problems with this formulation. Cicourel cites no exemplar of a base rule—rather, he furnishes readers with a reiteration of Schutz's inventory of the rules *presupposed* in orderly social interaction (reciprocity of perspectives, etcetera clause, normal-form typifications, commonsense equivalence classes), but these are very different from set interpretive schemata allegedly *employed* by the actor to provide symbolic representations of experiential data.

This attack, although clothed in obscure language, seems to make sense from a strict phenomenological orientation—but where does it leave the ethnomethodological distinction between external norms and interpretative or constructed rules? The same writer has this to say of Garfinkel's work, in a section entitled 'The Programme of Ethnomethodology' (Coulter, 1972, pp. 3–4):

> Garfinkel noted that 'norms' could be differentiated into sets of rules governing action in different senses. Firstly, there were scenes of action governed by rules which characterised what was going on in the first place, constitutive rules (specifying what to do), which depended upon the nature of the constitutive accent peculiar to the conjoint operations. In this sense, anyone coming across a scene of behavioural events could, by using his knowledge of the game-possible actions suggested by various possible constitutive accents, convert the appearances of behavioural events into a scene of orderly activities. Secondly, there were preferential rules (specifying how to do what is being done). If these were infringed, 'game-normalising' ploys would occur amongst participants. But, although games as such constitute a rather encapsulated model of social process, the infringement of preferential rules is not the critical variable in invoking indignation and cessation of interaction, as the general theory of normative order assumed; rather, the threat to the constitutive order to events as such is the key to social disorganisation.

Yet all of this is rather apparent if not downright obfuscation for there is obviously a distinction between challenging the nature of a game and challenging a move in a game—who on earth ever believed otherwise? Yet the same writer following Garfinkel goes on to add: 'As any social setting is self-organising with respect to its constitutive accent, it is unsatisfactory and unwarranted to import invariant categories into such settings to account for their production of rational properties of action.' But here lies the basis of our objection to ethnomethodology—namely that social organizations are not 'self-organising' with respect to their 'constitutive accent'. For the overriding practical aims and goals of most social organizations are given by the larger context of power and interest in the society in which they are contextually based. In any case, what would the distinction between 'constitutive rules' and 'preferential rules' be used for if we were to regard 'preferential rules' as equally necessary for the sustaining of order and organization. Coulter's arguments, like those of Garfinkel, Sacks, Cicourel, etc., all depend and insist upon the fluidity of rules and action, on the one hand, and yet ultimately, on the other hand, specify 'basic', 'constitutive', second-order typifications which are necessary to maintain social organization.[14] As Peter Lassman has pointed out (1970a, p. 6, our emphasis):

> Knowledge of the nature of interpretive rules is limited. Among the properties of interpretive procedures are those listed by Schutz and elaborated by Garfinkel, Cicourel, Churchill and Sacks. First among these is the existence of a *reciprocity of perspectives* whereby actors take for granted that each would probably have the same experiences of the immediate scene if they were to change places. Actors assume that others assume it of them that their descriptive accounts will be intelligible and recognisable features of a world known in common and taken for granted. But something more than a reciprocity of perspectives is required. Garfinkel suggests that there is an 'et cetera assumption' whereby actors 'fill in' or assume the existence of common understandings or relevances of what is being said on occasions when the descriptive accounts are seen as 'obvious' and even when not immediately obvious. *The reciprocity of perspectives and the et cetera assumption do not imply the existence or necessity of consensus. Agreement to sustain, terminate or begin interaction can occur despite the lack of conventional notions about the existence of substantive consensus to explain concerted action.* Garfinkel also suggests that the properties of practical reasoning (or interpretive procedures) can be viewed as a collection of

instructions to actors, by actors, and as a continual reflexive feedback for assigning meaning to environments. The interpretive procedures and their reflexive features provide a source of continuous instructions as social scenes develop.

He goes on to add (ibid.) that:

> To say this is to throw doubt upon the adequacy of the criteria that are given (if any) for deciding between different descriptions of social events. The fact that the actors whom sociology is trying to describe are themselves making descriptions of their own actions should not be regarded as a methodological advantage but rather as being, perhaps, its greatest methodological problem. The phenomenologists have grasped this fact but it is not yet clear what they want us to do about it.

Ethnomethodology is here turned upon itself—for either it provides some criteria for deciding upon the varying importance of the rules of everyday life: 'deep' and 'surface', 'constitutive' and 'preferential' and invalidates its own supposed inability to allow generalizations, or it relapses into microscopic description of the way in which social reality is established and unwarrantably acts upon the rejection of the assumption that the plasticity of common sense is shaped by larger power differences.

If we take the phenomenological import of ethnomethodology seriously, then it would seem to be committed either to the arbitrary and endless task of demonstrating how everyday life is constructed, or to revealing rules of interpretation necessary for its maintenance (something denied to them if they are to be consistent). Alvin Gouldner (1971, p. 392) has argued that the result of such an orientation is that there is:

> [A] strong tendency for each rule thus exposed to appear somewhat arbitrary, for each is assigned no distinct function or differential importance and is, in effect, interchangeable with a variety of others, all making some contribution to a stabilizing framework for interaction, to perform this stabilizing function, some other rule might conceivably do just as well.

It would seem to us that at base the ethnomethodological perspective is crudely empiricist. Ethnomethodologists recognize and study only one plane of social reality, individual consciousness. In rejecting general statements and concepts until they are reducible to member's consciousness, they falsely reduce all meaning to the meanings held by individual actors. They seem to believe that nothing is really fixed in the world, that the social world order is merely an ongoing, practical achievement of its members. But it is and it is not. Men create society, but not always in circumstances of their own choosing. Theoretically they deny the existence of a totality in the world, by denying the completeness of individuals. For in denying that members have internalized the values of a given social system—they go on to reject the reality of such structured values. In substance their project is atomistic, they see individuals as creating rules not social relationships. It is significant, therefore, that most of their work focuses on face-to-face interaction. For such action is 'apparently' relatively unstructured. In fact, of course, the 'taken for granted structuring of society' is rarely examined by members (unless they are part of a revolutionary group) because most day-to-day activity occurs within a very limited phenomenal world that 'everyone knows'.

Indeed the phenomenological reductions of ethnomethodology even abandons the considerations of ordering taken up by Schutz. Frank Pearce (1970, p. 8) puts this well when he notes that:

> There is a surprisingly selective use made by all the ethno-methodologists of the writings of Schutz. They do not use as an organising tool his concept of the 'life-plan'. He points out that when studying the individual actor in different social spheres his actions, motives, ends and means, and therefore projects and purposes are only elements among other elements forming a system. Any end is merely a means for another end; any project is projected within a system of higher order. For this very reason any choosing between projects refers to a previously chosen system of connected projects of a higher order. In our daily life our projected ends are means within a preconceived particular plan—and all these particular plans are subject to our plan for life as the most universal one which determines the subordinate ones even if the latter conflict with one another.
>
> This analytical construct of the life plan allows one to focus on the individual, social actor again and not merely as a member of a collectivity. It suggests that one must distinguish between meaning and significance. Two individuals may understand what is required in a situation, there is a substantive congruency over its meaning, but its significance differs.

This argument cannot be over-stressed: 'practical purposes' and individual 'mundane projects' are to be located within higher order life-plans.[15] It is precisely these normative life-plans, world views, or ideologies which constitute the cement which provides the beliefs necessary for the maintenance of social systems. Analysing social action, as analogous to game playing, can be overdone. Life is not a game, and only certain beliefs will sustain specific social systems. It is precisely in terms of the relationship between beliefs and action that ethnomethodology offers its contribution and its limitations. For whilst any description can be given for a piece of action, only some descriptions or motives will continually sustain an action. As L. Taylor and Graham (1972) argue:

> It is perhaps possible that the rules and procedures and assumptions which lie behind the ascription and citing of motives are arbitrarily distributed (albeit with collective aggregations) whilst the concrete statements to which they give rise are structurally differentiated. But this would be equivalent to saying that there were no relationships between words and grammar, between syntax and semantics. If motive is a way of conceiving social action, of giving intelligibility, then there are certain institutions which favour particular conceptions which deny motives to others on the grounds that their actions do not meet the procedural requirements which are a qualification for the award of a motive and thus for the conferral of words like purposive upon an individual's behaviour. Courts do not simply disbelieve the statements made by certain witnesses they also deny that they are doing motives. They question whether the defendant's behaviour is really action and therefore threaten the defendant's humanity by calling his action 'motiveless' even in the presence of statements which the witness has produced in reply to demands for accounts.

In fact, the differential availability of accounts to members is something which ethnomethodology cannot and does not study, yet it is precisely this problem which is at the basis of the distribution of motives which inform deviant behaviour. Our final assessment of ethnomethodology's contribution to the study of deviance is that in 'bracketing' away the question of social reality, it does not allow of any description of *the social totality* we assert to be productive of deviance.

7 Marx, Engels and Bonger on crime and social control

How closely juridical relations are linked with the development of these material forces arising from the division of labour is already clear from the historical development of juridical authority and the complaints of the feudal lords about the development of right. . . . It was just in the epoch between the rule of the aristocracy and the rule of the bourgeoisie, when the interests of two classes came into conflict, when trade between the European nations came to be important, and hence international relations themselves assumed a *bourgeois* character, it was just at that time that the power of the courts began to be important, and under the rule of the bourgeoisie, when this broadly developed division of labour became absolutely essential, the power of the courts reached its highest point. What the servants of the division of labour, the judges and still more the *professores juris*, imagine in this connection is a matter of the greatest indifference (Marx/Engels, *The German Ideology*, 1968, pp. 382–3).

Karl Marx, concentrating on problems of political economy and the relationships of capital and labour, did not write a great deal specifically on the subject of crime and deviance. There is little evidence that Marx had anything more than a passing interest in crime as an aspect of human behaviour. There is, however, an often overlooked but important section in *The German Ideology* (1845–6) on rights, crime and punishment (1965 ed., Lawrence & Wishart, pp. 342–79). Engels however does deal with crime at some length in his empirical work, *The Condition of the Working Class in England in 1844*.

For Engels, crime, like alcoholism, appeared largely as a form of 'demoralization'; a collapse of men's humanity and dignity, and an index, too, of societal decline. Demoralization was a consequence of capitalist industrialization. And working men in general, caught up in this process, had no choice in the matter (Engels, 1950, p. 130):

> If the influences demoralizing to the working-man act more powerfully, more concentratedly than usual, he becomes an offender as certainly as water abandons the fluid for the vaporous state at 80 degrees Réaumur. Under the brutal and brutalising treatment of the bourgeoisie, the working-man becomes precisely as much a thing without volition as water, and is subject to the laws of nature with precisely the same necessity; at a certain point all freedom ceases.

The demoralization engendered and tightly determined by capitalism leads to the spectre of disorder and of violence (ibid., p. 132):

> In this country, social war is under full headway, everyone stands for himself, and fights for himself against all comers . . . and this war grows from year to year, as the criminal tables show, more violent, passionate, irreconcilable. The enemies are dividing gradually into two great camps—the bourgeoisie on the one hand, the workers on the other. This war of all against all, of the bourgeoise against the proletariat, need cause us no surprise, for it is only the logical sequence of the principle involved in free competition. But it may well surprise us that the bourgeoisie remains so quiet and composed in the face of the rapidly gathering storm-clouds, that it can read all these things in the papers without, we will not say indignation at such a social condition, but fear of its consequences, of a universal outburst of that which manifests itself symptomatically from day to day in the form of crime.

In contrast to the cataclysmic perspective in Engels, Marx's own sparse writings on crime can be read superficially as explaining the functionality of crime in sustaining capitalist social relationships, and, in particular, its role in extending and maintaining the division of labour and occupational structures of early capitalist societies. In an ironic passage in *Theories of Surplus Value* entitled 'The apologist conception of the productivity of all professions', Marx (1964, p. 375) writes on crime as follows:

> A philosopher produces ideas, a poet poems, a clergyman sermons, a professor compendia and so on. . . . The criminal produces not only crimes but also criminal law, and with it the professor who gives lectures on criminal law and in addition to this the inevitable compendium in which this same professor throws his lectures onto the general market as 'commodities'. This brings with it augmentation of national wealth, quite

210

apart from the personal enjoyment which . . . the manuscript of the compendium brings to the originator himself.

This passage has often been incorrectly seen by criminologists to mean that Marx saw crime as performing an innovatory function, in particular, in extending the division of labour. The passage continues ironically:

> The criminal moreover produces the whole of the police and of criminal justice, constables, judges, hangmen, juries, etc., and all these different lines of business, which form equally many categories of the social division of labour, develop different capacities of the human spirit, create new needs, and new ways of satisfying them. Torture alone has given rise to the most ingenious mechanical inventions, and employed many honourable craftsmen in the production of its instruments.

Further (ibid., p. 375, our emphasis):

> The criminal produces an impression, partly moral and partly tragic, as the case may be, and in this way renders a 'service' by arousing the moral and aesthetic feelings of the public. He produces not only compendia on criminal law, not only penal codes and along with them legislators in the field, but also art, belles-lettres, novels and even tragedies . . . the criminal breaks the monotony and everyday security of bourgeois life. In this way he keeps it from stagnation, and gives rise to that uneasy tension and agility without which even the spur of competition would be blunted. *Thus he gives a stimulus to the productive forces.*

As the passage progresses, the irony becomes ever more clear. It is almost as though 'the war against crime' fulfils a crucial role in sowing contradictions and problems in capitalist social structure:

> The effects of the criminal upon the development of productive power can be shown in detail. Would locks ever have reached their present degree of excellence had there been no thieves? Would the making of bank-notes have reached its present perfection had there been no forgers? Would the microscope have found its way into the sphere of ordinary commerce but for trading frauds? Doesn't practical chemistry owe just as much to the adulteration of commodities and the efforts to show it up as to the honest zeal of production? Crime, through its constantly new methods of attack upon property, constantly calls into being new methods of defence, and so is as productive as strikes for the invention of machines.

That the 'war against crime' continues in the capitalist societies of our time, and that it calls forth new techniques of investigation, surveillance and control and, perhaps importantly, loss-reducing machinery is not in doubt. We may be entitled to a degree of scepticism, however, as to the centrality of crime (even in a period of 'societal breakdown') in the development of new technological devices and machinery by the capitalist powers. Elsewhere L. Taylor and I. Taylor (1968, pp. 29-32) have argued that:

The public outcry about crime, the press hysteria and even the publication (in Britain) of official documents on 'The War Against Crime' should not blind us to the reluctance of modern capitalism effectively to finance these particular 'military' operations. While there may be some little truth in gibes like 'Crime has become an industry', it is also true that its nationalised competititors (the Police, the courts and the correctional agencies) are so ill-prepared and ill-equipped that they can do little more than contain the competition. Television cameras for observing car-parks and computerised finger-printing are the most sophisticated 'machines' capitalism has financed in this unfinished war. They are scarcely capitalism's most notable technological achievements.

Put bluntly, identikits are hardly central to the stability of capitalism. Indeed, one commentator has thrown doubt on the independent contribution of 'innovation' in economic production in general to the stability of capitalist ecnomies, arguing that innovation and growth are independent of stability problems within a precariously-balanced system.[1]

However, it is clear that Marx's intentions in 'The apologist conception of the productivity of all professions' were ironic. As Paul Hirst has suggested, the passage is an attempt to ridicule the 'vulgar bougeois apology' wherein society is seen as divided morally into the 'upright' on the one hand and the 'depraved' on the other. 'Marx teases these vulgarians with the proposition that the most upright citizens depend for their livelihood on the criminal classes' (Hirst, 1972). There is no serious attempt to establish crime as a central dynamic in the system of capitalist production and innovation.

At the same time, there is little doubt that Marx is not simply concerned here to 'tease' the 'vulgar bourgeois apologists' but also to emphasize the criminal nature of capitalism as a system. As against the utilitarians and the positivists (in both the Comtian and Durkheimian traditions), Marx is asserting the possibility of a crime-free society by demonstrating, albeit ironically, the normal interdependence, not of an industrial society or a certain division of labour and crime, but quite specifically, of capitalist productive social relationships and crime. As Marx (1964, p. 375) himself suggested, 'a criminal produces crimes. If we look a little closer between these latter branches of production and society as a whole, we shall rid ourselves of many prejudices.' Marx's position is that, if we regard all activity as productive or (in the language of modern social science) as functional for the social system, then crime should be seen as functional too. Indeed, Marx quotes from Mandeville's *Fable of the Bees* and suggests that Mandeville, in showing that every kind of activity is productive, had followed the utimate logic of his position in arguing that '[if] evil ceases, the society must be spoiled, if not totally dissolved' (Mandeville, 1725, p. 474).

What Marx had seen more clearly than later functionalists, such as Durkheim, was that viewing activities in functional terms drives one into the absurd position of seeing crime as a necessary feature of society. For Marx and us it is not. This passage must be read as a polemic against functional analysis.

Marx's view of 'criminal man', like his view of man in general, was one in which man was both determined and determining. Thus, he was predominantly concerned at some points in his work, notably in *The German Ideology*, to attack the voluntaristic conceptions dominating the philosophies of his time. In one passage in this book (pp. 365–6) Marx shows how the 'vulgar bourgeois' view of crime is inextricably bound up with the view of law as resting on a general consensus of will:

> In actual history, those theoreticians who regarded *power* as
> the basis of right, were in direct contradiction to those who look
> on *will* as the basis of right—a contradiction which Saint
> Sancho[2] could have regarded also as that between realism (the
> child, the Ancient, the Negro, etc.) and idealism (the youth,
> the Modern, the Mongol, etc.). If power is taken as the basis of
> right, as Hobbes, etc., do, then right, law, etc. are merely the
> symptom, the expression of *other* relations upon which State
> power rests. The material life of individuals, which by no means
> depends merely on their 'will', their mode of production and
> form of intercourse, which mutually determine each other—
> this is the real basis of the State and remains so at all stages
> at which the division of labour and private property are still
> necessary, quite independently of the *will* of individuals. These
> actual relations are in no way created by the State power: on
> the contrary they are the power creating it. The individuals
> who rule in these conditions, besides having to constitute their
> power in the form of the *State*, have to give their will, which is
> determined by these definite conditions, a universal expression

as the will of the State, as law—an expression whose content is always determined by the relations of this class, as the civil and criminal law demonstrates in the clearest possible way. Just as the weight of their bodies does not depend upon their idealistic will or on their arbitrary decision, so also the fact that they enforce their own will in the form of law, and at the same time make it independent of the personal arbitrariness of each individual among them, does not depend on their idealistic will.

The idea that individuals freely or wilfully enter into contracts with the state, and that these contracts coalesce as law, ignores the material basis of power. Where material conditions express themselves as relationships of inequality and exploitation, as under capitalism, the idea that law bears anything other than a very indirect relation to will is utopian. It exists 'only in the imagination of the ideologist' (p. 367). And just as the law is the creation of material conditions rather than individual will, so (ibid.):

> Crime, i.e., the struggle of the isolated individual against the prevailing conditions, is not the result of pure arbitrariness. On the contrary, it depends on the same conditions as that rule. The same visionaries who see in right and law the domination of some independently existing, general will can see in crime the mere violation of right and law.

Only when the material forces are developed to the point that class domination, and the rule of the state, can be abolished, will it make any sense to talk of law as the reflection of will. Only under those circumstances, in other words, is it possible to conceive of a crime-free society. Part of the burden of the section on crime in *Theories of Surplus Value*, however, was to hold out such circumstances as a possibility, and to show that the abolition of crime is synonymous with the abolition of a criminogenic system of domination and control.

The contrast with Durkheim is instructive. For Durkheim both crime and the division of labour were normal: both of them external social facts. The form, content and meaning of criminality (and deviance) might vary substantially under different conditions in the division of labour. In Durkheim's ideal society, organized as a spontaneous system of occupational associations and relationships of production appropriate to individual aptitudes, crime and deviance would not be abolished: they would be expressions of the biological inequality of bodily endowments and individual receptivity to socialization into the spontaneous social order. For Marx, the division of labour and, therefore, crime, are not inevitable or normal, and he explicitly denies the utility of looking at individual differences (e.g. of will, but equally, implicitly, of biological endowment) in a situation where any kind of division of labour still obtains (ibid., p. 366): 'The material life of individuals . . . is the real basis of the State and remains so at all stages at which the division of labour and private property are still necessary, quite independently of the will of individuals.'

In conditions in which a Durkheimian spontaneous division of labour existed, that is, men would still be alienated from their productive activity, from their fellows, and from the society as a whole. 'A struggle of the isolated individual against the prevailing conditions', which in part would take the form of criminal action, would therefore ensue—but not, as in Durkheim, as a result of the existence of pathological individuals (an inevitable biological fact) but rather as a result of the alienations of all men whatever their particular (historically-defined) 'abilities'.

Whatever the form assumed by the division of labour, for Marx, crime is an expression of 'the struggle of the isolated individual against the prevailing conditions' whilst also being a struggle conditioned by those prevailing conditions. A dialectical tension is apparent between man as a determining actor (exercising free will) and man as an actor whose 'will' is a product of his times.

Just as this sense of tension has been ignored by commentators on Marxist political economy, so there has been a tendency in criminological textbook discussions to see Marx's criminology as a crude and one-dimensional economic determinism.[3] Particular attention has been given, by the ideologically-motivated, to empirical demonstrations of the positive and negative relationships between crime-rates and levels of unemployment, or the general level of economic activity measured on some 'objective' indices.[4]

Attention has also been given, however, to Marx's attacks on free will, and to the fact that, for example, in an article for the *New York Daily Tribune*, he makes use of the evidence on the 'regularity of crime' being produced by the 'moral statisticians'. The context is one in which Marx is mounting an attack on Hegel's philosophy of punishment. Where Hegel's argument was that punishment was a part of the rights of the free individual 'forced upon the individual by himself', Marx (1853) saw the criminal facing punishment as a 'slave of justice', and, implicitly, of course, of class justice. He writes that:

> [Hegel] elevates [the criminal] to the position of a free and self-determining being. Looking, however, more closely into the matter, we discover that German idealism here, as in most other instances, has but given a transcendental sanction to the

rules of existing society. Is it not a delusion to substitute for the individual with his real motives, with multifarious social circumstances pressing upon him, the abstraction of 'free will' —one among the many qualities of man himself? This theory, considering punishment as the result of the criminal's own will, is only a metaphysical expression of the old *jus talionis*, eye against eye, tooth against tooth, blood against blood.

Marx observed however that Quetelet in his 'excellent and learned book' had in 1829 been able to predict 'with astonishing certainty . . . not only the amount but all the different crimes committed in France in 1830' (Marx, 1853). It followed then, that 'the fundamental conditions of modern *bourgeois* society in general . . . produce an average amount of crime in a given national fraction of society' (ibid.). Indeed, says Marx, apparently at one with Quetelet's philosophy of 'moral statistical analysis', crimes, 'observed on a great scale' demonstrate 'the regularity of physical phenomena' (ibid.). In his reaction against the utilitarians and the 'bourgeois apologists', Marx finds uneasy company with positive scientists—at least in seeing crime as a more or less direct expression of material conditions. The temporary alliances—for strategical or illustrative material—with social determinists have laid Marx open to the charge of *economic* determinism (and the absence of a sense of dialectic between economic conditions and individual reaction to economic conditions).

But Marx's view of the constraints under which men operate is in fact very much more developed than that of the social positivists. His reaction against individualism took the form of a social explanation stressing the material conditions, the ideological superstructure of social control and the reaction of men to such constraints. In another article for the *New York Daily Tribune*—at a time in his life when, it is alleged, he was taken up with the paramount importance of the economic determination of action[5]—Marx spelt out what could be seen as a qualified 'social reaction' position in his discussion of the English criminal statistics of 1844–58. Referring to the statistical decrease in crime between 1854 and 1858, he writes (1859, our emphasis):

> The apparent decrease in crime, however, since 1854, is to be exclusively attributed to some technical changes in British Jurisdiction; to the juvenile offenders' act in the first instance, and, in the second instance, to the operation of the Criminal Justice Act of 1855, which authorizes the Police Magistrates to pass sentences for short periods with the consent of the prisoners. Violations of the law are generally the offspring of the economical agencies beyond control of the legislator, but, as the working of the Juvenile Offenders' Act testifies, it de-

pends to some degree on official society to stamp certain violations of its rules as crimes or as transgressions only. *This difference of nomenclature, so far from being indifferent, decides on the fate of thousands of men, and the moral tone of society. Law itself may not only punish crime, but improvise it.*

Not only was Marx not an economic determinist: he was also not unaware of the ways in which, as Edwin Lemert, a contemporary theorist of deviance, has put it, 'social control can lead to deviation' —in the sense that relatively arbitrary decisions by the police, the magistracy, or, indeed, the state can lead to different (criminal or non-criminal) outcomes.[6]

Ahead of his times as he was in this respect, Marx was at one with his contemporaries in seeing crime and rule-breaking as concentrated in 'the dangerous classes'—for him, the *Lumpenproletariat*. His explanation of this concentration, however, was quite distinctive. The criminal classes were criminal because they were the *Lumpenproletariat*, because they were unproductive (and therefore unorganized) workers. The members of the *Lumpenproletariat* were double parasitical. They did not contribute to the production of goods and commodities; and, moreover, they created a livelihood out of the goods and commodities produced only (and exclusively) by the productive workers (Hirst, 1972, pp. 49–52). Criminal activity was therefore necessarily an expression of a false and 'pre-political' form of individualistic consciousness. Marx's theoretical and practical concern with the organized working class as the agency of revolution, therefore, is indissolubly bound up with his disdain for the *Lumpenproletariat*, and is also perhaps responsible for the brevity with which he deals with the forms of consciousness and activity obtaining in that section of the population. It was not only a question of Marx's own personal and rather conventional morality therefore: rather his dislike for the 'dangerous classes' was a part of his general theory on the nature of proletarian and political consciousness.

It remains the case, however, that the discussion of the 'dangerous classes' and of crime is brief, and that Marx's authentic position on crime is never really fully spelt out. We are never really given systematic discussion of the criminal law and criminal activity under conditions of the forced division of labour (under capitalism) and we are not really given any picture of the crime-free society in which the division of labour has been abolished. Also, importantly, for our purposes here, the discussion of criminal motivation is extremely truncated.

In so far as attention is paid by Marx to the question of causation and motivation, the picture is not so much of criminals rationally

217

engaging in a redistribution of wealth in an individualistic fashion, but is rather a caricature of what Gouldner (1968) has called 'man on his back', that is, a man demoralized and brutalized by the day-to-day experience of employment (and unemployment) under industrial capitalism, but a man still able to grasp at the necessities of life through theft and graft. Though the criminal life might be a necessary response to the closing-off of life-chances under capitalism, it is depicted eventually as the response of the demoralized, and little attention is paid to the variety of ways in which a man might choose his options, the ways in which he might attempt to create a viable and moral existence in all but impossible conditions.

In other words, Marx and Engels, in their sparse empirical references to crime, did tend to subsume the question of humanity—or the rationality of human action—to the larger questions of political economy. Criminal action, in practice, is understood—in terms of the interests demanded by the structure of political economy as more or less 'false conscious' an adjustment to the society rather than as an inarticulate striving to overcome it.

Again in common with many classical, or liberal, thinkers, Marx and Engels's perspective on crime is one in which a relationship between economic conditions and the amount of crime is assumed. More specifically, crime is often seen to be a product of inequitable economic relationships in a context of general poverty. However, as George Vold (1958, p. 18) has shown quite thoroughly, the only conclusion deriving from attempts to demonstrate this assumed relationship is that, 'assumptions involving *either* positive or negative relationships with economic conditions may be supported with some show of statistical significance' (our emphasis).

Moreover, as Vold shows, there appears to be a strong case for working with a correlation between upturns in legitimate and illegitimate economic activity under modern capitalism. Hermann Mannheim, after examining the vastly differing conclusions of the investigations of (amongst others) Enrico Ferri (1886b) (into the movements of French criminality between 1826 and 1878), Georg von Mayr (1867) (into the correlations between theft and the price of grain in Bavaria between 1835 and 1861) and Dorothy S. Thomas (1925) into the correlations between business cycles and various social phenomena (ranging from crime through to geographical mobility), arrives at a similarly sceptical conclusion. For him, specific problems reside in elucidating the mediatory effect of unemployment, the distribution of occupations, and rather more subjective features of life, like 'job-satisfaction' and 'monotony of existence', before any certain statement about the relationship between criminality and economic conditions can be approached (Mannheim, 1965, pp. 572–91). That is, no simple solution to the debate about economic determinism and crime is likely until there is more clarity about the kind of crime under discussion,[7] some agreement on how to weight or index criminal and economic trends, and some greater understanding of the mediating role played by different social arrangements developed to sustain economic production in different societies. In so far as Marx and Engels, in writing of crime, are guilty of assuming a negative relationship between economic conditions and crime, they go close to adopting a form of economic determinism which, despite many claims to the contrary, they do not exhibit in other areas of their work.

Indeed, one of the most telling features of Marx's statements on crime is their a-typicality when compared to the vast body of 'orthodox Marxism'. If Marxism offers us anything of value in understanding the ways in which social conflict is generated, sustained, and helps to shape the kind and amount of criminal and deviant activity at large, we are more likely to find it in Marx's general theory than we are in the more specific statements made in response to isolated empirical challenges.

In part, Marxism stands or falls on the basis of certain assumptions it makes about the nature of man. Where other social theories (e.g. as developed by Durkheim and Weber) operate with implicit assumptions about man's nature, Marx made his starting-point a quite explicit philosophical anthropology of man (cf. Walton and Gamble, 1972, ch. 1). In *The Economic and Philosophical Manuscripts of 1844* Marx (p. 126) is concerned to show that man is distinct in a crucial and precise way from the members of the animal world:

> Man is a *species-being* not only in the sense that he makes the community (his own as well as those of other things) his object both practically and theoretically, but also (and this is simply another expression of the same thing) in the sense that he treats himself as the present living species, as a *universal* and consequently free being.

The bulk of Marx's later work is concerned with the demonstration of the ways in which man's social nature and consciousness have been distorted, imprisoned or diverted by the social arrangements developed over time. These social arrangements are the product of man's struggle to master the conditions of scarcity and material underdevelopment. These social arrangements, developed as a response to man's domination by poverty, imprison man tightly in social relationships of an exploitative nature and alienate men from men, and thus from the objects of their labour. Man is struggling to be free, but cannot realize freedom (or himself as a fully-conscious,

219

'sensuous' species-being) until such time as he is free of the exploitative relationships which are outmoded and unnecessary.

The continuing debates over Marxism in sociology and philosophy, (as well as within socialist movements) in the twentieth century, therefore, have had to do with problems of consciousness, contradictions and social change. That is, the image of society offered out by classical Marxism is one of competing social groups, each with a distinct set of interests and cultural world views, caught within a network of essentially temporary (or historically-specific) social arrangements, which in their turn are more or less likely to be revolutionized in periods of crisis. Capitalism, as a set of social relationships, is conceptualized as the most highly-developed form of social exploitation, within which are sown the seeds of man's leap to a liberating consciousness. Capitalism 'contains the seeds of its own destruction' not only in the sense that it creates the technology whereby physical and material need may be satisfied, but also because it prevents a more sophisticated set of social relationships developing alongside such productive forces.

A full-blown Marxist theory of deviance, or at least a theory of deviance deriving from a Marxism so described, would be concerned to develop explanations of the ways in which particular historical periods, characterized by particular sets of social relationships and means of production, give rise to attempts by the economically and politically powerful to order society in particular ways. It would ask with greater emphasis the question that Howard Becker poses (and does not face), namely, who makes the rules, and why? A Marxist theory would attempt, that is, to locate the defining agencies, not only in some general market structure, but quite specifically in their relationship to the overweening structure of material production and the division of labour. Moreover, to be a satisfactory explanation, a Marxist theory would proceed with a notion of man which would distinguish it quite clearly from classical, positivist, or interactionist 'images' of man. It would assume, that is, a degree of consciousness, bound up with men's location in a social structure of production, exchange and domination, which of itself would influence the ways in which men defined as criminal or deviant would attempt to live with their outsider's status. That is, men's reaction to labelling by the powerful would not be seen to be simply a cultural problem—a problem of reacting to a legal status or a social stigma: it would necessarily be seen to be bound up with men's degree of consciousness of domination and subordination in a wider structure of power relationships operating in particular types of economic context. One consequence of such an approach—which, it must be stated, has been conspicuous for its absence in deviancy theory—would be the possibility of building links between the insights of interactionist theory, and other approaches sensitive to men's subjective world, and the theories of social structure implicit in orthodox Marxism.[8] More crucially, such a linkage would enable us to escape from the strait-jacket of an economic determinism and the relativism of some sub-jectivist approaches to a theory of contradiction in a social structure which recognizes in 'deviance' the acts of men in the process of actively making, rather than passively taking, the external world. It might enable us to sustain what has until now been a polemical assertion, made (in the main) by anarchists and deviants themselves, that much deviance is in itself a political act, and that, in this sense, deviance is a property of the act rather than a spurious label applied to the amoral or the careless by agencies of political and social control.

In later chapters, the attempt will be made to spell out the elements of a theory which could achieve these linkages. For the purposes of this chapter, it is sufficient to note (and important to understand) that what passes for Marxism in the textbooks on deviancy in no way approaches (or attempts) a resolution of these questions. It is not merely that the Marxism in the textbooks is necessarily a distortion of Marxism—in the way that Marx dealt with crime; it is also that the development of Marxism in the direction of a social psychology of consciousness and an understanding of rational actors involved in action choices has been delayed—and indeed has been obstructed—since the time of Marx's work.

The late 1960s and early 1970s have witnessed a resurgence of Marxist social theory, not only in the form of translations of pre-viously obscure works by Marx himself (Hobsbawm, 1965; Mc-Lellan, 1971), but also in the works of interpreters with non-sectarian credentials (Avineri, 1969; Lukacs, 1971a; Meszaros, 1970; Walton and Gamble, 1972). There has been a move away from the barren and purely formal attempts of writers to claim a Marxist pedigree towards a more thoroughgoing and unflinching confrontation of Marxism and social theory at large. In this book, we attempt to demonstrate the utility of such a confrontation for the understanding and faithful rendition of what passes for criminal and deviant behaviour in an antagonistic, late capitalist society. Later chapters will spell out the implications of such a confrontation more fully. Here, we shall pause to consider the contributions and limitations of what has previously been characterized as 'the Marxist view', and turn them to the attempts made by others, operating in alternative traditions, to explain the antagonisms and conflicts of an advanced society, and their contribution to crime and deviance, in specifically non-Marxist (or anti-Marxist) fashion.

Willem Bonger and formal Marxism

In the study of crime and deviance, the work of Willem Bonger (1876–1940), professor at the University of Amsterdam, and author, amongst other pieces, of the monumental *Criminality and Economic Conditions* (1916), *An Introduction to Criminology* (1935) and *Race and Crime* (1943), has assumed the mantle of the Marxist orthodoxy —if only because (with the exception of untranslated writers inside the Soviet bloc) no other self-proclaimed Marxist has devoted time to a full-scale study of the area.

Bonger's criminology is an attempt to utilize some of the formal concepts of Marxism in the understanding of the crime-rates of European capitalism in the late nineteenth and early twentieth centuries. Importantly, however, Bonger's efforts appear, for us, not so much the application of a fully-fledged Marxist theory as they are a recitation of a 'Marxist catechism' in an area which Marx had left largely untouched—a recitation prompted by the growth not of the theory itself, but by the growth of a sociological pragmatism. Bonger must, therefore, be evaluated in his own terms,[9] in terms of the competence of his extension of the formal concepts of Marxism to the subject-matter, rather than in terms of any claim that might be made for him as *the* Marxist criminologist.

In at least two respects, Bonger's analysis of crime differs in substance from that of Marx. On the one hand, Bonger is clearly very much more seriously concerned than Marx with the causal chain linking crime with the precipitating economic and social conditions. On the other, he does not confine his explanations to working-class crime, extending his discussions to the criminal activity of the industrial bourgeoisie as defined by the criminal laws of his time. Whilst differing from Marx in these respects, however, Bonger is at one with his mentor in attributing the activity itself to demoralized individuals, products of a dominant capitalism.

Indeed, in both Marx and Bonger, one is aware of a curious contradiction between the 'image of man' advanced as the anthropological underpinning of 'orthodox' Marxism[10] and the questions asked about men who deviate.

The starting point of Bonger's exposition in *Criminality and Economic Conditions* (1916, p. 401) is in fact a rather ambiguous set of questions, involving in particular, the curious notion of 'the criminal thought':

The etiology of crime includes the three following problems:
First. *Whence does the criminal thought in man arise?* [our emphasis]. Second. What forces are there in man which can prevent the execution of this criminal thought, and what is their

origin? Third. What is the occasion for the commission of criminal acts?

The criminal thought, which runs through the bulk of Bonger's analysis of crime, is seen as the product of the tendency in industrial capitalism to create 'egoism' rather than 'altruism' in the structure of social life. It is apparent that the notion performs two different functions for Bonger, in that he is able to argue, at different points, that, first, 'the criminal thought' is engendered by the conditions of misery forced on sections of the working class under capitalism and that, second, it is also the product of the greed encouraged when capitalism thrives. In other words, as an intermediary notion, it enables Bonger to circumvent the knotty problem of the relationship between general economic conditions and the propensity to economic crime.[11]

Now, whilst the ambiguity in the notion may help Bonger's analysis, it does not stem directly from his awareness of dual problems. For Bonger, it does appear as an autonomous psychic and behavioural quality which is to be deplored and feared; 'the criminal thought', and its associated 'egoism' are products of the brutishness of capitalism, but at the same time they do appear to 'take over' individuals and independently direct their actions.

The Marxist perspective, of course, has always emphasized the impact that the dominant mode of production has had on social relationships in the wider society, and, in particular, has spelt out the ways in which a capitalist means of production will tend to 'individuate' the nature of social life. But to understand that 'egoism' and 'individuation' are products of particular sets of social arrangements is to understand that egoism and individuation have no force or influence independently of their social context. For Bonger, the 'criminal thought'—albeit a product of the egoistic structure of capitalism—assumes an independent status as an intrinsic and behavioural quality of certain (criminal) individuals. It is enormously paradoxical that a writer who lays claim to be writing as a sociologist and a Marxist should begin his analysis with an assumed individual quality (which he deplores) and proceed only later to the social conditions and relationships sustaining and obstructing the acting-out of this quality.[12]

In the first place, the emphasis in Bonger on 'the criminal thought' as an independent factor for analysis is equivalent to the biological, physiological and sociological (or environmental) factors accorded an independent and causative place in the writings of the positivist theorists of crime. The limitations of this approach have been pointed out, amongst others, by Austin T. Turk (1964b, pp. 454–5):

Students of crime have been preoccupied with the search for an

223

explanation of distinguishing characteristics of 'criminality', almost universally assuming that the implied task is to develop scientific explanations of the behaviour of persons who deviate from 'legal norms'. The quest has not been very successful . . . the cumulative impact of efforts to specify and explain differences between 'criminal' and 'non-criminal' cultural and behaviour patterns is to force serious consideration of the possibility that there may be *no* significant differences between the overwhelming majority of legally identified criminals and the *relevant* general population, *i.e.* that population whose concerns and expectations impinge directly and routinely upon the individuals so identified.

More succinctly (ibid., p. 455): 'the working assumption has been that *crime* and *non-crime* are classes of behaviour instead of simply labels associated with the processes by which individuals come to occupy ascribed . . . *statuses* of criminal and non-criminal.'

It is a comment on the nature of Bonger's Marxism that the actor is accorded such an idealistic independence; when to have started with a model of a society within which there are conflicting interests and a differential distribution of power would have revealed the utility of the criminal law and the 'criminal' label (with a legitimating ideology derived from academia) to the powerful élites of capitalist society. In fact, of course, a criminology which proceeds in recognition of competing social interests has two interrelated tasks of explanation. Certainly it has the task of explaining the causes for an individual's involvement in 'criminal' behaviour: but, prior to that, it has the task of explaining the derivation of the 'criminal' label (whose content, function and applicability we have argued will vary across time, across cultures, and internally within a social structure).

One cannot entirely avoid the conclusion that Bonger's analysis, irrespective of the extent to which it is guided by a reading and acceptance of Marxist percepts, is motivated (and confused) by a fear of those with 'criminal thoughts'.

For Bonger 'criminal thought' is by and large a product of the lack of moral training in the population. Moral training has been denied the proletariat, in particular, because it is not the essential training for work in an industrializing society. The spread of 'moral training' is the antidote to 'criminal thoughts', but, since such an education is unlikely under the brutish capitalism of the imperialist period, capitalism—or more precisely, the economic conditions (of inequality and accumulation)—are indeed a cause of crime.

In so far as Bonger displays any concern for the determinant nature of social relationships of production, he does so in order to illustrate the tendencies of different social arrangements to encourage egoism and 'criminal thoughts' in the population at large. As against the ameliorarist school, which saw an inevitable advance of man from conditions of primitive and brutish living to societies in which altruistic relationships would predominate, Bonger (1969, p. 28), in fundamental agreement with the value placed on altruism and liberalism, identified the advent of capitalism with the break in the process of civilizing social relationships:

> We cannot speak of the diminution of egoism, but of the moderating of violence in the course of time. It cannot be maintained that a capitalist who tried by a lockout to force his workmen to break with their union, in order that he may escape the danger of a decrease in his profits through a strike, and who in this way condemns them and their families to hunger, is less egoistic than the slave-owner driving his slaves to harder work. The former does not use force—it is useless—he has surer weapons at his command, the suffering with which he can strike his workmen; he seems less egoistic, but in reality he is as egoistic as the latter. . . . Capitalism is a system of exploitation in which, in place of the exploited person being robbed he is compelled by poverty to use all his powers for the benefit of the exploiter.

Moreover, Bonger comments (ibid., p. 29): 'The fact that the duty of altruism is so much insisted upon is the most convincing proof that it is not generally practised.'

The demise of egoism, and the creation of social conditions favourable to the 'criminal thought' parallels, for Bonger, the development of social arrangements of production as described by Marx.

Under 'primitive communism', production is seen to have been organized for social consumption and not for exchange, poverty and wealth were universally experienced (depending on the season and the geography of the individual community) and the subordination of men to nature was all but total. Thus, writes Bonger (1969, p. 35):

> primitive men feel themselves to be first of all the members of a unit . . . they not only abstain from acts harmful to their companions, but come to their aid whenever they can . . . they are honest, benevolent and truthful towards the members of their group and . . . public opinion has a great influence among them. The cause of these facts is to be found in *the mode of production which brought about a uniformity of interest in the persons united in a single group, obliged them to aid one another in the difficult and uninterrupted struggle for existence,*

225

and made men free and equal, since there was neither poverty nor riches, and consequently no possibility of oppression.

Under capitalism, the transformation of work from its value for use to its value for exchange (as fully described by Marx) is responsible for the 'cupidity and ambition', the lack of sensitivity between men, and the declining influence of men's ambitions on the actions of their fellows. Bonger writes (ibid., p. 37):

> As soon as productivity has increased to such an extent that the producer can regularly produce more than he needs, and the division of labour puts him in a position to exchange his surplus for things that he could not produce himself, at this moment there arises in man the notion of no longer giving to his comrades what they need, but of keeping for himself the surplus of what his labour produces, and exchanging it. Then it is that the mode of production begins to run counter to the social instincts of man instead of favouring it as heretofore.

Capitalism, in short (ibid., p. 40), 'has developed egoism at the expense of altruism'.

'Egoism' constitutes a favourable climate for the commission of criminal acts, and this, for Bonger, is an indication that an environment in which men's social instincts are encouraged has been replaced by one which confers legitimacy on asocial or 'immoral' acts of deviance. The commission of these acts, as Bonger explicitly states in *Introduction to Criminology*, has a demoralizing effect on the whole of the body politic.

Bonger's substantive analysis of types of crime, covering (in *Economic Conditions and Criminality*) a range of 'economic crimes', 'sexual crimes', 'crimes from vengeance and other motives', 'political crimes' and 'pathological crimes', is taken up with a demonstration of the ways in which these crimes are causatively linked with an environment encouraging egoistic action. Even involvement of persons born with 'psychic defects' in criminal activity can be explained in terms of these enabling conditions (Bonger, 1916, p. 354):

> These persons adapt themselves to their environment only with difficulty . . . have a smaller chance than others to succeed in our present society, where the fundamental principle is the warfare of all against all. Hence they are more likely to seek for means that others do not employ (prostitution, for example).

The whole of Bonger's analysis, however much it is altered or qualified at particular points in his discussion, rests on the environmental determinism of his 'general considerations'. In a social structure encouraging of egoism, the obstacles and deterrents to the emergence of the presumably ever-present 'criminal thought' are weakened and/or removed; where as, for example, under primitive communism, the communality was constructed around, and dependent upon, an interpersonal altruism. Capitalism is responsible for the free play granted to the pathological will, the 'criminal thought' possessed by certain individuals.

The bulk of Bonger's work, indeed, so far from being an example of dialectical procedure, is a kind of positivism in itself, or at least an eclecticism reminiscent of 'inter-disciplinary' positivism. Where the general theory appears not to encompass all the facts (facts produced by positivist endeavour), mediations of various kinds are introduced. In Bonger, it is possible to find examples of the elements of anomie theory, differential opportunity theory and, at times, the frameworks of structural-functionalism (much of it well in advance of its time). In his discussion of economic crime, for example, Bonger (1969, p. 108) approached a Mertonian stance on larceny:

> Modern industry manufactures enormous quantities of goods without the outlet for them being known· The desire to buy must, then, be excited in the public. Beautiful displays, dazzling illuminations, and many other means are used to attain the desired end. The perfection of this system is reached in the great modern retail store, where persons may enter freely, and see and handle everything—where, in short, the public is drawn as a moth to a flame. The result of these tactics is that the cupidity of the crowd is highly excited.

And Bonger is not unaware of the general, or the more limited, theories of criminality and deviance produced by the classical thinkers of his time and earlier. Where appropriate, Bonger attempts to incorporate elements of these competing theorists, though always in a way which subordinates their positions to his own 'general considerations'.[13] On Gabriel Tarde's 'law of imitation', for example, which purports to explain criminality as a function of association with 'criminal types', Bonger writes (1969, p. 85):

> In our present society, with its pronounced egoistic tendencies, imitation strengthens these, as it would strengthen the altruistic tendencies produced by another form of society. . . . It is only as a consequence of the predominance of egoism in our present society that the error is made of supposing the effect of imitation to be necessarily evil.

Our concern here is not to dispute particular arguments in Bonger for their own sakes, but rather to point to the way in which a single-factor environmentalism is given predominance, with secondary considerations derived from the body of existing literature being introduced eclectically. That is, Bonger's method, though resting on an environmentalism explicitly derived from Marx, appears in the final analysis as a method reminiscent of the eclectism practised by positivist sociologists operating with formal concepts lacking a grounding in history and structure.

This eclectic approach is accompanied by a crudely statistical technique of verification and elaboration. We are presented, amongst other things, with statistical demonstrations of the relationship between levels of educational attainment and violent crime, declines in business and 'bourgeois' crime (fraud, etc.), degrees of poverty and involvement in sexual crime (especially prostitution), crimes of 'vengeance' and the season of the year and many more.[14] Consistently, the objective is to demonstrate the underlying motivation as being bound up with an egoism induced and sustained by the environment of capitalism. So, for example, with 'crimes of passion' (Bonger, 1969, p. 160):

> We must notice . . . one kind of crime of passion, the revenge
> of a woman seduced and then abandoned. Besides sexual
> jealousy there are, in these cases, other motives playing their
> part. Often the woman has not given herself for love alone, but
> also with the prospect of a marriage, or a betterment of her
> economic position. It is not sexual vengeance that is the sole
> motive here then, but also vengeance for economic reasons.

And, lest we should think that egoism is directly a product of poverty and subordination, as opposed to being a central element of a general moral climate, Bonger is able to offer explanations of crime among the bourgeoisie. These crimes he sees to be motivated by need, in cases of business decline and collapse, or by cupidity. In the latter case, 'what [men] get by honest business is not enough for them, they wish to become richer' (ibid., p. 138). In either case, Bonger's case is contingent on the moral climate engendered by the economic system (ibid.):

> It is only under special circumstances that this desire for
> wealth arises, and . . . it is unknown under others. It will be
> necessary only to point out that although cupidity is a strong
> motive with all classes of our present society, it is especially so
> among the bourgeoisie, as a consequence of their position in
> the economic life.

Now, Bonger's formal Marxism does enable him to make an insightful series of comments about the nature of the deprivations experienced under capitalism. Judged in Bonger's own terms—that is, in terms of the social positivism of his time—his work surpasses much that was, and is, available. Notably, Bonger's discussion of the effects of the subordination of women (and its contribution to the aetiology of female criminality) and of 'militarism' (in sustaining an egoistic and competitive moral climate) seem far ahead of their time. Writing of the criminality of women, for example, Bonger (1969, p. 58) asserts that:

The great power of a man over his wife, as a consequence of his economic preponderance, may equally be a demoralizing cause. It is certain that there will always be abuse of power on the part of a number of those whom social circumstances have clothed with a certain authority. How many women there are now who have to endure the coarseness and bad treatment of their husbands, but would not hesitate to leave them if their economic dependence and the law did not prevent. Holmes, the author of 'Pictures and Problems from London Police Courts', who for years saw all the unfortunates who came before these tribunals, says in this connection: 'A good number of Englishmen seem to think they have as perfect a right to thrash or kick their wives as the American has to "lick his nigger" '.

The contemporary ring of these comments is paralleled in Bonger's comments, made, it should be remembered, at the time when the 'Marxist' parties of Europe found their members rushing to the 'national defence' in the 'Great War' (Bonger, 1969, p. 78): 'The harmful circumstances [of militarism] . . . will disappear only in the country where an army is exclusively for the purpose of defence, to repulse an enemy that wishes to destroy democratic institutions.'

Thus, whilst much of Bonger's formal Marxism appears as a form of abstracted and eclectic positivism when viewed across its canvas, he still derives a considerable benefit and understanding from the Marxist perspective in his sensitivity to the demoralizing and destructive consequences of the forms of domination characteristic of a capitalist society.

Paradoxically, however, this sensitivity does not extend to an understanding of the nature of domination and social control in defining and delineating the field of interest itself, namely what passes for crime and deviance in societies where 'law' is the law determined by powerful interests and classes in the population at large.

Bonger's lack of scepticism about the social content of the law is all the more surprising in view of the bows he makes to Marxism in early sections of his central texts. In *Criminality and Economic Conditions* (p. 24), he writes:

In every society which is divided into a ruling class and a class

229

ruled, penal law has been principally constituted according to the will of the former. . . . In the existing penal code, hardly an act is punished if it does not injure the interests of the dominant classes as well as the other, and if the law touching it protects only the interests of the other.

Elsewhere, Bonger (1936, p. 2) asserts that 'there are instances where an action stamped as criminal is not felt to be immoral by anybody.' But these statements, and others like them, are made in passing and do not constitute the basis for the thoroughgoing analysis of the structure of laws and interests. And Bonger is ambivalent throughout on the role of social control in the creation of crime. He seems aware only in certain cases, of 'societal reaction' in determining degrees of apprehension. So, for example (Bonger, 1969, p. 60): 'the offences of which women are most often guilty are also those which it is most difficult to discover, namely those committed without violence. Then, those who have been injured are less likely to bring a complaint against a woman than against a man.'

But later, in dealing with sexual crimes in general, Bonger uncritically accepts the official statistics of apprehension as an indication of 'the class of the population that commits these crimes' (p. 150).

In fact, Bonger's position is that the law (and its enforcement)—whilst certainly the creation of a dominant class—is a genuine reflexion of some universal social and moral sentiment. This is most clearly put in *An Introduction to Criminology* (p. 3): 'One might compare moral and criminal laws, respectively with two concentric circles, of which the former would be the larger.'

The manifest explanation for the inclusion within the criminal law of sanctions controlling behaviour which is not directly harmful to the class interests of the powerful is that the working classes themselves are not without power. That is, one supposes, it is in the interests of the powerful to operate a system of general social control in the interests of order (within which individual and corporate enterprise can proceed unimpeded). However, there is more than a suspicion that Bonger's equation of social control with a universal moral sentiment is based on a belief he shares with the bourgeoisie in order for its own sake. Socialism is preferable to capitalism because it is more orderly (Bonger, 1969, p. 168):

We have now reached the end of our remarks upon the etiology of these crimes, and have shown that the principle causes are, first, the present structure of society, which brings about innumerable conflicts; second, the lack of civilisation and education among the poorer classes; and, third, alcoholism, which is in turn a consequence of the social environment.

Bonger's formal Marxism, therefore, tells us that the solution to the problems of criminality is not so much to challenge the labels and the processing of capitalist law as it is to wage a responsible and orderly political battle for the reform of a divisive social structure. Even in the case of political opposition, a crucial distinction is to be drawn between responsible activity (the acts of a noble man) and the irresponsible and pathological activity—especially that of the anarchist movement (characterized, argues Bonger, by 'extreme individualism', 'great vanity', 'pronounced altruistic tendencies' 'coupled with a lack of intellectual development').

Since, as Bonger realizes, 'vain and excitable individualists are fairly numerous, yet almost none become active anarchists', he feels it necessary to explain anarchist involvement in a classically-positivist manner. We are told the life history of various anarchists in order to point to the uneasy childhoods they allegedly experienced; and the suggestion is made that anarchism is the creed of the low in intellect. The importance of anarchism as a political movement, however, like the importance of other forms of crime, is dependent on material and economic circumstance (Bonger, 1969, p. 181):

> No one can deny that there are as many persons predisposed to anarchistic crimes in a country like Germany as there are in Italy, for example. Yet anarchistic crimes do not occur in Germany for the good reason that the material conditions there are so much better than in Italy, and the degree of intellectual development of the working people is so much higher: the German working-man derides the 'naiveté' of the anarchists, and detests their futile crimes.

Given the original assumptions of Bonger's Marxism, this distaste for disorderly and individualistic activity can be easily characterized, as one might expect, as pathological. It is indicative, too, of Bonger's motivating disposition that it is only in the discussion of the political crimes of which he approves that any doubt is cast on the justifications of the criminal label (ibid., p. 174):

> It would be a waste of time to insist upon the fact that these acts [political crimes] have nothing in common with criminals but the name. Most criminals are individuals whose social sentiments are reduced to the minimum, and who injure others purely for the satisfaction of their own desires. The political criminals of whom we are speaking, on the other hand, are the direct opposite; they risk their most sacred interests, their

231

liberty and their life, for the benefit of society; they injure the ruling class only to aid the oppressed classes, and consequently all humanity. . . . While the ordinary criminal is generally 'l'homme canaille' . . . the political criminal is 'homo nobilis'.

Doubt is cast upon the criminal label here, largely, it must be said, because Bonger is able to empathize with the actor under consideration. Elsewhere in his discussion, there is no attempt on Bonger's part to put himself 'in the position of the other', or any attempt to empathize with the acts of a criminal as a solution to a human dilemma. This is most apparent, as with many other writers in the area, in the discussion of sexual offences. Writing of rape, Bonger asserts (ibid., p. 149): 'First of all it must be remembered that this crime is not the act of a pervert but of a brute.'

Indeed, one of the persistent themes running through Bonger's critique of capitalism is an essentially moralistic and idealistic belief in the role of socialism in controlling 'evil' (ibid., p. 164):

In the working circles in which socialism is beginning to make its way, there is growing little by little, an interest in things other than those which formerly occupied working-men in their leisure hours. They begin to become civilised and to have an aversion to the coarser amusements.

Bonger's failure to take issue with the dominant values and standards enshrined in the criminal law (which indeed he understands to be part of a universal and perhaps an absolute or natural value system) leads him into what Matza has called the correctional perspective on deviance. Crudely put, the correctional perspective has to do with understanding a social phenomenon only to the point of being able to rid society of the phenomenon in question. The correctional perspective has the additional feature of continually and successfully suppressing essential feaures of the phenomenon, characterized by subsuming them under one or other amorphous label, or sometimes by offering little or no description of the phenomenon, prior to advancing one's explanation. Either way, Matza argues, the correctional perspective 'loses the phenomenon' (p. 17).[15]

In contrast to the correctional perspective, Matza (1969, p. 10) advances the appreciative or naturalistic perspective on deviant behaviour. This is seen to involve:

The tacit purging of a conception of pathology by new stress on human *diversity*, and the erosion of a simple distinction between deviant and conventional phenomena, resulting from an intimate familiarity with the world as it is . . . [yielding] a more sophisticated view stressing complexity.

'Appreciating' as distinct from romanticizing a deviant pheno-menon involves most importantly the understanding (and faithful representation) of the individual deviant actor and his motivational accounts. There is some recognition, too, of the need to provide the explanatory links between these motivations and the structural context in which the deviant actor moves. The thrust of the argument, for 'appreciation', of course, centres around the assumption that men are guided in action by purposes and motives, keenly felt and experienced, and that to ignore or underplay these purposes and motives in one's descriptive and explanatory account is an act of bad faith and a faulty portrayal of the world as it is.

Bonger's correctional perspective is just such an account. Only in certain cases does Bonger accord a complexity of motive to his deviant actors. This complexity seems to appear when the general schema (depending on the egoism of the moral climate) collapses in the face of actual empirical instances. In dealing with 'economic crimes' (induced by poverty) Bonger writes (1969, p. 104):

> The same act may be at once *egoistic* and *altruistic*, and this is the case with some crimes committed from poverty, when an individual steals in order not to have those in his charge die of hunger. What conflicts of duty our present society creates!

Thefts induced by poverty, therefore, can, for Bonger, be both altruistic and rational. It is difficult to understand, though, how and by what criteria, Bonger denies such a rationality and altruism to other forms of crime. What Bonger calls 'crimes of vengeance', what he calls 'political crimes' (i.e. the activity of anarchists), and indeed the whole gamut of 'economic crimes' could all in theory be motivated by altruism as defined by Bonger in his general considerations. That is, they could all be the product of men's attempts to solve dilemmas of poverty, demoralization and a lack of control over life in general —produced by a climate of egoism but resolved in terms of men acting individually and collectively in an altruistic manner. Indeed, the very labels applied to crime by the powerful, and discussed rather uncritically by Bonger, could themselves be contradictory. What might be understood by the powerful as a crime of vengeance— larceny of an employer's home, refusal to pay one's rent, a with-drawal of dowry—could all be acts of altruism committed in order to support a family, or seen by the actor as legitimate means of making a living in a society of inequality and financial exploitation. In starting from the concept of crime as officially defined, Bonger, like the positivists he debated, laid himself open to the mistakes of his predecessors, and laid his subjects open to the correctional endeavours of a positive criminology.

In 'appreciative' accounts of human deviance, in contrast, we are presented with actors exercising degrees of choice and possessing a dignity of their own. For Matza, and for some of the writers in 'the Chicago School' in particular, even the apparently most 'demoralized' of men—caught in the most hopeless of circumstances (e.g. as a hobo, or an inhabitant of Skid Row cities) could exercise a choice and construct a life-project of sorts. For Bonger, however, the picture is ever and always a picture of determination. Bonger (1936, p. 23) sees human beings as involved in a web of circumstances determining their actions in largely irrevocable manner; but human beings, none the less, who have to take responsibility for their choice of action:

> Determinism teaches us that every human being, without exception, is to be held accountable for his actions; not on the grounds of an imaginery free will, but because of the fact that he is a member of society, and that this society must take measures to protect itself.

In discussing empirical examples, however, Bonger is often compelled to 'appreciate' the complex nature of human choice and its relationship to determining circumstances. In his discussion of 'economic crime', for example, Bonger (1969, p. 36) needs to spell out the range and variety of 'criminal' and other adaptations to poverty:

> Three expedients offer themselves to one who has fallen into the blackest poverty: mendicity, theft and suicide. It is partly chance (opportunity, etc.) and partly the individual predisposition which fixes what anyone under the conditions named will become, whether a mendicant or a thief.

Conclusion

For us, the outstanding feature of Bonger's essentially correctional perspective is that, quite aside from the premises on which it operates (the contingency of criminality on an egoistic moral climate), it does not reveal a consistent social psychology, or, by the same token, a systematic social theory. At one moment, the actor under consideration is seen to be inextricably caught up in a determined and identifiable set of circumstances (or, more properly, a set of economic relationships); at another, he appears as the victim of an assumed personal quality ('the criminal thought') sustained and (often) apparently developed by the moral climate of industrial capitalism.

In so far as a social theory reveals itself in Bonger, the central assumptions on which it is built appear to be Durkheimian in nature rather than to derive from the avowedly Marxist theory of its

234

author. Criminal man is consistently depicted not so much as a man produced by a matrix of unequal social relationships, nor indeed as a man attempting to resolve those inequalities of wealth, power and life-chances; rather, criminal man is viewed as being in need of social control. 'Socialism', in this perspective, is an alternative and desirable set of social institutions, which carry with them a set of Durkheimian norms and controls. 'Socialism' thus expressed is the resort of an idealist, wishing for the substitution of a competitive and egoistic moral climate by a context in which the co-operativeness of men is encouraged[Socialism is preferable to capitalism, most of all, because it will control the baser instincts of man, Bonger does not assert that the 'egoistic' man will 'wither away' under socialism: it is only that the social relationships of socialism will not reward the endeavours of an egoist.]

Now this social theory is not Marxist, or at least it does not meet the full requirements of a Marxist theory of deviance. Socialism is seen to arise, in this theory (as to some extent it does in the work of Edouard Bernstein) because it is preferable idealistically to the brutish alternatives of capitalist development; and, moreover, when it arises, it will assume a power over and above men as a means of controlling their thoughts and instincts. Bonger does not explain how this process of evangelism is to proceed, or indeed whether the agency of change is to be men struggling to abolish the constraints over their own lives and work. One has the impression that Bonger, with Bernstein, sees socialism as the ultimate consequence of sustained and responsible pressure by the intellectual leaderships of social democratic parties with formally Marxist programmes. If this is so, it is hard to see how this perspective differs in any crucial respect from the reformist perspectives of the liberals whom Bonger engages in formal polemic—except only in the content of the concepts with which the intellectual warfare is waged. It is certainly very difficult to equate Bonger's socialism with that envisaged by Marx as the culmination of a struggle for the control of the material means of production, and the realization of a classless society. It is perhaps not so hard to equate his socialism with that of the leadership of the Soviet bloc, which are currently engaged in their own 'war' against crime, utilizing the characteristically empiricist methodology of positivistic social science.

In some ways, it is inaccurate to endow Bonger's work with the status of a theory. Though he works with hypotheses, and makes his assumptions and terminological indebtedness plain enough to see, his method remains eclectic and, at times, urbane. Whilst this eclecticism may have been prompted by a felt need to reveal a familiarity with all alternative theorists (in order to rebut them), it is not an eclecticism that is conclusively linked with a total social theory.

Levels of analysis are confused, individual and social psychologies merged, and, in the end, the distinction between 'structure' and 'action', 'base' and 'superstructure', 'contradiction' and 'change', and 'power' and 'interest' not so much discussed as ignored.

What we want to offer in our concluding chapters is the element of a social theory which resolves these difficulties. Such a theory would certainly take Bonger's argument about the 'individuation' of relationships under capitalism, without accepting it as some autonomous personal quality continually at war with alternative, altruistic social arrangements. It would take too the implication in Bonger about the political nature of crime—whilst extending this implication to acts of deviance which Bonger relegates to the level of individual pathology (some sex crimes) or collective psychosis (anarchism). It would start with crime as human action, as reaction to positions held in an antagonistic social structure, but also as action taken to resolve those antagonisms. It would, in brief, involve a model— suggested but not followed thoroughly by Marx himself—of the dialectics of human action—however, or for whatever reason they tend to be defined as 'criminal' in particular historical periods by the powerful. Hopefully, too, it would not proceed in fear of an assumed human nature—in need of control and constraint—but would rather proceed to understand the relationship of criminal action, and an understanding of its dynamics, to human liberation.

8   The new conflict theorists

Theories of crime and deviance, like social theories in general, are in part creations of their time. Much of the sociological literature on deviance that we have discussed in earlier chapters is characterized, in the last analysis, by a consensual view of society, a view which, above all else, depends upon the assumption that there is some fundamental agreement among men as to the goals of social life, and the rules, or norms, which should govern the pursuit of those goals. This view is usually associated with the pioneering work of Talcott Parsons, and the 'structural-functionalist' school of American sociology, though the paradigm of consensus has been apparent in sociological theorizing from the days of Durkheim and Comte. The paradigm has been challenged at various times, but it is significant that the challenges have been most effective during periods of political uncertainty, or, in other words, during periods when men are less than secure about the stability, permanence, or legitimacy of existing social arrangements.

Formally, of course, the alternative paradigm to the consensual view, deriving from Durkheim and extended by Parsons, is the paradigm of conflict, whether in the form of a continuing conflict within market situations over the distribution of scarce resources (as in Weber) or in the form of conflicts deriving from men's struggle to abolish the divisions imposed by the arrangements of material production (as in Marx). These alternatives, in their classical form, have not, however, been adopted in the challenges made to the consensual paradigm in social theory. The challenges made by 'the new conflict theorists' to the paradigmatic theories of structural-functionalism, appear to have been prompted, not so much by a re-examination of the classical social theorists, but rather by events in the real world which have thrown the assumptions of 'consensus' into doubt.

Ralf Dahrendorf's formulation of a conflict theory of society,

237

based on a view of conflict over 'authority' in society, whilst ostensibly the product of theoretical discussions in the 'Thursday evening seminar' at the London School of Economics, appears above all to be informed by an awareness of the social conflicts in Europe in the middle fifties (Dahrendorf, 1959, p. 162):

> Evidently, the uprising of the 17th June (in East Berlin, in 1953) is neither due to nor productive of integration in East German society. It documents and produces not stability, but instability. It contributes to the disruption, not the maintenance, of the existing system. It testifies to dissensus rather than consensus.

How, whilst Dahrendorf identifies his task as being to supersede Marxist theory in the explanation of these events, his work appears to have been welcomed and developed (by American sociologists, in particular) because it arrived at a non-Marxist formulation which developed (rather than denied) the fundamental assumptions about consensus in society. As Hugh Stretton has noted (1969, p. 329): 'Dahrendorf insists [that his work] is only an addition, a supplement but not a replacement for the catalogue of integrationist questions.'

At about the time that Dahrendorf was making his challenge to the dominant paradigm of consensus in social theory, George Vold was in the process of producing the first criminological textbook to accord a significant place to crime as a product of social conflict. In his case, the attempt is to make use of Simmel's 'theory of group conflict' in order to explain those acts of crime and deviance which arise in situations of political and social inequality. Vold appears concerned to account for criminal acts arising out of wartime situations (the application of 'criminal' labels to conscientious objectors), out of labour disputes (violence committed against strike-breakers in order to ensure the solidity of a union's struggle) and, most crucially, from acts of protest, especially in cases of racial segregation (in the United States and in South Africa). The use of Simmel's theory, phrased by Vold in terms of a psychological assumption about the fundamental need of men to be members of, and loyal to, 'a group', is grafted on to the general treatment of crime and deviance residually—to account for events that other approaches (and, in particular, those deriving from the consensual view of society) appear to ignore or to leave unexplained. Importantly, with Vold (1958, pp. 204–5) as with Dahrendorf, such 'conflict' as is introduced in the general analysis, is limited in scope, and is treated as contributory to the dynamism of the existing set of social relationships:

As social interaction processes grind their way through varying kinds of uneasy adjustment to a more or less stable equilibrium of balanced forces in opposition, the resulting condition of relative stability is what is usually called social order or social organization. But it is the adjustment, one to another, of the many groups of varying strengths and of different interests that is the essence of society as a functioning reality.

The work of Dahrendorf and Vold, then, prompted by the concern to account for what went unaccounted for in existing consensus theory, that is, the diminution of open class conflict but the persistence of conflict in other forms, in no way represented a fundamental challenge to the dominant paradigms of the time. What they did do was to enlarge the range of what Stretton (1969) calls 'the catalogue of integrationist questions'.

We shall deal with Dahrendorf's work in some detail later, for the second challenge to consensus theories in crime and deviance, expressed in the recent work of the American criminologists, Austin Turk (1964a; 1964b; 1966; 1967; 1969) and Richard Quinney (1964; 1965a; 1965b; 1970a; 1970b; 1972) to a lesser extent, rests on the resurrection of the range of questions posed by Dahrendorf some ten years earlier (1958; 1959; 1968). The work of Turk and Quinney is quite clearly the result of a reflection on recent events in the United States, and the inability of existing theorization not only to account for these events but also to render them meaningful.

Turk, in the preface to *Criminality and Legal Order* (1969, p. vii), admits that:

> Embarrassment provided much of the initial push that led to the writing of this book. I was embarrassed at my lack of good answers when confronted by students who wondered, some-what irreverently, why criminology is 'such a confused mish-mash' . . . Some of these students were especially bothered by the 'unreality' of criminological studies, by which they meant the lack of sustained attention to connections between the theories and statistics about crime, and what they heard every day about relations among social conflicts, political maneuvers, and law violation and enforcement.

Quinney (1970b, ch. 1), even more quizzically, is concerned that a theory of crime must relate to 'the problematic nature of our exist-ence', recognizing that 'the mind is unable to frame a concept that corresponds to an objective reality', and that therefore the theory must 'give meaning' to our 'contemporary experiences'.

At a time when agencies of social control in America have recently been celebrating a decline in the volume of increase in crime (as expressed in the official statistics) and at a time when radicals and liberals alike have depicted the American legal apparatus unambiguously as a weapon wielded by the powerful in suppressing black and student movements, it is scarcely surprising that theorists of crime and deviance should want such a return to a conflict view of society. In reacting against the dominant paradigm of consensus and value-agreement, however, the new conflict theorists appear to be more concerned with the 'contemporary experience' of America than they do with the classical legacy of theorists of conflict. In this chapter, our preoccupation is with a form of theory which attempts to account for deviance as an expression of the structural conflict in unequal societies.

Austin Turk and Ralf Dahrendorf

In an essay which has assumed the status of a catechism on the 'new conflict theory', Dahrendorf (1958, p. 116) compares the assumption of consensus theorization with the assumptions underpinning the visions of utopian thinkers. In these utopias as, for example, in the Brave New World of Aldous Huxley, there is little on which to disagree. 'Strikes and revolutions are as conspicuously absent from utopian societies as are parliaments in which organized groups advanced their conflicting claims for power.'

For Dahrendorf (p. 119), much of the theorization in sociology is characterized by a 'utopian' lack of realism:

> The social system, like utopia, has not grown out of familiar reality. Instead of abstracting a limited number of variables and postulating their relevance for the explanation of a particular problem, it represents a huge and allegedly all-embracing superstructure of concepts that do not describe, propositions that do not explain, and models from which nothing follows. At least they do not describe or explain (or underlie explanations of) the real world with which we are concerned.

New analytical tools are required (Dahrendorf, 1959, p. 162):

> The integration model tells us little more than that there are certain 'strains' in the 'system'. In fact, in order to cope with problems of this kind we have to replace the integration theory of society by a different and, in many ways, contradictory model.

The contradictory model (summarized in the slogan 'out of utopia into conflict') is one in which conflict is recognized as extending beyond the class conflict of Marxist theory to conflict within what Dahrendorf, following Weber, terms 'imperatively co-ordinated associations'. These associations, the basic unit of social organization in Dahrendorf (1959, p. 171) are the amalgam of two (and only two) aggregates of position—positions of domination (or possession of authority) and positions of subjection (to authority):

> There are a large number of imperatively co-ordinated associations in any given society. Within every one of them we can distinguish the aggregates of those who dominate and those who are subjected. But since domination in industry does not necessarily involve domination in the State, or a church, or other associations, total societies can present a picture of a plurality of competing dominant (and, conversely, subjected) aggregates.

Operationalizing the notion of an 'imperatively co-ordinated association' within which the conflict is about authority in general, of course, entails a rejection of the centrality of class as the source of social conflict (ibid., p. 139):

> If we define classes by relations of authority, it is *ipso facto* evident that 'economic classes', i.e. classes within economic organizations, are but a special case of the phenomenon of class. Furthermore, even within the sphere of industrial production it is not really economic factors that give rise to class formation, but a certain type of social relations which we have tried to comprehend in the notion of authority.

The substitution of 'authority' for 'class' as the central source of dissensus in society has direct implications for the way in which we approach the study of crime and deviance. Most importantly, criminology and deviancy theory must develop a technique for identifying the crucial relationships of authority and subject in particular historical periods and in particular cultural settings.

Acceptance of this framework involves (as is illustrated in the work of Austin Turk (1969, p. 35)) a specific direction for work in the areas of crime and deviance:

> The study of criminality becomes the study of relations between the statuses and roles of legal *authorities*—creators, interpreters, and enforcers of right-wrong standards for individuals in the political collectivity—and those of *subjects*—acceptors or resisters but not makers of such law creating, interpreting and enforcing decisions.

What is at issue in this perspective is the notion of authority. If men act in accordance not with their position in a class structure, but in accordance with their position in a pluralistic society wherein a range of authority-subject relationships determine action, then some

241

clarity about the constituents of authority is required before general theory can be erected. Turk's concern is to construct a general theory of 'criminalisation'—specifying the conditions under which a subject in an authority-subject relationship will be defined as 'criminal'—and a theory which is applicable to any society (since it follows from the premises of Turk's position that all societies will be characterized by role-differentiation between authority and subject). Turk needs then to specify not only the conditions under which men will accept authority but also the reasons for men accepting authority at all.

In attempting to do this, Turk is not helped by the Weberian typology of authority. As he himself points out, Weber's distinction between charismatic, traditional and rational-legal forms of authority, whilst useful in characterizing existing social arrangements, does not constitute an explanation of why men will accept subjection at the hands of others in the first place. The alternative explanation, deriving from structural-functionalism, that men accept authority because they have internalized the norms of the total society, is rejected too, since to accept such an explanation would be to see deviance as 'undersocialization'.

Turk (1969, p. 42) offer a third alternative:

> This is basically the idea that people, both eventual authorities and eventual subjects, learn and continually re-learn to interact with one another as, respectively, occupants of superior statuses and inferior statuses and performers of dominating and submitting roles. That the learning process is never completed —implying that authority-subject relationships are never finally stabilized—is insured by the fact that modifications are introduced into any fragment of thought or behavior by the peculiarities of individual combinations of physical attributes and experiences as both an organism and a social animal who uses symbols.

It is by retreating to the atomistic view of the individual—and indeed by describing that individuality in part in organismic terms—that Turk is able to posit the inevitability of authority-subject differentiation. No actor can ever be free because (ibid., p. 42): 'His personal behavioral norms and his personal symbol-using patterns can do no more than approximate the social and cultural norms by which a grouping is identified.'

Authority-subject relationships are accepted (and learnt), therefore, in order that a social order, within which an infinite number of 'individuals' (in the strong sense of the word) coexist, can actually persist.

The stabilization of authority-subject relationships requires the continual conflict of interests implied by individual differences. For, if ambiguity were to arise about the locus of authority and power, it follows that men would not learn to perform their subordinate roles as effectively as they must (ibid., p. 43): 'Authorities have to learn and relearn to act appropriately, as do subjects.'

↙ The norms that are learnt are summarized as the *norms of domination*, and the *norms of deference*. These norms are universal to all sets of social arrangements, irrespective of the particular form the arrangements take. Even in time of change (ibid., p. 48), 'assuming the relatively powerful hold on long enough, most people will become conditioned to the new arrangements, and authority, and therefore law, will again come into existence.'

For Turk, then (p. 48), 'lawbreaking is taken to be an indicator of the failure or lack of authority; it is a measure of the extent to which rulers and ruled, decision-makers and decision-acceptors, are not bound together in a stable authority relationship.'

At the basis of Turk's rather tautological theory of criminalization is a view of conflict over social norms—not in the sense of the failure of some individuals to internalize dominant norms, but in the sense that different people relate to different sets of norms, depending on their own individual bio-social experience—some of which norms are institutionalized as norms of domination, others of which are assigned the status of deference. Conflict, and the assignation of a criminal status to various kinds of behaviour, will depend on the congruence or lack of congruence between social norms and the cultural evaluation of the norms.

The distinction between cultural and social norms is central to Turk's theory of criminalization, since the attempt is to spell out a predictive and explanatory typology tracing through the relative probability of criminalization for individuals in particular role-positions (authority or subject positions) in particular cultural contexts. Turk dwells on the range of cultural alternatives in any society—subcultures of youth, ethnic subcultures, and class sub-cultures are mentioned—and, whilst recognizing that such a range could be endless,[1] Turk selects as 'variables' the cultures of age, sex and race-ethnicity as the crucial indicators of differential cultural evaluation of social norms. Though no direct statement or evidence is offered in support of this choice, one can only assume that it has to do with what Turk, with other informed criminologists, knew about the distribution of criminality in the social structure in the first place. If this is the case, it is, of course, difficult to understand why the 'variable' of social class membership should be omitted (since 'social class' is highly correlated, at least with officially recorded criminality in the statistics) except that to use social class would be to recognize that a predictive social theory would have to

243

account for qualitatively different social structures—where 'authority' takes the form, quite specifically, of class power, as distinct from the power made necessary by normative differentiation.

Turk's position is that an actor's age, sex and racial group membership will determine the extent to which he relates to the norms of domination. In contemporary American society, for example, a middle-aged or old white woman is less likely to conflict with 'authority' than a black youth (whatever his class position). This seems obvious, and a small finding in itself. But it is Turk's explanation of this obvious finding which is at issue. Since 'most people will become conditioned to . . . arrangements' in an authority structure, the task is to explain why some do not. The 'norm resisters' (the actors who are supposed to condition themselves to the norms of deference) are, it turns out, 'relatively unsophisticated'.

Turk (1966, p. 648) asserts that the term 'sophistication' is intended to mean 'the knowledge of patterns in the behavior of others which is used in attempts to manipulate them', but in the substantive analysis that follows it is not 'knowledge of other's patterns' which influences discussion so much as it is a fear of the 'unsophisticated' in the very conventional sense of the term. In the final analysis, then, the criminality of the norm resisters is the result of their lack of sophistication coupled with a lack of clear-headed determination on the part of authority (the norm-enforcers).

Turk attempts to substantiate this with a highly tendentious reference to the work of Sykes and Matza (1957) on the 'techniques of neutralization'. Turk comments (1969, p. 57n): '[Their] interpretation is that such techniques are used to justify violation of norms actually shared with the authorities. However, it may be that "denial of the victim", etc., reflect no more than the lack of verbal skills and the immaturity of delinquent boys than normative consensus.'

For Turk, normative dissensus is inevitable between juvenile delinquents confronted by authority because of the psychological and other immaturities of the delinquent himself (and, in particular, his inability to verbalize) (ibid., p. 57):

> Because people vary in their ability to use symbols and justify
> cultural norms, both sides, particularly subordinates, who are
> less likely to have symbol-using skills than authorities, may
> resort to relatively unsophisticated excuses (rationalizations)
> for not acting in specific instances in accord with some cultural
> norm.

Presumably, for Turk, lack of sophistication, like the existence of authority-subject relationships themselves, is a universal and inevitable product of the infinite variability of individual experience. And, lest we should suspect that the use of a terminology of this kind reflects the introduction of values of the investigator, Turk quickly reminds us (p. 58) that a sociology of conflict must identify 'independently the patterns of conflict and . . . analyze these patterns in the neutral, testable language of science instead of the partisan, value-orientated language of involvement.' And it is on the basis of such a 'neutral' appraisal of the evidence that Turk is led into offer advice and prescriptions to authority-holders (not in this society, of course—in any society). It is not, after all, that delinquency is simply the product of lack of sophistication—which is inevitable. It can be eradicated (Turk, 1969, p. 58):

> Where an attribute or act has been integrated into a system of relationships, implying that it is a part of some role which the individual performs, then we can expect that some kind and degree of coercion will be required to break the behavior pattern or to eliminate the attribute. In this connexion, it is noteworthy that efforts to reform or educate the stigmatized so that their stigma is removed have been characterized historically by the reluctance of reformers and educators to recognize that their work depends ultimately upon the application of force to break apart the social and cultural contexts in which the undesired patterns originate and are maintained.

Lest he be misunderstood, and lest it be thought that he is still operating in the abstract language of a theory without immediate reference to existing social arrangements, Turk goes on to comment that (ibid.):

> There are indications that some authorities are beginning to understand that such norm violations as juvenile misconduct, family disorganization, indifference to hygiene, personality disorder, and lack of usable work skills constitute insoluble problems until and unless a total, determined attempt is made to destroy the structures of values and social relationships— the cultural and social structures—creating and perpetuating the unwanted patterns of language and behavior, and to force people (impolitic phrasing!) into the structures that lead to 'good'.

When it comes to empirical reference, then, Turk's theory of criminalization is a theory about the possession or lack of possession of the skills, values, organization, and goals of existing authoritative individuals and groups. Authority is about the domination of the unsophisticated, the juvenile delinquents, the broken family, the unhygienic, the disordered personality and those without 'usable work skills' by the sophisticated 'norm enforcers'. And the complex typology that is advanced as an offshoot to the abstract theorization

245

on the relationship between role-differentiation and normative dissensus is really a descriptive matrix which confirms (for the naïve) the fact that the young, the masculine, and the members of minority racial groups are more likely than most to be criminalized in contemporary American society.

It is not only that this kind of élitist conclusion is small reward for the struggles of abstract theorization. It is also that Turk's 'conflict theory' of deviance alerts us to the limitations and dangers of abstracted theorization, prompted only by the attempt to make theory superficially relevant to immediate experience. Turk's work is permeated by an acceptance of the fact that authority-subject relationships—in what he calls (after Dahrendorf) 'imperatively co-ordinated associations'—must necessarily be relationships of domination and subjection. Were it to be otherwise, the demoralized and the unhygienic—the very same spectres that haunt the work of Bonger—could fail to learn (or could unlearn) their roles as subjects, dominated by a legitimate authority. The fact of demoralization and delinquency is neither a product of subjection nor an attempt to struggle against such a subjection. Deviance is a failure of the authoritative to enforce their norms (as Turk would say, 'impolitic phrasing') so forcing people 'into the structures that lead to good'.

Turk's conflict theory, in short, appears to be informed by two outstanding fears. In the first place, one detects in Turk as one detects in Bonger,[2] a fear of the deviant (though one senses in Turk an admiration for, indeed a stimulus from, the political deviant)—or, more precisely, a fear of what the 'norm resister' might be able to do if authority-subject relationships were to be dissolved. Second, however, one detects in Turk a fear about theory and knowledge—a fear that existing theorization on crime and deviance, by virtue of its incompleteness or its manifest failure to recognize and give methodological status to processes of social conflict, might lose what credibility it possesses. The book starts with a homily on the inability of Turk's students to detect a 'realism' in existing theory. Turk presents us with a 'conflict theory' which is realistic in so far as it posits a series of 'conflict moves' which are familiar to the reader. In this respect, Turk's conflict theory is likely to achieve the kind of legitimacy within professional sociology that has been achieved by conflict theorists of the wider society, like Coser, and, in particular, Dahrendorf. An unsurprising observation, since Turk's indebtedness to Dahrendorf is clear.

But recognition of the existence of conflict, and the need to incorporate that conflict (and a 'sense of realism') into a general theory, is not all that is at stake. What is *also* at stake is the way in which conflict is conceptualized in the first instance. With Dahrendorf, Turk requires us to see conflict as being the product of men's individuality, and as having its focus on the possession of authority. In Dahrendorf, we are asked to accept conflict over authority within 'imperatively co-ordinated associations' as the fundamental form of social conflict (transcending the conflict implied in Marxist theory), and we are asked to do so on the grounds that 'capitalism' itself as a system has been replaced by what Dahrendorf (1959, p. 136) calls 'the post-capitalist society'. That is '[the] tie between the concept of class and the possession of, or exclusion from, effective property limits the applicability of a class theory to a relatively short period of European social history.'

'Post-capitalist society' is characterized by the separation of ownership and control. Because the worker in a factory is not directly commanded by the owners of industry, his conflict is not with the owners any longer or with any system they represent so much as it is with the managers and foremen exercising authority over him in the immediate workplace. Moreover, in the post-capitalist society, since the consumer status of the worker is relatively high, the conflict for property begins to operate at the point of consumption as well as at the point of production. Thus, conflictual relations can arise on the basis of authority-subject relationships in the market-place. This diffuses—and defuses—the centrality of industrial conflict of the kind given emphasis in Marx—in that the opponents of the worker are merely occupants of what Dahrendorf would call 'dissociated roles'. This dissociation of roles, as we indicated earlier, implies the relegation of class conflict to a minor role in the development and dynamics of the post-capitalist society, and, in the way in which this position is adapted by Turk, underpins the attempt to spell out the range of authority-subject relationships in the 'post-capitalist society'—in order that a theory of criminalization can properly be constructed.

At this stage, we have two questions to ask of such an approach to a general theory of post-capitalist society. First, we must ask how such an approach measures up to what we have called the formal requirements of a theory (of deviance). Second, we have to ask whether there are grounds for holding to the theory at all, and indeed whether it is a theory (or whether it is merely description).

Turk's conflict theory, like subcultural theory and other approaches of the social positivists, offers out an account of the processes leading to the reaction of social control agencies to an initial infraction, and an implicit account of the infraction itself. 'Crime', for Turk, is 'a status' accorded norm resisters whose realism and sophistication are inadequate to anticipate the results of their actions; the action itself results from the normative conflict existing in any society at any stage of development (it is, that is, the direct product of the idiosyncratic socialization of individuals with a greater likelihood

247

of a criminal label being applied to individuals caught within particular cultural contexts, of age, sex, and ethnicity). There is no concern in Turk for the outcome of criminalization; that is, the extent to which the application of a criminal or deviant status is likely to be used by the norm resister as a means of adapting to his new-found status. Though the stress in Turk is unambiguously on the impact of social control on deviant individuals, we are not given an account of that impact in terms of the individual's adaptation to 'criminalization'.

But it is in the light of what we might call the 'substantive requirements of theory' that Turk's version of social conflict is most lacking. Central to any social theory of deviance there is an image of the men involved in acts which lead to 'criminalization' and an account of the effects of those acts and the attribution of a status to it. Once made explicit, such an image of man enables us to test out the theory for the presence of a consistent and tenable set of operating assumptions. The evidence we have available about men is that they are caught in a dialectic of control and resistance to control; that they are at one and the same time the creatures and the creators of a constraining structure of power, authority and interest. Within this dialectic, men weave their path in a variety of ways: our interpretation of their actions must accurately represent the range of responses men can make to similar contingencies, and must recognize in these choices the actions of conscious men operating in accordance with motives freely chosen albeit within a range of limited alternatives. Turk's theory of conflict is initially promising in this respect, stressing as it does that (1969, p. 53): 'a sociological theory of interaction is required; moreover, it must be a theory of interaction among groupings and categories of people rather than a social psychological explanation of patterns among individuals.'

Whenever Turk retreats from his level of abstracted theorization, however, the image of men underlying his sociological theory of interaction reveals itself. Despite the fact that Turk's position is totally dependent on a set of assumptions about the consciousness of men—the way in which they relate to the world in general, and authority in particular—Turk devotes only a few lines to the subject. And he reveals only that he is a pessimist (ibid., p. 44):

> [There is] the view that political protest results from the failure
> of a social order to satisfy basic human needs. Apart from the
> very tricky business of deciding what are and what are not
> *basic* and *human* and *needs*, it is noteworthy that deprivation
> does not necessarily imply political dissidence. ... The
> stability of an authority relationship appears to depend far less
> upon subjects' conscious or unconscious belief in the rightness

or legitimacy of the rank order than upon their having been *conditioned to accept as a fact of life that authorities must be reckoned with as such.*

Turk's view is essentially descriptive: but even as a description it is contentious. We can be sure that an adequate description of deviance and dissent—the acts of men who have not been 'conditioned to accept the authorities as fact of life' requires something more in the way of a description of human consciousness than is allowed by the adoption of the terminology of behaviourist psychology. More importantly, however, there is in Turk no attempt to *explain* how authority relationships are linked with, or derive from, the wider system of social stratification.

Authority, stratification and criminalization

It is just such an explanation that Dahrendorf, on whom Turk is otherwise so dependent, attempted in his *Essays in the Theory of Society* (1968). Not content merely to describe the existence of systems of stratification (whether in the form of differentiation into rank or differentiation of power) and the forms they assumed in different societies, Dahrendorf is concerned in this work to examine the adequacy of the various sociological statements advanced to *explain the origins and causes of inequality.* A large part of his concern, as against Marx and other writers who argued for the possibility of a society without stratification, is to show that (Dahrendorf, 1968, p. 36): 'because there are norms and because sanctions are necessary to enforce conformity of human conduct, there has to be inequality of rank among men'; and that (ibid., p. 38): 'a third fundamental category of sociological analysis belongs alongside the two concepts of norm and sanction: that of institutional power.'

The argument is developed via a critique of Talcott Parsons's statement of the functionalist position on stratification. Parsons's original essay on the question, published in 1940, had taken as an ontological assumption the idea that men need to evaluate each other differently. Thirteen years later, Parsons published a revised version of the same essay (1954) in which 'he relates the existence of a concept of evaluation to the mere probability, not the necessity, of inequality'. But, as Dahrendorf points out, this empirical probability may reflect not an ontological given (a feature of men's individual essence) so much as it does a social necessity (a feature of the moral pressures imposed socially on the individual).

Dahrendorf accepts Parsons's empirical observation—that men do evaluate each other differently, rather than accepting each other on a universal and equal basis—but explains this in terms of the development of norms, and of law, to regulate the behaviour of men living in a human collectivity. At certain points in the development of society, norms become necessary to prevent the disintegration of the collectivity into individual warfare, and (Dahrendorf, 1968, p. 34): 'once there are norms that impose inescapable requirements on people's behavior and once their actual behavior is measured in terms of these norms ... a rank order of social status is bound to emerge.' But it is only really when it is necessary, in the development of a society, to ensure conformity to the norms by the development of sanctions rewarding compliance and punishing deviance, that Dahrendorf's third element in what he calls the 'trinity' of sociological analysis emerges: the factor of institutionalized power. The fact that conformity is rewarded and deviance punished implies that social groups—'the person(s) most favourably placed in society'— exist which have the power to establish those sanctions. A part of the sociological explanation of inequality, therefore, is an explanation of the ability of certain social groups to enforce a power to sanction (whether this be, for example, in the factory, the consumer outlet, the socializing agencies, or society at large): but it is only a part of the explanation, and, most importantly, it is a subsidiary to the explanation of the changes in the types of norms appropriate to the control and guidance of societies at different periods in the development of stratified societies. Social change in Dahrendorf, rather like social change in Durkheim, is the product of the struggle of groups to bring about a revolution in norms and values: to bring the stratification system and the system of moral evaluation (like the collective conscience) back into line with the realities of a changing industrial society (a change in the division of labour) (ibid., p. 42): 'the upper class of a bygone epoch may retain its status position for a while under new conditions. Yet normally we do not have to wait long for such processes as the "déclassement of the nobility" or the "loss of functions of property" which have occurred in several contemporary societies'.

Thus, the prevalence of values and norms appropriate to society at particular points in its development, so far from being an integrative feature of social organization (as in functionalist accounts), is intrinsically explosive and disruptive. Dahrendorf urges that we come to terms with a situation of ongoing conflict and the inevitability of continual protest against systems of stratification and evaluation. The 'utopia' of order and equilibrium—associated both in functionalist sociology and some common-sense ideologies with freedom—is, in fact, the antithesis of freedom. Order and stability will quickly coalesce into the domination by one interest group over the rest of society, whilst (ibid., p. 42): 'the existence of social inequality ... is an impetus toward liberty because it guarantees a society's ongoing dynamic, historical quality.'

Turk's formal conflict theory stands indicted, then, not simply as an unhelpful description of social inequalities which Dahrendorf at least attempted to explain: it also stands indicted as a formal theory which informally attempts to stabilize the ongoing dynamic of social conflict and thus, in Dahrendorf's terms, to bring about a 'utopian' totalitarianism. So far from being a theory which appreciates the merits of deviant action not only in itself but also for its contribution to the defence of freedom in divided social organizations, Turk's conflict theory is an exercise in retrenchment. Dahrendorf's vision is of 'permanent *rea*djustment'; Turk's is one of the permanent adjustment of the subordinate to the powerful, under present social arrangements.

The fact that a writer (like Turk) calls for 'a sociological theory of interaction between groups' (instead of resting content with the assumption of system-integration), should not blind us to the prescriptions that follow from the formal theory developed by that writer. This book attempts to offer out a sociological theory of interaction between groups: but it also attempts to address the fact that men caught in a dialectic of control and resistance do break through the structures of authority and domination, and that we have to take a value position on the actions of men who do this.

Dahrendorf's dynamic equilibrium, adding the phenomenon of permanent readjustment to the 'catalogue of integrationist questions', does not take this process of questioning far enough. For the fact is that Dahrendorf's own ontological assumptions are questionable. At the base of Dahrendorf's 'conflict theory' is the view that sanctions are necessary to ensure normative compliance. This necessity arises out of men's ability constantly to innovate, re-create and change the social conditions under which they live—in acts of revolt, political struggle and revolution.[3] What Dahrendorf does not confront is the possibility that under certain conditions a revolution in social arrangements could precipitate moral and social consensus. Like Weber, Dahrendorf assumes (and it is an assumption) that moral consensus was lost with the collapse of *Gemeinschaft* societies. But the development of industrialization—under capitalism—introduced a distinctive form of stratification, quite unlike the symbolic systems of stratification and evaluation existing in pre-industrial societies: stratification based on an individual's possession or lack of possession of income, his position in a system of industrial production, and, in the final analysis, a system of stratification based on social class, however defined, as an indicator of one's position and life-chances in a divided industrial society. The claim made by Dahrendorf, and those who model their writings on his theory of social conflict, to have transcended the Marxist scheme is not proven until such time as they can demonstrate not that normative agreement *or* the enforcement of normative compliance is necessary to the functioning of a human society (for that is a tautology), but rather that the specific structures which make the enforcement of compliance a necessary feature of social order (i.e. capitalist social relationships) are inevitable.

We see no reason for such an act of faith. In the meantime, however, Dahrendorf's view of conflict continues to inform the writings of the new criminologists, with the usual mistranslation occurring in the textbook interpretations. For 'permanent readjustment'—literally interpreted—to occur, and for Dahrendorf's liberal democracy to persist, both classes—'authorities' and 'subjects'—would have to acquiesce in any compromise or agreement. But the classes—whether employers and workers, or prison guards and inmates—are not equal, and do not derive equal benefit from continuing adjustments; so that unless one assumes, as Turk tends to, that men can be conditioned into domination, there will presumably always be attempts by the dominated to change the nature of their subjection, to refuse acquiescence if not finally to abolish their subjection.[4] Unless the dominators are prepared to relinquish authority voluntarily, the 'permanent adjustment' of Dahrendorf, and the process of conditioning in Turk, must always be a form of repression, and, under capitalism, it must always be a form of overt or covert class domination. So long as authority takes the form of domination, that is, authority will always be problematic, and, by the same token, any acts of deviance or dissent must be taken to be acts of resistance (however inarticulately expressed or formulated). Only when authority is both substantively and formally under control of its subjects—that is, only when authority is merely an administrative instrument of the interests of men as a whole—can one assume the persistence (in the sense implied by Dahrendorf) of some kind of 'permanent readjustment'. A truly post-capitalist society is not, as in Dahrendorf and the new conflict theorists of deviance, a society in which there is simply a recognized plurality of interests or a plurality of moral values and an ongoing readjustment of the power they wield: it is a society in which authority as such is divorced from the domination of men by men. It is also a society in which the power to 'criminalize'—if not abolished—is made subject to a genuine, rather than simply powerful, consensus.

Richard Quinney and the social reality of crime

Dahrendorf and Turk reacted to the crises of existing theory by adding to the 'catalogue of questions' to be given a theoretical compass. A tendency to equilibrium was cemented, in the work of Dahrendorf, by the continuing impetus to change and reform provided by social conflict; and deviancy, in Turk, was a product of the healthy regeneration of authority-subject relations between norm-enforcers and norm-resisters.

In an earlier chapter, we document the development of pheno-menological and ethnomethodological approaches to social life and deviance. Richard Quinney's work on deviance and crime, whilst not so explicit in its phenomenological emphasis as some of these writers, is characterized by the attempt to create 'an understanding of crime that is relevant to our contemporary experiences' (Quinney, 1970b) and an understanding that has as one of its explicit assump-tions the assertion 'that we have no reason to believe in the objective existence of anything' (p. 4).

Many of Quinney's statements about a theoretical orientation to the social reality of crime seem to be the product more of the author's own existential *Angst* than they are the result of clear-headed theoretical analysis. It is unclear from Quinney's existential preamble to his latest text why we should believe in the social reality of crime at all. Indeed, at one point (p. 316) Quinney suggests that 'crime begins in the mind' and that what happens is that 'crime is a definition of human conduct that becomes part of the social world'. As we shall attempt to show in this chapter, Quinney's solipsist disbelief in the objective existence of anything leads him into a crude view of social life in which a central problem is the integration of societal and individual interest. We can now see that much American criminology and sociology of deviance of the kind discussed in chapter 5 is a product of just such a confused relativist position. To say that an action is open to a number of different definitions (i.e. that it can be understood in terms of different 'social realities') is not to say that objective consequences do not follow from the definition of an action as criminal as against its being interpreted as acceptable.

Indeed, it is this continuing relativistic confusion which leads to an imprecise conception of the relevance of values to theorization (I. Taylor and Walton, 1970). Quinney (1970b, p .v), consistent with his disbelief in objectivity, simply asserts that a relevant criminology will be infused with personal values: 'It is my hope that the theory of the social reality of crime has the power of forcing us to consider libertarian ideals. I contend that a relevant criminology can be attained only when we allow our personal values to provide a vision for the study of crime.'

This uncritical subjectivism is inextricably associated with the in-dividualistic focus of Quinney's theoretical endeavours. His intention is to demonstrate the ways in which structures of power, authority and interest have given rise to a series of all but infinite 'subjective, multiple social worlds'.

253

In each of these social worlds, 'social reality' (consisting, for example, of the way in which social rules and laws are recognized and understood, and, thus, the way in which behaviour deviating from those rules is defined as deviant, criminal or simply odd) will be a highly idiosyncratic interpretation. Of course, the powerful in a society will be continually attempting to enforce their definition of reality, and they will, apart from anything else, be able to marshal the force of law to their aid. But there will also be the possibility that laws are unknown or unrecognized in the population at large, that there will be differential understanding of, or support for, the laws at different points in the society, or, indeed, the development of interests opposed to the law and its rationale—all of these possibilities obstructing the attempt of the powerful to enforce their definition of reality. It is also possible that law and rules—though thoroughly understood and well communicated—cannot be accepted by some of the groups in a society at all: law in these circumstances can only be understood as repressive domination of one reality by another (bearing no relationship to the 'playing-off' of interests).

Quinney (1970b) is concerned to cast doubt on the universal force of rules and laws in a society, and, in so doing, to emphasize the heuristic importance not only of an actor's definition of a situation (in the narrow sense) but also an actor's total 'subjective, social world':

> Though the content of the actions is shaped by the social and cultural location of the person in society, actions are ultimately the product of each individual (p. 274).
>
> Crime begins in the mind. In this sense a conceptual reality of crime is constructed. But the consequence of such construction is a world of actions and events; that is, a phenomenal reality. The whole developmental complex of conception and phenomenon, in reference to crime, is the construction of the social reality of crime (p. 316).

But Quinney is not a total relativist: he is interested in the patterning of the 'subjective, social world' by the interests existing in 'politically-organized society'. His analysis of modern industrial society in these terms is intended to illustrate the way in which social reality (e.g. the reality of conformity or deviance)—though individually chosen, interpreted and developed—is the product of coercion and conflict in an unequally structured society. It is out of the understanding of the dialectic between coercion by interests and subjective freedom within externally determined limits that Quinney's critique of one-sided criminologies emerges. And implicitly this understanding is intended to be of relevance for students of social life and students of deviance in understanding the complex mix of

254

coercion and choice that informs the action of our fellow human beings. What is at issue, therefore, is not the uneven and problematic nature of the 'fit' between external structures in a society and the subjective worlds of its individual members (as might be the case if Quinney were exclusively taken up, in a way that Berger and Luckmann, on whom Quinney is considerably dependent, tend to be).[5] Rather, what is at issue is the nature of the society itself, or the way in which Quinney depicts society as a preamble to his empirical discussion.

What the conflict theorists of deviance have (perhaps unwittingly) accomplished is to place the classical debates of social theory in the centre of our understanding of deviance. The whole thrust of their perspectives is that society is riven with antagonisms of a kind that even middle-range anomie theory is inadequate to depict. Conflict theorists of deviance, that is, unlike sociological theorists working in the traditions of structural-functionalism and, in particular, unlike psychological or inter-disciplinary thinkers (who concentrate primarily on the nature or function of the deviant act or actor), build the theoretical bridge to the area of dispute over the nature of general social structure.

But few criminologists and deviancy theorists are equipped for such excursions; and Turk and Quinney are unmistakably unwilling travellers. Turk, for reasons we have described, avoids a thoroughgoing analysis of structure by a return to Dahrendorf. Quinney seems to resolve the problem in a variety of ways.

In the first place, he attempts to maintain the 'dialectic' between the external world and his actors' 'subjective, social worlds' at a highly abstract level of generality, dependent on a modified version of C. Wright Mills's notion of 'institutional orders' (Gerth and Wright Mills, 1964, pp. 25–6).

For Quinney (1970b, p. 38) the 'institutional orders' define the content and direction of 'interests' (values, norms and ideological orientations) in a society. These 'institutional orders' are:

> (1) the *political*, which regulates the distribution of power and authority in society; (2) the *economic*, which regulates the production of goods and services; (3) the *religious*, which regulates the relationship of man to a conception of the supernatural; (4) the *kinship*, which regulates sexual relations, family patterns and the procreation and rearing of children; (5) the *educational*, which regulates the formal training of the society's members, and (6) the *public*, which regulates the protection and maintenance of the community and its citizens.

Within each 'institutional order' are contained 'segments' of society: 'segments' are not clearly defined, but apparently are the various groups held together in the common recognition and evaluation of an interest. 'Institutional orders' are the processes or organizations through which a segment will characteristically pursue its interests (ibid., pp. 36–42).

The convenience of this distinction for Quinney's premises is its relevance for his initial assertions about the autonomy of 'subjective, social worlds'. Within a segment, presumably, actors united in holding to similar subjective experiences of reality come together in order to pursue their interests—in a fashion circumscribed by the external constraints of institutional order. The distinction thus serves to maintain the integrity and causal independence of an actor's phenomenal reality.

A second merit of such a generalized conception of social structure for Quinney is that it enables the elaboration of empirical evidence in an apparently substantial manner. That is, in order to demonstrate the existence of some relationship between deviance and the antagonisms or contradictions in a social structure (that is, that society is fundamentally characterized by conflict rather than tendency to equilibrium or consensus), it is only necessary for Quinney to present evidence of deviance from societal norms or expectations which can be said in some way to result from 'conflict' or 'strain'. In fact, of course, there is a variety of theorization, not only in relation to deviance but to social behaviour in general, which recognizes the existence of such strains and conflicts, and there is also considerable empirical data on conflicts of interest and value deriving from these (highly diverse) perspectives. Quinney's examples of processes of conflict, arising out of the differences of interest in 'politically-organised society' are of an extremely catholic range. A chapter on 'Interest in the formulation of criminal law', in his major text, appears to rest on an examination of the peculiar form that the protestant ethic was forced to assume in a frontier society during the Puritan settlement of America, with some attention being devoted to the classical anthropological notion of conflict between cultures in a migratory situation.

So, Quinney (1970b) argues:

The Indians who were subject to colonial law were not judged by their own customary law but according to the interests of the settlers in England (p. 54).

The English common law on political crime was eventually adopted by the states and the federal government. What had seemed oppressive in the hands of the British became the law for Americans to impose on those who would appear to endanger their government (p. 58).

The purpose of law for the Puritans was the accomplishment of

God's will in a society bound together by a religious and political covenant. Authority of the state was thus religiously condemned (p. 64).

But this is immediately followed, in an examination of 'Application of criminal definition', by a diffuse explanation of the way in which (for example) police discretion in the advanced form of American society is not so much a function of broad social values (bound up with a 'religious and political covenant') as it is a function of specific organizational imperatives. So, the well-known finding of Piliavin and Briar (1964) that demeanour is the most important determinant of arrest in police encounters with juveniles is seen as reflection of societal conflict in much the same way as, for example, the need for a police organization to maintain a good 'clear-up' rate within its jurisdiction is also explicable in terms of underlying currents of strain within society.

Again, in discussion the effects of societal organization on behaviour, Quinney strays between contradictory positions, remaining faithful only to a perspective of some underlying conflict at the base of behaviour and its definition. At one point, Quinney (1970b, p. 233) will show awareness of the emphasis in 'labeling' theory:

Behavior patterns themselves are neither criminal nor non-criminal. They are merely behavior patterns, and their criminality is determined by the actions of others, who act according to other behavior patterns. Criminality is a construct, beyond the quality of specific behaviors, that is formulated and applied by the power segments of society.

At another (p. 229), Quinney can argue that: 'conformity to the law has never been an overwhelming obsession in America. ... The frontier experience called for an individuality that made each man a law unto himself.' With each man 'a law unto himself', deviance must necessarily have been a widespread behaviour, a property of the act itself.

Although Quinney's argument is that the persistence of the frontier heritage in a society divided into different social classes and ethnic groups in a more urbanized and industrialized context renders different behaviour patterns more or less liable to criminal definition, it is difficult to accept his assertion that actors commit themselves in action they know to be criminal in the way that they involve themselves in non-criminal action. Indeed, the evidence Quinney offers out, in his discussion of behaviour patterns in the various social classes and ethnic groups, seems to support (as indeed his arguments themselves suggest) the existence of contracultures at different points in American society. Slipping between a 'labelling' perspective

257

and a perspective based on subcultural theory, or between explanations of arrest rooted in the values of the society and the needs of an organization, the only consistency is a stress on some ambiguous idea of conflict.

Our argument is not that empirical research on differential apprehension, arrest or labelling of rule-breakers does not reveal a set of conflicts of interest. It *is* the case, however, that the recitation of findings from fundamentally different perspectives[6] does not help us in the erection of a generally coherent, but detailed, explanatory model of social conflict and its relationship to the codification of laws (and the structuring of rules) and their enforcement.

In C. Wright Mills's critique of pluralism, for example, in *The Power Élite*, it is not simply that a pluralism of interests is not reflected in an equality of power (or ability to enforce interest) among the various interest groups. Mills shows that the majority of the citizens in the United States do not even belong to any organization large enough to be politically significant. That is, in Quinney's terms, there are 'segments' of the population who do not even enter the arena of 'institutional order'. Further, Mills argues, even those members of a society who do belong to an organization (e.g. a trade union, a farmers' organization, a tenants' association) are not easily or necessarily, by virtue of being members of such organizations, able to develop anything like a coherent, structural view of the political process. This fact is attributed, in particular, to the bureaucratization of these organizations and the concern of their leaderships to obstruct the full expression of the interests of their members. Thus, the assumption implicit in pluralist theory—that the differentiation of social life and organization facilitates the playing-off of interest in a fluent and egalitarian fashion—is not an assumption borne out by the facts of institutional order. Finally, Mills observes, the pluralist model fails to analyse the differential social location of interests. Some interests may be very powerfully or efficiently organized—but only at the middle-level of institutional order. Other interests, less well-ordered in themselves, may, by virtue of their location at the centre of power, be able to enforce their interests by default. It is not only that power is more or less organized: it is also that some forms of power are more crucially possessed than others.

In short, Mills (1957, p. 266) would argue that 'we must revise and relocate the received conceptions of an enormous scatter of valid interests.' The élite model of American power developed by Mills is an attempt to account for the empirical fact that most people in that advanced society do *not* feel that they are able to realize their interests within existing institutional orders. Our criticisms of the views of social structure now being thrown up by the new conflict theory in American sociology (and criminology) would turn upon the debates between the élite and ruling-class models of advanced society, but they would not countenance a return to a pluralist model in any form.

Quinney's pluralistic and abstract conception of the social structure, however, is highly amenable to a catholic use of supporting studies, and it simultaneously enables him to eschew a detailed examination of the nature, genesis, content and development of whatever he means by 'social structure'.

A third advantage of Quinney's attempt to pitch analysis at such a general level is that he is able, in the face of all the evidence, to maintain that 'control' and 'power' are not antagonistic to his expressed ideals of justice and individual liberty. Quinney *is* aware of the theoretical *naïveté* involved in assuming that the differentiation of interests is in some way reflected in an equal balance of power, or a pluralism of interests, internally within a society. As he says (1970b, p. 41):

> Groups that are equal in power may well check each other's
> interests, but groups that have little or no power will not have
> the opportunity to have their interest represented in public
> policy. The consequence is government by a few powerful
> private interest groups. Furthermore, the politics of private
> interests tends to take place outside the arena of the public
> governmental process.

Although this rejection of the conception of pluralism, so dominant in contemporary political science, may not be a throughgoing critique, it serves Quinney well in his pursuit of an optimistic resolution to our present discontents. This resolution he phrases in tentative fashion (ibid., pp. 41–2):

> If there is to be any check in this contemporary condition, it is
> in the prospect that the 'public interest' will take precedence
> over private interests. Interest groups, *if for no other reason
> than their concern for public relations*, may bow to the
> commonweal. Optimistically, the public interest may become
> an ideal fulfilled, no matter what the source of private power.[7]

But optimism and pessimism are subjective predispositions rather than theoretical cornerstones. In fact, Quinney's theoretical position on this question is riven with ambiguities, for even Quinney is aware that there are serious theoretical objections to any position which suggests that the government (or the state) will act in the common good merely because of some public relations concern for neutrality. Immediately after advancing the government as a potential guardian of the 'public interest' he himself indicates that any

259

government strong enough to assume this role may lead in the opposite direction (ibid., p. 42): 'the fallacy in any expectation of the achievement of the public good through the "public interest" is that the government which could foster such a condition will become again in a new age an oppressive interest in itself. That age in fact, seems to be upon us.'

This ambivalence about the beneficence of government stems from Quinney's untenable distinction between the interests of the isolated individual and the overweening 'politically-organized society'. His analysis is not so much a theoretical position as it is a utopian hope for the delicate balancing of the interests of government, monopoly corporations, of the whole range of interests within advanced society —and the interests of the individual (ibid., p. 42, our emphasis):

> In raw form, we cannot hold optimistically to either govern-
> ment by private interests or public interest by government
> largesse. The future for *individual man* appears to lie in some
> form of protection from both forms of government. Decentral-
> ized government offers some possibility for *the survival of
> the individual* in a collective society.

Quinney's abandonment of structural analysis, for an abstract reference to a possible decentralization of government in the interests of the individual man, derives in part from the continuing juxta-position of man and society. If we are truly interested in the utility of conflict perspectives, then we have to address ourselves to the kind of structural reorganization which would render individual, societal and industrial interests identical. Quinney does not do this.

Classical social theory, however, was very much taken up with these questions, and indeed Quinney's goals of justice and individual freedom underpinned approaches as far apart as those of Marx and Durkheim.

Marx, for example, refused in his theory to allow of any distinction between man and society. Marx was a realist rather than a utopian in the sense that, seeing that men were divided by conflicts of interest, he sought to abolish the major structural forms which gave rise to the conflicts. All this is well known, and it is therefore surprising that Quinney, as a conflict theorist, periodically referencing his indebtedness to Marxian formulations (1970b, p. 38) should move in another direction. The separation of man (the 'individual' involved in a subjective social world, and pursuing a set of highly segmentary interests) and society (an amalgam of unequal institutional orders falling under the sway of one dominant view of social reality—the government's) is a fundamental dichotomy for Quinney. Thus, the social reality of crime and society, for Quinney, is an analysis of the interaction between bits of society and some Robinson Crusoe-like individual (who periodically strikes alliances within institutional orders with the similarly minded). For Marx (1844, p. 137) however, 'just as society produces man as man, so is society produced by him. Activity and mind, both in their content and their mode of existence, are social; social activity and social mind.'

The importance of this understanding for a thoroughgoing analysis of crime is that crime is structured within a given society. It is not just that the codification, enforcement and acting-out of conformity and deviance are products of a myriad of interacting sets of interests, which themselves are patterned into institutional orders. Importantly, for Marx (1931, pp. 31–2) it is the conditions of labour and production that shape the society in a highly specific form and (if understood) can explain the genesis of deviant and criminal acts and the necessity to label such acts as such:

> There is a prevalent tradition that in certain periods robbery constituted the only source of living. But in order to be able to plunder, there must be something to plunder; i.e. there must be production. And even this method of plunder is determined by the method of production. A stock-jobbing nation, for example, cannot be robbed in the same manner as a nation of shepherds.
>
> In the case of the slave the instrument of production is robbed directly. But when the production of the country in whose interest he is robbed must be so organized as to admit of slave labour, or (as in South America, etc.) a system of production must be introduced adapted to slavery.
>
> Laws may perpetuate an instrument of production, e.g. land, in certain families. These laws only assume an economic importance if extended landed property is in harmony with the system of production prevailing in society, as is the case for example in England. In France agriculture had been carried on on a small scale in spite of the large estates, and the latter were, therefore, broken up by the Revolution. But how about the legislative attempt to perpetuate the minute subdivision of the land? In spite of these laws land ownership is concentrating again. The effect of legislation on the maintenance of distribution and its resultant influence on production must be made particularly clear.

Even this seemingly radical view on crime, stressing its relationship to structural changes within societal order, is not peculiar to Marx. Durkheim (1964b, p. 387), also in contrast to Quinney, refused to see man and society as antagonistic elements but was concerned to demonstrate what social forces set men against each other:

> The task of the most advanced societies is, then a work of

justice. That they, in fact, feel the necessity of orientating themselves in this direction is what we have already shown and what everyday experience proves to us. Just as the ideal of lower societies was to create or maintain as intense a common life as possible, in which the individual was absorbed, so our ideal is to make social relations always more equitable, so as to assure the free development of all our socially useful forces.

Moreover, again unlike Quinney and in contradistinction to popular misconception about his views, Durkheim saw that justice was not simply a question of readjusting interests and values, or searching for a force independent of government and private interest, but understood that a prerequisite of a social reality that did not result in extreme anomie (or, for example, crime) was a structural reorganization directed as the resolution of inequality (Durkheim, 1964b, p. 377):

> In short, labour is divided spontaneously only if society is constituted in such a way that social inequalities exactly express natural inequalities. But, for that, it is necessary and sufficient that the latter be neither enhanced nor lowered by some external cause. Perfect spontaneity is, then, only a consequence and another form of this other fact—absolute equality in the external conditions of the conflict.

It is a pity that Quinney fails at crucial points in his analysis to refer to the thinking of classical theorists (especially as these thinkers were themselves taken up with the dilemmas of Quinney's introduction). His failure to engage these social theories on the question of men's relationship to society leads him away from a structural analysis of the forces conducive to crime and disorder (*and* the protection of the individual from a repressive law and social control) to an abstracted refuge in legal reform. All of Quinney's eclectic collection of instances of conflict produce nothing more than a sociology of civil liberties; they say little about the structure of civil society as such (Quinney, 1970b, p. 42):

> Protection must be sought in procedural law, a law that must necessarily be removed from the control of private groups or public government. The challenge for law of the future is that it creates an order providing fulfilment for individual values that are now within our reach, values that paradoxically are imminent because of the existence of interests from which we must now seek protection. A new society is coming: can a law be created apart from private interests which assures individual fulfilment within a good society?

This prescription (and cry of anguish) succinctly expresses the existential and programmatic dilemmas of Quinney's approach to the social reality of deviance. Oppression in the social structure threatens the ability of isolated individuals to pursue and realize interests, whilst emphasizing the need for individuals to come together in the defence of those interests. What appears to be argued, therefore, is that an understanding of the way in which the powerful in particular societies will attempt to enforce their definition of reality should lead us into formulating a counter-culture, united in the defence of the liberal and individualistic traditions of Anglo-Saxon law.

Now, whilst this conclusion may reveal a certain consistency, it is dependent on a set of assumptions about the relationship of law and interest, and, ultimately, on a crude atomistic model of the social structure of advanced industrial society. The fact that Anglo-Saxon procedural law is built around the defence of individual interest has to be understood in terms of the contexts in which such law developed, and the interests protected by the individualistic emphasis in precedents and enforcements.

The centrality of 'individualism' in the Anglo-Saxon law is closely connected with the rise of the state as an instrument for the regulation of economic and commercial relations (Kennedy, 1970, p. 16):

> Just as the national State came to recognize and guarantee, as well as create, civil laws relating to market relations, private property, labour, imports, exports, tariffs, it likewise came to have full power to create and impose criminal laws which related to the same institutions of capitalism. Under the ethic of individual responsibility, any citizen, even one forgiven by his kin or community, could be penally sanctioned as an individual by an abstract State and without much probability of reprisal against the State on the part of those who had forgiven him. With the advent of the formally rational State, punishment was no longer an act of war. And any violation of criminal law—defined by the State—came to be seen as a harm against the State.

The replacement of the social relationships (and the penal arrangements) of feudalism by the relationships of capital and labour, that is, represented a fundamental alteration in the content, function and jurisdictions of law. It is not only that crimes which were previously settled in blood feuds between kin-groups came to receive sanction under the formal laws of the state; it is also that these crimes came to be conceived in terms of individual transgressions for which individual men should bear responsibility. This was not simply the victory of a specific interest group over another for historically-

263

specific reasons; it was also the victory of an ethic of individualism which informed and underpinned an economic and social system at an early stage in its development. The structure and function of laws as a whole in advanced capitalist society can be seen as a reflection of this ethic, rather than as the cumulation of the activities of independent and autonomous interest groups arising in different historical periods (Kennedy, 1970, p. 16):

> Apart from the older harms criminal laws were established primarily for the protection and development of the institutions of capitalism. The reference here is not simply to penal sanctions against robbery, theft, burglary, or other violations of private property. It is to penal sanctions which directly controlled the manner in which social structure would develop in cities. It is to penal sanctions which had direct bearings on determining the organization of the division of labour in society and consequently upon the class structure of commercial settlements.

To understand that formal law is connected with the alliance of capital and the state, in this way, is to understand that the sanctioning of behaviour as criminal and ability to enforce punishment is fundamentally bound up with the control of the state. In particular, it has been argued (Kennedy, 1970) that the structure of formal law under such circumstances will be so constituted as to create two kinds of citizenship and responsibility. The labour forces of industrial society (whether employed or not, and at whatever level of qualification—so long as they are sellers of labour) will be bound by criminal law and by penal sanction. The state and the owners of labour will be bound only by a civil law which regulates their competition between each other. It is not only that there is differential application of law: it is also that the state and the owners of capital and labour—irrespective of particular battles between interest groups at particular moments of historical development—are 'beyond incrimination' and, most significantly, beyond the criminal sanction.

It is in these respects that Quinney's atomistic conception of society, containing and subsuming a mass of interest groups, is an inadequate basis on which to build a programme for the defence of individual interests and civil liberties. For if the state appears to be bent on a path of repression and restriction of individual rights, this progression must reflect some kind of fundamental crisis in the relationship of state and individual, and, more precisely, in the relationship between those sellers of labour who are subject to the force of law and those owners of capital and labour who are—by virtue of the institutional arrangements of state—'beyond incrimination'.

And if such a fundamental crisis is developing, then it follows that the state's monopoly over the control and direction of law will be reformed accordingly (removal of the individual right not to self-incriminate, increase in the powers granted to police to enter and search and removal of the right to strike from the labour force, etc.). The individualistic ethic of Anglo-Saxon law was never an instrument for the arbitration of equal interests (an ethic—and an instrument— to which all were subject); but it is even less likely to assume such a function when individualism is in the process of sacrifice to new institutional demands.

Quinney is not alone in his continuing determination to see the law as an agency for the protection of rights, liberties and interests. American and British literature, for example, in the area of race relations, is very much taken up with the role of the law as an agency of change, and as an institutional weapon against discrimination. This tradition—ultimately, it has been argued, stemming from a utilitarian view of law (Schur, 1968, especially pp. 33–6)—has led many sociologists into the study of law in particular cultures and in different historical periods. The thrust of this work has been directed at undermining the utilitarian view of law—that is, the law as some reflection of public opinion, or more precisely, men's calculative and purposive actions made in the pursuit of happiness—and replacing it with a view of law as social control (the 'legal realist' approach to law) (Schur, 1968, pp. 43–50). In his introduction to the reader *Crime and Justice in Society*, Quinney (1969) is involved in demonstrating the way in which law assumes the shapes demanded by currently powerful interest, and he marshalls a considerable and catholic variety of evidence to illustrate this position.

Particular stress is laid on the work of William Chambliss and Jerome Hall, whose work in this area is rapidly assuming centrality in the sociology of law at large. In the work of Hall (1952), the trespass laws, embodied in Carrier's case of 1473, were the result of the necessity to protect the burgeoning properties of the mercantilists (particularly in wool and textiles) and their traders; in the case of vagrancy, in Chambliss's interpretation (1964, pp. 67–77), legislation was necessitated by the need to force unemployed vagrants, who might otherwise have existed on the giving of alms, into employment on low wages in agriculture. Quinney summarizes these researches by commenting that the legal changes were 'brought about by powerful interest groups' and moves on to evidence other research supporting such a conclusion (e.g. the liquor trade and its lobby during the period of prohibition in the United States).

The reaction against the utilitarian view of law, however, in favour of the view of law as an instrument of social control in the hands of 'powerful interest groups', does not take us far enough in our understanding of the dynamics of law. Just as the 'pluralistic' model of society—as has been pointed out in many critiques—tends to be circular and thus unfalsifiable—since it is always possible abstractly to separate out a new 'interest' as having replaced an old; so it is possible to see the evolution of law as reflecting such a simple process of replacement. The problem with this position is that it can never specify the conditions under which law would not be simply an instrument of a currently powerful interest. Thus, it can never specify the conditions under which there is the optimum chance for guaranteeing individual liberties and freedom for people who are not affiliated to the powerful interest groups of the day.

Thus far, our assessment of the work of Richard Quinney and Austin Turk has proceeded along two lines of criticism. We have attempted to show that the new conflict theories they advance for consideration by sociologists of crime and deviance are subject to the limitations of the approaches from which they stem—respectively, the 'conflict-functionalism' of Ralf Dahrendorf and the pluralist models of society derived from American political science. We have, in that sense, indicated that the substance of the new conflict theories is *not* especially new. We have also attempted to demonstrate that the substantive theorization of Quinney and Turk is inadequate to the purposes of the authors themselves. In Turk's case, although he may have answered his students' pleas for a more systematic 'criminology', it is by no means clear that his systematization will be acceptable as a means of linking conceptualization with a way out of the crisis of American institutions. Turk's 'conflict theory of society', whilst giving order to theorization, accepts the retrenchment of existing orders of domination and repression. Quinney's desire for a theory which makes sense of social reality, and 'the contemporary experience', is hardly satiated by a view of society dominated by the circulating 'interests' of an ordered society: we have shown that some interests are more central than others, and that some interests, in particular, are—within the existing institutional order—thoroughly 'beyond incrimination'. Such a perspective may be some kind of basis on which to build a theory of crime which has the power 'of forcing us to consider libertarian ideals': it is *not* the basis for the defence, extension or institutionalization of such ideals. We have, by implication, drawn rather similar conclusions about the excursions recently made by sociologists (in America in particular) into the study of law.

But the re-emergence of a conflict perspective in the study of crime is a promising development. Amongst other things, it holds out the prospect of theorization and empirical study characterized by a sense of history. In particular, we can hope to see studies of law and crime which are informed, not by a static conception of pathological and/or anomic individuals colliding with a simple and taken-for-granted set of institutional orders, but rather by a conception of the complex interaction between developments in institutional and social structures and the consciousness of men living within such structures. The development of labelling theory, which we have discussed in chapter 5 (and which also arises out of the reaction against simple models of social structures, social processes and individual consciousness), promises to infect the new conflict approaches with a sense of psychology, too; in stressing the extent to which men's behaviour can be the product of the social reactions of others as much as it is the reaction of self to internal or material exigencies (psychological or financial needs).

In these respects, the new conflict theories fare well in fulfilling a few of the formal requirements of a general theory. But, if there is one respect in which they fail to meet these requirements, it is at the most fundamental level of all. That is, the conception of human action, not only in Turk and Quinney but also, to varying extents, in Marx, Bonger and Vold, is still a conception of the criminal man as pathological. Of course, the new conflict theorists do not retreat to the pathologies of early positivism; but the stress remains on the way in which men's criminal behaviour and behaviour in general are *determined*. It may be that the criminal behaviour of, for example, thieves, is determined by the unequal possession and distribution of wealth in a society; or it may be that the political deviance of contemporary radicals (prepared to face the force of law) is determined by the monopoly of defining power by the state or the rule-enforcers. But the overwhelming impression is one of determination at the expense of *purpose* and *integrity*. Whether they are discussing the genesis of behaviour or the derivation of labels, the new conflict theorists see a relatively simple relationship between power and interest, and the consciousness of men (as being formed in conjunctures of such interests). For the time being, we shall only comment that such a conception undermines or understresses an alternative view of men as purposive creators and innovators of action. In particular, it leads to an approach to crime in which action is merely and simply a product of powerful interests or unequal society—as opposed to being the product of purpose individual or collective action taken to resolve such inequalities of power and interest. It tends to suggest that one can only be a deviant when one is seen or described as a deviant by the powerful interests of the day or when one is in a disadvantaged position in such an unequal society. In so doing, the conflict approach is in danger of withdrawing integrity and purpose—or idiosyncracy—from men: and, thus, is close to erecting a view of crime as non-purposive (or pathological) reaction to external circumstance.

267

9 Conclusion

The insulation of criminology from sociology in general—symbolized institutionally in America in Robert Merton's insistence on placing the study of crime in the Department of Social Administration at Columbia—is rapidly being broken down. The 'social reaction theorists' in drawing attention to the activities of the rule-creators and enforcers (cf. Emerson, 1969; Lemert, 1970), and David Matza, in emphasizing the role of Leviathan in the signification of behaviours in terms of the demands of state, have redirected criminological attention to the grand questions of social structure and the overweening social arrangements within which the criminal process is played out. We are confronted once again with the central question of man's relationship to structures of power, domination and authority—and the ability of men to confront these structures in acts of crime, deviance and dissent—we are back in the realm of social theory itself.

This book has attempted to provide an implicit account of the uneven history of criminology's relationship to the social sciences. Starting with an account of the classical utilitarian approach to the protection of the individual from excessive punishment, and moving through the varieties of biological, psychological and social positivism, we have attempted to provide an immanent critique of various positions from a vantage point which stresses the importance of the initiative of state, and its entrepreneurial representatives, in defining and sanctioning certain forms of behaviour at certain points in time: and we have suggested that an adequately *social* theory would need to be free of the biological and psychological assumptions that have been involved in the various attempts to explain the actions of the men who do get defined and sanctioned by the state as deviant and react against those definitions, in different historical circumstances.

268

Thus far, the book has operated within a relatively modest or limited perspective. The sociology with which we have urged a reconciliation has remained ambiguous: we have been content to say that such a sociology must be fully social (unbroken by the assertions of biological or other non-social assumptions) and that it must be able to account (in a historically informed fashion) for men's imprisonment within social structures that constrain his possibilities. We have not been able to specify, for example, the limitations of a sociology that is itself insulated from an economic understanding of structural forces (cf. Gordon, 1971; Pearce, 1973) or that has been developed entirely within the confines of a developing or developed capitalist society (Heather, forthcoming; L. Taylor and Robertson, 1972). We have not had space enough to draw out sufficiently cross-cultural evidence about the forms assumed by criminal and deviant action, and structures of social control, in pre-capitalist societies or in societies where there is an explicit attempt to break down the culture of capitalist societies (cf. Loney, 1973).

We have, however, attempted to open out the criminological debate by pointing to certain *formal* and *substantive* requirements of a fully social theory of deviance, a theory that can explain the forms assumed by social control and deviant action in 'developed' societies (characterized—we have argued—by the domination of a capitalist mode of production, by a division of labour involving the growth of armies of 'experts', social workers, psychiatrists and others who have been assigned a crucial role in the tasks of social definition and social control, and, currently, by the necessity to segregate out—in mental hospitals, prisons and in juvenile institutions—an increasing variety of its members as being in need of control).

We have not, at this point, gone far beyond what we might call an immanent critique of existing theory. Rather, we have been concerned to develop a model which contains all the elements, some of which are lacking in individual examples of the existing literature on crime and deviance. And, despite the fact that we have continually stressed the need for a sense of history in the kind of explanations offered out of crime, deviance and control (a sense of history that is almost totally absent in existing criminological *theory*[1]), we have not had the space here to enter into any detailed historical explanations.[2] It is obvious that our endeavours need now to be supplemented with a concrete application of the formal model, resulting from the immanent critique of existing thinkers, to empirical cases: and, in particular, to situations in which a different form of production, a different division of labour and a different form of crime are all alleged to obtain. Given the nature of our premises, spelt out in the substantive requirements of the theory later in this conclusion, such an onerous enterprise would only be useful if the purpose for carrying it out was clear. And one of the central purposes of this critique has been to assert the possibility—not only of a fully social *theory*—but also of a society in which men are able to assert themselves in a fully social fashion. With Marx, we have been concerned with the social arrangements that have obstructed, and the social contradictions that enhance, man's chances of achieving full sociality —a state of freedom from material necessity, and (therefore) of material incentive, a release from the contraints of forced production, an abolition of the forced division of labour, and a set of social arrangements, therefore, in which there would be no politically, economically, and socially-induced need to criminalize deviance. We shall expand on this later: for the time being, it is clearly essential to spell out the elements of the formal model that emerge out of the immanent critique.

The *formal* requirements of this theory are concerned with the scope of the theory. It must be able to cover, and sustain the connections between:

1   The wider origins of the deviant act

The theory must be able, in other words, to place the act in terms of its wider structural origins. These 'structural' considerations will involve recognition of the intermediate structural questions that have traditionally been the domain of sociological criminology (e.g. ecological areas,[3] subcultural location,[4] distribution of opportunities for theft) (cf. Armstrong and Wilson, 1973) but it would place these against the overall social context of inequalities of power, wealth and authority in the developed industrial society. Similarly, there would be consideration of the questions traditionally dealt with by psychologists concerned with the structures conducive to individual breakdown, that is with an individual's exclusion from 'normal' interaction (Hepworth, 1970; 1972). But, again, there would be an attempt, as in the later work of the anti-psychiatry school, to place these psychological concerns (e.g. with the schizophrenic nature of the bourgeois nuclear family) in the context of a society in which families are just one part of an interrelating but contradictory structural whole. The move would be away from the view of man as an atomistic individual, cut off within families or other specific subcultural situations, insulated from the pressures of existence under the prevailing social conditions.

The wider origins of the deviant act could only be understood, we would argue, in terms of the rapidly changing economic and political contingencies of advanced industrial society. At this level, the formal requirement is really for what might be called *a political economy of crime.*

270

2 Immediate origins of the deviant act

It is, of course, the case, however, that men do not experience the constraints of a society in an undifferentiated fashion. Just as subcultural theorists, operating in the anthropological tradition, have argued that the subcultural notion is useful to explain the different kinds of ways in which men resolve the problems posed by the demands of a dominant culture (Downes, 1966a, ch. 1), so we would argue that an adequately social theory of deviance must be able to explain the different events, experiences or structural developments that precipitate the deviant act. The theory must explain the different ways in which structural demands are interpreted, reacted against, or used by men at different levels in the social structure, in such a way that an essentially deviant choice is made. The formal requirement, at this level, that is, is for a *social psychology of crime*: a social psychology which, unlike that which is implicit in the work of the social reaction theorists, recognizes that men may *consciously* choose the deviant road, as the one solution to the problems posed by existence in a contradictory society (cf. Hepworth, 1970; 1972; L. Taylor, 1972).

3 The actual act

Men may choose to engage in particular solutions to their problems, without being able to carry them out. An adequate social theory of deviance would need to be able to explain the relationship between beliefs and action, between the optimum 'rationality' that men have chosen and the behaviours they actually carry through. A working-class adolescent, for example, confronted with blockage of opportunity, with problems of status frustration, alienated from the kind of existence offered out to him in contemporary society, may want to engage in hedonistic activities (e.g. finding immediate pleasure through the use of alcohol, drugs, or in extensive sexual activities) or he may choose to kick back at a rejecting society (e.g. through acts of vandalism). He may also attempt to assert some degree of control over, for example, the pace at which he is asked to work (cf. L. Taylor and Walton, 1971) or the ways in which his leisure time interests are controlled (cf. I. Taylor, 1971a; 1971b; S. Cohen, 1972a). But he may find that these options themselves are not easily achieved. Cloward and Ohlin have argued that adolescent 'drop-outs' in the United States, failures in the legitimate society, can also experience 'double-failure' in being rejected in delinquent subcultures themselves. Deviant individuals can find that they are rejected by other deviants (as 'uncool', physically inadequate or unattractive, or generally undesirable). Whilst we would argue that there is always a relationship between individual choice (a set of beliefs) and action it is not necessarily a simple one: an adolescent boy could choose the hedonistic, the rejective or the assertive options without there being any chance of sustaining them. Adjustments of some kind would then be necessitated. The formal requirement at this level then is for an explanation of the ways in which the actual acts of men are explicable in terms of the rationality of choice or the constraints on choice at the point of precipitation into action. The formal requirement, here, is for an account of real *social dynamics* surrounding the actual acts.

4 Immediate origins of social reaction

Just as the deviant act itself may be precipitated by the reactions of others (e.g. as a result of an adolescent's attempt to win acceptance as 'cool' or 'tough' in a subculture of delinquency, or from a business-man's attempt to show ability as a sharp practitioner) so the sub-sequent definition of the act is the product of close personal relation-ships. A certain behaviour may encourage a member of the actor's family or peer group to refer that actor to a doctor, to a child guidance clinic, or to a psychiatrist (because that behaviour is seen to be odd). Or another behaviour may result in the individual being reported to the police by people outside the individual's immediate family circle or friendship group (because he has been acting sus-piciously, or actually been seen committing an illegal act). In both instances, there is a degree of choice on the part of the social audience: it may be thought that the behaviour *is* odd, but that it is preferable to keep it in the family; or it may be thought that although the individual *has* been acting suspiciously or has been behaving illegally, it would be too troublesome to involve the police.

Even when the formal agencies of social control themselves—in particular, the police, but also the various agencies of the 'Welfare State'—directly apprehend the individual in the course of his law-breaking (which is relatively rare), a degree of choice is exercised by the agent in his reaction to the deviant. The complex mix of classical liberalism (emphasizing, for example, 'police discretion' and the role of the local constable as a part-time social worker) and the lay theories of criminality (emphasizing what a real criminal, hooligan, junkie, or 'villain' actually looks like)[5] contributes to the moral climate and lays down the boundaries within which informal social reaction to deviance is likely to occur.

The requirement at this level is for an explanation of the immediate reaction of the social audience in terms of the range of choices available to that audience. The requirement, in other words, is for a *social psychology of social reaction*: an account of the contingencies and the conditions which are crucial to the decision to act against the deviant.

5   Wider origins of deviant reaction

In the same way that the choices available to the deviant himself are a product of his structural location, primarily, and, secondarily, his *individual* attributes (his acceptability to significant others—both those involved in legitimate activity and those who are engaged in rule-breaking activity of one kind or another), so the social psychology of social reaction (and the lay theories of deviance behind it) is explicable only in terms of the position and the attributes of those who instigate the reaction against the deviant. It is obviously the case that members of a law-breaker's immediate family group are far less likely to react against his activity than those who are strangers to him.[6] But it is also the case that the 'lay' theories of criminality and deviance adhered to by strangers will vary enormously: social work ideology (with its positivistic stress on reform) is continually at odds with the more classically punitive ideologies of correctional institutions and their controllers; police ideology is sometimes at odds with the philosophies of courtroom practice (in particular, the adjudicatory powers of the non-professional jury);[7] and even amongst those without formal positions in the structure of social control (the 'public') the lay theories found to be acceptable will vary across the contours of social class, ethnic group and age (Simmons and Chambers, 1965).

The predominant tendencies in criminological treatments of the wider origins of deviant reaction, so far as they have been dealt with at all, have been to see these as located in occupational groups and their particular needs (Box, Dickson), in a set of rather ambiguously defined set of pluralistic interests (Quinney, Lemert), in authority-subject relationships within 'imperatively-coordinated associations' (Turk), or in simple superordinate-subordinate political relationships (Becker). All of these treatments of the sources of reactions against the deviant are, of course, implicit political sociologies of the state; and, as we have attempted to make clear throughout, few criminologists have really grappled in an effective way with the debates about social structure in the traditions of grand social theory. In particular, few criminologists have been able to deal with the ways in which the political initiatives that give rise to (or abolish) legislation, that defined sanctionable behaviour in society or ensure the enforcement of that legislation, are intimately bound up with the structure of the *political economy* of the state. Sutherland's treatment of white-collar crime, for example, was informed hardly at all by an examination of the ways in which white-collar infractions were (and are) functional to industrial-capitalist societies at points in their development: rather it was concerned with illuminating what he saw to be the inequitable use of law in controlling behaviour in defiance of formally-defined rules of conduct (cf. Pearce, 1973). The fact that the political sociologies of crime in criminology remain implicit and ambiguous is some indication of the extent to which criminology has moved away from the concerns of the classical social thinkers. We saw, in chapter 3, how it was impossible for Durkheim to conceive of crime and deviance without his conceiving also of a certain set of productive social arrangements overarched by a certain collective conscience (a forced division of labour being associated with 'functional rebellion' as well as with the 'skewed deviant' adaptation). We saw also how for him it was impossible to talk of the dimunition of crime without talking politically of the abolition of the forced division of labour, the abolition of inherited wealth, and the setting up of occupational associations in tune with (politically enforceable) social arrangements based on a biological meritocracy. In chapter 7 we saw that Marx's political sociology of crime was also inextricably bound up with a political critique and a clear-headed analysis of existing social arrangements. For him, crime was expression of men's situation of constraint within alienating social arrangements—and in part an indication of a struggle to overcome them. The fact that criminal action was no political answer in itself to those situations was explained in terms of the political and social possibilities of the *Lumpenproletariat* as a parasitical agency on the organized working class itself. We shall develop our earlier critiques of these two positions a little later: for the time being, it is sufficient to mention them not only as evidence of the *dilution of theory* in twentieth-century investigations of crime but also as an indictment of the *depoliticization* of the issues involved in the classical discussions in social theory on crime, accomplished and applauded by those who carry out work in the field of contemporary 'applied' criminology.

For the moment it is sufficient to assert that one of the important formal requirements of a fully social theory of deviance, that is almost totally absent in existing literature, is an effective model of the political and economic imperatives that underpin on the one hand the 'lay ideologies' and on the other the 'crusades' and initiatives that emerge periodically either to control the amount and level of deviance (cf. Manson and Palmer, 1973) or else (as in the cases of prohibition, certain homosexual activity, and, most recently, certain 'crimes without victims') to remove certain behaviours from the category of 'illegal' behaviours. We are lacking a *political economy of social reaction.*

6 The outcome of the social reaction on deviant's further action

One of the most telling contributions of the social reaction theorists to an understanding of deviance was their emphasis on the need to understand deviant action as being, in part, an attempt to come to terms by the rule-breaker with the reaction against his initial infraction. As we argued in chapter 5, one of the superficial strengths of the social reaction perspective was its ability to see the actor as using the reaction against him in a variety of ways (that is, in exercising choice). This we saw to be an advance on the deterministic view of the impact of sanctions on further behaviour in positivistic views of 'reform', 'rehabilitation', and, most particularly, 'conditioning'. We also argued, however, that the notion of secondary deviation was undialectical; that is, that it could have the same status as an explanation of what the social reaction theorists separate out as primary deviation, and that, in reality, it might be impossible to distinguish between the causes of primary and secondary deviation.

A fully social theory of deviance—premised on the notion of man as consciously involved (however inarticulately) in deviant choices— would require us to see the reaction he evolves to rejection or stigmatization (or, for that matter, sanction in the form of institutionalization) as being bound up with the conscious choices that precipitated the initial infraction. It would require us to reject the view which is paramount in Lemert's discussion of secondary deviation (1967, p. 51) viz. that 'most people drift into deviance by specific actions rather than by formed choices of social roles and statuses' and that, because of this, they unintentionally, unwittingly and (implicitly) rather tragically enter what Lemert terms a 'staging area set up for an ideological struggle between the deviant seeking to normalize his actions and thoughts, and agencies seeking the opposite' (p. 44). Actually, Lemert, as we implied in chapter 5, is not able to show that the problems faced by the deviant are always the result of his being apprehended and reacted against (either formally or informally) in this rather straightforward sense. He writes at one point (ibid., p. 48) that:

> Becoming an admitted homosexual ('coming out') may endanger one's livelihood or professional career, but it also absolves the individual from failure to assume the heavy responsibilities of marriage and parenthood, and it is a ready way of fending off painful involvements in heterosexual affairs.

In other words, the act of breaking through what Gouldner has termed the normalized repression of everyday routine expectations, consciously and wittingly, does not always require precipitation in the form of social reaction. It only requires one to know one's enemy

275

and to know how to deal with the stigmatization and exclusion that may then result. Just as a homosexual preparing to 'come out' may take a long time to prepare his revelation (and thus be consciously prepared for the reaction against him), so any deviant can be understood as having some degree of consciousness of what to expect in the event of apprehension and reaction. A fully social explanation of the outcome of social reaction to the further actions of the apprehended deviant, therefore, would be one in which the deviant actor is always endowed with some degree of consciousness about the likelihood and consequences of reaction against him, and in which his subsequent decisions are developed from that initial degree of consciousness.[8] All those writers who see deviants as 'naive' must now realize that they are dealing with a minority of deviants, even in situations where the degree or extent of social reaction is unexpected (because, for example, of a moral panic amongst the powerful about a particular kind of offence, or because a campaign of control has been instigated against it—as in the case of the white adolescents who received unexpectedly heavy sentences for their role during the Notting Hill race riots in 1959), it would still be important to have a social explanation of the ways in which the deviants responded to their sentences with a degree of consciousness about 'the law' which they had developed before they had had a formal contact with it.

In a fully social theory, then, the consciousness conventionally allowed deviants in the secondary deviation situation would be seen as explicable—at least in part—in terms of the actors' consciousness of the world in general.

7 The nature of the deviant process as a whole

The formal requirements of a fully social theory are formal in the sense that they refer to the *scope* of the theoretical analysis. In the real world of social action, these analytical distinctions merge, connect and often appear to be indistinguishable. We have already indicted social reaction theory, which is in many ways the most sophisticated rejection of the simpler forms of positivism (concentrating as they do on the pathologies of the individual actor), as one-sidedly deterministic: in seeing the deviant's problems and consciousness simply as a response to apprehension and the application of social control. Positivistic explanations stand accused of being unable to approach an explanation not only of the *political economy* of crime (the background to criminal action) but also of what we have called the *political economy*, the *social psychology* and the *social dynamics* of social reaction to deviance. And most of the classical and earlier biological psychological positivists (whom we discussed

276

in the first two chapters) are unable to offer out even a satisfactorily social explanation of the relationship between the individual and society: the individual in these accounts appears by and large as an isolated atom unaffected by the ebb and flow of social arrangements, social change, and contradictions in what is, after all, a society of social arrangements built around the capitalist mode of production.

The central requirement of a fully social theory of deviance, however, is that these formal requirements must not be treated simply as essential factors all of which need to be present (in invariant fashion) if the theory is to be social. Rather it is that these formal requirements must all appear in the theory, as they do in the real world, in a complex, dialectical relationship to one another. Georg Lukacs's criticism of Solzhenitsyn's early work is instructive here, if only because it is so well applicable to the work of Goffman, Garfinkel, Becker, Lemert and other thinkers who have been concerned with the impact that 'social control' (whether institutional or otherwise) has on its victims. Writing of Solzhenitsyn's early work on the prison camp (which Lukacs correctly takes as a metaphor intended to apply to the whole society), Lukacs (1971b) observed that:

Solzhenitsyn's development . . . of [his] technique from his first story not only, of necessity, increases the number of prisoners whose life is shown . . . it also demands that the initiators and organisers of this internment of large masses of people must also be depicted on a wider basis and more concretely. . . . Only thus does the 'place of action' receive its concrete socially determined significance. . . . In the last resort it is a social fact that the internment camp confronts both its victims and its organisers spontaneously and irresistibly with its provocative basic questions . . .

Working our way through the *substance* of the various theories of crime and deviance, we have found not only that the number of prisoners (by analogy, the number of criminals and deviants) 'whose life is shown' has increased but also the fact that the theories have been more or less inadequate to cope with the 'provocative basic questions' posed by the persistence of crime, deviance and dissent.

The great merit of Solzhenitsyn, using the skills and the techniques of the novelist, is that he is able, in a way that many formal models in existing social theory are not, to encompass the substance of man in his many manifestations. Man is both determined by the fact of his imprisonment, and also determining, in the sense that he creates (and is able to struggle against) his own imprisonment. Some men (the guards) have interests (up to a point) in the maintenance of imprisonment; others (the inmates, their relatives and sympathizers) do not. There is, in Solzhenitsyn's 'prison', a sense of the contingencies and sequences that may lead some men to imprison others: a view of the social and political origins of repression and the segregation of deviants. There is some conception too, of the real political, material and symbolic imperatives that lie at the back of such sequences and processes. And, finally, there is an implicit prescription in Solzhenitsyn, a *politics* for which he is now experiencing exclusion and segregation himself, a politics which implies that man is able consciously to abolish the imprisonment that he consciously created.

It may well be, as Lukacs's criticism implies, that these substantive features of Solzhenitsyn's writings are not held together and continuously, in an ongoing dialectic of resistance and control. Nevertheless, Solzhenitsyn's attempts to achieve this fare well by comparison with many sociological excursions into the area. The substantive history of twentieth-century criminology is, by and large, the history of the empirical emasculation of theories (like those of Marx and Durkheim) which attempted to deal with the whole society, and a history therefore of the depoliticization of criminological issues.

The new criminology

The conditions of our time are forcing a reappraisal of this compartmentalization of issues and problems. It is not just that the traditional focus of applied criminology on the socially deprived working-class adolescent is being thrown into doubt by the criminalization of vast numbers of middle-class youth (for 'offences' of a hedonistic or specifically oppositional nature) (S. Cohen, 1971c; I. Taylor, 1971d). Neither is it only that the crisis of our institutions has deepened to the point where the 'master institutions' of the state, and of the political economy, are unable to disguise their own inability to adhere to their own rules and regulations (cf. Kennedy, 1970; Pearce, 1973). It is largely that the total interconnectedness of these problems and others is being revealed.

A criminology which is to be adequate to an understanding of these developments, and which will be able to bring politics back into the discussion of what were previously technical issues, will need to deal with the society as a totality. This 'new' criminology will in fact be an *old* criminology, in that it will face the same problems that were faced by the classical social theorists. Marx (1951) saw the problem with his usual clarity when he began to develop his critique of the origins of German idealism (328–9):

The first work which I undertook for a solution to the doubts which assailed me was a critical review of the Hegelian

278

philosophy of right, a work the introduction to which appeared in 1844 in the *Deutsch-Französische Jahrbücher* published in Paris. My investigations led to the result that legal relations as well as the forms of state to be grasped neither from themselves nor from the so-called general development of the human mind, but rather have their roots in the material conditions of life, the sum total of which Hegel, following the example of Englishmen and Frenchmen of the eighteenth century, combines under the name 'civil society', that however the anatomy of civil society is to be sought in political economy.

We have argued here for a political economy of criminal action, and of the reaction it excites, and for a politically-informed social psychology of these ongoing social dynamics. We have, in other words, laid claim to have constructed the formal elements of a theory that would be adequate to move criminology out of its own imprisonment in artifically segregated specifics. We have attempted to bring the parts together again in order to form the whole.

Implicitly, we have rejected that contemporary trend which may claim for itself the mantle of a new criminology, or a new deviancy theory, and which presumably claims to find a solution to our present discontents largely in the search for the sources of individual meaning. Ethnomethodology, however, is a historical creature too: its pedigree goes back to the phenomenological contemplations that were so prominent in an earlier period of uncertainty and doubt: the collapse of European social democracy and the rise of fascism. Phenomenology looks at the prison camp and searches for the *meaning* of the 'prison' rather than for its alternative; and it searches for the meaning in terms of individual definitions rather than in terms of a political explanation of the necessity to imprison.

Indeed, one of the recurring criticisms we have had of many of the theorists discussed in this book is the way in which they place men apart from society. The view of man in society is sometimes *additive* (in the sense that environmental 'factors' are seen as having a more or less significant impact of some fundamental fact of human nature—as in Eysenck); sometimes it is *discontinuous* (in that there is a recognition of interplay between man and social influences, but an interplay which is curtailed by men's differential ability to be socialized—as in Durkheim—or in the appropriateness of certain social patterns for different men in different periods—as in Durkheim and in Merton), and when there is a fusion of man and society, it is only in terms of man's given biological or psychological pathologies (which, for example, force him to gravitate into delinquent areas, as in Shaw and Mackay and the early ecologists).

Phenomenology and ethnomethodology make the break between man and society by reifying experience and meaning, as specifics in their own right, which we cannot take (for granted) to be socially determined in any currently identifiable manner.

Increasingly, it is becoming clear that the contemplation and suspension involved in these (and other) traditions are not enough. There is a crisis not just in social theory and social thought (Gouldner, 1971) but in the society itself. The new criminology must therefore be a normative theory: it must hold out the possibilities of a resolution to the fundamental questions, and a social resolution.

It is this normative imperative that separates out the European schools of criminology from the eclecticism and reformism in professional American sociology (cf. Nicolaus, 1969).[9] The domination of orthodox positivism over European criminology has been most clearly challenged recently by the emergence of a social welfare-oriented criminology in Scandinavia, centring particularly around the Institute of Criminology and Criminal Law at the University of Oslo, and by the beginnings of a politically-informed 'structuralism' in the formation of the National Deviancy Conference in Britain.

The new Scandinavian criminology, which has been several years in the making (N. Christie, 1965; 1968; 1971; Mathieson, 1965; 1972) has been fundamentally concerned with the description and explanation of the forms assumed, as the titles of their publications imply, by the 'aspects of social control in welfare-states'. Working in relatively underpopulated societies, and in the urban centres where the major bureaucracies of the city and the university were constantly meeting up and interpenetrating, the Scandinavian criminologist originally took on a role and an ideology not unlike that of the early Chicago ecologists—or indeed the role of the cautious rebel as advocated by Merton. That is, they acted as agitators of public opinion *and* advisers to governments on questions of prison administration, the reform of juvenile training schools, preventive programmes and the like. The result of this interpenetration was not so much the alleviation of social problems or of social control as it was the co-optation of the new criminologists. The new criminology has now split, on friendly terms, into two distinct tendencies: on the one hand, the poetic social democratic, and the other, the direct action revolutionary.

The first tendency is described by Nils Christie (1971):

We have not made clear that our role as criminologists is not first and foremost to be received as useful problem-solvers, but *as problem-raisers*. Let us turn our weakness into strength by admitting—and enjoying—that our situation has a great resemblance to that of artists and men of letters. We are working on a culture of deviance and social control. . . . Changing times create new situations and bring us to new crossroads. Together with other cultural workers—because these fields are central to all observers of society—but equipped with our special training in scientific method and theory, it is our obligation as well as pleasure to penetrate these problems. Together with other cultural workers, we will probably have to keep a constant fight going against being absorbed, tamed, and made responsible, and thereby completely socialised into society—as it is.

For Thomas Mathieson and others, however, the limitations of the original social welfare approach to social control did not dissolve simply into the problem of avoiding personal co-option. For him, the problem, even in the relatively benign atmosphere of Scandinavia, was action; to change society 'as it is': not simply to describe 'The Defences of the Weak' but to organize them. The normative prescription of the new Scandinavian criminology led to the formation of the K.R.U.M., a trade union for inmates of Scandinavian prisons, and a union which was able, two years ago, to co-ordinate a prison strike across three national boundaries and across several prison walls (Mathieson, 1972).

Something of the same dilemma faces the normative criminology of the kind being developed in Britain (cf. S. Cohen, 1971; I. Taylor, 1971d; Rock, 1973; Rock and McIntosh, 1973) and advocated via an immanent critique of other explanations of crime, deviance and dissent in these pages. The retreat from theory is over, and the politicization of crime and criminology is imminent. Close reading of the classical social theorists reveals a basic agreement; the abolition of crime *is* possible under certain social arrangments. Even Durkheim, with his notion of human nature as a fixed biological given, was able to allow for the substantial diminution of crime under conditions of a free division of labour, untramelled by the inequalities of inherited wealth and the entrenchment of interests of power and authority (by those who were not deserving of it).

It should be clear that a criminology which is not normatively committed to the abolition of inequalities of wealth and power, and in particular of inequalities in property and life-chances, is inevitably bound to fall into correctionalism. And all correctionalism is irreducibly bound up with the identification of deviance with pathology. A fully social theory of deviance must, by its nature, break entirely with correctionalism (even with social reform of the kind advocated by the Chicagoans, the Mertonians and the romantic wing of Scandinavian criminology) precisely because, as this book

281

has attempted to show, the causes of crime must be intimately bound up with the form assumed by the social arrangements of the time. Crime is ever and always that behaviour seen to be problematic within the framework of those social arrangements: for crime to be abolished, then, those social arrangements themselves must also be subject to fundamental social change.

It has often been argued, rather misleadingly, that for Durkheim *crime* was a normal social fact (that it was thus a fundamental feature of human ontology). For us, as for Marx and for other new criminologists, *deviance* is normal—in the sense that men are now consciously involved (in the prisons that are contemporary society and in the real prisons) in asserting their human diversity. The task is not merely to 'penetrate' these problems, not merely to question the stereotypes, or to act as carriers of 'alternative phenomenological realities'. The task is to create a society in which the facts of human diversity, whether personal, organic or social, are not subject to the power to criminalize.

Notes

1 Classical criminology and the positivist revolution

1 Although, as we shall see, Hobbes's theory of social contract, in contrast to that of the utilitarians, saw force as a necessary element for the enforcement of contract in an unequal society.

2 We shall see in the following chapters how social theorists like Durkheim and Marx have attempted to resolve the problems of definition and action involved in the notion of an 'equal' distribution of property.

3 Neo-classicists and positivists alike usually point to the establishment of the Elmira Reformatory as the first reformative penal institution—a progressive institution in that it did not expect its inmates to reform themselves during the course of rational and moral reflexion. Willem Bonger, avowedly a Marxist, but in reality (as we argue in chapter 7) a positivist, described this development in the following terms (1969, p. 83):

> It is possible to practice a . . . system, which takes its origin from the idea that the crime does not proceed from the free will, but from causes which it will be necessary to try to remove, in place of inflicting a useless punishment. It is to the credit of the State of New York that it should be the first to put into practice this sort of a system of combating crime [in the Elmira Reformatory]. An effort is made to make a man of the criminal, to turn him into a strong and sound individual; he is taught a trade, his mind is elevated, his feeling of honour revived; in short, everything is done that is necessary to stimulate the development of what is human in the man.

The ability to exercise free choice, in Bonger, and in the neo-classical revisions, was to a certain (and increasing) degree an environmental question.

4 Comte's 'positive science'—the parent of many an infant positivism—was framed with a view to practice when the necessary and sufficient stage of human civilization had been realized. It was, in this sense, a science of the future, and the task of the positive scientist, as much as anything else, was to hasten society along the civilizing road.

5 For a recent, and very comprehensive, account of the social processes

involved in the compilation of the criminal statistics, see Box (1971, ch. 6).

6 Cf. Perks Committee (1967) for an outline of some such measures with regard to the British statistics. Also, for the situation in America see Winslow (1968, ch. 3).

7 The search for models of the criminal process (from apprehension to disposition) has now come to take on a cybernetic form. The problem of crime in these accounts is basically an engineering problem: how best to process particular segments of behaviour with a view to certain (scientifically specifiable) outcomes (cf. Wilkins, 1964).

8 This is fundamentally the position taken by two American authors (who would disclaim a positivist pedigree)—Herman and Julia Schwendinger (1970, pp. 123–57). Under attack from defenders of the legalistic conception of crime, the Schwendingers have redefined their notion of 'human rights' (1971, pp. 71–82).

9 To this extent, the definition of natural crime is similar to the 'standard deviation' definition used by Wilkins (1964, ch. 4).

10 Cf. our discussion in chapter 6.

11 The only explicit statement by a radical positivist which attempts to respond to Tumin's critique is a footnoted comment by Merton himself (1966, p. 821). He writes: 'it should . . . be noted that this problem [of measuring the net balance of effects], which has at least been identified in functional sociology as a focus of inquiry and analysis, is of course implicit in other sociological analyses of social disorganization and deviant behaviour.' In fact, of course, the problem is only a problem if the concern in the analysis is to measure as distinct from simply to understand behaviour; if one is concerned, in Matza's terms, to 'correct' as distinct from to 'appreciate' the behaviour. The problem of measurement is not, *pace* Robert Merton, a problem in sociologies that do not subscribe to the positive faith.

12 It is characteristic of radical positivists that one of their most important contemporary representatives can dedicate one of his major works 'To Gary: in the hope that he will grow up in a society more interested in psychology than politics' (Eysenck, 1954).

13 Cf. our discussion of Eysenck in chapter 2.

14 Namely the idea that the world is bifurcated into the wicked and the virtuous. Thoroughgoing classicism would in fact maintain that all men are subject to the temptations of crime set against the virtues of a ubiquitous reason.

15 Cf. Jock Young's discussion of 'absolutism' (1970; 1971a, ch. 3). Cf. also the discussion of the relationship between consensus and forms of social organization (feudalism, capitalism, etc.) by Mark Kennedy (1970).

2 The appeal of positivism

1 For a discussion of 'the ethos of productivity' as a central tenet of consensual politics and the defusion in the mass media of realities which threaten it, see J. Young (1972b; 1973b).

2 Cf. Jack Douglas (1967, p. 21) in which Douglas, referring to *Suicide*, argues that 'Durkheim seems to have been at his best in developing the ideas he had taken from the moral statisticians.'

3 Cf. the account of Bonger's work in chapter 7.

4 Note that each individual is scored, by Sheldon, on a seven point scale in terms of the extent to which he measures up to each ideal somatype. There is a quantitative continuum from extreme ectomorph to extreme endomorph with mesomorphs in the middle. Once again, sharp qualitative differences are disallowed.

5 Conrad, in fact, uses Kretschmer's distinction between the *pybric* and the *leptosomatic* body types, which corresponds roughly to Sheldon's distinction between the mesomorph and the endomorph.

6 Hans Eysenck in *Fact and Fiction in Psychology* (1965) quotes approvingly Sheldon's suggestion that mesomorph/endomorphs are more likely to be extraverted and ectomorphs to be introverted (Sheldon, 1940).

7 The tendency amongst biological positivists has been to use inmates as subjects (with outsiders as the control group). The convenience of this group for research purposes is obvious: few contact and refusal problems are likely to be encountered. The problem is however that biological positivists have tended to see inmates as generally representative of the potentially or actually criminal, rather than as a highly-sifted, processed and (therefore) unrepresentative section of those at risk of apprehension and incarceration.

8 For an illuminating critique of this debate, see Sarbin and Miller (1970).

9 The presence of a Y chromosome ensures that a baby is male, and, as we shall see, the chromosome debate is concerned entirely with male chromosomal abnormality. *Female* chromosome abnormality arises when there is an additional X chromosome, or when one X chromosome is missing, i.e. the XXX and XO combinations respectively.

10 The sex chromosome abnormality theory is also exceptional in that, unlike most of the contemporary positivist accounts, it does posit a qualitative difference between the criminal and the non-criminal: that is, in the possession or non-possession of the extra Y chromosome. Theories involving biological homeostasis, for example, biochemical theories of mental illness, might also do this. We will not be dealing with this area in this text.

11 Although this is not at all the impression one would gather from some discussions of the sex chromosomal debate in the mass media.

12 For an examination of this concept, see Sarbin (1969).

13 This is based on the article by S. Kessler and R. Moos, 'The XYY karyotype and criminality' (1970).

14 Eysenck and Trasler both base their theory of crime on classical conditioning and the autonomic nervous system. To them crime is seen as a lack of learning social norms in a conditioned fashion. An alternative behaviourist theory of crime is based primarily on rational learning (operant conditioning) and the central nervous system. Here crime is normal and social, learnt because it has been positively reinforced in

the past. Such an approach is absent in Eysenck because he fails to consider the possibility of elaborate criminal values and techniques which can be learnt—rather, for him crime occurs as an outburst of pre-social covetousness, it is raw impulse unstemmed by the social reflexes of the conditioned conscience. For a discussion of a behaviourist theory based on operant conditioning, see chapter 4, where we deal with Burgess and Akers's reformulation of Sutherland's principles.

15 The other two personality dimensions he uses are emotionality— stability and psychoticism—and normality, both of which, like introversion-extraversion, are based on the autonomic nervous system. We shall concentrate on introversion-extraversion for simplicity's sake.

16 This conception of man has some affinity with Gordon Allport's conception of the Leibnizean, creative nature of man, rather than the passive determined Lockean nature as exhibited in the work of Eysenck (see Allport, 1955). But, we shall argue later, the first theorist to operate with a fully social conception of man was Karl Marx.

17 See Eysenck, 1953, pp. 180 et seq., where he argues extensively for social relativism.

18 Note the tension here between Eysenck's élitism and his appeal to the consensus. The trained psychologist knows best for society and, therefore, presumably can ascertain who are the really socially dangerous deviants. Thus he can, as in 'The technology of consent' suggest that 'private' deviancy in the general realm is permissible yet the 'public' deviancy of strikes theatens the social system and demands ameliorative action.

19 A critique that stemmed from Ferri's attack on the work of Lombroso in the late nineteenth century.

3 Durkheim and the break with 'analytical individualism'

1 For a contemporary discussion of the limitations of marginalist economic theory see Walton and Gamble (1972).

2 John Rex (1969, p. 128) puts this in a nutshell:

> Durkheim was an Alsatian Jew who was born in 1858 and grew up in a turbulent period of French history, marked by the defeat of the Franco-Prussian war, the setting up of the Third Republic, and the weakening of traditional educational institutions dominated by the church. Himself an agnostic, Durkheim devoted himself to the search for a new secular and scientific social ethics which could serve to bind the new French society together.

3 Although, as we shall see, the concept of human nature—at the basis of his concept of a spontaneous division of labour—had a central *biological element*, the relationship between structure and human needs was fundamentally a question of the structural arrangement of labour (a question which was resolvable in terms of social rather than biological science).

4 See pp. 76–8.

5 So, as Giddens (1971c, p. 221) puts it; 'egoism' is thus identified solely

with the 'pre-social' and is portrayed as wholly foreign to the 'penetration of the individual by society'.

6 Durkheim, indeed, contrary to many misconceptions, had a very modest view of the contribution of science. He wrote that the scientists' 'first duty is to make a moral code for [themselves]. Such a work cannot be improvised in the silence of the study; it can only arise through itself, little by little, under the pressure of internal causes which make it necessary' (1964b, p. 409).

7 There is some dispute over this point in the literature: Giddens (1971c) argues that although the collective conscience is weakened, in an organic society, a new form of representation has become necessary to institutionalize individualism, whilst Lukes (1971, p. 195) argues that, because of ambiguities in Durkheim's assumptions, the question is irresoluble: 'pre-social, organically-given factors play a crucial role at various points in his theories—as, for example, in one major strand in his account of anomie, namely the notion of unrestrained and limitless (organic-psychic) desires, and also in his conception of natural distribution of talents, and his doctrine about the biologically-given characteristics of womanhood.' In the final analysis, for all Durkheim's emphasis on the advance of the social alongside the division of labour, he retains his biological premises.

8 An astonishing number of textbooks and commentaries in criminology adopt this simplistic interpretation of Durkheim. Cf. for example, Mannheim (1965, p. 501), Radzinowicz (1966, pp. 87–8) and Schafer (1969, pp. 245–6).

9 We would concur with Anthony Giddens (1971c, p. 226) when he points to Durkheim's failure 'to consider the theoretical significance of the possibility that moral obligations *themselves* may be "factual" elements in the horizon of the acting individual. A person (or a group) may acknowledge the existence of the obligations, or take account of them in orienting his conduct, without feeling any strong commitment to them. Such action is not necessarily "criminal" in the sense of directly flouting the moral prescriptions in question. But it rests neither solely upon fear of the sanctions, which would be invoked as punishment for transgression, nor solely upon moral commitment.'

4 The early sociologies of crime

1 The orthodox interpretation of Merton is in terms of a complete break with Durkheim. Thus Lukes (1967, p. 135) asserts that 'most writers have followed Merton in discarding Durkheim's theory of human nature'. As will become obvious as this chapter develops, this is a one-sided simplification and is based on a misunderstanding of Durkheim's notion of human nature which was examined in chapter 3.

2 Merton himself claims that this adaptation must be 'the most common and widely diffused', since otherwise 'the stability and continuity of society could not be maintained'. In his substantive discussion of social order, however, great reliance is placed on the innovator, who hastens along the American Dream and the individualization of society. It is

this myth of success in the future (available to those who save, postpone gratification and work) that really sustains the Mertonian society. And no empirical example is offered of the conformist: in practice, it might be difficult to separate him out from the ritualist.

3 Cf. Richardson and Spears (1972), especially papers by Joanna Ryan, John Rex and the editors: 'Eysenck ... has attempted to provide a psychometric justification for the *status quo*. He can give a superficial impression of having a persuasive case because he represents such concepts as IQ as imperfect but objective and value free ... [but] claims for objectivity must be based on a careful analysis of the covert assumptions in concepts as well as on obedience to certain rules of argument and logic' (p. 194).

4 For a discussion of 'retreatism' both in Merton and in Cloward and Ohlin and the 'absolutist' negation of bohemian values, see Young (1972a, ch. 4).

5 Cf. Young (1972a) where it was found that a fundamental factor in deviant behaviour was the thwarting of expressive aspirations (i.e. in Mertonian terms 'expressive anomie') and that many student subcultures actively disdained instrumentality and material success. For a theoretical statement of the notion of the 'optimum balance' as an expression of rationality, see I. Taylor and Walton (1970).

6 Cf. the essay 'Paranoia and the dynamics of exclusion' in Lemert (1967).

7 See Weber's discussion of the three types of legitimate authority in *The Theory of Social and Economic Organization* (1966).

8 To be discussed in chapter 5.

9 Cf. some of Martin Nicolaus's perceptive comments on 'The professional organization of sociology: a view from below' (1969).

10 For a recent statement of this argument see Lee Braude (1970, pp. 1–10).

11 Sprout and Sprout (1965, p. 83) argue that 'free-will environmentalism' is characterized by the notion of the environment affecting an individual's free will in order that he behaves in a certain specifiable way. They contrast this version of human ecology with 'possibilism' where 'the milieu does not compel or direct man to do anything. The milieu is simply there—clay, sometimes malleable, sometimes refractory, but clay nonetheless at the disposal of man the builder.'

12 The discussion of 'problem housing estates' in Britain is a case in point. Wilson (1963) and others have discussed the possibility that the problematic nature of some housing estates can be seen as a result (a) of the deliberate dumping by housing committees of families or individuals seen to be 'troublesome' (b) of the differential willingness and ability of certain kinds of individuals to pay a certain level of rent, and (c) of the way in which different kinds of people perceive the nature of an estate, i.e. its appropriateness for them. An earlier study of 'Radby' suggested that the presence of high delinquency rates on certain streets in this Midlands mining town (on what were called the 'black streets') was a function of the existence of families that were carriers of delinquent values (Carter and Jephcott, 1954). In these studies and in others (cf. in particular, Taft, 1933), the implication is

often that a certain kind of person gravitates towards a certain kind of area or zone (a street or an estate), because of his personal characteristics or, as is the emphasis in the Radby studies, because of his membership of a family group supportive of pathological values.

Even where the contemporary urban researcher is aware of the activities of (for example) the housing committee in labelling individuals as appropriate for residential placing in a certain area, there is no break with the analogy of selection: the activities of the housing committee are rarely seen to be unnatural (or wrong). This problem is examined more fully in an important text: Baldwin, Bottoms and Walker, *The Urban Criminal* (1973). Some of the methodological problems of this kind of ecological research are examined in Hirschi and Selvin (1967).

13 There was always tension in late nineteenth- and early twentieth-century ecology in England between a social reforming focus on the structural inequalities productive of delinquency and an ambivalence towards the delinquents and the demoralized produced by those conditions. The work of Henry Mayhew and Jack London displays—in a contradictory fashion—an explanation of the conditions they vividly describe in terms of a modified social Darwinism *and* a prescription in terms of, respectively, liberal and socialist reconstruction. Much the same is true of the work of Charles Booth and Sidney and Beatrice Webb (Cf. Levin and Lindesmith, 1937). In these respects they are very similar in concern to Bonger, whom we discuss at greater length in chapter 7.

14 Downes, for example, has argued that the crucial problem for adolescents in East London is their lack of opportunity in the 'market for leisure'. Unlike Rex and Moore, however, he sees the boys' situation in that market as inextricably linked with, rather than distinct from, their position (primarily) in the labour market, and, to a lesser extent (given low status of the area in general) their chances of advancement through the education 'market'. Writing in 1966, he characterized the reaction of boys to the existing market opportunities as one of 'dissociation' (that is, as rejection of the value traditionally placed by workers on the importance of work which is brought about by the paucity of either expressive or instrumental satisfaction in available work roles). But this displacement of the frustrations engendered at work and in school on to a primary focus on leisure time is only feasible for so long as boys have meaningful access to leisure, and an ability to pay. The 'Rocker' who cannot afford a 'motor' is no 'Rocker' at all. With commendable foresight, Downes (1966a, p. 264) argued that:

if automation is allowed to constitute the prospect of under and unemployment in this [working class] sector ... the raw deal [they experience] will worsen into no deal at all. If the sizeable rump of non-skilled young male workers become convinced of their own expendability, their reaction in terms of delinquency could well be explosive, and assume fully-fledged contracultural proportions.

The scale and intensity of 'skinhead' activity in Britain in 1972—a youth group which is largely composed of unskilled male workers—testifies to David Downes' foresight, and also to the fact that this struggle faced by adolescents is in part a struggle for jobs.

15 O'Neill's terminology here, and his general prespective, are derived from Herbert Marcuse, who, in *Eros and Civilisation* and in *One-dimensional Man*, makes the abolition of public and private spheres a central plank of his platform. Psychology dissolves into politics as a part of this polemic. For an extrapolation and critique of Marcuse's position on this, see Walton and Gamble (1972).

16 Cf. the excellent discussion of the ways in which the lay theory of criminality in the police force incorporates some crucial assumptions about the identity and character of those who move in public space, in Box (1971, ch. 6).

17 A concise urban ecology of 'natural areas' which was concerned to identify the subjective definitions of these areas by the locally powerful could, for example, tell us much more than we now know about the differential exercise of magisterial and police discretion (cf. Armstrong and Wilson, 1973). For example, in the apprehension of and sentencing of juveniles at play on the street, or drug-users in their homes, in terms of the home territories of these various rule-breakers. This would be a considerable development theoretically and empirically—provided that it is not asserted, with the pure phenomenologists, that the 'contours' of the ongoing interaction are not determined by individual consciousness. As we shall see in chapter 6, in the section on 'The phenomenological project', the orthodox phenomenological position sees everyday individual experience as primary, and asserts that anything beyond that is a reification—a position we reject as idealistic and also as unpromising by itself in the construction of a social theory of deviance.

18 Hirschi and Selvin, in an important technical critique of ecological criminologists working in the Shaw and Mackay tradition (notably Lander) have pointed to the 'false criteria of causality' implicit in their continuing use of an eclectic correlational or factor analysis (Lander, 1954; Hirschi and Selvin, 1967).

19 It is not only that Shaw and Mackay insisted on the existence of some pathogenic factor within the delinquent area itself (which gave rise to all the other conditions—e.g. to lack of hygiene, to overcrowding and to disorder). They also quite explicitly rejected the view that the 'delinquent area' might in part be the creation of social control—the consequence of local housing policies (the dumping of those defined as undesirable) or local police practices. They also rejected the idea that the persistence of high delinquency rates in an area could in any way be a result of what we have called the 'phenomenological perception of the ecology of the city'. Terence Morris (1957, p. 77) was the first to highlight these limitations in Shaw and Mackay's one-sided ecology of the delinquent area. Accepting, in faith, Shaw's conclusion (1929) 'that the difference between rates [of delinquency in different areas was] quite out of proportion to ... difference in police strength [in these different areas]', Morris goes on to comment that 'whether there exist variations in police attitudes to offenders from different areas (essenti-

ally different social classes] is, however, quite another matter'. In common with anthropologists working on the delinquent area like Walter Miller (1958) (insisting on the impermeability and oppositional nature of lower-class 'focal concerns'), and like Oscar Lewis (1961; 1966) with his emphatic view of the localized and falsely-conscious 'culture of poverty', Shaw and Mackay have no conception of the variability of social reaction or of the ways in which an area can be assigned a reputation (by agencies of the wider society) to which the inhabitants of the area will have to react, and from which they will find it hard to escape.

20 For Shaw and Mackay (1931) the only factor that could throw the existence or stability of consensus into doubt was the conflict of cultures which would immediately accompany rapid migration. But, ultimately, Shaw and Mackay asserted, assimilation would occur and thus, the dominant culture reassert itself over these other traditions. They write (1942, p. 435): 'the fact that in Chicago the rates of delinquents for many years have remained relatively constant . . . despite successive changes in the nativity and nationality of the population, supports emphatically the conclusion that delinquency-producing factors are inherent in the community.'

21 In this discussion we will limit ourselves to the recent formulation of differential association theory (Sutherland and Cressey, 1966) rather than pointlessly attacking earlier formulations.

22 See our discussion of motives and consciousness in chapter 5.

23 This is close to the concept of 'dissociation' used by David Downes (1966a) to characterize the origins of working-class youth cultures. In *The Drugtakers*, Young (1971a) has utilized the concept of anomie in this extended sense to explain the origins of illicit drug subcultures. Something of the same theory can be seen in the discussion of the 'powerlessness' of the young soccer supporter and the sources of the drift into hooliganism (I. Taylor, 1969; 1971a; 1971b).

24 For a discussion of the meritocratic myth and moral indignation see Young (1972b).

5 Social reaction, deviant commitment and career

1 In the 1972 edition of *Human Deviance, Social Problems and Social Control*, Edwin Lemert has reproduced his paper, previously published in 1968, entitled 'Social problems and the sociology of deviance'. In many ways, the argument presented in this paper bears superficial resemblance to the one we have advanced in this book. However, at no point in the argument, which amounts to a re-write of his former position, does Lemert abandon the concepts of 'primary deviation' and 'secondary deviation' or call for what we see to be essential, that is, a look at the causes or origins of primary deviation. In fact, Lemert seems to be shedding himself of the responsibility which his own work (along with that of Becker, Kitsuse and Erikson, whom he cites as giving rise to a crude, labelling approach to deviancy) demands.

2 An exception here is Kai Erikson, whose work is explicitly functionalist. Indeed, a recent defender of the labelling approach, Edwin Schur (1971, p. 29), has agreed 'that certain applications of the functional approach are fully consistent with, even required by, the labelling approach'.

3 The same might not apply throughout Britain: for example, the definitions placed on events in Northern Ireland are obviously open to political dispute.

4 A particularly rigid version of the sequence of interaction leading to deviation is given in Lemert's early work (1951, p. 77) where he discusses, under the unfortunate heading 'sociopathic individuation', the stages of secondary deviation through which the individual must pass if his 'role conceptions' are to be 'reinforced'. These stages are (1) primary deviation; (2) social penalties; (3) further primary deviation; (4) stronger penalties and rejections; (5) further deviation, perhaps with hostilities and resentment beginning to focus upon those doing the penalizing; (6) crisis reached in the tolerance quotient, expressed in formal action by the community stigmatizing of the deviant; (7) penalties; (8) ultimate acceptance of the deviant social status and efforts at readjustment on the basis of the associated role.

   Schur (1971) quotes this sequence approvingly. For us, the whole sequence is to be regarded as hypothetical. Most importantly, the sequence could just as well account for primary as for secondary deviation (if we are to take the assumption of symbolic interactionism with the seriousness they deserve).

5 In arguing for such a possibility, Lemert (1967, p. 51) reinterprets Matza's notion of drift into deviance, suggesting that 'drift is not an informed choice'. For Matza, and for us, this limited and deterministic notion of drift would (for slightly different reasons) be unacceptable. Where DeLamater poses four questions, Lemert himself is content with only two: the origins of the behaviour and the social reaction to it.

7 Lemert's essay, 'Legal commitment and social control' in Lemert (1967) and the various papers on the determinants of referral in Wheeler (1968) all demonstrate an awareness of the sometimes complex relationship between formal and informal agencies of social control.

8 Hence, the attempts by Wilkins (and others) to erect a cybernetic model of deviancy amplification systems for explaining deviant processing must be seen to be mechanistic and over-determined (Wilkins, 1964).

9 This recognition, as we shall see, infuses the work of Austin Turk, who, in advocating a return to a conflict model of society, argues for the unambiguous repression of deviant roles and patterns by the one (dominant) interest. See our discussion in chapter 8.

6 American naturalism and phenomenology

(We would like to acknowledge our debt in this chapter to the following British sociologists: Jeff Coulter, Stuart Hall, Peter Lassman, Frank Pearce, Wes Sharrock and Laurie Taylor.)

1 Within these modes, the rebel and the bohemian are to be identified in

terms of an intellectual consciousness, where the critique of society involved in delinquency is always *implicit*.

2 In seeming to rest content with the view of delinquent accounts as neutralization, Matza, as we shall see, is never really able to tell us what a non-neutralizing account really looks like. The suspicion is that this is bound up with Matza's failure—in the final analysis—to break with the static view of human possibilities we have identified with positivism. Indeed, immediately prior to working through neutralization with Sykes, Matza was conducting work related to 'The extent of delinquency in the U.S.' (cf. Teeters and Matza, 1959). It is hard to see how a truly dialectical approach to the study of deviant motivation should find anything of value in head-counting research.

3 It is of course the case that individual adolescents are under adult (that is, parental) surveillance and are, to varying extents, dependent on adults materially and financially, but only during certain periods of the day, when they are not at school or work. When they are at school, at work, or out of the home, however, they are in *collective* situations and are subjected to cultural pressures (e.g. from their peers, the mass media, the 'underground', the revolutionary left, and (if they are black) the black power movement)—none of which is easily reducible to the conventional and individualistic 'subterranean' leisure values of the dominant society. Matza's adolescent (unlike, paradoxically the subcultural adolescent) often appears as an isolated individual: immune from social pressures other than the most conventional. This *individualism* is reflected, as we shall see, in the focus of explanation at the level of individual motivation—in 'drift'—rather than on the impact on individuals of structural contradictions (unemployment) or cultural innovation (the growth of a politicized underground).

4 Discussing the limitations of anomie theory (postulating as it does the internalization of success goals throughout the population) Laurie Taylor (1968a, p. 97) has drawn attention to 'the consistently reported findings of relatively low occupational and educational aspirations among the young from those socio-economic groups in which delinquents are over-represented'.

5 An additional criticism of Matza's view of subcultural recruitment is that its three components are conceptualized in an *additive* fashion. It is difficult to see this as methodologically very different from the models of subcultural recruitment in Cohen and Cloward and Ohlin, with their 'positive delinquents' emerging: the very animal whose existence Matza seeks (by his exhortation of free will) to deny.

6 How, for example, could Matza's theory of demoralization and disreputability account for the political emergence and the rejection of the 'delinquent role' by Malcom X (the hustler), Eldridge Cleaver (the rapist) and George Jackson (the petty recidivist) (cf. Malcom X, 1966; Cleaver, 1968; Jackson, 1970). Matza (1969b, p. 193) has argued, against Valentine, that 'the meaningful question . . . is whether black rebellion will become organized, whether the alliance between students and blacks can ever materialize, and, most of all, whether organized labour can conceivably be shaken from its established lethargy to ally

with an unemployed underclass and return to its occasional militancy.' None of these conditions has really been fulfilled (and certainly not in conjunction) but the 'demoralized' blacks and Puerto Ricans (and the inmates of Attica and other American prisons) *are* asserting their 'reputability' and rejecting a delinquent status and consciousness.

7 Robin Blackburn makes much the same point as we are making about Matza in his discussion of the Affluent Worker Studies (of Luton car workers). Goldthorpe and Lockwood suggested that workers were becoming increasingly instrumental and that, therefore, protest was unlikely. Blackburn recalls that scarcely one month after the publication of Goldthorpe's early findings, the workers broke into open rebellion. As Blackburn (1967, p. 51) says of workers imprisoned within the structure of capitalist society 'their consciousness is likely to become volatile as a consequence of even quite minor adjustments of established understandings'.

8 This section was written before the benefit of 'members' talk with ethnomethodologists such as David Sudnow and Harvey Sacks. In the light of conversations with them, it would appear that much of our criticism is 'outsiders' criticism and is only one possible reading of the literature.

Indeed, Sacks in particular has convinced the authors that there is *no necessary* incompatibility between the work in *The New Criminology* and the work and discovery of micro-structural phenomena by ethnomethodologists.

9 Cf. an interesting assessment and criticism of Alfred Schutz's 'phenomenological sociology' by Barry Hindess (1972, p. 24). Hindess argues that the direction of the phenomenology of Schutz is based on the unwarranted assumption that 'the world of "objective mind" can be reduced to the behaviour of individuals.'

10 A statement of the ethnomethodological position on 'decontextualised meanings' is given by Jeff Coulter (1971, pp. 303–4). In this paper, he argues: 'As there can be no generalised contexts, no all-embracing mode of enquiry and no purge of the indexicality of accounts, so there can be no finality in the interpretations offered of socially accomplished settings and assembled events. There is finality for members of these settings and participants in these events, but it is marked with a (generally unstated) subordinate clause or cut-off point—'for all practical purposes'.

11 The following discussion does not pretend to be a full coverage of the ethnomethodological contribution to the study of deviance. Moreover, it does not deal with the rapidly emerging differences between ethnomethodologists and other sociologists working in the phenomenological tradition. See, for example, the footnotes to Coulter (1971), in which he criticizes Cicourel for his view of ethnomethodology as work necessary to the construction of more rational methods. Coulter, like Garfinkel (1968b), criticizes any attempt to search for invariants which would enable us to move beyond the study of indexicality. Thus Coulter (1971, p. 325) also criticizes Peter McHugh (1968) by stating that:

McHugh asserts the possibility of the sociologist constructing 'hard' rules out of those observed by him, in the course of interaction. It is unclear what would differentiate the two sorts of rules, and why the sociologist's should be regarded as 'hard'. We are back with Schutz's 'typification' or 'second order' constructs in a context where they are hardly apposite.

A close examination of the work of Garfinkel, Sacks, Bittner, Cicourel, Douglas, Sudnow and McHugh will show that their work varies immensely in the extent to which it is consistent with the rigorous limitations imposed by phenomenological imperatives. On the first page of *The Social Organization of Juvenile Justice*, Cicourel (1968), argues: 'case studies should be designed to reveal *invariant* properties of the social arrangements observed and interpreted. To suggest there are *invariant* properties discernible in case studies means the researcher must search for and demonstrate the *generalizability* of his findings as applied to all forms of social organization.' Another example is McHugh, who argues that he is no longer interested in ethnomethodology but that he is doing 'analysis'. Now, whatever analysis may be, it looks as though McHugh's previous search for 'hard rules' means that he envisages that one can use these 'hard' or necessary rules as a basis for generalization out of specific situations. McHugh himself does just this in 'A commonsense conception of deviance' (Douglas, 1970a, p. 85). He states: 'Underlying these matters is the analytic idea that deviance must be conceived in terms of the character of rules and their treatment by members, not concrete acts and their treatment or concrete persons and their treatment. It is the rules to which we look in our creation of moral assessments, enforcements, exemptions, and so on.'

McHugh goes on to argue in a number of other papers, published and unpublished, that ethnomethodology fails to grasp properly that there are a number of basic forms of life, i.e. art, science, and commonsense.

Now most of the differences between phenomenological sociologists seem to centre on divergences around the question of how much human behaviour is rule-following and how much is not. The middle way in this debate seems to be simply to study *rule use* (cf. Zimmerman and Wieder, 'Ethnomethodology and the problem of order', and 'The practicalities of rule use', both in Douglas (1971b).)

12 Parsons is a clear example of a theorist who attempts to explain deviancy largely in terms of under-socialization, that is the failure to internalize need-dispositions.

13 This section relies on an unpublished paper by Peter Lassman of the University of Birmingham (1970b).)

14 It is a typical feature of the studies that have been conducted by ethnomethodologists that they frequently start with or involve assertions which are generalizations, which indicate invariance, and hide a highly organized view of society. Generalizations of this order abound in the work of Harold Garfinkel. For example, in his article 'Passing and the managed achievement of sex status in an "intersexed" person' (in

Garfinkel, 1968a, ch. 5) he glibly asserts that: 'every society exerts close controls over the transfers of persons from one status to another. Where transfers of sexual statuses are concerned, these controls are particularly restrictive and rigorously enforced' and 'from the standpoint of persons regarded as normally sexed, their environment has a perceivedly normal sex composition. This composition is rigorously dichotomized into the "natural" i.e. moral entities of male and female.' It was pointed out to the authors that Garfinkel's argument, apart from being empirically incorrect (anthropological evidence to the contrary abounds) espouses a rigid dichotomizing between those members who are totally imprisoned by culture and those who (on occasion, the sane members) are totally free. As one British trans-sexual sociologist, Carol, formerly, David Riddell commented, implicit in this rigorous and unjustified dichotomy is Garfinkel's view of society. Riddell's unpublished paper 'Transvestism and the tyranny of gender' (1972), is a devastating critique of this position. Egon Bittner (1963, p. 935) makes similarly unjustifiable assumptions in his work. He has this to say: 'the radical can never win an argument in the long run if experience is defined as the relevant test of validity, as it must be if the creed pertains to existential and moral matters'. Commenting on this assertion in an unpublished paper, Frank Pearce (1970, p. 8) suggests: '[Bittner] makes the unjustifiable assumption that radical projects for transforming the world can never be realized—one would think that the successful revolutions in various parts of the world would undermine this view'.

The purpose of giving these examples is not merely to indicate that ethnomethodologists can be wrong empirically but also to show that they find it impossible to follow their own phenomenological imperatives.

15 See Alfred Schutz (1951).

7 Marx, Engels and Bonger on crime and social control

1 For this commentator, Michael Kidron (1968), the problem is to locate a mechanism of stabilization outside the assumed causal link between productivity and a steady level of employment and improved living standards. For Kidron, this link is the necessarily wasteful expenditure on arms in the 'permanent arms economies' of west and east.

2 Saint Sancho is one of the pejorative nicknames used by Marx in *The German Ideology* for Max Stirner, the 'Young Hegelian' philosopher, author of *Der Einzige und sein Eigenthum*.

3 Sutherland and Cressey (1966, p. 54), for example, make no bones about their assessment: 'The socialist school of criminology, based on the writings of Marx and Engels, began about 1850 and emphasized economic determinism'. Mannheim (1965, pp. 444–6) seems to think that Marx had written of crime as a direct reflection of the conflict of classes, and discusses Marx only with a view to challenging his model of social class. Radzinowicz (1966, p. 42) on the basis of a single quotation

from Marx identifies what he calls 'the economic interpretation of society' and asserts that its expositors (e.g. Bonger) have regarded it as the interpretation of history *tout court*. Similarly abbreviated discussions, misunderstandings and caricatures of Marxist thought are to be found in the works of Stephen Shafer (1969), Edwin Schur (1971) and, in relationship to Marx's alleged functionalism, in Lewis Coser (1956).

4 Cf. discussion on pages 218–19 and also George Vold (1958, pp. 159–82).

5 This is the period which Hirst (1972, p. 36), following Althusser, calls the 'Historical Materialist' period in Marx's writings, a period in which 'the economic structure of society is the condition of existence of the superstructure, it is the foundation on which this superstructure rests, and therefore prescribes certain definite limits to what can be erected upon it'. For a discussion of our differences with Hirst on this, and other questions, see I. Taylor and Walton (1972).

6 The substance of the 'social reaction' perspective—and the relationships between 'social control agencies' to the central structures of power and authority—are discussed in chapter 5.

7 It may be that *different types of crime* are affected (encouraged or discouraged) by a variety of economic conditions (cf. the discussion in I. Taylor and L. Taylor (1972)).

8 One attempt to achieve these links in general terms was made by Ernest Becker (1965, pp. 108–34).

9 We are not here concerned to enter into a debate with J. M. Van Bemmelen as to why Bonger became a criminologist. Bemmelen's psychoanalytical interpretation of Bonger's writings (and the moral passion sustaining them) may indeed have some truth behind them— Bonger may have been motivated by a hatred of the nuclear family and the functions it performed as a training ground for Dutch industry during the late nineteenth century. But this hardly says anything about the essential truth of Bonger's writings. J. M. Van Bemmelen, 'Willem Adrian Bonger', *Journal of Criminal Law, Criminology and Police Science*, vol. 46, no. 3 (Sept–Oct 1955) reprinted in H. Mannheim (ed.) *Pioneers in Criminology*, London: Stevens, 1960.

10 The debate about orthodox Marxism continues with the publication in English of Lukacs's *History and Class Consciousness* (1971a). An earlier translation of the essay 'What is Orthodox Marxism?' appeared in the British quarterly journal *International Socialism*, 24, spring 1966, translated by M. Phillips and C. Posner, pp. 10–14.

The contrast between what we are calling formal Marxism and orthodox Marxism is well put in the following passage (p. 10) from the earlier translation:

Orthodox Marxism does not mean uncritical acknowledgment of the results of Marx's research, nor does it mean 'faith' in this or that thesis, nor the exegesis of a sacred book. Where Marxism is concerned, orthodoxy refers far more to method exclusively. It implies the scientific conviction that the Marxist dialectic is the correct method of investigation and that this method cannot be developed, extended or made more profound except in the spirit of its founders.

Further, it implies that all attempts to overcome or 'improve' it have led and had to lead to shallowness, triviality, and eclecticism.

Central to the *Marxist method* is the 'anthropologising of man', cf. Walton, Gamble and Coulter (1970a, pp. 259–74; 1970b). Our point here is precisely that Bonger's tendency to abstract Marxist concepts for use in a purely formal fashion leads him into a 'shallowness, triviality and eclecticism'.

11 Bonger's emphasis on the importance of 'egoism' under capitalism in producing crime is, of course, totally unMarxist. Marx castigated the German idealist philosophers for taking up a similar position. For Marx, capitalism is characterized by the existence of interests, and specifically of class interests, rather than by the particular moral climate engendered by particular capitalist formations. Under capitalism, says Marx, it is an 'obvious falsification' to argue that the criminal is activated solely by some desire to offend against the 'Holy' ideas of the state (as in Hegelian metaphysics): the criminal *needs* the goods he steals: he has real, material rather than 'ideal' interests (cf. Marx and Engels, 1968, pp. 381–3).

12 Indeed, Marx could well have been referring to Bonger when he wrote of the German idealists (Stirner, Bauer, etc.) that:

> The very same ideologists who could imagine that right, law, State, etc. arose from a general concept, the final analysis perhaps the concept of man, and that they were created for the sake of this concept—*these same ideologists can, of course, also imagine that crimes against a concept are committed out of sheer wantonness*, that crimes, in general, are nothing but a mockery of concepts and are only punished in order to give satisfaction to the insulted concepts. (Marx/Engels, *The German Ideology*, 1968 edition, p. 381, our emphasis).

13 Bonger subordinates, in this way, the work of Quetelet, on the constancy of forms of crime, and even Rousseau on the social contract, to his 'general' (that is, economic) considerations.

14 That Bonger is involved in a straightforwardly positivistic methodology is revealed in his continuing stress on the need to isolate alcoholism as an independent variable, highly associated with the advent of 'the criminal thought'. On the relation between chronic alcoholism and criminality, he writes: 'Notwithstanding their divergences the percentages in the different countries are generally very high, and in every case much higher than among the non-criminal population' (1969 ed. p. 76).

15 Cf. discussion of Matza in chapter 6.

8 The new conflict theorists

1 As we indicated earlier, it is only by asserting that individual experience is almost entirely idiosyncratic that Turk is able to assume a continuing and inevitable condition of dissonance between men and the culture in which they live.

2 The fact that Turk should share with Bonger not only a view of a

society in conflict, but also a moral distaste for the 'demoralized' (the *Lumpenproletariat* in Bonger) may partly explain the otherwise para-doxical fact that Turk should take time off to edit a new edition of Bonger's *Criminality and Economic Conditions* (allegedly *the* Marxist statement on crime) in 1969.

3 Dahrendorf's ontological assumptions seem to flow directly from his observation of the East German revolt, mentioned earlier: it must have been difficult for a man in his position, in 1953, to accept a functionalist ontology unquestioningly.

4 For a recent account of the way in which inmates resist the deprivations and 'loss of self' involved in sentences of long-term imprisonment under maximum security conditions, see L. Taylor and S. Cohen (1972).

5 It is important, however, to take note of Quinney's fundamentally *reified* image of man—wherein the ontological assumption is that man is involved in a quest for an orderly and consistent understanding of society (in Turk the ontological premise appears to develop shape as a quest for order in the society itself). Quinney derives this ontology from his reading of the work of Peter Berger and Thomas Luckmann on *The Social Construction of Reality* (1966). For a criticism which takes issue with this reified, i.e. non-social image of man, see Walton and Gamble (1972, ch. 2).

6 For example, 'liberal' research in which the merits of allowing in-dividual police officers (or law enforcers generally) a degree of dis-cretion (in the desire to minimize legal stigmatization of deviants) as against bureaucratically-informed research which proceeds in the belief that social control be effectively extended to all aspects and instances of law-breaking.

7 This statement is reminiscent of James Burnham's much criticized suggestion in *The Managerial Revolution* that the separation of owner-ship and control in industry would encourage a balance of the public and private interests of the corporation: a balance which, he alleged, would be very much a change from the corporate pursuit of profit. For a devastating critique of this thesis, see Ralph Miliband (1969).

9 Conclusion

1 There are, of course, empirical histories of crime and its control. The most notable treatments of the English history of crime are J. J. Tobias (1967) and Leon Radzinowicz (3 vols, 1948–56).

2 One of the consequences of our inability to enter into such a concrete historical treatment is that the concepts of crime and deviance (and, indeed, dissent) appear to be used interchangeably at different points in the text. This is, of course, the case in all the existing textbook treatments of the subject which are not taken up with the historically changeable nature of the phenomenon in question. A very modest attempt has been made to grapple with this problem in Taylor and Taylor (1972).

3 A highly suggestive attempt to wed the concerns of ecological analysis

with the wider context of power, authority and political domination is made by Gail Armstrong and Mary Wilson (1973).

4 The largely uncharted history of youth subcultures in Britain since the war is at last being attempted against the background of some kind of structural analysis. (Cf. S. Cohen, 1971a; 1972a; 1972b; P. Cohen, 1972; Rock and Cohen, 1970; Willis, 1972.)

5 The notion of 'lay theories of criminality' is taken up by Box (1971, pp. 180-1) in a discussion of the particular 'theories' informing the everyday exercise of police discretion. He writes:

> In order to cope with the chaos of an infinite number of suspects, the police develop theories on the causes of crime and the nature of the criminal. These theories are refractions of professional theories, past and present, which have been transmitted, like rumours, from the writings of 'experts' through the mass media and into the heads of the lay public, including policemen, who then mould and slightly recast them to fit in with their occupational experiences, and to facilitate occupational performances.

One of the central features of lay theories, as adopted by the police and the magistracy in particular, is what one of the present authors has termed its 'absolutist' view of society. In this version of 'theory', deviants are divided into the real—committed, pathological—types (e.g. the drug-pusher, or, as in Yablonsky, the disturbed sociopath who wins positions of authority in working-class fighting gangs and in the middle-class communes of hippies) on the one hand, and the misled innocents on the other (the immature and stupid youth who buys—under pressure—from the ruthless pusher; or the ordinary street-kid who follows a gang leader because he has no healthy youth club leader as an alternative focus of identification). Cf. the discussion of the ways in which policemen encourage the drug-user to accept this distinction in exchange for sympathetic treatment in court, in Young (1971b, pp. 188-9).

6 This is evidenced, most significantly, in the low rate of reportability of certain kinds of sexual offences (e.g. forcible rape)—a large proportion of which (contrary to media representation) occur within family groups or amongst relatively close acquaintances (cf. for example, Menachem Amir, 1967; 1971).

7 From time to time, of course, attempts are made by one interest group to win other groups to its own version of lay theory. At the time of writing, for example, proposals are being mooted by the Criminal Law Revision Committee (under pressure from the Police Federation, the press and others) to the Home Secretary in the United Kingdom, to withdraw certain safeguards traditionally accorded defendants. The net effect of these proposals (centring around the withdrawal of the right to remain silent, the placing of the accused in the witness-box and the admissibility of forcibly obtained confessions) would be that the lay theory of the non-professional juries would be replaced as the decisive courtroom reality by the lay theory adhered to by the police (cf. Michael Zander, *Guardian*, 7 April 1972).

8 It is worth noting that studies of prison subcultures are moving precisely in this direction. Where many writers have adopted a view of inmates as relatively passive and malleable creatures of institutional regime, capable at most of what Goffman terms 'secondary adjustment' in the face of the mortification of imprisonment, there has been a tendency in recent literature towards an examination of 'what the inmates bring with them'. This tendency has been most noticeable in studies of adult prisons, and in a sense is an inevitable consequence of the rise of the prison movement in the United States (especially amongst blacks and especially in California), the inmate unions in Scandinavia, some acts of resistance in British maximum security prisons and the formation of the Preservation of Rights of Prisoners. Cf. L. Taylor and S. Cohen (1972); and also, in a less detailed and empirical fashion, John Irwin and Donald Cressey (1962). Less dramatic evidence of the connections between the consciousness of *juvenile* delinquents prior to apprehension and their 'adjustments' in juvenile institutions is presented in an unpublished paper 'Theories of action in juvenile correctional institutions', by Ian Taylor (1971c).

9 The eclecticism of American criminology and deviancy theory is probably explicable partly in terms of a critique of American social thought in general, of the kind that Gouldner is currently engaged in. For the time being we can characterize the two central themes in American criminology as reformism and millenarianism, both of which have in common a theoretical naïveté and a normative incongruity. Criminal lawyers like Sanford Kadish and 'radical' sociologists like Howard Becker can both identify the 'care-taking institutions' as 'overcriminalizing' American youth and American deviants in general, and argue for change at the attitude level amongst the guardians of public order (Kadish, 1968; Becker, 1967; 1972). The more radical wing can respond to the politicization of deviance and the rise of a prison movement amongst the black *Lumpenproletariat* by polemics which pass for theory, calling for the removal of a legal system which is unjust in its choice of victims (Quinney, 1972). The continuing crisis of American institutions, and the continuing polarization of social forces within the society, may result in a clarification of criminological politics, and a revival of theory to accompany it. As yet, these possibilities exemplify themselves only in an embryonic sociology of law (Chambliss and Siedman, 1971) and in a return to social history (Quinney, 1971b; Weis, 1971)—both of these tendencies basing themselves on an ambiguous middle-range 'theory' of interest group conflict. They are open to all the limitations of the new conflict theorists in general (cf. our comments in chapter 8).

Bibliography

AKERS, RONALD L. (1967), 'Problems in the sociology of deviance: social definitions and behavior', *Social Forces*, 46, 455–65.

AKERS, R., BURGESS, R. and JOHNSON, W. (1968), 'Opiate use, addiction and relapse', *Social Problems*, 15, 459–69.

ALIHAN, M. A. (1938), *Social Ecology: A Critical Analysis*, New York: Columbia University Press; reference here to 1960 ed., New York: Cooper Square.

ALLEN, F. A. (1960), 'Raffaele Garofalo', in H. MANNHEIM, ed. (1960).

ALLPORT, G. (1955), *Becoming*, New Haven: Yale University Press.

AMIR, MENACHEM (1967), 'Patterns of forcible rape', in M. B. CLINARD and R. QUINNEY, eds, *Criminal Behavior Systems*, New York: Holt, Rinehart & Winston, pp. 60–74.

AMIR, MENACHEM (1971), *Patterns in Forcible Rape*, University of Chicago Press.

ARMSTRONG, GAIL and WILSON, MARY (1973), 'City politics and deviancy amplification', in L. TAYLOR and I. TAYLOR, eds (1973).

AUBERT, VILHELM and MESSINGER, SHELDON (1958), 'The criminal and the sick', *Inquiry*, 1, 137–60.

AVINERI, SHLOMO (1969), *The Social and Political Thought of Karl Marx*, Cambridge University Press.

BALDWIN, J., BOTTOMS, A. E. and WALKER, M. A. (1973), *The Urban Criminal*, London: Tavistock.

BALL, D. W. (1967), 'An abortion clinic ethnography', *Social Problems*, 14, 293–301.

BECCARIA, C. (1804), *Essay on Crimes and Punishments* (originally published as *Dei delitti e delle pene*, 1764); reference here to essay on Beccaria in H. MANNHEIM, ed (1960). (See also, Beccaria, *Of Crimes and Punishments*, Oxford University Press, 1964).

BECKER, ERNEST (1965), 'Mills' social psychology and the great historical convergence on the problem of alienation', in I. L. HOROWITZ, ed., *The New Sociology*, Oxford University Press.

302

BECKER, HOWARD S. (1960), 'Notes on the concept of commitment', *American Journal of Sociology*, 66, 32–40.

BECKER, HOWARD S. (1963), *Outsiders: Studies in the Sociology of Deviance*, New York: Free Press.

BECKER, HOWARD S. ed. (1964), *The Other Side: Perspectives on Deviance*, New York: Free Press.

BECKER, HOWARD S. (1967), 'Whose side are we on?', *Social Problems*, 14 (3), 239–47.

BECKER, HOWARD S. (1971), *Sociological Work*, London: Allen Lane.

BECKER, HOWARD S. (1972), 'Labelling theory revisited', in ROCK and MCINTOSH, eds (1972).

BERGER, BENNET M. (1963), 'On the youthfulness of youth culture', *Social Research*, 30 (4), 319–42.

BERGER, PETER and LUCKMANN, THOMAS (1966), *The Social Construction of Reality*, New York: Doubleday; London: Allen Lane.

BERNSTEIN, BASIL (1972), *Class, Codes and Control*, London: Routledge & Kegan Paul (2 vols).

BITTNER, EGON (1963), 'Radicalism and the organization of radical movements', *American Sociological Review*, 28, 928–39.

BITTNER, EGON (1965), 'The concept of organization', *Social Research*, 32 (3), Autumn, 239–55.

BITTNER, EGON (1967a), 'The police on Skid-Row: A study of peace-keeping', *American Sociological Review*, 32 (5), 699–715.

BITTNER, EGON (1967b), 'Police discretion in the emergency apprehension of mentally ill persons', *Social Problems*, 14 (3), 278–92.

BLACK, M. and METZGER, D. (1969), 'Ethnographic description and the study of law', in S. A. TYLER, ed., *Cognitive Anthropology*, New York: Holt, Rinehart & Winston.

BLACKBURN, ROBIN (1967), 'The unequal society', in A. COCKBURN and R. BLACKBURN, eds, *The Incompatibles*, Harmondsworth: Penguin.

BLUM, ALAN F. and MCHUGH, PETER (1971), 'The social ascription of motives' *American Sociological Review*, 36, February, 98–109.

BONGER, WILLEM (1916), *Criminality and Economic Conditions*, Boston: Little, Brown and Co.

BONGER, WILLEM (1935), *An Introduction to Criminology*, London: Methuen.

BONGER, WILLEM (1943), *Race and Crime*, New York: Columbia University Press.

BONGER, WILLEM (1969), *Criminality and Economic Conditions*, Bloomington: Indiana University Press (abridged and with an introduction by AUSTIN T. TURK).

BOX, STEVEN (1971a), *Deviance, Reality and Society*, London: Holt, Rinehart & Winston.

BOX, STEVEN (1971b), 'Review of David Matza's *Becoming Deviant*', *Sociology*, 4 (3), 403–4.

BRAUDE, LEE (1970), 'Park and Burgess: an appreciation', *American Journal of Sociology*, 76.

BROSMONT, B. (1856), *Du Suicide et de la folie suicide*, Paris: Baillière.

BURGESS, R. and AKERS, R. (1966), 'A differential association-reinforcement theory of criminal behaviour', *Social Problems*, 14, 128–47.

303

BURNHAM, JAMES (1943), *The Managerial Revolution*, London: Putnam.

CARMICHAEL, STOKELY (1968), 'Black Power', in D. COOPER, ed., *The Dialectics of Liberation*, London: Penguin, pp. 150–74.

CARTER, M. P. and JEPHCOTT, P. (1954), 'The social background of delinquency', unpublished, University of Nottingham Library.

CASEY, M., *et al.* (1966), 'Sex chromosome abnormalities in two state hospitals for patients requiring special security', *Nature*, 5 February, 641–3.

CHAMBLISS, WILLIAM J. (1964), 'A sociological analysis of the law of vagrancy', *Social Problems*, 12 (1), 67–77, reprinted in W. G. CARSON and P. WILES, eds, *Crime and Delinquency in Britain: A Book of Readings*, London: Martin Robertson, 1970.

CHAMBLISS, WILLIAM J. ed. (1969), *Crime and the Legal Process*, New York: McGraw-Hill.

CHAMBLISS, WILLIAM J. and SIEDMAN, ROBERT B. (1971), *Law, Order and Power*, Massachusetts: Addison-Wesley.

CHAPMAN, DENNIS (1968), *Sociology and the Stereotype of the Criminal*, London: Tavistock.

CHRISTIE, NILS (1961), 'Scandinavian criminology', *Sociological Inquiry*, 38, 134–48.

CHRISTIE, NILS, *et al.* (1965; 1968; 1971), *Scandinavian Studies in Criminology*, London: Tavistock; Oslo: Universitetsforlaget (3 vols).

CHRISTIE, NILS (1971), 'Scandinavian criminology facing the 1970's', in CHRISTIE, *et al.* (1971), pp. 121–49.

CHRISTIE, R. (1956), 'Some abuses of psychology', *Psychological Bulletin*, 53, 439–51.

CICOUREL, AARON V. (1968), *The Social Organization of Juvenile Justice*, New York: Wiley.

CICOUREL, AARON V. (1970), 'Basic and normative rules in the negotiation of status and role', in DREITZEL, ed. (1970), pp. 4–45.

CLEAVER, ELDRIDGE (1969), *Soul on Ice*, London: Cape.

CLOWARD, RICHARD and OHLIN, LLOYD (1960), *Delinquency and Opportunity: a Theory of Delinquent Gangs*, Chicago: Free Press.

COCKETT, R. (1971), *Drug Abuse and Personality in Young Offenders*, London: Butterworth.

COHEN, ALBERT K. (1955), *Delinquent Boys: the Culture of the Gang*, Chicago: Free Press.

COHEN, ALBERT K. (1965), 'The sociology of the deviant act: anomie theory and beyond', *American Sociological Review*, 30 (1), 5–14.

COHEN, ALBERT K. (1966), *Deviance and Control*, Engelwood Cliffs: Prentice-Hall.

COHEN, PHIL (1972), 'Subcultural conflict and working class community', *Working Papers in Cultural Studies* (2), 5–52 (Centre for Contemporary Cultural Studies, University of Birmingham).

COHEN, STANLEY (1966), 'Vandalism', *New Education*, 2, October.

COHEN, STANLEY (1967), 'Mods, Rockers and the Rest: community reactions to juvenile delinquency', *Howard Journal*, 13; reprinted in W. G. CARSON and P. WILES, eds, *Crime and Delinquency in Britain: A Book of Readings*, London: Martin Robertson, 1970, and in J. B. MAYS, ed., *Delinquency: The Family, School and Social Group*, London: Longman, 1972.

COHEN, STANLEY (1968), 'The politics of vandalism' *New Society*, 324, 12 December, 872–8 (also in *The Nation*, 11 November 1968).

COHEN, STANLEY (1969), 'Ideological and criminal violence', *Phalanx*, 2, University of Durham.

COHEN, STANLEY ed. (1971a), *Images of Deviance*, Harmondsworth: Penguin (for the National Deviancy Conference).

COHEN, STANLEY (1971b), 'Directions for research on adolescent group violence and vandalism', *British Journal of Criminology*, 11 (4), 319–40.

COHEN, STANLEY (1971c), 'Protest, unrest and delinquency: convergences in labels or behaviour?', paper given to the International Symposium on Youth Unrest, Tel-Aviv, 25–27 October (forthcoming in publication of proceedings).

COHEN, STANLEY (1972a), *Moral panics and folk devils*, London: Mac-Gibbon & Kee.

COHEN, STANLEY (1972b), 'Breaking out, smashing up, and the social context of aspiration', in B. RIVEN, ed., *Youth at the Beginning of the Seventies*, London: Martin Robertson.

COHEN, STANLEY (1972c), 'Criminology and the sociology of deviance in Great Britain: a recent history and a current report', in ROCK and MCINTOSH, eds (1972).

COHEN, STANLEY (1972d), 'Property destruction: motives and meanings', in C. WARD, ed., *Vandalism and Architecture*, London: Architectural Press.

COHEN, STANLEY and ROCK, PAUL (1970), 'The Teddy Boys', in V. BOGDANOR and R. SKIDELSKY, eds, *The Age of Affluence*, London: Macmillan, 288–320; reprinted in 1972 in Macmillan Student Editions.

COHEN, STANLEY and TAYLOR, LAURIE (1970), 'The experience of time in long-term imprisonment', *New Society*, 431, 31 December, 1156–59.

COHEN, STANLEY and TAYLOR, LAURIE (1971), 'The closed emotional world of the security prison', *New Edinburgh Review*, 15, November, 4–8.

COHEN, STANLEY and TAYLOR, LAURIE (1972), *Psychological Survival: The Experience of Long-Term Imprisonment*, Harmondsworth: Penguin.

COMFORT, ALEX (1950), *Authority and Delinquency in the Modern State*, London: Routledge & Kegan Paul.

COMFORT, ALEX (1967), *The Anxiety Makers*, London: Nelson.

COMTE, AUGUSTE (1842), *The Positive Philosophy* (see 1853 ed. translated by H. MARTINEAU, Trübner).

COMTE, AUGUSTE (1854), *Cours de Philosophie positive*, Paris.

CONRAD, KLAUS (1963), *Der Konstitutionstypus* (2nd ed.), Berlin: Springer.

COSER, LEWIS (1956), *The Functions of Social Conflict*, London: Routledge & Kegan Paul.

COSER, LEWIS (1960), 'Durkheim's conservatism and its implications for his sociological theory', in WOLFF, ed. (1960).

COULTER, JEFF (1970), 'Marxism and symbolic interactionism', unpublished working paper, Department of Sociology and Anthropology, University of Manchester.

COULTER, JEFF (1971), 'Decontextualised meanings; current approaches to *verstehende* investigations', *Sociological Review*, 19 (3), 301–23.

COULTER, JEFF (1973), 'The ethnomethodological programme in contemporary sociology', *The Human Context* (forthcoming).

CRESSEY, DONALD R. (1953), *Other People's Money*, Chicago: Free Press.

CRESSEY, DONALD R. (1962), 'Role theory, differential association and compulsive crimes', in ARNOLD ROSE, ed., *Human Behaviour and Social Processes*, London: Routledge & Kegan Paul, 443–67.

DAHRENDORF, RALF (1958), 'Out of Utopia: toward a reconstruction of sociological analysis', *American Journal of Sociology*, 67, September, 115–27.

DAHRENDORF, RALF (1959), *Class and Class Conflict in an Industrial Society*, London: Routledge & Kegan Paul.

DAHRENDORF, RALF (1968), *Essays in the Theory of Society*, Stanford University Press; references here are to the section 'On the origin of inequality among men'; reprinted in A. BETEILLE, ed., *Social Inequality*, Harmondsworth: Penguin, 1969.

DARWIN, CHARLES (1871), *Descent of Man*, London: John Murray.

DELAMATER, JOHN (1968), 'On the nature of deviance', *Social Forces*, 46 (4), June, 445–55.

DENZIN, N. K. (1969), 'Symbolic interactionism and ethnomethodology: a proposed synthesis', *American Sociological Review*, 34 (6).

DICKSON, DONALD T. (1968), 'Bureaucracy and morality: an organisational perspective on a moral crusade', *Social Problems*, 16 (2), 143–56.

DOUGLAS, JACK D. (1967), *The Social Meanings of Suicide*, Princeton University Press.

DOUGLAS, JACK D. ed. (1970a), *Deviance and Respectability: the Social Construction of Moral Meanings*, London and New York: Basic Books.

DOUGLAS, JACK D. ed. (1970b), *The Impact of Sociology*, New York: Appleton-Century-Crofts.

DOUGLAS, JACK D. (1971a), *The American Social Order: Social Rules in a Pluralistic Society*, New York: Free Press.

DOUGLAS, JACK D. ed. (1971b), *Understanding Everyday Life: Toward the Reconstruction of Sociological Knowledge*, London: Routledge & Kegan Paul.

DOWNES, DAVID (1966a), *The Delinquent Solution*, London: Routledge & Kegan Paul.

DOWNES, DAVID (1966b), 'The gang myth', *The Listener*, 75 (1933), 14 April, 534–7.

DOWNES, DAVID and ROCK, PAUL (1971), 'Social reaction to deviance and its effect on crime and criminal careers' *British Journal of Sociology*, 22 (4), 351–64.

DREITZEL, H. P. (1970), *Recent Sociology No. 2*, New York: Collier-Macmillan.

DURKHEIM, EMILE (1912), *The Elementary Forms of the Religious Life*; reference here to 1954 ed., Chicago: Free Press.

DURKHEIM, EMILE (1914), 'Le Dualisme de la nature humaine et ses conditions humaines', *Scientia*, 15; translated and reprinted as 'The dualism of human nature', in WOLFF, ed. (1960).

DURKHEIM, EMILE (1952), *Suicide: A Study in Sociology*, London: Routledge & Kegan Paul.

DURKHEIM, EMILE (1953), *Sociology and Philosophy* (translated by D. F. POCOCK), Chicago: Free Press.

DURKHEIM, EMILE (1957), *Professional Ethics and Civic Morals*, London: Routledge & Kegan Paul.

DURKHEIM, EMILE (1962), *Socialism and Saint-Simon*, London: Routledge & Kegan Paul.

DURKHEIM, EMILE (1964a), *Rules of Sociological Method*, New York: Free Press.

DURKHEIM, EMILE (1964b), *The Division of Labour in Society*, New York: Free Press.

EMERSON, R. (1969) *Judging Delinquents: Context and Process in the Juvenile Court*, Chicago: Aldine Press.

ENGELS, FRIEDRICH (1950), *The Condition of the Working Class in England in 1844*, London: Allen & Unwin.

ERIKSON, KAI T. (1962), 'Notes on the sociology of deviance', *Social Problems*, 9, Spring; reprinted in H. S. BECKER, ed. (1964).

ESQUIROL, J. E. D. (1839), *Des Maladies mentales*, Paris (*Mental Maladies: A Treatise on Insanity* (translated by E. K. Hunt), New York and London: Hafner, 1966).

ESSLIN, MARTIN (1971), 'Solzhenitsyn and Lukacs' *Encounter*, 37 (3), March, 47–51.

EYSENCK, HANS (1953), *Uses and Abuses of Psychology*, Harmondsworth: Penguin.

EYSENCK, HANS (1954), *The Psychology of Politics*, London: Routledge & Kegan Paul; New York: Humanities Press, 1963.

EYSENCK, HANS (1965), *Fact and Fiction in Psychology*, Harmondsworth: Penguin.

EYSENCK, HANS (1969), 'The technology of consent' *New Scientist*, 26, June.

EYSENCK, HANS (1970), *Crime and Personality* (revised ed.), London: Paladin.

EYSENCK, HANS and EYSENCK, S. (1970), 'Crime and personality: an empirical study of the three-factor theory', *British Journal of Criminology*, 10, 225–39.

FARNER, J. A. (1880), *Crimes and Punishments*, London: Chatto & Windus.

FERRI, ENRICO (1886a), 'Polemica in difesa scuola criminale positiva', in FERRI, LOMBROSO, GARAFALO and FIORETTI, eds, *Studi sulla criminalita*, Turin: Bocca (2nd ed., 1901).

FERRI, ENRICO (1886b), 'Studi sulla criminalita in Francia del 1826 al 1878', in Ferri (1886a).

FERRI, ENRICO (1895), *Criminal Sociology*, London (abridged ed.), London: Unwin.

FERRI, ENRICO (1901), *The Positive School of Criminology* (English ed. published in 1908 by C. H. Kerr & Co, Chicago).

FERRI, ENRICO (1929), *Criminal Sociology*, Boston: Little, Brown & Co.

FYVEL, T. R. (1961), *The Insecure Offenders*, Harmondsworth: Penguin.

GARFINKEL, HAROLD (1960), 'The rational properties of scientific and common sense activities', *Behavioral Science*, 5 (1), 72–83.

GARFINKEL, HAROLD (1962), 'Common sense knowledge of social structure:

the documentary method of interpretation', in J. M. SCHER, *Theories of the Mind*, Collier-Macmillan.

GARFINKEL, HAROLD (1968a), *Studies in Ethnomethodology*, New York: Prentice-Hall.

GARFINKEL, HAROLD (1968b), Taped conversations, in HILL and CRITTENDEN, eds (1968).

GAROFALO, RAFFAELE (1914), *Criminology*, Boston: Little, Brown & Co; Patterson-Smith, 1968.

GERTH, HANS and WRIGHT MILLS, C. (1964), *Character and Social Structure*, New York: Harcourt, Brace & World; London: Routledge & Kegan Paul, 1954.

GIBBONS, DONALD C. (1968), *Society, Crime and Criminal Careers*, London: Prentice-Hall.

GIBBONS, DONALD C. and JONES, J. F. (1971), 'Some critical notes on current definitions of deviance', *Pacific Sociological Review*, 14 (1), 20–37.

GIBBS, JACK P. (1966), 'Conceptions of deviant behavior: the old and the new', *Pacific Sociological Review*, 9, Spring.

GIDDENS, ANTHONY (1971a), *Capitalism and Modern Social Theory; An Analysis of the Writings of Marx, Durkheim and Max Weber*, Cambridge University Press.

GIDDENS, ANTHONY (1971b), 'Durkheim's political sociology', *Sociological Review*, 19 (4), November, 477–519.

GIDDENS, ANTHONY (1971c), 'The "Individual" in the writings of Emile Durkheim', *European Journal of Sociology*, 12 (2).

GLASER, DANIEL (1956), 'Criminality theory and behavioral images', *American Journal of Sociology*, 61, 433–44.

GLUECK, SHELDON and GLUECK, ELEANOR (1950), *Unraveling Juvenile Delinquency*, New York: Harper & Row.

GLUECK, SHELDON and GLUECK, ELEANOR (1956), *Physique and Delinquency*, New York: Harper & Row.

GOFFMAN, ERVING (1968), *Stigma: Notes on the Management of Spoiled Identity*, Harmondsworth: Penguin.

GOLD, MARTIN (1970), *Delinquent Behavior in an American City*, California: Wadsworth Publishing Co.

GORDON, D. M. (1971), 'Class and the economics of crime', *Review of Radical Political Economics*, 3 (3), 51–75.

GORING, CHARLES (1913), *The English Convict*, London: HMSO.

GOULD, JULIUS (1969), 'Auguste Comte' in T. RAISON, ed., *The Founding Fathers of Social Science*, Harmondsworth: Penguin.

GOULDNER, ALVIN W. (1968), 'The sociologist as partisan: sociology and the welfare state', *The American Sociologist*, May, 103–16.

GOULDNER, ALVIN W. (1971), *The Coming Crisis of Western Sociology*, London: Heinemann Educational; New York: Basic Books, 1970.

GRUPP, S. E. ed. (1968), *The Positive School of Criminology: Three Lectures by Enrico Ferri*, University of Pittsburgh Press.

GUERRY, A. M. (1863), *Statistique Morale de l'Angleterre comparée avec la statistique morale de la France*, Paris; reference here to RADZINOWICZ (1966), 35 and 139.

HALL, JEROME (1952), *Theft, Law and Society*, Indianapolis: Bobbs-Merrill.

HALL, STUART (1972), 'Deviancy, politics and the media' in ROCK and MCINTOSH, eds (1972).

HARGREAVES, DAVID H. (1967), *Social Relations in the Secondary School*, London: Routledge & Kegan Paul.

HART, H. L. A. (1962), 'Punishment and the elimination of responsibility', Hobhouse Memorial Lecture, no. 31; reprinted in H. L. A. HART, *Punishment and Responsibility*, Oxford University Press, 1968.

HEATHER, JUDITH (forthcoming), 'An analysis of law and social change (with special reference to China)', M. Phil. thesis, University of London.

HEPWORTH, MIKE (1971), 'Deviants in disguise: blackmail and social acceptance', in S. COHEN (1971a), 192–218.

HEPWORTH, MIKE (1972), 'Missing persons', in ROCK and MCINTOSH, eds (1972).

HILL, R. J. and CRITTENDEN, K. S. eds, (1968), *Proceedings of the Purdue Symposium on Ethnomethodology*, no. 1, Institute for the Study of Social Change, Department of Sociology, Purdue University.

HINDELANG, MICHAEL J. (1970), 'The commitment of delinquents to their misdeeds: do delinquents drift?', *Social Problems*, 17, 502–9.

HINDESS, BARRY (1972), 'The phenomenology of Alfred Schutz', *Economy and Society*, 1 (1), February, 1–27.

HIRSCHI, TRAVIS (1969), *The Causes of Delinquency*, University of California Press.

HIRSCHI, TRAVIS and SELVIN, HANNAN (1967), *Delinquency Research: An Appraisal of Analytic Methods*, New York: Free Press.

HIRST, PAUL Q. (1972), 'Marx and Engels on crime, law and morality', *Economy and Society*, 1 (1), February, 28–56.

HOBSBAWM, ERIC (1965), *Pre-Capitalist Economic Formations* (by Karl Marx), London: Lawrence & Wishart.

HOGHUGHI, M. and FORREST, A. (1970), 'Eysenck's theory of criminality', *British Journal of Criminology*, 10, 240–54.

HOLLANDER, PAUL (1969), 'A converging social problem: juvenile delinquency in the Soviet Union and the United States', *British Journal of Criminology*, 9 (2), April, 148–66.

HOROWITZ, I. L. and LIEBOWITZ, M. (1968), 'Social deviance and political marginality', *Social Problems*, 15 (3), 280–96.

HORTON, JOHN (1964), 'The dehumanization of anomie and alienation: a problem in the ideology of sociology', *British Journal of Sociology*, 15, 283–300.

HORTON, JOHN (1966), 'Order and conflict theories of social problems as competing ideologies', *American Journal of Sociology*, 71, May, 701–713.

HUNTER, H. (1966), 'YY chromosomes and Klinefelter's Syndrome', *The Lancet*, 30 April.

IRWIN, JOHN and CRESSEY, DONALD (1962), 'Thieves, convicts and the inmate culture', *Social Problems*, 10 (2), Fall, 142–55; reprinted in H. S. BECKER, ed. (1964).

JACKSON, GEORGE (1970), *Soledad Brother*, Harmondsworth: Penguin.

KADISH, SANFORD (1968), 'The crisis of overcriminalization', *American Criminal Law Quarterly*, 7, 17.

309

KENNEDY, MARK (1970), 'Beyond incrimination: some neglected facets in the theory of punishment', *Catalyst*, 5, Summer, 1–37.

KESSLER, S. and MOOS, R. (1970), 'The XYY karyotype and criminality', *Journal of Psychiatric Research*, 7, 153–70.

KIDRON, MIKE (1968), *Western Capitalism since the War*, London: Weidenfeld & Nicolson.

KITSUSE, JOHN I. (1962), 'Societal reaction to deviant behavior: problems of theory and method', *Social Problems*, 9, Winter, pp. 247–56; reprinted in H. S. BECKER, ed. (1964).

KITSUSE, JOHN I. and CICOUREL, AARON V. (1963), 'A note on the uses of official statistics,' *Social Problems*, 11, 131–9.

KOESTLER, ARTHUR (1964), *The Act of Creation*, London: Hutchinson.

KRETSCHMER, ERNST (1921), *Körperbau und Charakter*, Berlin: Springer; see also, English ed. (1964), *Physique and Character*, New York: Cooper Square (translated by W. J. H. SPROTT).

KUHN, THOMAS (1970), 'The logic of discovery or psychology of research?', in I. LAKATOS and A. MUSGRAVE, eds, *Criticism and the Growth of Knowledge*, Cambridge University Press.

LAING, RONALD (1967), *The Politics of Experience and the Bird of Paradise*, Harmondsworth: Penguin.

LAMBERT, JOHN R. (1970), *Crime, Police and Race Relations*, London: Institute of Race Relations/Oxford University Press.

LANDER, B. (1954), *Towards an Understanding of Juvenile Delinquency*, New York: Columbia University Press.

LASSMAN, PETER (1970a), 'Theoretical aspects of ethnomethodology', unpublished working paper, Department of Sociology, University of Birmingham.

LASSMAN, PETER (1970b), 'Some recent discussions in the philosophy of social science' unpublished working paper, Department of Sociology, University of Birmingham.

LEMERT, EDWIN M. (1948), 'Some aspects of a general theory of sociopathic behavior', *Proceedings of the Pacific Sociological Society*, State College of Washington, 16, 23–9.

LEMERT, EDWIN M. (1951), *Social Pathology*, New York: McGraw-Hill.

LEMERT, EDWIN M. (1967), *Human Deviance, Social Problems and Social Control*, New York: Prentice-Hall.

LEMERT, EDWIN M. (1968), 'Social problems and the sociology of deviance', in DAVID L. SILLS, ed., *International Encyclopedia of the Social Sciences*, New York: Crowell Collier and Macmillan, Inc., vol. 14, 452–8; reprinted as chapter 1 of 1972 ed. of *Human Deviance, Social Problems and Social Control*.

LEMERT, EDWIN M. (1970), *Social Action and Legal Change: Revolution within the Juvenile Court*, Chicago: Aldine Press.

LEVIN, Y. and LINDESMITH, A. (1937), 'English ecology and crime of the past century', *Journal of Criminal Law and Criminology*, 27, 801–16; reprinted in W. G. CARSON and P. WILES, eds, *Crime and Delinquency in Britain: A Book of Readings*, London: Martin Robertson, 1970.

LEWIS, OSCAR (1961), *The Children of Sanchez*, New York: Random House.

LEWIS, OSCAR (1966), *La Vida: a Puerto Rican Family in the Culture of Poverty: San Juan and New York*, New York: Random House.

LICHTMAN, RICHARD (1970), 'Symbolic interactionism and social reality', *Berkeley Journal of Sociology*, 15.

LINDESMITH, A. and LEVIN, Y. (1937), 'The Lombrosian myth in criminology', *American Journal of Sociology*, 42, 653–71.

LITTLE, A. (1963), 'Professor Eysenck's theory of crime: an empirical test on adolescent offenders', *British Journal of Criminology*, 4, 152–63.

LOMBROSO, CESARE (1876), *L'Uomo Delinquente*, Milan: Hoepli (5th ed., Turin: Bocca).

LOMBROSO, CESARE (1911), Introduction to Gina Lombroso Ferrara: *Criminal Man According to the Classification of Cesare Lombroso*, New York: Putnam.

LOMBROSO, CESARE (1913), *Crime: its Causes and Remedies*, Boston: Little, Brown & Co.

LONEY, MARTIN (1973), 'Social control in Cuba', in L. TAYLOR and I. TAYLOR, eds (1973).

LUKACS, GEORG (1966a), 'What is orthodox Marxism?', *International Socialism*, 24 (translators, M. PHILLIPS and C. POSNER).

LUKACS, GEORG (1966b), 'Existentialism or Marxism?', in G. NOVACK, ed., *Existentialism versus Marxism*, New York: Delta Books, 134–53.

LUKACS, GEORG (1971a), *History and Class Consciousness*, London: Merlin Press.

LUKACS, GEORG (1971b), *Solzhenitsyn*, London: Merlin Press.

LUKES, STEVEN (1967), 'Alienation and anomie' in P. LASLETT and W. G. RUNCIMAN, eds, *Philosophy, Politics and Society* (3rd series), Oxford: Blackwell.

LUKES, STEVEN (1971), 'Prolegomena to the interpretation of Durkheim', *European Journal of Sociology*, 12 (2).

LYMAN, S. M. and SCOTT, M. B. (1970), 'Territoriality: a neglected sociological dimension', in LYMAN and SCOTT, *A Sociology of the Absurd*, New York: Appleton-Century-Crofts; reprinted in D. I. DAVIES and K. HERMAN, eds, *Social Space: Canadian Perspectives*, Toronto: New Press, 1971.

MCHUGH, PETER (1968), *Defining the Situation: The Organization of Meaning in Social Interaction*, Indianapolis: Bobbs-Merrill.

MCHUGH, PETER (1970), 'A commonsense conception of deviance', in DOUGLAS, ed. (1970), 61–88.

MCINTOSH, MARY (1971), 'Changes in the organization of thieving', in S. COHEN, ed. (1971a), 98–133.

MACINTYRE, ALASDAIR (1962), 'A mistake about causality in the social sciences', in P. LASLETT and W. G. RUNCIMAN, eds, *Philosophy, Politics and Society* (2nd series), Oxford: Blackwell.

MCKENZIE, R. D. (1933), *The Metropolitan Community*, New York: McGraw-Hill.

MCKINNEY, J. C. and TIRYAKIAN, E. A. (1970), *Theoretical Sociology: Perspectives and Developments*, New York: Appleton-Century-Crofts.

MCLELLAN, DAVID, ed. (1971), *Marx's Grundrisse*, Oxford: Blackwell.

MACPHERSON, C. B. (1962), *The Political Theory of Possessive Individualism*, Oxford University Press.

MALCOLM X (1966), *The Autobiography of Malcolm X*, London: Hutchinson.

MANDEVILLE, BERNARD DE (1725), *The Fable of the Bees*, Originally published 1714; reference here to 1725 edition, London: J. Tonson.

MANKOFF, MILTON (1970), 'Power in advanced capitalist society: a review essay in recent élitist and Marxist criticism of pluralist theory', *Social Problems*, 17 (3), 418–30.

MANKOFF, MILTON (1971), 'Societal reaction and career deviance: a critical analysis', *The Sociological Quarterly*, 12, Spring.

MANNHEIM, HERMANN, ed. (1960), *Pioneers in Criminology*, London: Stevens.

MANNHEIM, HERMANN (1965), *Comparative Criminology*, London: Routledge & Kegan Paul.

MANSON, I. and PALMER, J. (1973), *The Dirty Old Man on the Last Tube: The Social Response to Pornography*, London: Davis-Poynter.

MARX, KARL (1844), *The Economic and Philosophical Manuscripts of 1844*; reference here to 1964 ed., New York: International Publishers.

MARX, KARL (1845), *Third Thesis on Feuerbach*; reference here to Foreign Languages Publishing House, Moscow (no date); reprinted in MARX and ENGELS, *The German Ideology*, London: Lawrence & Wishart, 1965 ed., 660.

MARX, KARL (1853), 'Capital punishment', *New York Daily Tribune*, 18 February; reprinted in T. B. BOTTOMORE and M. RUBEL, eds, *Karl Marx: Selected Writings in Sociology and Social Philosophy*, Harmondsworth: Penguin, 1963, 233–5.

MARX, KARL (1859), 'Population, crime and pauperism', *New York Daily Tribune*, 16 September.

MARX, KARL (1951), Preface to *A Contribution to the Critique of Political Economy*, in *Marx-Engels Selected Works*, vol. 1, Foreign Languages Publishing House, Moscow.

MARX, KARL (1963), *The Economic and Philosophical Manuscripts of 1844*; reference here to citations in T. B. BOTTOMORE and M. RUBEL, ed., *Karl Marx: Selected Writings in Sociology and Social Philosophy*, Harmondsworth: Penguin.

MARX, KARL (1964), *Theories of Surplus Value*, Part 1 (translated by E. Burns), Lawrence & Wishart.

MARX, KARL (1971), *Grundrisse der politische Oekonomie*; reference here to translation and abridged edition by DAVID MCLELLAN (1971).

MARX, KARL and ENGELS, F. (1965), *The German Ideology*, London: Lawrence & Wishart.

MARX, KARL and ENGELS, F. (1968), *Selected Works*, London: Lawrence & Wishart.

MATHIESON, THOMAS (1965), *The Defences of the Weak: A Study of a Norwegian Correctional Institution*, London: Tavistock.

MATHIESON, THOMAS (1972), *Beyond the Boundaries of Organizations*, California: Glendessary Press.

MATZA, DAVID (1961), 'Subterranean traditions of youth', *Annals of the American Academy of Political and Social Science*, 338, 102–18.

MATZA, DAVID (1964), *Delinquency and Drift*, New York: Wiley.

MATZA, DAVID (1967), 'The disreputable poor' in R. BENDIX and S. M.

LIPSET, *Class, Status, and Power* (revised ed.), London: Routledge & Kegan Paul.

MATZA, DAVID (1969a), *Becoming Deviant*, New York: Prentice-Hall.

MATZA, DAVID (1969b), Reply to Charles Valentine's 'Culture and poverty', *Current Anthropology*, 10 (2–3), April–June, 192–4.

MATZA, DAVID (1971), 'Poverty and disrepute', in R. K. MERTON and R. NISBET, eds, *Contemporary Social Problems* (3rd revised ed.), New York: Harcourt, Brace & World, 601–56.

MATZA, DAVID and SYKES, GRESHAM (1961), 'Juvenile delinquency and subterranean values', *American Sociological Review*, 26, 712–19.

MAYS, JOHN B. (1954), *Growing Up in the City*, Liverpool University Press.

MEAD, G. H. (1918), 'The psychology of punitive justice', *American Journal of Sociology*, 23, 577–602.

MERTON, R. K. (1938), 'Social structure and anomie', *American Sociological Review*, 3, 672–82.

MERTON, R. K. (1957), *Social Theory and Social Structure* (revised ed.), New York: Free Press.

MERTON, R. K. (1964), 'Anomie, anomia and social interaction', in M. B. CLINARD, ed., *Anomie and Deviant Behaviour*, New York: Free Press, 213–42.

MERTON, R. K. (1966), 'Social problems and sociological theory' in R. K. MERTON and R. NISBET, eds, *Contemporary Social Problems*, New York: Harcourt, Brace & World.

MESZAROS, ISTVAN (1970), *Marx's Theory of Alienation*, London: Merlin Press.

MILIBAND, RALPH (1969), *The State in Capitalist Society*, London: Weidenfeld & Nicolson.

MILLER, WALTER B. (1958), 'Lower-class culture as a generating milieu of gang delinquency', *Journal of Social Issues*, 15, 5–19; reprinted in M. WOLFGANG, L. SAVITZ and N. JOHNSTON, eds, *The Sociology of Crime and Delinquency*, London: Wiley, 1962; New York: Wiley, 1970.

MORRIS, TERENCE (1957), *The Criminal Area*, London: Routledge & Kegan Paul.

NICOLAUS, MARTIN (1969), 'The professional organisation of sociology: a view from below', *Antioch Review*, Fall, 375–87.

O'NEILL, JOHN (1968), 'Public and private space', in TREVOR LLOYD and JACK MACLEOD, *Agenda 1970: Proposals for a Creative Politics*, University of Toronto Press; reprinted in D. I. DAVIES and K. HERMAN, eds, *Social Space: Canadian Perspectives*, Toronto: New Press, 1971.

PARK, ROBERT E. (1929), 'Sociology', in W. GEE, ed., *Research in the Social Sciences*, New York: Macmillan.

PARK, ROBERT E. (1936), 'Human ecology', *American Journal of Sociology*, 42 (1), July, 15.

PARSONS, TALCOTT (1940), 'An analytical approach to the study of stratification', *American Journal of Sociology*, 45, 841–62.

PARSONS, TALCOTT (1954), *Essays in Sociological Theory*, (revised ed.), Chicago: Free Press.

PEARCE, FRANK (1970), 'On ethnomethodology', unpublished paper delivered to the Fifth National Deviancy Symposium, April 1970.

313

PEARCE, FRANK (1973), 'Crime, corporations and the American social order', in L. TAYLOR and I. TAYLOR, eds (1973).

PEARCE, FRANK and HAYES, MIKE (1973), *Crime, Politics and the State*, London: Routledge & Kegan Paul.

PERKS COMMITTEE (1967), *Report of the Departmental Committee on the Criminal Statistics*, Cmnd. 3448, London: HMSO.

PHILLIPSON, MICHAEL (1971), *Sociological Aspects of Crime and Delinquency*, London: Routledge & Kegan Paul.

PHILLIPSON, MICHAEL and ROCHE, MAURICE (1971), 'Phenomenological sociology and the study of deviance', unpublished paper delivered to the 1971 Annual Conference of the British Sociological Association.

PILIAVIN, S. and BRIAR, S. (1964), 'Police encounters with juveniles', *American Journal of Sociology*, 52, 206–14.

PRICE, W. *et al.* (1966), 'Criminal patients with XYY sex chromosome complement', *The Lancet*, 1.

PRICE, W. *et al.* (1967), 'Behaviour disorders and patterns among XYY males identified at a maximum security hospital', *British Medical Journal*, 1, 533–6.

PSATHAS, G. (1968), 'Ethnomethods and phenomenology', *Social Research*, 35.

QUETELET, A. (1842), *Treatise on Man*, Paris: Bachelier (first published in 1835 as *Sur l'homme et le développement de ses facultés ou Essai de physique sociale*, 2 vols).

QUINNEY, RICHARD (1964), 'Crime in political perspective', *American Behavioral Scientist*, 8, December, 19–22.

QUINNEY, RICHARD (1965a), 'A conception of man and society for criminology', *Sociological Quarterly*, 6, Spring, 119–27.

QUINNEY, RICHARD (1965b), 'Is criminal behaviour deviant behaviour?', *British Journal of Criminology*, 5, April, 132–42.

QUINNEY, RICHARD, ed. (1969), *Crime and Justice in Society*, Boston: Little, Brown & Co.

QUINNEY, RICHARD, ed. (1970a), *The Problem of Crime*, New York: Dodd, Mead & Co.

QUINNEY, RICHARD (1970b), *The Social Reality of Crime*, Boston: Little, Brown & Co.

QUINNEY, RICHARD (1972), 'The ideology of law: notes for a radical alternative to legal oppression', *Issues in Criminology*, 7 (1), Winter, 1–36.

RADZINOWICZ, LEON (1948–56), *History of the English Criminal Law*, London: Stevens (3 vols).

RADZINOWICZ, LEON (1966), *Ideology and Crime: A Study of Crime in its Social and Historical Context*, London: Heinemann Educational.

REX, JOHN (1969), 'Emile Durkheim' in T. RAISON, ed., *The Founding Fathers of Social Sciences*, London: Penguin.

REX, JOHN (1971a), *Race Relations and Sociological Theory*, London: Weidenfeld & Nicolson.

REX, JOHN (1971b), 'Sociological theory and deviancy theory', unpublished paper delivered to the 1971 Annual Conference of the British Sociological Association.

REX, JOHN and MOORE, ROBERT (1967), *Race, Community and Conflict: a*

314

Study in Sparkbrook, London: Institute of Race Relations/Oxford University Press.

RICHARDSON, K. and SPEARS, D. eds (1972), *Race, Culture and Intelligence*, Harmondsworth: Penguin.

RICHTER, M. (1960), 'Politics and Political Theory' in WOLFF, ed. (1960).

RIDDELL, CAROL (1972), 'Transvestism and the tyranny of gender', unpublished paper delivered to the Tenth National Deviancy Conference, April 1972.

ROCK, PAUL (1973), *A Sociology of Deviance*, London: Hutchinson.

ROCK, PAUL and COHEN, STANLEY (1969), 'The Teddy Boys', in V. BOGDANOR and R. SKIDELSKY, eds, *The Age of Affluence 1951–1964*, London, Macmillan, 288–320.

ROCK, PAUL and MCINTOSH, MARY, eds (1973), *Deviance and Social Control*, London: Tavistock (for the British Sociological Association).

ROSENTHAL, ROBERT (1968), *Pygmalion in the Classroom: Teacher Expectation and Pupil's Intellectual Development*, New York: Holt, Rinehart & Winston.

ROUSSEAU, JEAN-JACQUES (1762), *Le Contrat Social* (see *Du Contrat Social*, Garnier: Harrap, 1966).

SACKS, HARVEY (1963), 'Sociological description', *Berkeley Journal of Sociology*, 8.

SARBIN, T. (1969), *The Myth of the Criminal Type*, Connecticut: Center for Advanced Studies, Wesleyan University.

SARBIN, T. and MILLER, J. (1970), 'Demonism revisited: the XYY chromosomal anomaly', *Issues in Criminology*, 5, Summer, 195–207.

SCHAFER, STEPHEN (1969), *Theories in Criminology*, New York: Random House.

SCHEFF, THOMAS J. (1966), *Being Mentally Ill: A Sociological Theory*, Chicago: Aldine Press.

SCHUR, EDWIN M. (1968), *Law and Society: A Sociological View*, New York: Random House.

SCHUR, EDWIN M. (1969), 'Reactions to deviance: a critical assessment', *American Journal of Sociology*, 75, 309–22.

SCHUR, EDWIN M. (1971), *Labeling Deviant Behavior: its Sociological Implications*, New York: Random House.

SCHUTZ, ALFRED (1943), 'The problem of rationality in the social world', *Economica*, 10, 130–49.

SCHUTZ, ALFRED (1944), 'The stranger: an essay in social psychology', *American Journal of Sociology*, 49, May, 499–507.

SCHUTZ, ALFRED (1945), 'On Multiple Realities', *Philosophy and Phenomenological Research*, 5, 533–76.

SCHUTZ, ALFRED (1951), 'Choosing among projects of action', *Philosophy and Phenomenological Research*, 12 (2), December, 161–84.

SCHUTZ, ALFRED (1953), 'Commonsense and scientific interpretation of human action', *Philosophy and Phenomenological Research*, 14 (1), 1–38.

SCHUTZ, ALFRED (1967), *The Phenomenology of the Social World* (translators GEORGE WALSH and FREDERICK LAMBERT) Northwestern University Press.

SCHWENDINGER, HERMAN (1961), *The Instrumental Theory of Delinquency*, unpublished Ph.D. thesis, University of California.

SCHWENDINGER, HERMAN and JULIA (1970), 'Defenders of order or guardians of human rights?', *Issues in Criminology*, 5 (2), Summer.

SCHWENDINGER, HERMAN and JULIA (1971), 'The continuing debate on the legalistic approach to the definition of crime', *Issues in Criminology*, 7 (1), Winter.

SCOTT, P. D. (1956), 'Gangs and delinquent gangs in London', *British Journal of Delinquency*, 7, July.

SELLIN, THORSTEIN (1962a), 'The conflict of conduct norms', extract from *Culture, Conflict and Crime*, New York: Social Science Research Council, 1938, 63–70, in M. WOLFGANG, L. SAVITZ and N. JOHNSON, eds, *The Sociology of Crime and Delinquency*, London: Wiley, 1962; New York: Wiley, 1970.

SELLIN, THORSTEIN (1962b), 'A sociological approach to the study of crime causation', extract from SELLIN (1962a), 17–32, in M. WOLFGANG, L. SAVITZ and N. JOHNSTON, eds, *The Sociology of Crime and Delinquency*, London: Wiley, 1962; New York: Wiley, 1970.

SELLIN, THORSTEIN and WOLFGANG, MARVIN (1969), 'Measuring delinquency', in T. SELLIN and M. WOLFGANG, eds, *Delinquency: Selected Studies*, New York: Wiley.

SHAW, CLIFFORD R. et al. (1929), *Delinquency Areas*, University of Chicago Press.

SHAW, CLIFFORD R. and MACKAY, HENRY D. (1931), *Social Factors in Juvenile Delinquency: a Study of the Community, the Family and the Gang in Relation to Delinquent Behavior*, National Commission on Law Observance and Enforcement: Report on the Causes of Crime, vol. II, Washington : US Government Printing Office.

SHAW, CLIFFORD R. and MACKAY, HENRY (1942), *Juvenile Delinquency and Urban Areas*, Chicago University Press.

SHELDON, W. (1940), *Varieties of Human Physique*, New York: Harper & Row.

SIMMONS, J. L. and CHAMBERS, H. (1965), 'Public stereotypes of deviants', *Social Problems* 13, 223–32.

SIMMONS, J. L. (1969), *Deviants*, California: Glendessary Press.

SKOLNICK, JEROME (1966), *Justice Without Trial*, New York: Wiley.

SPROUT, HAROLD and SPROUT, MARGARET (1965), *The Ecological Perspective: with Special Reference to International Politics*, Princeton University Press.

STINCHCOMBE, ARTHUR L. (1963), 'Institutions of privacy in the determination of police practice', *American Journal of Sociology*, 69, 150–60.

STRETTON, HUGH (1969), *The Political Sciences*, London: Routledge & Kegan Paul.

SUTHERLAND, EDWIN H. and CRESSEY, DONALD R. (1966), *Principles of Criminology*, Philadelphia: J. P. Lippincott; references here to 7th ed.

SWANSON, G. (1968), 'Review symposium of Harold Garfinkel', *American Sociological Review*, 33, 122–4.

SYKES, GRESHAM and MATZA, DAVID (1957), 'Techniques of neutralization: a theory of delinquency', *American Sociological Review*, 22, December, 664–70; reprinted in M. WOLFGANG, L. SAVITZ and N. JOHNSTON, eds,

316

The Sociology of Crime and Delinquency, London: Wiley, 1962; New York: Wiley, 1970.

TAFT, DONALD R. (1933), 'Testing the selective influence of areas of delinquency', *American Journal of Sociology*, 38, 699–712.

TAPPAN, PAUL (1962), 'Who is the criminal?', *American Sociological Review*, 12, February, 96–102; reference here to reprinted version in M. WOLFGANG, L. SAVITZ and N. JOHNSTON, eds, *The Sociology of Crime and Delinquency*, London: Wiley, 1962; New York: Wiley, 1970.

TARDE, GABRIEL (1912), *Penal Philosophy*, Boston: Little, Brown & Co.

TAYLOR, IAN (1969), 'Hooligans: soccer's resistance movement', *New Society*, 358, 7 August, 204–6.

TAYLOR, IAN (1971a), 'Soccer consciousness and soccer hooliganism', in S. COHEN, ed., (1971a), 134–64.

TAYLOR, IAN (1971b), ' "Football mad"—a speculative sociology of soccer hooliganism', in ERIC DUNNING, ed., *The Sociology of Sport: A Selection of Readings*, London: Cass.

TAYLOR, IAN (1971c), 'Theories of action in juvenile correctional institutions', unpublished paper given to the First Anglo-Scandinavian Seminar in Criminology, Norway, September 1971.

TAYLOR, IAN (1971d), 'The new criminology in an age of doubt', *New Edinburgh Review*, 15, November, 14–17.

TAYLOR, IAN and TAYLOR, LAURIE (1972), 'Changes in the motivational construction of deviance', *Catalyst*, 6.

TAYLOR, IAN and WALTON, PAUL (1970), 'Values in deviancy theory and society', *British Journal of Sociology*, 21 (4), 362–74.

TAYLOR, IAN and WALTON, PAUL (1971), 'Hey, Mister, This is what we really do; some observations on vandalism in play', *Social Work Today*, 2 (12), 25–7; reprinted in C. WARD, ed., *Vandalism and Architecture*, London: Architectural Press (forthcoming).

TAYLOR, IAN and WALTON, PAUL (1972), 'Radical deviancy theory and Marxism: a reply to Paul Hirst', *Economy and Society*, 1 (2), 229–33.

TAYLOR, LAURIE (1968a), 'Alienation, anomie and delinquency theory', *British Journal of Social and Clinical Psychiatry*, 7, 93–105.

TAYLOR, LAURIE (1968b), 'Erving Goffman: an evaluation', *New Society*, 323–8.

TAYLOR, LAURIE (1970), 'Review of Matza: *Becoming Deviant*', *British Journal of Criminology*, 10 (3), July, 288–91.

TAYLOR, LAURIE (1971), *Deviance and Society*, London: Michael Joseph.

TAYLOR, LAURIE (1972), 'The significance and interpretation of replies to motivational questions: the case of sex offenders', *Sociology*, 6 (1), January, 23–40.

TAYLOR, LAURIE and COHEN, STANLEY (1972), *Psychological Survival: The Experience of Long-Term Imprisonment*, Harmondsworth: Penguin.

TAYLOR, LAURIE and GRAHAM, HILARY (1972), 'Grammars and vocabularies: alternative approaches to a sociology of motivation', mimeo, Department of Sociology, University of York.

TAYLOR, LAURIE and TAYLOR, IAN (1968), 'We are all deviants now' *International Socialism*, 34, 28–32.

TAYLOR, LAURIE and TAYLOR, IAN, eds (1973), *Politics and Deviance*, Harmondsworth: Penguin (for the National Deviancy Conference).

TAYLOR, LAURIE and ROBERTSON, ROLAND (1972), 'Problems in the comparative analysis of deviance', in ROCK and MCINTOSH, eds (1972).

TAYLOR, LAURIE and WALTON, PAUL (1971), 'Industrial sabotage: motives and meanings', in S. COHEN (1971a).

TEETERS, NEGLEY K. and MATZA, DAVID (1959), 'The extent of delinquency in the US', *Journal of Negro Education*, Summer, 210–11.

THOMAS, DOROTHY S. (1925), *Social Aspects of the Business Cycle*, London: Routledge & Kegan Paul.

TOBIAS, J. J. (1967), *Crime and Industrial Society in the Nineteenth Century*, London: Batsford (Penguin, 1972).

TRASLER, GORDON (1962), *The Explanation of Criminality*, London: Routledge & Kegan Paul.

TRICE, H. M. and ROMAN, P. M. (1970), 'Delabeling, relabeling and alcoholics anonymous', *Social Problems*, 17, Spring, 538–46.

TUMIN, MELVIN (1965), 'The functionalist approach to social problems', *Social Problems*, 12, Spring, 379–88.

TURK, AUSTIN T. (1964a), 'Toward construction of a theory of delinquency', *Journal of Criminal Law, Criminology and Police Science*, 55 (2), June, 215–29.

TURK, AUSTIN T. (1964b), 'Prospects for theories of criminal behaviour', *Journal of Criminal Law, Criminology and Police Science*, 55, December, 454–61.

TURK, AUSTIN T. (1966), 'Conflict and criminality', *American Sociological Review*, 31, June, 338–52.

TURK, AUSTIN T. (1967), 'Psychiatry vs the law: therefore?' *Criminologica*, 5 (3), November, 30–5.

TURK, AUSTIN T. (1969), *Criminality and the Legal Order*, Chicago: Rand McNally & Co.

TURNER, RALPH (1960), 'Sponsored and contest mobility in the schools system', *American Sociological Review*, 25 (5), 855–67.

VALENTINE, CHARLES (1968), *Culture and Poverty: Critique and Counter-Proposals*, University of Chicago Press.

VAN BEMMELEN, J. M. (1960), 'Willem Adrian Bonger', in H. MANNHEIM, ed. (1960).

VENESS, THELMA (1962), *School-leavers*, London: Methuen.

VOLD, GEORGE (1958), *Theoretical Criminology*, Oxford University Press.

VON MAYR, G. (1867), 'Statistik der gerichtlichen Polizei in Königreiche Bayern', in *Beiträge zur Statistik im Königreiche Bayern*, Munich.

WALSH, DERMOT (1969), 'The social adjustment of the physically handicapped with special reference to crime and deviance', unpublished Ph.D. thesis, University of London.

WALTON, PAUL (1973), 'Social reaction and radical commitment: the case of the Weathermen', in L. TAYLOR and I. TAYLOR, eds (1973), Harmondsworth: Penguin.

WALTON, PAUL and GAMBLE, ANDREW (1972), *From Alienation to Surplus Value*, London: Sheed & Ward.

318

WALTON, PAUL, GAMBLE, ANDREW and COULTER, JEFF (1970a), 'Philosophical anthropology in Marxism', *Social Research*, 37 (2), Summer, 259–74.

WALTON, PAUL, GAMBLE, ANDREW and COULTER, JEFF (1970b), 'Marx's image of man', *Social Theory and Practice*, 1 (2), Fall.

WATSON, J. B. (1925), *Behaviourism*, London: Kegan Paul.

WEBER, MAX (1966), *The Theory of Social and Economic Organization*, New York: Free Press.

WEIS, JOSEPH G. (1971), 'Dialogue with David Matza', *Issues in Criminology*, 6 (1), Winter, 33–53.

WERTHMAN, CARL (1969), 'Delinquency and moral character', in D. R. CRESSEY and D. A. WARD, eds, *Delinquency, Crime and Social Process*, New York: Harper & Row, 613–32.

WHEELER, STANTON, ed. (1968), *Controlling Delinquents*, New York: Wiley.

WHYTE, WILLIAM F. (1943), *Street Corner Society*; reference here to revised ed., University of Chicago Press, 1957.

WILKINS, LESLIE (1964), *Social Deviance: Social Policy, Action and Research*, London: Tavistock.

WILLIS, PAUL (1972), 'The motorbike within a subcultural group', *Working Papers in Cultural Studies*, 2, Centre for Contemporary Cultural Studies, University of Birmingham, 53–70.

WILSON, BRYAN R. (1970), *Rationality*, Oxford: Blackwell.

WILSON, ROGER (1963), *Difficult Housing Estates*, London: Tavistock.

WINSLOW, ROBERT (1968), *Crime in a Free Society: selections from the President's Commission on Law Enforcement and the Administration of Justice*, California: Dickenson.

WOLFF, KURT, ed. (1960), *Emile Durkheim et al.: Writings on Sociology and Philosophy*, New York: Harper & Row.

WOOTTON, BARBARA (1959), *Social Science and Social Pathology*, London: Allen & Unwin.

WRIGHT MILLS, C. (1943), 'The professional ideology of social pathologists', *American Journal of Sociology*, 49 (2), September; reprinted in I. L. HOROWITZ, ed., *Power, Politics and People*, Oxford University Press, 1967, 525–52.

WRIGHT MILLS, C. (1957), *The Power Elite*, Oxford University Press.

WRIGHT MILLS, C. (1966), 'Social psychology for liberals', in I. L. HOROWTIZ, ed., *Sociology and Pragmatism*, Oxford University Press, 260–78; see also extract from G. P. STONE and H. A. FABERMAN, eds, *Social Psychology Through Symbolic Interation*, New York: Ginn & Co., 1970, 42–53.

WRIGHT MILLS, C. (1967), 'Situated actions and vocabularies of motive', *American Sociological Review*, 5 (6), December, 1940; reference here to reprinted version in I. L. HOROWITZ, ed. *Power, Politics and People*, Oxford University Press, 439–51.

WRONG, DENNIS (1961), 'The oversocialized conception of man', *American Sociological Review*, 26, 184–93.

YABLONSKY, LEWIS (1962), *The Violent Gang*, New York: Macmillan.

YABLONSKY, LEWIS (1968), *The Hippie Trip*, New York: Pegasus Books.

YOUNG, JOCK (1970), 'The zookeepers of deviancy', *Catalyst*, 5, 38–46.

YOUNG, JOCK (1971a), *The Drugtakers: the Social Meaning of Drug Use*, London: MacGibbon & Kee/Paladin.

YOUNG, JOCK (1971b), 'The role of the police as amplifiers of deviancy, negotiators of reality and translators of fantasy: some consequences of our present system of drug control as seen in Notting Hill', in s. COHEN (1971a), 27–61.

YOUNG, JOCK (1971c), 'Drugs and the media', *Drugs and Society*, 1, 14–18.

YOUNG, JOCK (1972a), 'The student drugtaker: the subculture of drug use in a London college', unpublished Ph.D. thesis, University of London.

YOUNG, JOCK (1972b), 'The consensual myth: the portrayal of the drugtaker in the mass media' in ROCK and MCINTOSH, eds (1972).

YOUNG, JOCK (1973a), 'The Hippie Solution: an essay in the politics of leisure', in L. TAYLOR and I. TAYLOR, eds (1973).

YOUNG, JOCK (1973b), *Media as Myth*, London: Paladin.

YOUNG, JOCK and COHEN STANLEY, eds (1973), *Mass Media and Social Problems:* London: Constable.

ZORBAUGH, HARVEY (1925), 'Natural Areas of the City', in R. BURGESS, ed., *The City*, University of Chicago Press.

Index

Veblen, Thorstein, 177
Vold, George, 238–9

wealth, inherited, 87–8
Weber, Max, 194

Werthman, Carl, 191–2
Wilkins, Leslie, 12
women, deprivation, of, 83–4
Wrong, Dennis, 204

International Library of Sociology

Edited by
John Rex
University of Warwick

Founded by
Karl Mannheim
as The International Library of Sociology
and Social Reconstruction

*This Catalogue also contains other Social Science
series published by Routledge*

Routledge & Kegan Paul   London and Boston
68-74 Carter Lane London EC4V 5EL
9 Park Street Boston Mass 02108

Contents

● *Books so marked are available in paperback*
All books are in Metric Demy 8vo format (216 × 138mm approx.)

GENERAL SOCIOLOGY

Belshaw, Cyril. The Conditions of Social Performance. *An Exploratory Theory. 144 pp.*

Brown, Robert. Explanation in Social Science. *208 pp.*

Cain, Maureen E. Society and the Policeman's Role. *About 300 pp.*

Gibson, Quentin. The Logic of Social Enquiry. *240 pp.*

Homans, George C. Sentiments and Activities: *Essays in Social Science. 336 pp.*

Isajiw, Wsevold W. Causation and Functionalism in Sociology. *165 pp.*

Johnson, Harry M. Sociology: *a Systematic Introduction. Foreword by Robert K. Merton. 710 pp.*

Mannheim, Karl. Essays on Sociology and Social Psychology. *Edited by Paul Keckskemeti. With Editorial Note by Adolph Lowe. 344 pp.*
    Systematic Sociology: *An Introduction to the Study of Society. Edited by J. S. Erös and Professor W. A. C. Stewart. 220 pp.*

Martindale, Don. The Nature and Types of Sociological Theory. *292 pp.*

● **Maus, Heinz.** A Short History of Sociology. *234 pp.*

Mey, Harald. Field-Theory. *A Study of its Application in the Social Sciences. 352 pp.*

Myrdal, Gunnar. Value in Social Theory: *A Collection of Essays on Methodology. Edited by Paul Streeten. 332 pp.*

Ogburn, William F., and **Nimkoff, Meyer F.** A Handbook of Sociology. *Preface by Karl Mannheim. 656 pp. 46 figures. 35 tables.*

Parsons, Talcott, and **Smelser, Neil J.** Economy and Society: *A Study in the Integration of Economic and Social Theory. 362 pp.*

● **Rex, John.** Key Problems of Sociological Theory. *220 pp.*

Stark, Werner. The Fundamental Forms of Social Thought. *280 pp.*

FOREIGN CLASSICS OF SOCIOLOGY

● **Durkheim, Emile.** Suicide. *A Study in Sociology. Edited and with an Introduction by George Simpson. 404 pp.*
    Professional Ethics and Civic Morals. *Translated by Cornelia Brookfield. 288 pp.*

● **Gerth, H. H.**, and **Mills, C. Wright.** From Max Weber: *Essays in Sociology. 502 pp.*

Tönnies, Ferdinand. Community and Association. *(Gemeinschaft und Gesellschaft.) Translated and Supplemented by Charles P. Loomis. Foreword by Pitirim A. Sorokin. 334 pp.*

SOCIAL STRUCTURE

Andreski, Stanislav. Military Organization and Society. *Foreword by Professor A. R. Radcliffe-Brown. 226 pp. 1 folder.*

- **Cole, G. D. H.** Studies in Class Structure. *220 p.*
- **Coontz, Sydney H.** Population Theories and the Economic Interpretation. *202 pp.*
- **Coser, Lewis.** The Functions of Social Conflict. *204 pp.*
- **Dickie-Clark, H. F.** Marginal Situation: *A Sociological Study of a Coloured Group. 240 pp. 11 tables.*
- **Glass, D. V.** (Ed.). Social Mobility in Britain. *Contributions by J. Berent, T. Bottomore, R. C. Chambers, J. Floud, D. V. Glass, J. R. Hall, H. T. Himmelweit, R. K. Kelsall, F. M. Martin, C. A. Moser, R. Mukherjee, and W. Ziegel. 420 pp.*
- **Glaser, Barney,** and **Strauss, Anselm L.** Status Passage. *A Formal Theory. 208 pp.*
- **Jones, Garth N.** Planned Organizational Change: *An Exploratory Study Using an Empirical Approach. 268 pp.*
- **Kelsall, R. K.** Higher Civil Servants in Britain: *From 1870 to the Present Day. 268 pp. 31 tables.*
- **König, René.** The Community. *232 pp. Illustrated.*
- **Lawton, Denis.** Social Class, Language and Education. *192 pp.*
- **McLeish, John.** The Theory of Social Change: *Four Views Considered. 128 pp.*
- **Marsh, David C.** The Changing Social Structure in England and Wales, 1871-1961. *272 pp.*
- **Mouzelis, Nicos.** Organization and Bureaucracy. *An Analysis of Modern Theories. 240 pp.*
- **Mulkay, M. J.** Functionalism, Exchange and Theoretical Strategy. *272 pp.*
- **Ossowski, Stanislaw.** Class Structure in the Social Consciousness. *210 pp.*

SOCIOLOGY AND POLITICS

- **Crick, Bernard.** The American Science of Politics: *Its Origins and Conditions. 284 pp.*
- **Hertz, Frederick.** Nationality in History and Politics: *A Psychology and Sociology of National Sentiment and Nationalism. 432 pp.*
- **Kornhauser, William.** The Politics of Mass Society. *272 pp. 20 tables.*
- **Laidler, Harry W.** History of Socialism. *Social-Economic Movements: An Historical and Comparative Survey of Socialism, Communism, Co-operation, Utopianism; and other Systems of Reform and Reconstruction. 992 pp.*
- **Mannheim, Karl.** Freedom, Power and Democratic Planning. *Edited by Hans Gerth and Ernest K. Bramstedt. 424 pp.*
- **Mansur, Fatma.** Process of Independence. *Foreword by A. H. Hanson. 208 pp.*
- **Martin, David A.** Pacificism: *an Historical and Sociological Study. 262 pp.*
- **Myrdal, Gunnar.** The Political Element in the Development of Economic Theory. *Translated from the German by Paul Streeten. 282 pp.*
- **Verney, Douglas V.** The Analysis of Political Systems. *264 pp.*
- **Wootton, Graham.** Workers, Unions and the State. *188 pp.*

FOREIGN AFFAIRS: THEIR SOCIAL, POLITICAL AND ECONOMIC FOUNDATIONS

Bonné, Alfred. State and Economics in the Middle East: *A Society in Transition. 482 pp.*
  Studies in Economic Development: *with special reference to Conditions in the Under-developed Areas of Western Asia and India. 322 pp. 84 tables.*
Mayer, J. P. Political Thought in France from the Revolution to the Fifth Republic. *164 pp.*

CRIMINOLOGY

Ancel, Marc. Social Defence: *A Modern Approach to Criminal Problems. Foreword by Leon Radzinowicz. 240 pp.*
Cloward, Richard A., and **Ohlin, Lloyd E.** Delinquency and Opportunity: *A Theory of Delinquent Gangs. 248 pp.*
Downes, David M. The Delinquent Solution. *A Study in Subcultural Theory. 296 pp.*
Dunlop, A. B., and **McCabe, S.** Young Men in Detention Centres. *192 pp.*
Friedlander, Kate. The Psycho-Analytical Approach to Juvenile Delinquency: *Theory, Case Studies, Treatment. 320 pp.*
Glueck, Sheldon, and **Eleanor.** Family Environment and Delinquency. *With the statistical assistance of Rose W. Kneznek. 340 pp.*
Lopez-Rey, Manuel. Crime. *An Analytical Appraisal. 288 pp.*
Mannheim, Hermann. Comparative Criminology: *a Text Book. Two volumes. 442 pp. and 380 pp.*
Morris, Terence. The Criminal Area: *A Study in Social Ecology. Foreword by Hermann Mannheim. 232 pp. 25 tables. 4 maps.*
Trasler, Gordon. The Explanation of Criminality. *144 pp.*

SOCIAL PSYCHOLOGY

Bagley, Christopher. The Social Psychology of the Child with Epilepsy. *320 pp.*
Barbu, Zevedei. Problems of Historical Psychology. *248 pp.*
Blackburn, Julian. Psychology and the Social Pattern. *184 pp.*
● **Fleming, C. M.** Adolescence: *Its Social Psychology: With an Introduction to recent findings from the fields of Anthropology, Physiology, Medicine, Psychometrics and Sociometry. 288 pp.*
● The Social Psychology of Education: *An Introduction and Guide to Its Study. 136 pp.*
Homans, George C. The Human Group. *Foreword by Bernard DeVoto. Introduction by Robert K. Merton. 526 pp.*
  Social Behaviour: *its Elementary Forms. 416 pp.*

Klein, Josephine. The Study of Groups. *226 pp. 31 figures. 5 tables.*
Linton, Ralph. The Cultural Background of Personality. *132 pp.*
Mayo, Elton. The Social Problems of an Industrial Civilization. *With an appendix on the Political Problem. 180 pp.*
Ottaway, A. K. C. Learning Through Group Experience. *176 pp.*
Ridder, J. C. de. The Personality of the Urban African in South Africa. *A Thematic Apperception Test Study. 196 pp. 12 plates.*
● **Rose, Arnold M.** (Ed.). Human Behaviour and Social Processes: *an Interactionist Approach. Contributions by Arnold M. Rose, Ralph H. Turner, Anselm Strauss, Everett C. Hughes, E. Franklin Frazier, Howard S. Becker, et al. 696 pp.*
Smelser, Neil J. Theory of Collective Behaviour. *448 pp.*
Stephenson, Geoffrey M. The Development of Conscience. *128 pp.*
Young, Kimball. Handbook of Social Psychology. *658 pp. 16 figures. 10 tables.*

SOCIOLOGY OF THE FAMILY

Banks, J. A. Prosperity and Parenthood: *A Study of Family Planning among The Victorian Middle Classes. 262 pp.*
Bell, Colin R. Middle Class Families: *Social and Geographical Mobility. 224 pp.*
Burton, Lindy. Vulnerable Children. *272 pp.*
Gavron, Hannah. The Captive Wife: *Conflicts of Household Mothers. 190 pp.*
George, Victor, and **Wilding, Paul.** Motherless Families. *220 pp.*
Klein, Josephine. Samples from English Cultures.
  1. Three Preliminary Studies and Aspects of Adult Life in England. *447 pp.*
  2. Child-Rearing Practices and Index. *247 pp.*
Klein, Viola. Britain's Married Women Workers. *180 pp.*
  The Feminine Character. *History of an Ideology. 244 pp.*
McWhinnie, Alexina M. Adopted Children. *How They Grow Up. 304 pp.*
Myrdal, Alva, and **Klein, Viola.** Women's Two Roles: *Home and Work. 238 pp. 27 tables.*
Parsons, Talcott, and **Bales, Robert F.** Family: *Socialization and Interaction Process. In collaboration with James Olds, Morris Zelditch and Philip E. Slater. 456 pp. 50 figures and tables.*

SOCIAL SERVICES

Bastide, Roger. The Sociology of Mental Disorder. *Translated from the French by Jean McNeil. 264 pp.*
Carlebach, Julius. Caring For Children in Trouble. *266 pp.*
Forder, R. A. (Ed.). Penelope Hall's Social Services of Modern England. *352 pp.*
George, Victor. Foster Care. *Theory and Practice. 234 pp.*
  Social Security: *Beveridge and After. 258 pp.*

● **Goetschius, George W.** Working with Community Groups. *256 pp.*

Goetschius, George W., and **Tash, Joan.** Working with Unattached Youth. *416 pp.*

Hall, M. P., and **Howes, I. V.** The Church in Social Work. *A Study of Moral Welfare Work undertaken by the Church of England. 320 pp.*

Heywood, Jean S. Children in Care: *the Development of the Service for the Deprived Child. 264 pp.*

Hoenig, J., and **Hamilton, Marian W.** The De-Segration of the Mentally Ill. *284 pp.*

Jones, Kathleen. Lunacy, Law and Conscience, *1744-1845: the Social History of the Care of the Insane. 268 pp.*

Mental Health and Social Policy, 1845-1959. *264 pp.*

King, Roy D., Raynes, Norma V., and **Tizard, Jack.** Patterns of Residential Care. *356 pp.*

Leigh, John. Young People and Leisure. *256 pp.*

Morris, Pauline. Put Away: *A Sociological Study of Institutions for the Mentally Retarded. 364 pp.*

Nokes, P. L. The Professional Task in Welfare Practice. *152 pp.*

Timms, Noel. Psychiatric Social Work in Great Britain (1939-1962). *280 pp.*

● Social Casework: *Principles and Practice. 256 pp.*

Trasler, Gordon. In Place of Parents: *A Study in Foster Care. 272 pp.*

Young, A. F., and **Ashton, E. T.** British Social Work in the Nineteenth Century. *288 pp.*

Young, A. F. Social Services in British Industry. *272 pp.*

SOCIOLOGY OF EDUCATION

Banks, Olive. Parity and Prestige in English Secondary Education: a Study in Educational Sociology. *272 pp.*

Bentwich, Joseph. Education in Israel. *224 pp. 8 pp. plates.*

● **Blyth, W. A. L.** English Primary Education. *A Sociological Description.*

1. Schools. *232 pp.*
2. Background. *168 pp.*

Collier, K. G. The Social Purposes of Education: *Personal and Social Values in Education. 268 pp.*

Dale, R. R., and **Griffith, S.** Down Stream: *Failure in the Grammar School. 108 pp.*

Dore, R. P. Education in Tokugawa Japan. *356 pp. 9 pp. plates*

Evans, K. M. Sociometry and Education. *158 pp.*

Foster, P. J. Education and Social Change in Ghana. *336 pp. 3 maps.*

Fraser, W. R. Education and Society in Modern France. *150 pp.*

Grace, Gerald R. Role Conflict and the Teacher. *About 200 pp.*

Hans, Nicholas. New Trends in Education in the Eighteenth Century. *278 pp. 19 tables.*

● Comparative Education: *A Study of Educational Factors and Traditions. 360 pp.*

Hargreaves, David. Interpersonal Relations and Education. *432 pp.*
● Social Relations in a Secondary School. *240 pp.*
Holmes, Brian. Problems in Education. *A Comparative Approach. 336 pp.*
King, Ronald. Values and Involvement in a Grammar School. *164 pp.*
● **Mannheim, Karl,** and **Stewart, W. A. C.** An Introduction to the Sociology of Education. *206 pp.*
Morris, Raymond N. The Sixth Form and College Entrance. *231 pp.*
● **Musgrove, F.** Youth and the Social Order. *176 pp.*
● **Ottaway, A. K. C.** Education and Society: *An Introduction to the Sociology of Education. With an Introduction by W. O. Lester Smith. 212 pp.*
Peers, Robert. Adult Education: *A Comparative Study. 398 pp.*
Pritchard, D. G. Education and the Handicapped: *1760 to 1960. 258 pp.*
Richardson, Helen. Adolescent Girls in Approved Schools. *308 pp.*
Simon, Brian, and **Joan** (Eds.). Educational Psychology in the U.S.S.R. *Introduction by Brian and Joan Simon. Translation by Joan Simon. Papers by D. N. Bogoiavlenski and N. A. Menchinskaia, D. B. Elkonin, E. A. Fleshner, Z. I. Kalmykova, G. S. Kostiuk, V. A. Krutetski, A. N. Leontiev, A. R. Luria, E. A. Milerian, R. G. Natadze, B. M. Teplov, L. S. Vygotski, L. V. Zankov. 296 pp.*
Stratta, Erica. The Education of Borstal Boys. *A Study of their Educational Experiences prior to, and during Borstal Training. 256 pp.*

SOCIOLOGY OF CULTURE

Eppel, E. M., and **M.** Adolescents and Morality: *A Study of some Moral Values and Dilemmas of Working Adolescents in the Context of a changing Climate of Opinion. Foreword by W. J. H. Sprott. 268 pp. 39 tables.*
● **Fromm, Erich.** The Fear of Freedom. *286 pp.*
The Sane Society. *400 pp.*
● **Mannheim, Karl.** Diagnosis of Our Time: *Wartime Essays of a Sociologist. 208 pp.*
Essays on the Sociology of Culture. *Edited by Ernst Mannheim in co-operation with Paul Kecskemeti. Editorial Note by Adolph Lowe. 280 pp.*
Weber, Alfred. Farewell to European History: *or The Conquest of Nihilism. Translated from the German by R. F. C. Hull. 224 pp.*

SOCIOLOGY OF RELIGION

Argyle, Michael. Religious Behaviour. *224 pp. 8 figures. 41 tables.*
Nelson, G. K. Spiritualism and Society. *313 pp.*

Stark, Werner. The Sociology of Religion. *A Study of Christendom.*
  Volume I. *Established Religion. 248 pp.*
  Volume II. *Sectarian Religion. 368 pp.*
  Volume III. *The Universal Church. 464 pp.*
  Volume IV. *Types of Religious Man. 352 pp.*
  Volume V. *Types of Religious Culture. 464 pp.*
Watt, W. Montgomery. Islam and the Integration of Society. *320 pp.*

SOCIOLOGY OF ART AND LITERATURE

Beljame, Alexandre. Men of Letters and the English Public in the Eighteenth Century: *1660-1744, Dryden, Addison, Pope. Edited with an Introduction and Notes by Bonamy Dobrée. Translated by E. O. Lorimer. 532 pp.*
Jarvie, Ian C. Towards a Sociology of the Cinema. *A Comparative Essay on the Structure and Functioning of a Major Entertainment Industry. 405 pp.*
Rust, Frances S. Dance in Society. *An Analysis of the Relationships between the Social Dance and Society in England from the Middle Ages to the Present Day. 256 pp. 8 pp. of plates.*
Schücking, L. L. The Sociology of Literary Taste. *112 pp.*
Silbermann, Alphons. The Sociology of Music. *Translated from the German by Corbet Stewart. 222 pp.*

SOCIOLOGY OF KNOWLEDGE

Mannheim, Karl. Essays on the Sociology of Knowledge. *Edited by Paul Kecskemeti. Editorial note by Adolph Lowe. 353 pp.*
Stark, Werner. The Sociology of Knowledge: *An Essay in Aid of a Deeper Understanding of the History of Ideas. 384 pp.*

URBAN SOCIOLOGY

Ashworth, William. The Genesis of Modern British Town Planning: *A Study in Economic and Social History of the Nineteenth and Twentieth Centuries. 288 pp.*
Cullingworth, J. B. Housing Needs and Planning Policy: *A Restatement of the Problems of Housing Need and 'Overspill' in England and Wales. 232 pp. 44 tables. 8 maps.*
Dickinson, Robert E. City and Region: *A Geographical Interpretation. 608 pp. 125 figures.*
  The West European City: *A Geographical Interpretation. 600 pp. 129 maps. 29 plates.*
●   The City Region in Western Europe. *320 pp. Maps.*

Humphreys, Alexander J. New Dubliners: *Urbanization and the Irish Family. Foreword by George C. Homans. 304 pp.*

Jackson, Brian. Working Class Community: *Some General Notions raised by a Series of Studies in Northern England. 192 pp.*

Jennings, Hilda. Societies in the Making: *a Study of Development and Redevelopment within a County Borough. Foreword by D. A. Clark. 286 pp.*

Kerr, Madeline. The People of Ship Street. *240 pp.*

● **Mann, P. H.** An Approach to Urban Sociology. *240 pp.*

Morris, R. N., and **Mogey, J.** The Sociology of Housing. *Studies at Berinsfield. 232 pp. 4 pp. plates.*

Rosser, C., and **Harris, C.** The Family and Social Change. *A Study of Family and Kinship in a South Wales Town. 352 pp. 8 maps.*

RURAL SOCIOLOGY

Chambers, R. J. H. Settlement Schemes in Africa: *A Selective Study. 268 pp.*

Haswell, M. R. The Economics of Development in Village India. *120 pp.*

Littlejohn, James. Westrigg: *the Sociology of a Cheviot Parish. 172 pp. 5 figures.*

Williams, W. M. The Country Craftsman: *A Study of Some Rural Crafts and the Rural Industries Organization in England. 248 pp. 9 figures. (Dartington Hall Studies in Rural Sociology.)*

The Sociology of an English Village: *Gosforth. 272 pp. 12 figures. 13 tables.*

SOCIOLOGY OF INDUSTRY AND DISTRIBUTION

Anderson, Nels. Work and Leisure. *280 pp.*

● **Blau, Peter M.,** and **Scott, W. Richard.** Formal Organizations: *a Comparative approach. Introduction and Additional Bibliography by J. H. Smith. 326 pp.*

Eldridge, J. E. T. Industrial Disputes. *Essays in the Sociology of Industrial Relations. 288 pp.*

Hetzler, Stanley. Technological Growth and Social Change. *Achieving Modernization. 269 pp.*

Hollowell, Peter G. The Lorry Driver. *272 pp.*

Jefferys, Margot, *with the assistance of Winifred Moss.* Mobility in the Labour Market: *Employment Changes in Battersea and Dagenham. Preface by Barbara Wootton. 186 pp. 51 tables.*

Millerson, Geoffrey. The Qualifying Associations: *a Study in Professionalization. 320 pp.*

Smelser, Neil J. Social Change in the Industrial Revolution: *An Application of Theory to the Lancashire Cotton Industry, 1770-1840. 468 pp. 12 figures. 14 tables.*

Williams, Gertrude. Recruitment to Skilled Trades. *240 pp.*

Young, A. F. Industrial Injuries Insurance: *an Examination of British Policy.* *192 pp.*

ANTHROPOLOGY

Ammar, Hamed. Growing up in an Egyptian Village: *Silwa, Province of Aswan. 336 pp.*
Brandel-Syrier, Mia. Reeftown Elite. *A Study of Social Mobility in a Modern African Community on the Reef. 376 pp.*
Crook, David, and **Isabel.** Revolution in a Chinese Village: *Ten Mile Inn. 230 pp. 8 plates. 1 map.*
The First Years of Yangyi Commune. *302 pp. 12 plates.*
Dickie-Clark, H. F. The Marginal Situation. *A Sociological Study of a Coloured Group. 236 pp.*
Dube, S. C. Indian Village. *Foreword by Morris Edward Opler. 276 pp. 4 plates.*
India's Changing Villages: *Human Factors in Community Development. 260 pp. 8 plates. 1 map.*
Firth, Raymond. Malay Fishermen. *Their Peasant Economy. 420 pp. 17 pp. plates.*
Gulliver, P. H. Social Control in an African Society: a Study of the Arusha, Agricultural Masai of Northern Tanganyika. *320 pp. 8 plates. 10 figures.*
Ishwaran, K. Shivapur. *A South Indian Village. 216 pp.*
Tradition and Economy in Village India: *An Interactionist Approach. Foreword by Conrad Arensburg. 176 pp.*
Jarvie, Ian C. The Revolution in Anthropology. *268 pp.*
Jarvie, Ian C., and **Agassi, Joseph.** Hong Kong. *A Society in Transition. 396 pp. Illustrated with plates and maps.*
Little, Kenneth L. Mende of Sierra Leone. *308 pp. and folder.*
Negroes in Britain. *With a New Introduction and Contemporary Study by Leonard Bloom. 320 pp.*
Lowie, Robert H. Social Organization. *494 pp.*
Mayer, Adrian C. Caste and Kinship in Central India: *A Village and its Region. 328 pp. 16 plates. 15 figures. 16 tables.*
Smith, Raymond T. The Negro Family in British Guiana: *Family Structure and Social Status in the Villages. With a Foreword by Meyer Fortes. 314 pp. 8 plates. 1 figure. 4 maps.*

DOCUMENTARY

Meek, Dorothea L. (Ed.). Soviet Youth: *Some Achievements and Problems. Excerpts from the Soviet Press, translated by the editor. 280 pp.*
Schlesinger, Rudolf (Ed.). Changing Attitudes in Soviet Russia.
2. *The Nationalities Problem and Soviet Administration. Selected Readings on the Development of Soviet Nationalities Policies. Introduced by the editor. Translated by W. W. Gottlieb. 324 pp.*

SOCIOLOGY AND PHILOSOPHY

Barnsley, John H. The Social Reality of Ethics. *A Comparative Analysis of Moral Codes. 448 pp.*

Douglas, Jack D. (Ed.). Understanding Everyday Life. *Toward the Reconstruction of Sociological Knowledge. Contributions by Alan F. Blum. Aaron W. Cicourel, Norman K. Denzin, Jack D. Douglas, John Heeren, Peter McHugh, Peter K. Manning, Melvin Power, Matthew Speier, Roy Turner, D. Lawrence Wieder, Thomas P. Wilson and Don H. Zimmerman. 358 pp.*

Jarvie, Ian C. Concepts and Society. *216 pp.*

Roche, Maurice. Phenomenology, Language and the Social Sciences. *About 400 pp.*

Sklair, Leslie. The Sociology of Progress. *320 pp.*

International Library of Social Policy

General Editor Kathleen Janes

Jones, Kathleen. Mental Health Services. *A history, 1744-1971. About 500 pp.*

Thomas, J. E. The English Prison Officer since 1850: *A Study in Conflict. 258 pp.*

Primary Socialization, Language and Education

General Editor Basil Bernstein

Bernstein, Basil. Class, Codes and Control. *2 volumes.*
1. *Theoretical Studies Towards a Sociology of Language. 254 pp.*
2. *Applied Studies Towards a Sociology of Language. About 400 pp.*

Brandis, Walter, and **Henderson, Dorothy.** Social Class, Language and Communication. *288 pp.*

Cook, Jenny. Socialization and Social Control. *About 300 pp.*

Gahagan, D. M., and **G. A.** Talk Reform. *Exploration in Language for Infant School Children. 160 pp.*

Robinson, W. P., and **Rackstraw, Susan, D. A.** A Question of Answers. *2 volumes. 192 pp. and 180 pp.*

Turner, Geoffrey, J., and **Mohan, Bernard, A.** A Linguistic Description and Computer Programme for Children's Speech. *208 pp.*

Reports of the Institute of Community Studies and the Institute of Social Studies in Medical Care

Cartwright, Ann. Human Relations and Hospital Care. *272 pp.*
    Parents and Family Planning Services. *306 pp.*
    Patients and their Doctors. *A Study of General Practice. 304 pp.*
Dunnell, Karen, and **Cartwright, Ann.** Medicine Takers, Prescribers and Hoarders. *About 140 pp.*
● **Jackson, Brian.** Streaming: *an Education System in Miniature. 168 pp.*
Jackson, Brian, and **Marsden, Dennis.** Education and the Working Class: *Some General Themes raised by a Study of 88 Working-class Children in a Northern Industrial City. 268 pp. 2 folders.*
Marris, Peter. Widows and their Families. *Foreword by Dr. John Bowlby. 184 pp. 18 tables. Statistical Summary.*
    Family and Social Change in an African City. *A Study of Rehousing in Lagos. 196 pp. 1 map. 4 plates. 53 tables.*
    The Experience of Higher Education. *232 pp. 27 tables.*
Marris, Peter, and **Rein, Martin.** Dilemmas of Social Reform. *Poverty and Community Action in the United States. 256 pp.*
Marris, Peter, and **Somerset, Anthony.** African Businessmen. *A Study of Entrepreneurship and Development in Kenya. 256 pp.*
Runciman, W. G. Relative Deprivation and Social Justice. *A Study of Attitudes to Social Inequality in Twentieth Century England. 352 pp.*
Townsend, Peter. The Family Life of Old People: *An Inquiry in East London. Foreword by J. H. Sheldon. 300 pp. 3 figures. 63 tables.*
Willmott, Peter. Adolescent Boys in East London. *230 pp.*
    The Evolution of a Community: *a study of Dagenham after forty years. 168 pp. 2 maps.*
Willmott, Peter, and **Young, Michael.** Family and Class in a London Suburb. *202 pp. 47 tables.*
Young, Michael. Innovation and Research in Education. *192 pp.*
● **Young, Michael,** and **McGeeney, Patrick.** Learning Begins at Home. *A Study of a Junior School and its Parents. 128 pp.*
Young, Michael, and **Willmott, Peter.** Family and Kinship in East London. *Foreword by Richard M. Titmuss. 252 pp. 39 tables.*

Medicine, Illness and Society
General Editor   W. M. Williams

Robinson, David. The Process of Becoming Ill.
Stacey, Margaret. *et al.* Hospitals, Children and Their Families. *The Report of a Pilot Study. 202 pp.*

Routledge Social Science Journals

The British Journal of Sociology. *Edited by Terence P. Morris. Vol. 1, No. 1, March 1950 and Quarterly. Roy. 8vo. Back numbers available. An international journal with articles on all aspects of sociology.*

Economy and Society. *Vol. 1, No. 1. February 1972 and Quarterly. Metric Roy. 8vo. A journal for all social scientists covering sociology, philosophy, anthropology, economics and history.*

Printed in Great Britain by Lewis Reprints Limited
Brown Knight & Truscott Group, London and Tonbridge

21972